Beyond Women's Words

Beyond Women's Words unites feminist scholars, artists, and community activists working with the stories of women and other historically marginalized subjects to address the contributions and challenges of doing feminist oral history.

Feminists who work with oral history methods want to tell stories that matter. They know, too, that the telling of those stories—the processes by which they are generated and recorded, and the different contexts in which they are shared and interpreted—also matters—a lot. Using Sherna Berger Gluck and Daphne Patai's classic text, *Women's Words*, as a platform to reflect on how feminisms have influenced the field of oral history, this collection brings together an international, multigenerational, and multidisciplinary group of authors whose work highlights the variety in understandings of, and approaches to, feminist oral histories.

Through five thematic sections, the volume considers Indigenous modes of storytelling, feminism in diverse locales around the globe, different theoretical approaches, oral history as performance, digital oral history, and oral history as community-engagement. *Beyond Women's Words* is ideal for students of oral history, anthropology, public history, women's and gender history, and Women's and Gender Studies, as well as activists, artists, and community-engaged practitioners.

Katrina Srigley is Associate Professor in the Department of History at Nipissing University, Ontario, Canada. Author of the award-winning monograph *Breadwinning Daughters: Young Working Women in a Depression-Era City* (2010), her current collaborative work with Nipissing First Nation focuses on the history of Nbisiing Anishinaabeg territory.

Stacey Zembrzycki teaches at Dawson College, Quebec, Canada. She is the author of *According to Baba: A Collaborative Oral History of Sudbury's Ukrainian Community* (2014) and its accompanying website www.sudburyukrainians.ca, and is co-editor of *Oral History Off the Record: Toward an Ethnography of Practice* (2013).

Franca Iacovetta is Professor of History at the University of Toronto, Canada, and co-editor of *Studies in Gender and History* at University of Toronto Press. A past president of the Berkshire Conference of Women Historians, she is author or editor of ten books, including the award-winning *Gatekeepers: Reshaping Immigrant Lives in Cold War Canada* (2006).

Beyond Women's Words

Feminisms and the Practices
of Oral History in the
Twenty-First Century

Edited by
Katrina Srigley,
Stacey Zembrzycki,
and Franca Iacovetta

 Routledge
Taylor & Francis Group

LONDON AND NEW YORK

First published 2018
by Routledge
2 Park Square, Milton Park, Abingdon, Oxon OX14 4RN

and by Routledge
711 Third Avenue, New York, NY 10017

*Routledge is an imprint of the Taylor & Francis Group,
an informa business*

British Library Cataloguing-in-Publication Data
A catalogue record for this book is available from the British Library

Library of Congress Cataloging-in-Publication Data
Names: Srigley, Katrina, 1973- editor. | Zembrzycki, Stacey, editor. |
Iacovetta, Franca, 1957– editor.
Title: Beyond women's words : feminisms and the practices of oral
history in the twenty-first century / edited by Katrina Srigley,
Stacey Zembrzycki, and Franca Iacovetta.
Description: Abingdon, Oxon ; New York, NY : Routledge, 2018. |
Includes bibliographical references and index.
Identifiers: LCCN 2017052691| ISBN 9780815357681
(hardback : alk. paper) | ISBN 9780815357711 (pbk. : alk. paper) |
ISBN 9781351123822 (ebook : alk. paper)
Subjects: LCSH: Women's studies—Methodology. | Women—
Research—Methodology. | Feminism—Research—Methodology. |
Oral history—Methodology.
Classification: LCC HQ1180 .B494 2018 | DDC 305.42—dc23
LC record available at https://lccn.loc.gov/2017052691

ISBN: 978-0-8153-5768-1 (hbk)
ISBN: 978-0-8153-5771-1 (pbk)
ISBN: 978-1-351-12382-2 (ebk)

Typeset in Galliard
by Florence Production Ltd, Stoodleigh, Devon, UK

For Sherna Berger Gluck, mentor, friend, inspiration

Contents

List of figures   xi
Biographies   xiii
Preface and acknowledgments   xx
Foreword   xxii
SHERNA BERGER GLUCK

Introduction   1
FRANCA IACOVETTA, KATRINA SRIGLEY,
AND STACEY ZEMBRZYCKI

SECTION 1
Reflections on women's words   25
Section introduction   27
LINDA SHOPES

1   **"That's not what I said": A reprise 25 years on**   31
    KATHERINE BORLAND

2   **The positionality of narrators and interviewers:**
    Methodological comments on oral history with
    Anglo-Indian schoolteachers in Bangalore, India   38
    SANCHIA DESOUZA AND JYOTHSNA LATHA BELLIAPPA

3   **When is enough enough?**   48
    DAPHNE PATAI

4   **Feminist oral histories of racist women**   56
    KATHLEEN BLEE

5 Emotion and pedagogy: Teaching digital
   storytelling in the millennial classroom   63
   RINA BENMAYOR

SECTION 2
Doing feminist oral history then and now   75
Section introduction   77
PENNY SUMMERFIELD

6 Talking about feminism: Reconciling fragmented
   narratives with the feminist research frame   81
   LYNN ABRAMS

7 "Are you only interviewing women for this?":
   Indigenous feminism and oral history   95
   LIANNE C. LEDDY

8 Living, archiving, and reflecting on feminism
   and activism in India: An oral history with
   Uma Chakravarti   109
   PONNI ARASU AND UMA CHAKRAVARTI

9 Locating lesbians, finding "gay women," writing
   queer histories: Reflections on oral histories,
   identity, and community memory   126
   VALERIE J. KORINEK

10 Memory, history, and contestations in present-day
   Iraq   137
   NADJE AL-ALI

SECTION 3
Decentering and decolonizing in feminist oral history   149
Section introduction   151
NAN ALAMILLA BOYD

11 Speaking private memory to public power: Oral
   history and breaking the silence on sexual and
   gender-based violence during the Khmer Rouge
   genocide   155
   THERESA DE LANGIS

12 Yarning up oral history: An Indigenous feminist
    analysis   170
    SUE ANDERSON, JAIMEE HAMILTON, AND
    LORINA L. BARKER

13 "This thing we are doing here": Listening and
    writing in the "Montréal Life Stories" project   184
    STÉPHANE MARTELLY

14 Intersubjective experiences and a depiction beyond
    written words: Doing ethnography with wartime
    children in northern Uganda   192
    GRACE AKELLO

15 Putting the archive in movement: Testimonies,
    feminism, and female torture survivors in Chile   204
    HILLARY HINER

SECTION 4
Feminists in the field: Performance, political
activism, and community engagement   217
Section introduction   219
PAUL ORTIZ

16 Storyweaving, Indigenous knowledge, and process
    in *Material Witness*   223
    PENNY COUCHIE AND MURIEL MIGUEL

17 Oral history for building social movements, then
    and now   236
    SARAH K. LOOSE, WITH AMY STARECHESKI

18 Women power and feminine solidarity: Oral history,
    life stories, and trauma in the context of an industrial
    disaster   244
    SUROOPA MUKHERJEE

19 Public homeplaces: Collaboration and care in oral
    history project design   252
    SADY SULLIVAN

20 Come wash with us: Seeking home in story   261
SHAHRZAD ARSHADI, HOURIG ATTARIAN,
KHADIJA BAKER, AND KUMRU BILICI

SECTION 5
Listening to and learning from stories in the
digital world   277
Section introduction   279
ANNA SHEFTEL

21 Feminist oral history practice in an era of digital
    self-representation   283
MARGO SHEA

22 The medium is political and the message is personal:
    Feminist oral histories online   298
MARY A. LARSON

23 Oral history's afterlife   304
ELISE CHENIER

24 Women's words from the archives   313
RUTH PERCY

25 "Shut the tape off and I'll tell you a story":
    Women's knowledges in urban Indigenous
    community representations   321
HEATHER A. HOWARD

    Index   336

Figures

5.1 Screen shots from *Fighting for my History* by Kristen
    LaFollette   68
5.2 2014 Festival poster   70
11.1 Nam Mon and her husband watch the interview excerpt on
    www.cambodiawomenshistory.com in Kampong Cham,
    12 September 2013   160
11.2 Prak Yoeun stands in front of her house in Kampong Speu,
    14 December 2013   162
11.3 Prak Yoeun is interviewed by You Sotheary, lead research
    assistant for the CWOHP, in Kampong Speu, on
    14 December 2013   163
13.1 Mafalda Nicolas Mondestin, *Chita pale* (Sit Down and Talk) 189
19.1 Audience break-out group at the second annual "What Are
    You? A Discussion About Mixed Heritage," Brooklyn
    Historical Society, 2012   254
19.2 Audience break-out group at "Science Fiction and
    Multiraciality: From Octavia Butler to Harry Potter,"
    Brooklyn Historical Society, 2013   255
19.3 Workshop participants: "Racial Realities: Writing about Race
    in the First Person," Brooklyn Historical Society, 2013   257
20.1 Our washtubs   262
20.2 Washing   263
20.3 Barika refugee camp, near Sulaymaniyah in Iraqi Kurdistan
    (Northern Iraq), November 2015   265
20.4 Piled up laundry during the performance, October 2015   266
20.5 Kawergosk Syrian refugee camp in the Kurdish region of
    Northern Iraq, near Erbil City, 2012   268
20.6 Historical Armenian fountains, Hebap/Ekinözu village
    (Havav in Armenian) Kovancılar district of Elazığ province,
    Turkey, October 2016   272
20.7 Barika refugee camp, near Sulaymaniyah in Iraqi Kurdistan
    (Northern Iraq), November 2015   273

20.8 Khadija pouring water over Hourig's hands with Hourig's
     great grandmother Lusya's bowl during the performance   274
25.1 Screen shot of the "First Story Toronto" mobile phone app
     showing pins marking historical and contemporary events   324
25.2 Screen shot of the "First Story Toronto" app page, featuring
     Verna Johnston   327
25.3 Two pages from the entry for Jeanette Corbiere-Lavell on
     the "First Story Toronto" app   330

Biographies

Editors

Katrina Srigley is Associate Professor of History at Nipissing University in North Bay, Ontario, Canada. Author of the award-winning monograph *Breadwinning Daughters* (2010), Srigley's scholarship explores the dynamics of memory making and storytelling. Her current work, in partnership with Nipissing First Nation, explores the history of Nbisiing Anishinaabeg territory by honoring Anishinaabeg ways of knowing, sharing, and documenting history.

Stacey Zembrzycki teaches at Dawson College in Montréal, Quebec, Canada. An award-winning oral and public historian of ethnic, immigrant, and refugee experiences, she is the author of *According to Baba* (2014) and its accompanying website, www.sudburyukrainians.ca, and co-editor of *Oral History Off the Record* (2013). Her current project explores the connections between mining, health, and the environment in Sudbury, Canada.

Franca Iacovetta is Professor of History at the University of Toronto, Canada, and past president of the Berkshire Conference of Women Historians (2011–2014). Author and editor of ten books on women, migration, and other topics, including, most recently, a volume in honor of Luisa Passerini, she is completing a book on women's pluralism and researching wartime internment memories.

Contributors

Lynn Abrams is Professor of Modern History at the University of Glasgow, UK, where she teaches oral history and women and gender relations. The author of *Myth and Materiality in a Woman's World: Shetland 1800–2000* (2005) and *Oral History Theory* (2nd edn., 2016), she is currently researching the technologies, psychologies, and mobilities of postwar womanhood.

Grace Akello is Associate Professor at Gulu University in northern Uganda and Coordinator of a Master of Medical Anthropology programme in East and Central Africa. A current fellow at the London School of Economics, UK, her publications focus on former child soldiers and children's coping mechanisms in contexts of war and HIV/AIDs as well as intersubjectivity and autoethnography.

Nadje Al-Ali is Professor of Gender Studies at SOAS, University of London, UK. A specialist of women and feminism in the Middle East, transnational migration and diaspora, and gendering violence, war, and peace, she has authored several books, including *Iraqi Women: Untold Stories from 1948 to the Present* (2007) and *What Kind of Liberation? Women and the Occupation in Iraq* (with N. Pratt, 2009).

Sue Anderson teaches Australian history at the University of South Australia. An oral historian, archaeologist, and cultural consultant with a long history of working with Indigenous communities, she authored *Doreen Kartinyeri: My Ngarrindjeri Calling* (2008). A past president of Oral History Australia, she is currently the Oceania Representative for the International Oral History Association.

Ponni Arasu is a queer feminist activist, theater practitioner, and lawyer who has worked in India and Sri Lanka. Her University of Toronto dissertation uses historical ethnography to trace political movements in Tamil Nadu between 1950 and 1970. She also recently created an oral archive of the Indian women's movement for the Indian Association of Women's Studies and Zubaan.

Shahrzad Arshadi is a Montréal-based Canadian-Iranian multidisciplinary feminist artist and human rights activist whose work uses photography, documentary film, writing, sound creation, and performance to address issues of memory, culture, and human rights. Her film, *Dancing for Change*, won the 2015 International Galawej Cultural Festival Award. In 2017, she received the Women of Distinction Inspiration Award from Montréal's Women's Y Foundation.

Hourig Attarian is Assistant Professor in the College of Humanities and Social Sciences at the American University of Armenia and a core member of Concordia University's Centre for Oral History and Digital Storytelling (COHDS), Canada. Anchored in the blurred genre of life history and autobiographical inquiry, her work draws together difficult memories and marginalized histories of violence within a framework of public pedagogy.

Khadija Baker is a Montréal-based interdisciplinary artist of Kurdish–Syrian descent. A PhD candidate at Concordia University's Centre for Interdisciplinary Studies in Society and Culture, Canada, she is also a core member of COHDS. She explores themes related to persecution, displacement, and memory by breaching the divide between artist, art, and public, and creating spaces for participation, exchange, understanding, and storytelling.

Lorina L. Barker is a descendant of the Wangkumara and Muruwari people from Northwest New South Wales, Adnyamathanha (Flinders Rangers, South Australia), the Kooma and Kunja (southwest Queensland), and the Kurnu-Baarkandji (Northwest New South Wales). An oral historian, she teaches modern Australian History, oral history, and local and community history in the School of Humanities at the University of New England in Armidale, NSW, Australia.

Jyothsna Latha Belliappa has degrees in Sociology and Women's Studies from Jawaharlal Nehru University, India, and the University of York, UK, and currently teaches at the Srishti Institute of Art, Design and Technology in Bangalore, India. The author of *Gender, Class and Reflexive Modernity in India* (2013), she is a consultant to educational institutions, industry, and the not-for-profit sector.

Rina Benmayor is Professor Emerita at California State University, Monterey Bay, USA, where she taught oral history, digital storytelling, and literature. Her publications include the co-authored *Telling to Live: Latina Feminist Testimonios* (2001) and co-edited *Memory, Subjectivities, and Representation: Approaches to Oral History in Latin America, Portugal, and Spain* (2016). She is past president of the International Oral History Association and the US Oral History Association.

Sherna Berger Gluck, Director Emerita of the Oral History Program and emerita Women's Studies faculty at California State University, Long Beach, USA, is a US women's historian. An activist-scholar, she interviewed and published on Palestinian women's movement leaders and grassroots activists. In 2000, she co-founded/directed Virtual Oral/Aural History (www.csulb.edu/voaha). Her current work addresses the promises and perils of oral history on the web.

Kumru Bilici is a Canadian-Turkish freelance journalist and photographer with an M.A. in Film Studies. Her research focuses on post-exilic Armenian "homecoming" documentary films and the traumatic post-memory of the 1915 genocide. She writes for *Agos*, a weekly newspaper in Istanbul, and is co-founder of *Voices in Dialogue*, an organization that promotes peaceful dialogue among people of Turkish, Armenian, and Kurdish descent.

Kathleen Blee is Distinguished Professor of Sociology and Bailey Dean of the Dietrich School of Arts and Sciences at the University of Pittsburgh, USA. Her many publications on racial violence and progressive social movements include *Inside Organized Racism* (2002), *Women in the Klan* (1991), *Making Democracy* (2012), and *The Road to Poverty* (with Dwight Billings, 2000).

Katherine Borland is Director of the Center for Folklore Studies and Associate Professor of Comparative Studies at Ohio State University, USA. She has written three books: *Creating Community* (2000), *Unmasking Class,*

Gender and Sexuality in Nicaraguan Festival (2006), and *International Volunteer Tourism* (co-edited with Abigail E. Adams, 2013).

Nan Alamilla Boyd is Professor of Women and Gender Studies at San Francisco State University, USA. A long-time volunteer at the GLBT Historical Society and founder of the society's oral history project, she authored *Wide Open Town* (2003) and co-edited *Bodies of Evidence* (2012).

Uma Chakravarti is a distinguished gender historian of India and long-time figure in India's women's movement. She has published seven books, including *Rewriting History* (1998), and produced the documentary *Fragments of a Past* (2010). Her honors include the J.P. Naik Fellowship from the Centre for Women's Development Studies, Delhi, and the Ingalls Fellowship from Harvard University, USA.

Elise Chenier is Professor of History at Simon Fraser University, Canada, Director of the Archives of Lesbian Oral Testimony (www.alotarchives.org), and creator of www.interracialintimacies.org, an online visualization of the oral history research and publication process. A scholar of lesbian and queer sexualities in the 20th century, she is writing a history of same-sex marriage practices in postwar America.

Penny Couchie is an Anishinaabe dancer, actor, teacher, and choreographer from Nipissing First Nation, Canada. She holds a degree in Aboriginal Studies and Drama and graduated from The School of Toronto Dance Theatre. In 2007, she co-founded Aanmitaagzi, which co-produced *Material Witness* with Spiderwoman Theater. A recipient of the 2016 KM Hunter Award in Dance, her recent works include *When Will You Rage?* and *Dances of Resistance.*

Theresa de Langis, a specialist in human rights and women, and peace and security, is Associate Professor of Global Affairs and Humanities at the American University of Phnom Penh, Cambodia. Her independent feminist research includes the "Cambodian Women's Oral History" project (www.cambodianwomensoralhistory.com), which collected testimonials of sexual and gender-based crimes under the genocidal Khmer Rouge regime (1970–1979).

Sanchia deSouza is a PhD candidate in the Department of History at the University of Toronto, Canada. Her doctoral research draws on the history of dairy production and consumption to examine animal–human relationships, trans-imperial and transnational circulation, and urban development in and around 20th century Bombay, India.

Jaimee Hamilton, a Ngunawal woman who grew up in New South Wales, Australia, is completing a PhD that focuses on Aboriginal social theory. She is interested in Indigenous feminism, pedagogies, and philosophies, as well as open-sourced learning, and has presented her work at numerous conferences. As a previous lecturer at the University of South Australia, she taught courses on Indigenous knowledges and philosophy.

Hillary Hiner is Assistant Professor of History at the Universidad Diego Portales in Santiago, Chile. A specialist of gender, feminism, violence, and memory in recent Chilean and Latin American history, she has conducted more than 160 oral histories throughout Chile for the state-funded Fondecyt project, *Una historia inconclusa: violencia de género y políticas públicas en Chile, 1990–2010*.

Heather A. Howard is Assistant Professor of Anthropology at Michigan State University, USA, and affiliated research faculty with the University of Toronto's Centre for Indigenous Initiatives, Canada. She has worked with Toronto's Indigenous community for over 20 years and is a co-founder and active member of First Story Toronto. She is the co-editor of *Feminist Fields: Ethnographic Insights* (1999), *Keeping the Campfires Going* (2009), and *Aboriginal Peoples in Canadian Cities* (2011).

Valerie J. Korinek is Professor of History at the University of Saskatchewan, Canada. The author and co-editor of three books on women's popular culture, feminist, and food histories, her latest book is *Prairie Fairies: A History of Queer Communities and People in Western Canada, 1930–1985* (2018). She is currently researching the history of queer marriage and the same-sex marriage industry in Canada and beyond.

Mary A. Larson is the Associate Dean for Special Collections and the Puterbaugh Professor of Library Service at the Oklahoma State University Libraries, USA. An anthropologist and oral historian, her research has focused on ethics in oral history, particularly relative to evolving technologies. She is also a past president of the US Oral History Association.

Lianne C. Leddy is Anishinaabe kwe from Serpent River First Nation (SRFN) and grew up in Elliot Lake, Canada. Assistant Professor of Indigenous Studies at Wilfrid Laurier University, Brantford, Canada, Leddy explores issues related to gender and the environment, as well as historical methods. Her work has appeared in the *Canadian Historical Review*, *Oral History Forum d'histoire orale*, *Herizons*, and several edited collections.

Sarah K. Loose is founder and co-coordinator of the Groundswell: Oral History for Social Change network and co-founder of Oregon's Interfaith Movement for Immigrant Justice. She uses oral history, popular education, community organizing, and participatory research to further movements for social and environmental justice, from the highlands of El Salvador to the rural communities of the Pacific Northwest.

Stéphane Martelly was born in Port-au-Prince and now lives in Montréal. Affiliate Assistant Professor in Concordia University's Theatre Department, she has published poetry (e.g. *Inventaire*, 2016), children's tales (e.g. *La Maman qui s'absentait*, 2011), and pictorial work (*Folie passée à la chaux vive*, 2010), as well as scholarly manuscripts (*Le Sujet opaque*, 2001; *Les Jeux du dissemblable. Folie, marge et féminine en littérature haïtienne contemporaine*, 2016).

Muriel Miguel (Kuna/Rappahannock) is founding member and Artistic Director of Spiderwoman Theater, the longest running Native American women's theater company in North America. She has co-written and directed all of Spiderwoman's shows (over 20). She is the recipient of numerous awards and fellowships, including an honorary Doctorate in Fine Arts for her work as a director, choreographer, and actor.

Suroopa Mukherjee teaches literature at Hindu College, Delhi University, India, and campaigns for the Bhopal gas tragedy. She was staff advisor of *We for Bhopal*, which created a magazine, *Hinterland*, and made the documentary film *Closer to Reality*. Her *Surviving Bhopal: Dancing Bodies, Written Texts, Oral Testimonials of Women in the Wake of an Industrial Disaster* (2010) has been widely acclaimed.

Paul Ortiz is Director of the Samuel Proctor Oral History Program and Associate Professor of History at the University of Florida, USA. The recipient of the Southern Regional Council's Lillian Smith Book Award and the César E. Chávez Action and Commitment Award, his publications include the co-edited volume *Remembering Jim Crow* (2001), *Emancipation Betrayed* (2006), and *An African American and Latinx History of the United States* (2016).

Daphne Patai is Professor Emerita of Languages, Literatures, and Cultures at the University of Massachusetts Amherst, USA. She has published a dozen books, including *Professing Feminism: Education and Indoctrination in Women's Studies* (rev. ed., 2003, with Noretta Koertge), and *What Price Utopia?: Essays on Ideological Policing, Feminism, and Academic Affairs* (2008). A recipient of fellowships from the Guggenheim Foundation, the National Endowment for the Humanities, and the National Humanities Center, she sits on the Board of Directors of the non-partisan Foundation for Individual Rights in Education, which defends First Amendment rights on campus.

Ruth Percy teaches British and American history at the University of Oxford, UK. A scholar of gender and class, and urban working-class women in the 19th and 20th centuries, her forthcoming book is entitled *"I Am Not a Feminist": Equality, Rights, and Working Women's Culture in London and Chicago, 1870s–1920s*.

Margo Shea is Assistant Professor of Public History at Salem State University, USA, where she teaches courses in heritage, public, local, and urban history, and museum studies. Trained in cultural geography, public history, and memory studies, her work focuses on the city of Derry/Londonderry, Northern Ireland. Her expertise also extends to community heritage, service-learning, and campus-community partnerships.

Anna Sheftel is Assistant Professor of Conflict Studies at Saint Paul University in Ottawa, Canada. Her many publications in oral history and ethics include the co-edited *Oral History Off the Record* (2013), winner of the Oral History Association's 2014 Book Award. Her current work focuses on Holocaust survivors in post-1945 Canada.

Linda Shopes is a consultant in oral and public history and freelance editor in humanities fields. She served on committees developing successive iterations of the US Oral History Association's Principles and Best Practices for Oral History; and is a past president of the association. From 2001 to 2013, she was co-editor of Palgrave Macmillan's *Studies in Oral History* series.

Amy Starecheski is Co-Director of Columbia University's Oral History M.A. Program, USA. A cultural anthropologist and oral historian, she co-authored *The Telling Lives Oral History Curriculum Guide*, served as a lead interviewer on the "September 11, 2001 Narrative and Memory" project, and facilitates the Practitioner Support Network for Groundswell. She published *Ours to Lose: When Squatters Became Homeowners in New York City* in 2016.

Sady Sullivan is a New York City-based oral historian who was Curator for the Columbia Center for Oral History Archives at Columbia University, USA (2014–2016). As Director of Oral History at the Brooklyn Historical Society (2006–2014), she created "Crossing Borders, Bridging Generations," an award-winning oral history project, racial justice dialogue series, and digital humanities site exploring mixed-heritage identity.

Penny Summerfield is Professor Emerita at the University of Manchester, UK. She was Professor of Modern History there from 2000 to 2016, and Professor of Women's History at Lancaster University, UK, from 1994 to 2000, where she co-directed the Centre for Women's Studies (1989–1994). She authored *Contesting Home Defence* (with Corinna Peniston-Bird, 2007) and *Reconstructing Women's Wartime Lives* (1998).

Preface and acknowledgments

Just over a quarter century after the publication of *Women's Words: The Feminist Practice of Oral History*, a landmark text in feminist oral history, we are pleased to present *Beyond Women's Words: Feminisms and the Practices of Oral History in the Twenty-First Century*. The 25 original chapters in this international, multigenerational, and multidisciplinary volume highlight the enormous degree of activity and introspection among feminists "doing" oral history in diverse contexts. They are intended to encourage new as well as ongoing conversations and debates in the field.

The book brings together a varied collection of scholars, students, Indigenous Elders, activists, artists, and community-based oral history practitioners from around the world and at different stages in their careers or life trajectories to address the practices, politics, and ethics surrounding oral history. The contributors reflect in enlightening ways on the dynamics of the interview process, the narratives that emerged from their research collaborations, the practical and methodological problems they encountered, and the political and ethical implications of their work. The volume combines continuing efforts to center the lives of historically edged-out, marginalized, or silenced groups of women—and others—with newer commentary about the impact, both positive and negative, of digital technologies. Written in clear and accessible prose, the chapters introduce uninitiated readers to the possibilities and limits of oral history.

The Introduction provides an overview of the project and situates the chapters in relation to each other and within broader contexts. It charts the evolution of feminist oral history and offers some suggestions for moving forward in the 21st century. The section introductions for the five central themes around which the volume is organized—Reflections on women's words; Doing feminist oral history: Then and now; Decentering and decolonizing in feminist oral history; Feminists in the field: Performance, political activism, and community engagement; and Listening to and learning from stories in the digital world—are written by leading scholars who provide valuable context for, and insight into, the chapters in each section.

Given that it aims to capture the different contexts in which feminists do oral history and encourage exchange across national and other borders, theoretical approaches, and methodologies, this volume required a collaborative effort among a diverse group of practitioners. As editors, we are thus delighted to thank our contributors for their critical involvement with what we view as an ongoing project in feminist oral history. We could not have met our goal of producing a volume that provides wide geographical coverage and features a truly remarkable range of researchers and narrators without their commitment to the feminist principles of collaboration, mutual respect, and solidarity in intellectual and political purpose. Without their hard work, this new edition would have taken much longer to produce. Importantly, we also acknowledge and say chi-miigwech to our Anishinaabeg, Ininiw, and Haudenosaunee colleagues, Elders, and Treaty partners for their respect, kindness, and wisdom.

At Routledge, we would like to thank Eve Setch, the Publisher for Modern Global History, for her generous and continuing support for the project, Zoe Thomson and Emma Sudderick for shepherding us through the volume's final production, and copy-editor Sandra Stafford for her sage editorial advice. We also thank Shivani Desai, a graduate of the University of Toronto, for her excellent assistance with manuscript preparation. We are deeply indebted to Kathryn Nasstrom, who provided invaluable support during the early stages of this project. She also read a draft of the Introduction, as did Susan Hill, Mary Jane McCallum, Lynn Abrams, Sherna Berger Gluck, and Linda Shopes. We are grateful to them for their thoughtful feedback. For graciously agreeing to participate in a book inspired by the pioneering volume she initiated, we thank Daphne Patai, whose current project, together with Ricardo Santhiago, is a follow-up volume to *Brazilian Women Speak: Contemporary Life Stories* (1988) based on new interviews with several dozen of the women Patai originally interviewed in Brazil in the 1980s.

Working together has been a remarkably rewarding experience for all of us. The intergenerational feminist relationships at the heart of this book—sustained by generosity, respect, and mentorship—shaped our work together in meaningful and lasting ways. Katrina and Stacey wish to thank Franca for continuing to be an inspiration to them. *Beyond Women's Words* is "breathtaking" for this reason, as well. Franca thanks Katrina and Stacey for accommodating her innumerable suggestions and telling her when to stop, and for their impressive insights, hard work, and sense of humor. We also thank our respective partners, Henning Helms, Robert Douglas, and Ian Radforth, for their continuing love, respect, and support, and for accommodating our needs when, on more than one occasion, work on this book became all-consuming. To our brilliant young daughters, Klarissa Srigley, Hannah Helms, and Liliya Douglas, we hope the relationships, knowledge, and social justice approaches in this book are integral to your worlds in joyful ways.

Finally, we thank Sherna Berger Gluck, without whom this volume would never have seen the light of day. We are tremendously grateful to Sherna, a deeply committed feminist oral historian whose scholarship and political activism are an inspiration. We thank her for her infectious enthusiasm, generosity, and sense of humor, for the brilliant insights and incisive feedback she provided, especially in the final stages of writing, and for her friendship. This volume is dedicated to her.

Foreword

Sherna Berger Gluck

I could barely hear my Canadian colleagues over the din of the noisy Vietnamese restaurant in Montréal where we gathered after a 2011 International Oral History Workshop at Concordia University. "It's really time for *Women's Words II*," they urged me. "I couldn't agree more," I told them, "and you have my blessing—as if you need it—so go for it!" Indeed, they did.

That Concordia workshop, co-organized by one of the three Canadian co-editors of *Beyond Women's Words*, Stacey Zembrzycki, marked the start of the conversation. It continued at the 2014 Berkshire Conference on the History of Women (the Big Berks), where another of the editors, Katrina Srigley, raised provocative questions about the state of feminist oral history in a session on *Women's Words* co-organized by Zembrzycki and Pamela Sugiman, which featured several of the eventual contributors to *Beyond Women's Words*, including this writer.

Squeezed in the crowd outside the door of the jam-packed session was the third co-editor, well-known historian Franca Iacovetta, who was the President of the Berkshire Conference of Women Historians and host of the 2014 Big Berks. Under her stewardship, that international conference, held for the first time outside the continental US, was notable for the highly visible and varied feminist oral history sessions and for its focus on transnational and Indigenous scholarship.

These three co-editors, each an accomplished author of women's history in her own right, also have impressive records of collaborative scholarship, much of which focuses on oral history and storytelling. Their creative, collaborative partnership now brings us this latest work in the 40 years of anthologizing English-language feminist oral history. The scope and breadth of this new collection of essays on the theory and practice of feminist oral history is, quite frankly, breathtaking, and represents both the staying power and the evolution of feminist oral history.

The first collection of women's oral history, published in the 1977 special issue of *Frontiers: A Journal of Women's Studies*, featured the growing number of mainly US-based feminists engaged in oral history projects, what we might identify as the first generation, or what Susan Armitage characterizes as the first stage.[1] Both the academics among them who were using oral history in their classrooms and the activists working in community-based projects were engaged in a recovery process, simultaneously documenting women's oppression and celebrating their agency. The relationship between the interviewers and the women whose lives they were recording was a major focus of this first generation, as was advocacy. Yet, despite a commitment to "diversity" and "inclusion," their work was marked by naïve assumptions that overlooked difference and the power differential between interviewer and narrator. Nothing reflects this more than my own *Frontiers* essay, "What's so special about women? Women's oral history," which is a source of embarrassment for me today.

It was not just embarrassment about some of our early thinking that led some of us to start talking about the need for an updated anthology. Rather, by the mid-1980s, the shifting discourse of feminist thinking emphasized difference and positionality, with the recognition of multiple subjectivities and intersectional identities becoming a central tenet.

Having rejected the idea of a *Frontiers* redux, it did not take much for me to embrace Daphne Patai's proposal for a new anthology; and so began our productive collaboration. Our rather artless call for papers, issued in July 1988, noted that we were seeking "theoretical and methodological problems relating to intersubjectivity, ethics, the interview process itself, the subsequent formation of spoken words into written texts and interpretation . . ."

The resulting 1991 anthology, *Women's Words: The Feminist Practice of Oral History,* featured many new voices of a second generation of feminist oral historians as well as new thinking by members of the first generation. A more nuanced and complex analysis of the interviewer–narrator relationship was a hallmark of the anthology, especially with its emphasis on intersubjectivity. Additionally, it problematized ethical issues and advocacy, with greater self-reflexivity leading to a serious questioning of earlier practices and assumptions. For example, my own work with Palestinian women certainly complicated my embrace of advocacy, as did Daphne Patai's Brazilian work, which led her to ask increasingly vexing ethical questions.[2] Although we were concerned that the multiple problems raised by *Women's Words'* contributors might discourage new users, ultimately we were convinced that the essays demonstrated how to get on with our work even as we confronted the problems they raised.

Despite its important contribution to feminist oral history and its continuing value, we cannot ignore the shortcomings of *Women's Words.* As in the 1977 *Frontiers* issues, US-based scholars and activists dominated, even among the contributors whose work was international; and there were neither Indigenous nor LGBTQ+ voices. The absence of the latter was largely a product of its time and the fact that much of this literature was just becoming public.[3] Additionally, even though the scholarship challenging the hegemonic historiography of feminism was in its early stages, we should have recognized a multiplicity of practices, using the less essentialist title of *Women's Words: Feminist PracticeS of Oral History.*

In any event, the staying power of *Women's Words* and its almost iconic status has been somewhat surprising. As late as 2007, Alistair Thomson described it as one of "the core texts for feminist oral history," placing it firmly in what he identified as the third paradigmatic shift in [Western] oral history.[4] Nevertheless, by the time of the 2011 International Workshop at Concordia University, it was apparent that it was time for a sequel.

It was not just a matter of filling in the gaps in *Women's Words*. Rather, global feminist thinking and activism, including the growing influence of North American women of color, and the re-visioning of LGBTQ+ scholarship, had led both to an expanded consciousness and to a different discourse. Western-dominated feminist thinking was increasingly displaced by an emphasis on decolonial intersectionality and transnational feminism.[5]

With their very thoughtful editorial decisions and creative framing, Srigley, Zembrzycki, and Iacovetta have captured the profound impact these developments have had on feminist oral history practiceS. As a result, *Beyond Women's Words* has expanded and internationalized earlier North American scholarship, moving Indigenous and LGBTQ+ voices from the margins; storytelling and autoethnography have also been added to the pantheon of feminist oral history practices.

What is most notable about *Beyond Women's Words* is the innovative work presented by a new generation of intersectional feminists from across the globe, adding their voices to those of second-generation contributors. While the themes of ethics, advocacy, interviewer–narrator relationships, and collective identity that characterized the earlier anthologies continue to be addressed, in *Beyond Women's Words* these are interrogated in increasingly nuanced analyses and through innovative performance art.

Featuring a third generation that is also engaging with the digital revolution places *Beyond Women's Words* in oral history's evolving fourth paradigm, as proposed by Alistair Thomson. At the same time that some of the contributors are creating new digital archives, and others are using interviews from existing digital archives, the various conundrums and ethical implications posed by the digital revolution are critically addressed—and with a distinctly feminist spin.

In other words, the compelling and engaging contributions to *Beyond Women's Words* deepen our understanding and appreciation of what feminist oral history practices look and sound like today. This does not necessarily render earlier work moot; or suggest that the three generations, or the "stages" of feminist oral history, have evolved in a linear fashion. Rather, some themes have endured, even as they play out in different ways. Perhaps it is more like the spiralling effect that Daphne Patai and I noted in our Afterword to *Women's Words*, where each successive turn on the spiral produces a view that is both similar and different.

March 2018

Notes

1 Most of these articles, as well as others in subsequent issues of *Frontiers*, were published in 2001 in Susan H. Armitage, Patricia Hard, Karen Weathermon, eds., *Women's Oral History: The Frontiers Reader* (Lincoln, NE: University of Nebraska Press, 2002). Also see Susan H. Armitage, "Stages of Women's Oral History," in *Oxford Handbook of Oral History*, ed. Donald A. Ritchie (New York: Oxford University Press, 2010), 169–185.

2 Gluck, "Advocacy Oral History: Palestinian Women in Resistance" and Patai, "US Academics and Third World Women: Is Ethical Research Possible?" in *Women's Words: The Feminist Practice of Oral History*, eds. Sherna Berger Gluck and Daphne Patai (New York: Routledge, 1991).

3 Because their ground-breaking oral history of the Buffalo lesbian community was still in the works, Elizabeth Laprovsky Kennedy and Madeline D. Davis were reluctant to contribute to *Women's Words*. *Boots of Leather, Slippers of Gold: The History of a Lesbian Community* (Routledge, first 1993; reprint 2014) was published two years after its release.

4 Alistair Thomson, "Four Paradigm Transformations in Oral History," *Oral History Review* 34, no. 1 (2007): 49–70.

5 See especially Maria Lugones, "Toward a Decolonial Feminism," *Hypatia* 25, no. 4 (2010): 742–759, and, more recently, Sara Salem, "Decolonial Intersectionality and a Transnational Feminist Movement," *The Feminist Wire*, last modified 17 April 2014, accessed 5 May 2017, www.thefeministwire.com/2014/04/decolonial-intersectionality/.

Introduction

Franca Iacovetta, Katrina Srigley,
and Stacey Zembrzycki

Feminists who work with oral history methods want to tell stories that matter.
They know, too, that the telling of those stories—the processes by which they
are generated and recorded, and the contexts in which they are shared and
interpreted—also matters—a lot. Forty years ago, pioneering woman's historian
Sherna Berger Gluck asserted that feminist oral historians like herself used oral
history to validate women's lives, highlight the rhythms of those lives, and
negotiate the dynamics of authority and power that shape, to quote Luisa
Passerini, another innovator, the "social relationship that is the interview."[1]
Engagement with practices informed by feminist principles was motivated by
a desire to share knowledge about women and other historically marginalized
subjects, and to revise and upend understandings of the past—and present.
Inspired as well by a commitment to advocate on behalf of women, feminists
sought to write impactful, even empowering, histories that would contribute
to meaningful social change. Since Gluck issued that declaration in the 1970s,
many important stories have been narrated, analyzed, and the methods by
which they were collected and shared subjected to careful reflection, producing
an impressive body of research, theory, and debate in the field of feminist oral
history, both inside and outside the academy.

Beyond Women's Words is an international, multigenerational, and multidisciplinary volume of essays that are variously situated at the intersections of
feminisms, broadly defined, and the practices, theories, and ethics of doing
oral history. It is organized around five main themes and includes a separate
introduction for each thematic section. Written by Linda Shopes, Penny
Summerfield, Nan Alamilla Boyd, Paul Ortiz (our lone male participant), and
Anna Sheftel, respectively, the section introductions discuss the theme in
question and the chapters related to it. Our introduction provides an overview
of the project as a whole.

Moving beyond

Our title reflects the multiple ways we have interpreted "moving beyond."
Of course, we stand more than 25 years beyond the publication of *Women's
Words*, the ground-breaking volume edited by Gluck and Daphne Patai that

2 Iacovetta, Srigley, and Zembrzycki

helped to lay a more critical and theoretical foundation for women's and feminist-informed oral history. In their respective essays, a diverse and multi-disciplinary group of feminist scholars honestly discussed and rigorously debated how the dynamics of power affect the process, content, and outcomes of interviews and the nature of the scholarship produced. Their analytical discussions regarding key concepts such as subjectivity (the ways in which consciousness, self-identity, behavior, and language shape memory), the positionality of both narrator and researcher (appreciating how context—including narrators' and interviewers' subjectivities—influences memories, memory-making, and its subsequent interpretation), and the possibility, or not, of developing fully egalitarian research methods helped to generate much subsequent research.

Given its landmark status, our volume contains, appropriately enough, reflections on *Women's Words* and feminist oral history more generally, beginning with a Foreword by Gluck. Three other contributors to the original *Women's Words*—Katherine Borland, Rina Benmayor, and Patai (a critic of certain recent trends in oral history)—build on earlier analyses regarding conflicts over authorial interpretation, oral history as transformative pedagogy, and the vexed ethics of white privileged academics interviewing marginalized women, to move beyond the 1991 volume in ways we discuss later.[2]

The volume is meant to capture some of the exciting research, insights, and debates that have engaged feminist scholars and activists prior to and since the publication of *Women's Words* and to encourage new and ongoing conversations.[3] It brings together a diverse collection of scholars, students, Indigenous Elders, activists, artists, and community-engaged and social-movement-based oral history practitioners from around the world, and at different points in their careers or life trajectories. With researchers and narrators from seven continents, the volume's broad regional coverage includes parts of North and South America, the United Kingdom of Great Britain and Northern Ireland, Asia, the Middle East, Africa, and Australia. In addition to current scholarship, much of it advocacy oriented, it highlights activist oral history, creative work, and performance derived from diverse modes of storytelling, and the impact of the "digital turn." Whereas *Women's Words'* inclusion of work outside North America consisted mainly of critical reflections on cross-cultural research conducted by US-based academics doing fieldwork on what some identified as "Third World" women, this volume includes work by scholars rooted in the southern regions they study as well as those who challenge the dichotomy between North and South, Western and non-Western, and traditional and modern.[4]

This project took hold with the 2014 Berkshire Conference on the History of Women (Big Berks), which co-editor Franca Iacovetta hosted at the University of Toronto. Earlier conversations about reengaging with *Women's Words* resulted in a very successful workshop co-organized by Stacey Zembrzycki and Pamela Sugiman.[5] The participants included Kathleen Blee, a scholar of racist movements in the United States whose chapter theorizes about writing feminist oral histories of unsympathetic subjects radically opposed to feminist goals of equality and social justice, and Lynn Abrams, whose chapter on women who reached maturity in post-1945 Britain reflects on the contradiction that emerged between the women's liberation narratives and their discomfort with the subject of feminism.[6] The workshop did not resolve Gluck's quandary: How do we define feminist oral history, which has long been described as research by, on, and for women, without being essentialist?[7] But the diverse group of workshop participants, like the many other oral historians across the conference's global program, certainly shared some basic understandings of feminist-informed oral history practices.[8] It was time for a volume devoted to feminist oral history in the 21st century.

Such a project could not adopt a simple linear approach to moving beyond. Certainly, one objective was to build on the strength of *Women's Words* by redressing some of its limitations. In her Foreword, Gluck herself identifies the absence of Indigenous and LGBTQ+ voices, too few researchers from outside the United States, and a title that did not reference a multiple set of feminist oral history practices. We could add little explicit discussion of sexuality and the body. Reviewers of the book praised (or acknowledged) its discussion of different interview techniques and interpretive frameworks, challenges of cross-cultural research, and issues related to advocacy. Some expressed concern (which the editors shared) that the focus on self-criticism and dilemmas might discourage subsequent work.[9] A few characterized the volume as post-modernist largely because of the anthropological essays that explicitly engaged the self-critical work in post-modern ethnography (which questioned scientific claims to produce objective knowledge through a focus on the anthropologist's subjectivity in shaping fieldwork observations and encouraged self-critical analysis of how that subjectivity, or positionality, shaped those interpretations of other people's cultures) and advocated reflexivity (the self-critical act of being aware of, and reflecting upon, one's presence, even intrusion, into the research process).[10] However, the book did not occasion the deeply polarized debates then occurring elsewhere, perhaps because the ethical issues addressed resonated with feminists across the political and theoretical spectrum.[11] But no one noted the failure to engage Indigenous modes of storytelling, an omission that spoke to the need for conversations that cross, and aim to bridge, disciplinary and epistemological divides.[12]

If noting the shortcomings of *Women's Words* captures some sense of what moving beyond means, it is also inadequate. Indeed, it can mistakenly paint a Whiggish view of history as but one main narrative that is improved on through periodic inclusion of new subjects or insights. Here, we have not restricted our contributions to work with a direct or sole lineage to *Women's Words*. For example, Valerie Korinek's chapter on the narratives, and silences, that surfaced in interviews with queer women in Canada's prairie west, draws on a now long-standing scholarship in LGBTQ+ oral history that has sought to decenter knowledge rooted in heteronormativity (the assumption that humans fall into two distinct genders, male and female, with natural roles to play in society).

The chapter by Uma Chakravarti and Ponni Arasu, which uses an inter-generational and activist narrative frame to map the politicization of Chakravarti, a pioneering feminist educator, scholar, and activist, draws on a rich South Asian praxis and scholarship. To be even more blunt, the contribution from Australia by Sue Anderson, Jaimee Hamilton, and Lorina Barker, which makes a compelling case for the feminist tradition of Indigenous women's yarning (storytelling), draws on thousands of years of cultural knowledge, history, and law to decolonize oral history.[13] Our recognition of these multiple contexts also explains why, as editors, we did not impose a strict requirement that contributors genuflect, intellectually speaking, before *Women's Words* if their own work reflected different influences.

Moving beyond in feminist oral history also involves decentering the scholarly hegemony of the United States and English-speaking world, an admittedly daunting task. As Canadians who live on the edge of the powerful United States, we are acutely sensitive to the geopolitical dynamics involved, but no less so than feminists located elsewhere, including those with histories shaped by entanglements with American imperialism. Pro-active efforts to redress the global imbalance through—for instance, transnational conferences—help to challenge assumptions about who sits at the center and margins of scholarly debate, but they have not permanently altered scholarly practices.[14] This is not to downplay the significant historiographies produced elsewhere—such as in the United Kingdom,[15] South Asia,[16] Latin America,[17] and for that matter Canada[18]—or the importance of international conversations in oral history.[19] Nevertheless, Anglophone dominance means that the (mostly un-translated) work of oral historians working in non-English-speaking countries—including much of the extensive Spanish-language literature on *testimonios*—remains sidelined.[20]

The related challenge of centering the stories of racial, sexual, refugee, undocumented, and other historically oppressed groups within different national or regional contexts, including that of the United States, and within key sites of knowledge-production, such as universities, remains an ongoing one. Here, Benmayor's analysis of the empowering impact a digital course on "Latina Life Stories" had on students from families of migrant Mexican farmworkers and Sady Sullivan's reflections on a collaborative community project she led in Brooklyn, New York, which involved mixed-heritage people, contribute to continuing efforts to decenter knowledge produced both within and outside mainstream institutions.[21] So, too, does Sarah Loose and Amy Starecheski's discussion of oral history's potential for social justice struggles and social-movement building, which also draws on engagements with international movements. These and other chapters extend as well the attention that some authors in *Women's Words* focused on the rewards (not just pitfalls) of oral history practices rooted in community-based projects.[22] However, given the critical role of oral history research with Black women and transgendered people in challenging dominant narratives in the US—and Canada—and making space for alternative ones, the absence of scholars in this fields in this project is a glaring one.[23]

Without diminishing either the international scope of *Women's Words* or its influence internationally, we see *Beyond Women's Words* as contributing towards further internationalizing feminist oral history.[24] Among the scholars located outside North America who draw insight from *Women's Words* but also extend the global focus are Theresa de Langis, who discusses the complex ethics surrounding the "Cambodian Women's Oral History" project, an advocacy project that helped to break the silence on the sexual brutality and gendered violence women suffered under the genocidal Khmer Rouge regime of the 1970s, and Hillary Hiner, who explores the practical and ethical dilemmas and findings that emerged from oral history research focused on the memory and trauma of feminist survivors of Chile's Pinochet dictatorship. In their reflections on an oral history project with Anglo-Indian school teachers in Bangalore, India, Sanchia deSouza and Jyothsna Latha Belliappa consider the positionality of both researcher and narrator, highlighting in particular the contexts in which the latter wielded power in the interview.

Keen to produce a volume that reflects the diverse contexts in which feminists are practicing oral history, we were delighted with the diversity of authors who replied to our call for papers. They included Suroopa Mukherjee, whose chapter on the 1984 Bhopal industrial disaster focuses on the protest voices and street performances that marked the rise of one of India's longest (and ultimately failed) women-led social justice movements. It also included those engaged in the digital turn, one of whom, Margo Shea, uses oral histories conducted with Catholic women in Northern Ireland to highlight how digital culture has altered modes of self-representation, understandings of oral history practice, and feminist engagements with heritage culture.

Another respondent was Elise Chenier, who uses her experience developing a digital archive of lesbian oral histories in Canada to write a how-to guide for creating such repositories. Like Korinek, Chenier also builds on and contributes to the growing scholarship in queer oral history.[25] In both cases, some reference is made to transgender oral history. Also noteworthy here is Hiner's chapter on Chile, which offers some insight into the experiences of lesbian and transgender trauma survivors. Overall, however, our volume does not adequately reflect the current outpouring of projects in transgender oral history.[26]

To ensure a greater cross-section of feminist oral history work, we also built on relationships forged through the Big Berks and beyond. In addition to the Indian specialists already named, medical anthropologist Grace Akello joined our project with a reflective piece on how a research project on the impact of war on northern Ugandan children compelled her to confront her own trauma. Relatedly, feminist anthropologist Nadje Al-Ali uses an oral history project with Iraqi refugee women in multiple locations of dispersal around the globe, and fieldwork related to Islamic State/ISIS sexual violence against women in Iraq, to reflect on the significance of positionality and the challenge of conveying "truths" through oral history. Together, these authors' participation meant greater representation of those working within explicitly anti-colonial feminist frameworks. Their projects center the stories, and lives, of women and children in South Asia, Africa, the Middle East, and in diaspora, and in contexts shaped by colonialism, authoritarianism, custodial violence, economic sanctions, militarization, and war.

With important exceptions,[27] until relatively recently, the large body of work that has been commonly recognized as oral history (as opposed to studies in folklore and oral tradition) showed little engagement with Indigenous oral histories.[28] Feminist efforts to more fully integrate the storytelling traditions of Indigenous peoples into our methodological and epistemological discussions of oral history will involve sustained consideration of those who have long been sharing stories in this tradition—such as Lee Maracle (Sto:lo) and Madonna Thunderhawk (Sioux)—and collaborative work on Indigenous ways of thinking about stories, storytelling, and documenting the past.[29] The observation applies equally to the extensive oral history work being produced by Indigenous scholars.[30]

Our efforts to encourage more explicit engagement with storytelling traditions that are both ancient and present, and key sites of knowledge- and meaning-making, also have a connection to the 2014 Big Berks. The significant presence of Indigenous participants at the conference was the result of a collaborative process of negotiation and relationship-building that occurred on an international scale. As co-chairs of the Indigenous program, historians Mary Jane McCallum and Susan Hill, and allied scholar Adele Perry, a conference program co-chair, played indispensable roles in attracting Indigenous activists, scholars, students, performers, filmmakers, and other artists whose presentations spoke powerfully to the importance of decolonizing knowledge rather than simply invoking the principle of inclusivity. McCallum and Hill, who have written incisively on the theme of decolonizing historical knowledge, are currently co-editing a volume on Indigenous women's histories that draws on the 2014 Big Berks.[31]

Following the conference, we initiated conversations with Indigenous intellectuals long engaged with women's words, informing them of our intentions to produce a book, and inviting them to help shape the project.[32] Among those who generously agreed to join us was performer and writer Penny Couchie (Anishinaabekwe, Nipissing First Nation), and her long-time mentor, internationally renowned writer, and founder of Spiderwoman Theater Muriel Miguel (Kuna and Rappahannock Nations). Presented in the form of a conversation, their chapter explores how story-weaving mobilizes key organizing principles of Anishinaabeg epistemology—creation stories, relationality, and non-linear time—to tell stories. They also included Anderson, Hamilton, and Barker, whose contribution on yarning is discussed earlier, and Lianne C. Leddy, who reflects on interviews conducted with Elders in her home community of Serpent River First Nation in northern Ontario, to discuss collective modes of knowledge-sharing and activism as well as Indigenous feminism(s). Finally, Heather Howard, who has long worked in relationship on Mississauga Anishinaabeg territory in Toronto, traces transformations in representations of urban Indigenous women's knowledge and orality as collected and disseminated by First Story Toronto, a long-time Indigenous community-based history project that recently developed a mobile phone app. Like the other contributions involving popular education and digital technology, Howard's essay is an important contribution to public history.[33]

In making meaningful engagements with Indigenous women's ways of storytelling and knowing a central goal for the 21st century, *Beyond Women's Words* confirms and extends a fundamental principle of oral history: that we build real understanding through relationship, not just inclusivity (which can easily slip into tokenism). At a time when Canada and other white settler societies have been rightly challenged to prioritize above all reconciliation with Indigenous peoples, we have tried to move beyond tokenism through the inclusion of Indigenous modes of storytelling, analysis, and reflection across the collection as a whole. As Eve Tuck and K. Wayne Yang note, "decolonization" is not simply a synonym (or metaphor) for social justice projects, but requires attention to the processes and effects of colonization on Indigenous peoples as well as active engagement with Indigenous ways of knowing.[34] A broader collective commitment to decolonizing knowledge can also aim to bridge the silos between oral history and what is viewed as oral tradition, and write more intertwined histories.

In related fashion, we have interpreted moving beyond in feminist oral history as an act of circling back to earlier, still incisive insights and exchanges that can be caricatured or forgotten with every new claim to historiographical advancement. (In a stronger rebuke, Patai decries the rush to claim methodological innovation when a report on findings might suffice.) The requirement of post-graduate university programs and scholarly publishing venues to produce "original" work has engendered training methods that can encourage a culture of discounting or forgetting elders, a term we use advisedly to refer broadly to elder members of a given community who have left a mark on it. One result is frequent dismissal of, or disregard for, the work of earlier scholars. By contrast, the lessons offered by Indigenous Elders, who gift their stories to younger members of their communities, and others, encourage respect for the wisdom of earlier generations. This more organic, and respectful, approach similarly informs the caution issued by scholars such as Susan Armitage and Penny Summerfield against reductionist portraits of early feminist oral history scholarship as merely recovering subjects.[35] At a time when the resurgence of extreme-right and xenophobic movements endanger the rights and histories of variously defined minorities across the globe, no stronger case can be made for doing recuperative work.[36]

Continuing the conversation(s)

Feminist oral history today looks very different than it did 40 years ago, thanks in large part to *Women's Words* and other significant analytical interventions published before, alongside, and since its appearance. Here, we offer a few sweeping generalizations. An initial optimistic, and naïve, embrace of oral history as women-centered research that would be undertaken by equal partners (interviewer and narrator), and necessarily validate women's lives, empower them, raise their consciousness, and rewrite history has undergone much revision as scholars have come to see how deeply fraught the oral history process can be.[37]

Frank reflection on and debate over the dangers of assuming the commonalities of gender over the differences forged by class, race, age, Indigeneity versus settler status, ability/disability, and other social categories has further sensitized feminists, and others, to the power dynamics shaping the interview and knowledge-production more generally. In one of the most cited essays in *Women's Words*, Judith Stacey addressed the ethical contradictions between feminist principles and the ethnographic method by asking "Can there be a feminist ethnography?" She answered this question by suggesting we might at best produce partially feminist studies, just as partial rather than whole "truths" are likely to emerge from our research.[38] The debates prompted by such insights have not led feminists to quit the craft but rather to modify earlier exaggerated, even utopian, claims about oral history's capacity to produce egalitarian and emancipatory scholarship without abandoning important goals, such as centering the voices of the historically marginalized. While we no longer view our objectives and methods as unproblematic, the continuing act of recording women's stories while seeking to explicate the cultural meanings of their memories has produced a rich and diverse body of work on women and other marginalized subjects.[39]

A continuing appreciation for the power of storytelling that is also reflected in this volume has intensified with the growth of research into the memories of survivors of traumatic and life-altering events, which for women has often involved sexual violence. A consequence in large part of the succession of wars, genocides, mass violence, and forced migrations that have shaped global realities in the late 20th and 21st centuries, this literature has powerfully demonstrated just how important narratives can be in aiding the healing process for survivors, though never in a linear way. More recently, attention has extended to witnesses and perpetrators.[40] The multidisciplinary scholarship also underscores the analytical value of insights into the fragmentary and contingent nature of memory, and its "living" quality. In other words, one's memories can be shaped as much by one's present circumstances and worldview as one's past—a point made years ago by Luisa Passerini and others.[41] Another noteworthy development is the growing importance of survivors' testimonies in landmark legal cases as well as political mobilizations. The truth and reconciliation commissions that have drawn on the testimonies of survivors of residential schools and apartheid have addressed the transgenerational trauma produced by colonialism.[42]

Given feminists' critical role in breaking the silence surrounding gender-based violence against women, it is fitting that *Beyond Women's Words* includes several chapters dealing with memory and trauma. In their aforementioned chapters on major oral history projects involving female survivors of the Khmer

Rouge and Pinochet dictatorship, de Langis and Hiner continue the important conversations regarding empowerment. A central question is whether and how oral histories informed by feminist sensibilities create the conditions that enable women to speak their truth to a powerful state that sanctioned and silenced their oppression. In addressing it, both authors reflect on their positionality as a "white American" and a "*gringa chilena*" (American-born but Chilean-raised) in their respective research, and confirm the value of the survivors' subjective truths. So too does Al-Ali, whose response to current post-modernist preoccupations with positing multiple, shifting, and contradictory interpretations of all texts, including the oral history record created by researcher and narrator, is to assert that "nihilism" is insufficient and dangerous when the lives of real women are at stake. Akello is engaged by questions of subjectivities and truths as well. As a Black African in a field (anthropology) long dominated by white Westerners, she (like others) acknowledges the cultural baggage that informs the ethnographic method as well as efforts to redress it.[43] Her introspective analysis of the troubling ailments that first disrupted her carefully ("scientifically") designed plans to interview the sick and harried child survivors of Uganda's civil war, and then prompted the revelation of how a shared trauma would indelibly shape her results, offers a poignant contribution to work on intersubjectivity (which seeks to understand how interaction between interviewer and narrator, and their respective subjectivities, affects the oral dynamics of the interview).

The two chapters with connections to the "Montréal Life Stories" project, a major oral history project on refugee and exile populations in that city, reflect on the potential, and (uneven) impact of storytelling on narrators through a focus on collective writing and performance, respectively.[44] They do so in ways that disrupt normative interview narrator structures. Stéphane Martelly writes evocatively about the breakthrough that occurred among a group of grieving Haitian women survivors of the 2010 earthquake resistant to project guidelines regarding interviews when, in the context of a creative writing class she ran, they reset the rules by which they collaboratively narrated their stories. As scholars and artists, Shahrzad Arshadi, Hourig Attarian, Khadija Baker, and Kumru Bilici have made the memories of violence, atrocity, and displacement in their respective Middle East and Near East nations, both inherited family memories and those based on their experiences, the fabric of their individual and collective work. Here, they address these themes through reflecting on a performance piece that focuses on doing laundry and telling stories.[45]

Women's Words and other work encouraged greater attention to every aspect of the interview—to understand it as a linguistic and social event and a performance. These and related insights, such that women narrators are prone to understatement, still resonate. A large and growing literature attests to feminist efforts to move beyond just listening to surface words, but instead to listen "in stereo" or to "listen deeply" to the refrains as well as gestures, silences, and other non-verbal clues that can help to unlock the personal scripts, cultural myths, and other codes by which people live.[46] From early on, feminists expressed disappointment with social scientific models of interviewing, whether by admitting to failing as the dispassionate scientist or noting the advantages of being personally forthcoming with one's "subjects" and even developing friendships with them.[47] A growing attention to subjectivity and intersubjectivity in the interview also meant more focus on the importance of empathy, not just rapport, and relationship to the interview process.[48] Additionally, there has been continuing willingness to discuss and learn from apparent failures. Here, we take two examples involving unexpected reactions to questions about feminism. When faced with narrators who ascribed to liberationist practices but not "second-wave" feminism, Abrams acknowledges feminism's uneven impact and suggests that posing such questions widens our conversations about feminism in important ways. For her part, Leddy's reflection on the limited impact of "whitestream" feminism on the Anishinaabekwe (women) Elders she interviewed prompts important reflections about the complex meanings of Indigenous womanhood.

Of course, feminists have not worked in isolation from other oral historians, as exemplified by their ongoing engagement with the influential work of leading male oral historians such as Alessandro Portelli, Alistair Thomson, Ronald Grele, and Michael Frisch. If the motives of both groups have not always been identical, there has been a widely shared (but not exclusive) mandate to focus on the voices of less powerful groups and write bottom-up histories that challenged dominant models, though feminists sought as well to challenge male-based articulations of class, work, militancy, and so on. As well, feminists have been centrally involved in the wider conversations and debates that, for instance, shifted attention away from critiques of "faulty" memories to that of making the creative process of memory-making itself the subject of analysis.[49] In addition, the standard oral history readers have been inclusive of feminist work.[50] There are also more specific examples that speak to the wider intellectual community that feminist and other oral historians shared. For example, the interest that feminist scholars Kathryn Anderson and Dana C. Jack showed, in shifting the focus in oral history from data gathering to interactive process, resonates with Ronald J. Grele's concept of an interview as a conversational narrative, articulated at roughly the same time Anderson and Jack were working.[51] Similarly, feminist efforts to "democratize" the interview and explore ways of sharing power with narrators are arguably compatible with Frisch's concept of shared authority—whose own book using the term also came out in 1991—but even more so with the recent emphasis on "sharing authority" (something of a re-interpretation of Frisch) in an oral history project. The later framework focuses on building and nurturing relationships between narrators and researchers before, during, and after the interview, and often leads to the creation of a collaborative outcome, such as a museum exhibit, walking tour, or performance.[52] Still, given the leading role that feminists have played in initiating major critiques, debates, and paradigmatic shifts in the field, it seems fair to ask, as an open-ended question for debate:

Why is it that male scholars, and a small group of male scholars in particular, are cited more consistently than feminists?[53]

Moving forward

In moving forward, feminists must seriously address the impact of the digital turn on our work. A decade ago, Alistair Thomson correctly predicted that digital technology would transform the craft.[54] Since then, Gluck has been vocal about the need to acknowledge the ethical fault lines that might undermine the democratizing potential of this technology, but few have heeded her call. How does the "quantum leap" in the dissemination of oral histories online, posted for many years after an interview is completed, affect what narrators tell us and who listens to these now public stories? What happens to trust? And the formal and informal agreements we make with our narrators?[55] Instead of tackling these questions, oral historians have forged ahead collectively, for the most part, using the Internet and both proprietary and open source software and their corresponding tools to hone their "post-documentary sensibility" in an effort to make the stories we collect "easier" to use, process, and share.[56] As Mary A. Larson explains here, the Internet and its platforms are largely masculine spaces. Designed by men, most oral history tools run counter to what oral history is at heart: an intimate encounter between people rooted in relationships forged over time and through the process of sharing stories.[57] Nor, as Susan Hill has pointed out, are Indigenous scholars likely to be "setting the agenda."[58] Since the digital is here to stay, we need to recognize the incompatibility between our feminist sensibilities, such as respect for narrators, and the digital's pace, openness, and impersonal, profit-driven nature.

Stories that are shared online, through websites or apps, or that are posted on social media, can create the illusion that we are experiencing intimate storytelling spaces. But, as Shea shows, access to intimacy in a digital realm is difficult, given that we tend to know little about the narrators themselves. And, as Gluck notes, the dynamics of storytelling surely change when narrators know their listeners will not be limited to those in the room. Since what is said, and what gets silenced, matters a lot, so do these issues. As for the power inherent in sharing stories, who exactly is empowered when those stories are shared? Howard stresses the need to fully consider these issues when digitizing Indigenous oral traditions. Can the digital decolonize knowledge while also protecting the cultural integrity of story? Or do we necessarily commodify stories by putting them online? In Howard's case, community members control the stories they tell and share through the app they collaboratively created, but when stories are shared online, on sites like Facebook, they become the property of the companies who operate those spaces.

We must consider as well who is listening online and who has the ability to share stories in the digital realm. The still real issues around digital accessibility and literacy affect women and LGBTQ+ people more than men, and the elderly more than younger generations. Class speaks to the exclusionary nature of the digital too; and, as Larson notes in this volume, privilege helps define who gets to listen and also which practitioners have the ability to "go digital" at all. Since most practitioners, do not possess the capacity to code, design software, or create websites, it means paying for expensive services they likely cannot afford. Under-funded community-based practitioners working with marginalized groups face particular challenges in this regard.

Also concerning is the time that must be invested in going digital, adding to the already onerous and daunting task of doing oral history. A well-indexed digital oral history collection is a joy to use, but most interviews actually remain on shelves in libraries (if not the dark corners of our closets), and researchers often read transcripts, themselves the result of laborious work. In her chapter on archived interview materials, Ruth Percy urges us not to aban-don the archives or the study of the memories of deceased subjects. But in highlighting what archived digital and analog collections can offer historians, she also reminds us that we remain as firmly tied to transcripts as ever. Here, too, privilege and funding largely determine what gets digitized. Moreover, in some cases the only records that remain in oral history collections are the original transcripts themselves, as archives once commonly addressed their storage challenges by destroying the original tapes. Notwithstanding our lofty goal of returning the aurality to the oral, it is also faster to read through a transcript than to listen to an interview in its entirety. We can try to interpret stories told to others in the past, but, as Percy appreciates, we will never fully understand the contexts in which they were shared. To engage with stories in the digital age, where the potential for democratization is circumscribed by the various ethical issues that require structures of authority, *real* shared authority, and even severe limitations on distribution and use, we need to re-think how we can proceed in an ethical manner that respects that humanism that is at the center of our diverse practices, feminist or otherwise.

Conclusion

Our reply to Gluck's question about moving beyond essentialist definitions of feminist oral history is to ask whether—given the huge range and diversity of work, and the challenges that lie ahead—the process of arriving at a definition would be unnecessarily limiting. Certainly, feminist oral history practices have shared some common goals, such as analyzing women's subordination within patriarchal structures and producing alternative histories rooted in women's experiences and truths. Without imposing a singular trajectory, we have noted some of the debates, shifts, and continuities. Feminist approaches to oral history, as Lynn Abrams notes, reveal distinctive features. Like most feminist researchers, they have "always rejected any pretense at objectivity," been acutely honest about oral history's limits, and offered "probably the most sustained practical and theoretical engagement with issues around subjectivity and intersubjectivity."[59] As we contemplate the future, an open-ended under-standing of the possibilities that feminisms hold for challenging inequalities and advocating for equality in whatever form is necessary within the context of the relationships that ground our work is a viable solution.

As for challenges, a key priority is to critically engage the relationship between feminism and colonialism as we think about developing a more inclusive feminist oral history moving forward. In 1995, Patricia Monture said she did not see feminism as removed from the colonial practices of her country (Canada).[60] That "whitestream" feminism has little traction among the Anishinaabekwe Elders of Serpent River First Nation (Leddy) signals the need to recognize the different origins and forms of feminisms. Similarly, at the 2014 Big Berks, Elder Lorraine Whiteduck Liberty (Nipissing First Nation) responded to a conversation about feminism's history and its utility for the way we live and make change in the world, in a manner that resonates here. She asked, with incredulity: "Don't you know you're equal?" For Whiteduck Liberty, her feminism is rooted in who she is as an Anishinaabekwe, in the long history of strong activist women in her life and culture, and within her way of living in the world. As the authors of *Indigenous Feminisms* point out, to engage in this work requires integrating Indigenous perspectives and recognizing that "a single normative definition remains impossible because Indigenous women's circumstances vary enormously throughout colonizing societies, where patriarchy dominates, and in Indigenous communities with distinct histories and cultural traditions."[61]

Instead of concerning ourselves with a definition of feminist oral history, we might allow the goals of the field—to story and re-story the past, challenge inequalities, and teach and empower through telling stories that matter—to be realized by honoring a variety of ways of knowing, sharing, and learning that do not abandon feminist politics to challenge inequalities, but, rather, as Nigerian author Chimanada Ngozi Adichie and Black feminist scholar bell hooks insist, work within and through a decolonized feminist perspective that is deeply contextual and attentive to varied histories.[62] Perhaps the true power of feminist oral history is emancipating it and ourselves from its constraints.

Notes

1 Sherna Berger Gluck, "What's So Special about Women? Women's Oral History," *Frontiers: A Journal of Women's Studies* 2, no. 2 (Summer 1977): 3–17; Luisa Passerini, "A Passion for Memory," *History Workshop Journal* 72 (2011): 241.
2 See Borland, Patai, and Benmayor in Sherna Berger Gluck and Daphne Patai, eds., *Women's Words: The Feminist Practice of Oral History* (New York: Routledge, 1991). The debate also includes important interventions by Gaytri Spivak, "Can the Subaltern Speak?" in *Marxism and the Interpretation of Culture*, eds. C. Nelson and E. Grossberg (Basingstoke: Macmillan Education, 1988), 271–313; Chandra Mohanty, *Feminism without Borders: Decolonizing Theory, Practicing Solidarity* (Durham: Duke University Press, 2003); Lila Abu-Lughod, *Do Muslim Women Need Saving?* (Cambridge: Harvard University Press, 2013).
3 Important discussions that inspired or were contemporary to *Women's Words* include the four theme issues of *Frontiers: A Journal of Women Studies* (published in 1977, 1983 and 1998) that were later compiled in Susan H. Armitage, Patricia Hard,

Karen Weathermon, eds., *Women's Oral History: The Frontiers Reader* (Lincoln, Nebraska: University of Nebraska Press, 2002); Susan Geiger, "Women's Life Histories: Method and Content," *Signs* 11, no. 2 (Winter 1986): 334–351; Geiger, "What's So Feminist about Women's History?" *Journal of Women's History* 2, no. 1 (1990): 169–182; Ann Oakley, "Interviewing Women: A Contradiction in Terms?" in *Doing Feminist Research*, ed. Helen Roberts (London: Routledge, 1981), 30–61; C. Bell and H. Roberts, eds., *Social Researching: Politics, Problems, Practice* (London: Routledge, 1984); Personal Narratives Group, eds., *Interpreting Women's Lives: Feminist Theory and Personal Narratives* (Bloomington: Indiana University Press, 1989), including essays by Luisa Passerini, Marjorie Mbiliny, and Marjorie Shostak; Daphne Patai, "Ethical Problems of Personal Narratives, or, Who Should Eat the Last Piece of Cake?" *International Journal of Oral History* 8, no. 1 (1987): 5–27.

4 The feminist scholarship (informed by what some have called Third World feminism) that offered the most sustained critique of cross-cultural research has also provided feminist oral historians with critical insights into writing transnational histories that decolonize understandings of "non-Western" women in conflict and in diaspora. As well as those noted above, see Chandra Mohanty, "Under Western Eyes: Feminist Scholarship and Colonial Discourse," *Boundary 2* 12, no. 3 (Spring–Autumn 1984): 333–358; Mohanty, "Under Western Eyes Revisited: Feminist Solidarity through Anti-Capitalist Struggle," *Signs* 28, no. 2 (2003): 499–535; Lila Abu-Lughod, *Writing Women's Words: Bedouin Stories* (Berkeley: University of California Press, 2008); Vijay Agnew, ed., *Diaspora, Memory and Identity: A Search for Home* (Toronto: University of Toronto Press, 2005); Nadje Al-Ali, *Iraqi Women: Untold Stories from 1948 to the Present* (London: Zed Books, 2007); Parin Dossa, *Racialized Bodies, Disabling Worlds: Storied Lives of Immigrant Muslim Women* (Toronto: University of Toronto Press, 2009); Nadia Jones-Gailani, *Iraqi Women in Diaspora: A Transnational Study of Women's Life Histories in Amman, Detroit, and Toronto* (Toronto: University of Toronto Press, forthcoming); South Asian Diaspora: South Asian Immigrants-Oral Histories, accessed 13 October 2017, http://guides.nyu.edu/c.php?g=276914&p=1846510.

5 Sugiman's many important essays on Japanese Canadian women's memories of internment include her much-cited "Passing Time, Moving Memories Interpreting Wartime Narratives," *Histoire Sociale/Social History* 37, no. 73 (May 2004): 51–79. Other workshop participants are part of a forthcoming theme section on feminist oral history in Katrina Srigley and Stacey Zembrzycki, eds., *Oral History Review* 45, no. 1 (Winter/Spring 2018).

6 Other workshop participants are part of a forthcoming theme section on feminist oral history in Katrina Srigley and Stacey Zembrzycki, eds., *Oral History Review* 45, no. 1 (Winter/Spring 2018).

7 Sherna Berger Gluck, "Personal Reflections on the Making of *Women's Words*: Looking Back, Looking Forward," 16th Berkshire Conference on the History of Women (Toronto, 2014); "Has Feminist Oral History Lost Its Radical/Subversive Edge," *Oral History* (Autumn 2011): 63–72, where she cites Bornat as asserting that *Women's Words* questioned feminism's essentialist direction (65–66).

8 Other oral history panels since published include Donna R. Gabaccia and Franca Iacovetta, eds., *Borders, Conflict-Zones and Memory: Scholarly Engagements with Luisa Passerini* (New York: Routledge, 2018), initially published as a theme issue of *Women's History Review* 25, no. 3 (2016).

9 "*Women's Words*: A Review Symposium," with Susan Armitage, George Lipsitz, and Gary R. Mormino, *Oral History Review* 20, nos. 1/2 (Spring–Fall, 1992): 105–111; Susan Geiger, *Signs* (review of three books) (Winter 1994): 499–503. The reviews consulted include Rebecca Maksel, *Journal of American Folklore History* 107, no. 424 (Spring 1994): 332–335; Nancy Porter, *Women's Studies Quarterly* 19, nos. 3/4 (Fall/Winter 1991): 150–153; Mary Blewett, "Good Intentions," *The*

Women's Review of Books IX, no. 5 (February 1992): 10–11; Carol L. Benton, "Review Essay: Performance: Ethical Concerns and Moral Dilemmas," *Text and Performance Quarterly* 13 (1993): 97–111; Lori E. Cole, *Pennsylvania History* 60, no. 4 (October 1993): 545–546; Marcia G. Synott, *Women's Studies International Forum* 16, no. 1 (January 1993): 83–84.

10 See the chapters written by Judith Stacey, Sondra Hale, and Claudia Salazar. Also see Armitage et al., "A Review Symposium," 106, 110; Elizabeth Tonkin noted the critiques of positivism in the *Journal of the History of the Behavioral Sciences* 31 (July 1995): 288. Later elaborations on post-modernism's impact on the field include Susan H. Armitage, "The Stages of Women's Oral History," in *Oxford Handbook of Oral History*, ed. Donald A. Ritchie (New York: Oxford University Press, 2010), 169–185; Valerie Yow, "'Do I Like Them Too Much': Effects of the Oral History Interview on the Interviewer and Vice Versa," *Oral History Review* 24, no. 1 (Summer 1997): 55–79.

11 This is not to suggest there was no debate over the claims, issued by post-structuralist and post-modernist scholars, that objective knowledge is unattainable and language has little if any relationship to lived experience. Other feminist interventions include Deborah Gordon, "Writing Culture, Writing Feminism: The Poetics and Politics of Experimental Ethnography," *Inscriptions* 3/4 (1988): 15; Frances E. Mascia-Lees, Patricia Sharpe, and Colleen Ballerino Cohen, "The Postmodernist Turn in Anthropology: Cautions from a Feminist Perspective," *Signs* 15 (1989): 7–33; Geiger, What's So Feminist?; Joan Scott, "Experience," in *Feminists Theorize the Political*, eds. Judith Butler and Joan W. Scott, (London: Routledge, 1992), 22–40; Joan Sangster, "Telling Our Stories: Feminist Debates and the Use of History," *Women's History Review* 3, no. 1 (1994): 5–28; Franca Iacovetta, "Post-Modern Ethnography, Historical Materialism, and De-centring the (Male) Authorial Voice: A Feminist Conversation," *Histoire Sociale Social History* 32, no. 64 (November 1999): 275–293.

12 Relevant work includes Julie Cruikshank, *The Social Life of Stories: Narrative and Knowledge in the Yukon Territory* (Lincoln: University of Nebraska Press, 2000); Heather Howard-Bobiwash, "'Like Her Lips to My Ear': Reading Anishnaabekweg Lives and Cultural Continuity in the City," in *Feminist Fields: Ethnographic Insights*, eds. Rae Bridgman, Sally Cole, and Heather Howard-Bobiwash (Peterborough: Broadview Press, 1999), 117–136; Kim Anderson, *Life Stages and Native Women: Memory, Teachings, and Story Medicine* (Winnipeg: University of Manitoba Press, 2011); Lianne Leddy, "Interviewing Nookomis and Other Reflections of an Indigenous Historian," *Oral History Forum d'histoire orale* 30 (2010): 1–18; Winona Wheeler, "Reflections on the Social Relations of Indigenous Oral Histories," in *Walking a Tightrope: Aboriginal People and their Representations*, eds. David McNab and Ute Lischke (Waterloo: Wilfrid Laurier Press, 2005), 189–214; Katrina Srigley and Autumn Varley, "Learning to Unlearn: Building Relationships on Anishinaabeg Territory," in *Indigenous Research: Theories, Practices and Relationships*, eds. Rochelle Johnston and Deborah McGregor (Toronto: Canadian Scholars Press, 2018); and the references in notes 28–32.

13 The relevant literatures in LGBTQ+, South Asian, and Indigenous oral history, respectively, are listed in three separate notes below.

14 For example, the Berkshire Conference of Women Historians, the International Federation for Research in Women's History, and the International Oral History Association.

15 A sample of UK literature includes the four theme issues of *Oral History* devoted to women's history (published in 1977, 1982, 1993, and 2002); Jill Liddington and Jill Norris, *One Hand Tied Behind Us* (London: Virago Press, 1978; 1984; 2000); Ann Oakley, *Becoming a Mother* (New York: Schoken Books, 1979);

Elizabeth Roberts, *A Woman's Place: An Oral History of Working-Class Women, 1880–1940* (Oxford: Blackwell, 1984); Carolyn Steedman, *Landscape for a Good Woman: A Story of Two Lives* (New Brunswick: Rutgers University Press, 1987); Penny Summerfield, *Reconstructing Women's Wartime Lives: Discourse and Subjectivity in Oral Histories of the Second World War* (Manchester: Manchester University Press, 1998); Lynn Abrams, *Myth and Materiality in a Women's World: Shetland 1800–2000* (Manchester: Manchester University Press, 2005); Penny Summerfield and Corinna Peniston-Bird, *Contesting Home Defence: Men, Women and the Home Guard in the Second World War* (Manchester: Manchester University Press, 2007). See also Joanna Bornat and H. Diamond, "Women's History and Oral History: Developments and Debates," *Women's History Review* 16, no. 1 (2007): 19–39, and the website: www.bl.uk/collection-guides/oral-histories-of-womens-history.

16 For the Indian subcontinent, where the classic anti-colonial women's oral history projects and texts came initially from activists, not academics, a small sample of the literature includes Uma Chakravarti and Nandita Haksar, *The Delhi Riots: Three Days in the Life of a Nation* (New Delhi: Lancer International, 1987); Ke Lalita et al., *"We Were Making History": Life Stories of Women and the Telangana Uprising* (New Delhi: Kali for Women, 1989); Urvashi Butalia, *The Other Side of Silence: Voices from the Partition of India* (Durham: Duke University Press, 2000); Urmilā Pawar, Meenakshi Moon, and Wandana Sonalkar, *We Also Made History: Women in the Ambedkarite Movement* (New Delhi: Zubaan Books, 2014); Ritu Menon, *Making a Difference: Memoirs from the Women's Movement in India* (New Delhi: Women Unlimited, 2011); Mallavika Sinha Roy, "Magic Moments of Struggle: Women's Memory of the Naxalbari Movement in West Bengal, India (1967–1975)," *Indian Journal of Gender Studies* 16, no. 2 (2009): 205–232. See also: www.cam.ac.uk/news/south-asian-oral-history-archive-goes-online.

17 A sample of work on *testimonios* includes (in English with the original publication date in Spanish): Moema Viezzer, *Let Me Speak! Testimony of Domitila, a Woman of the Bolivian Mines*, trans. Domitila Barrios de Chungara (New York: Monthly Review Press, 1978 [1977]); Rigoberta Menchú with Elizabeth Burgos-Debray ed., *I, Rigoberta Menchú: An Indian Woman in Guatemala*, trans. Ann Wright (London: Verso, 1984 [1983]); María Teresa Tula, *Hear My Testimony: María Teresa Tula, Human Rights Activist of El Salvador*, ed. and trans. Lynn Stephen (Boston: South End Press, 1994); Daniel James, *Doña María's Story: Life, History, Memory and Political Identity* (Durham: Duke University Press, 2000); Rosa Isolde Reuque Paillalef, *When a Flower Is Reborn: The Life and Times of a Mapuche Feminist*, ed. and trans. Florencia Mallon (Durham: Duke University Press, 2002). Historiographical treatments include Elizabeth Jelin, *Los trabajos de la memoria* (Madrid: Siglo XXI Editores, 2002); Troncoso Pérez, Lelya Elena, and Isabel Piper Shafir, "Género y memoria: articulaciones críticas y feministas," *Athenea Digital* 15, no. 1 (2015): 65–90.

18 A sample includes Daphne Read, ed., *The Great War and Canadian Society* (Toronto: New Hogtown Press, 1978); Varpu Lindström, *Defiant Sisters: A Social History of Finnish Immigrant Women in Canada* (Toronto: Multicultural History Society of Ontario, 1988); Ruth Frager, *Sweatshop Strife: Class, Ethnicity, and Gender in the Jewish Labour Movement of Toronto, 1900–1939* (Toronto: University of Toronto Press, 1992); Franca Iacovetta, *Such Hardworking People: Italian Immigrants in Postwar Toronto* (Montréal: McGill-Queen's University Press, 1992); Denyse Baillargeon, *Ménagères au temps de la Crise* (Montréal: Remue-ménage, 1991 [English trans. 1999]; Joy Parr, *The Gender of Breadwinners: Women, Men and Change in Two Industrial Towns, 1880–1950* (Toronto: University of Toronto Press, 1990); Joan Sangster, *Earning Respect: The Lives of Working Women in*

Small-Town Ontario, 1920–1960 (Toronto: University of Toronto Press, 1995); Marlene Epp, *Women without Men: Mennonite Refugees of the Second World War* (Toronto: University of Toronto Press, 2000); Nancy Janovicek, *No Place to Go: Local Histories of the Battered Women's Shelter Movement* (Vancouver: UBC Press, 2007); Joy Parr, *Sensing Change: Technologies, Environments, and the Everyday, 1953–2003* (Vancouver: UBC Press, 2010); Katrina Srigley, *Breadwinning Daughters: Young Working Women in a Depression-Era City, 1929–1939* (Toronto: University of Toronto Press, 2010); Stacey Zembrzycki, *According to Baba: A Collaborative Oral History of Sudbury's Ukrainian Community* (Vancouver: UBC Press, 2014); Rhonda Hinther, *Perogies and Politics: Canada's Ukrainian Left, 1891–1991* (Toronto: University of Toronto Press, forthcoming).

19 Oral history journals provide an important space for these conversations, as does the journal of the International Oral History Association (IOHA). Annual IOHA meetings tend to take place outside North America. There are active national oral history associations in India, Australia, New Zealand, Finland, and elsewhere.

20 Some of the *testimonio* literature is cited earlier and in the chapters by Hiner and Benmayor in this volume. Donna R. Gabaccia and Franca Iacovetta discuss the role that English-language publications played in disseminating Passerini's Italian-based scholarship in their introduction to *Borders, Conflict Zones, and Memory*.

21 Such efforts go back to the first feminist oral history issue, "Women's Oral History," published by *Frontiers: A Journal of Women Studies* 2, no. 2 (Summer, 1977). A small sample includes work on Asian American women, such as the oral history essays in Linda Trinh Vo and Marian Sciachitano, eds., *Asian American Women: The Frontiers Reader* (Lincoln: University of Nebraska Press, 2003); Evelyn Nakano Glenn, *Issei Nisei, War Bride: Three Generations of Japanese American Women in Domestic Service* (Philadelphia: Temple University Press, 1986); Judy Yung, *Unbounded Feet* (Berkeley: University of California Press, 1995); Yung, *Unbounded Voices: A Documentary History of Chinese Women in San Francisco* (Berkeley: University of California Press, 1999); Rhacel Salazar Parreñas, *Servants of Globalization: Women, Migration and Domestic Work* (Stanford: Stanford University Press, 2001).

22 See the chapters by Karen Olson and Linda Shopes, and Laurie Mercier and Mary Murphy.

23 In addition to Etter-Lewis's chapter in *Women's Words* and her *My Soul Is My Own: Oral Narratives of African American Women in the Professions* (New York: Routledge, 1993), this literature includes Elizabeth Clark Lewis, *Living In Living Out: African American Domestics in Washington D.C.* (Washington, D.C.: Smithsonian Institution Press, 1995); Patricia Hill Collins, *Black Feminist Thought: Knowledge, Consciousness, and the Politics of Empowerment* (Boston: Unwin Hyman, 1990); Kim Lacy Rogers, *Righteous Lives: Narratives of the New Orleans Civil Rights Movement* (New York: New York University Press, 1993); Anne Valk and Leslie Brown, *Living With Jim Crow: African American Women and Memories of the Segregated South* (New York: Palgrave Macmillan, 2010). The smaller but growing Canadian literature includes Mikada Silvera, *Silenced: Talks with Working Class Caribbean Women about their Lives and Struggles as Domestic Workers in Canada* (Toronto: Sister Vision Press, 1983, 1989); Dionne Brand (with Lois De Shield), *No Burden to Carry: Narratives of Black Working Women in Ontario, 1920s–1950s* (Toronto: Women's Press, 1991); Karen Flynn, *Moving Beyond Borders: A History of Black Canadian and Caribbean Women in the Diaspora* (Toronto: University of Toronto Press, 2011).

24 See the chapters by Patai on Brazilian women and Sondra Hale on Sudanese women. Earlier cross-cultural work includes Margaret Strobel, *Muslim Women in Mombasa, 1890–1975* (New Haven: Yale University Press, 1979); Claire Robertson, *Sharing*

the *Same Bowl: A Socio-Economic History of Women and Class in Accra, Ghana* (Bloomington: Indiana University Press, 1983). While most widely cited in the United States and Canada, *Women's Words*' reach extended to the United Kingdom, Europe, Asia, and elsewhere, having been cited in more than 1,000 publications.

25 A sample includes Elizabeth Lapovsky Kennedy and Madeleine Davis, *Boots of Leather, Slippers of Gold: The History of a Lesbian Community* (New York: Routledge, 1993, reprinted 2014); Becki L. Ross, *The House That Jill Built: Lesbian Nation in Formation* (Toronto: University of Toronto Press, 1995); Ann Cvetkovich, *An Archive of Feelings: Trauma, Sexuality, and Lesbian Public Cultures* (Durham: Duke University Press, 2003); Nan Alamilla Boyd, *Wide-Open Town: A History of Queer San Francisco to 1965* (Oakland: University of California Press, 2005); Horacio N. Roque Ramírez, "A Living Archive of Desire: Teresita la Campesina and the Embodiment of Queer Latino Community Histories," in *Archive Stories: Facts, Fictions, and the Writing of History*, ed. Antoinette Burton (Durham: Duke University Press, 2006), 111–135; Boyd, "Who Is the Subject? Queer Theory Meets Oral History," *Journal of the History of Sexuality* 17, no. 2 (May 2008): 177–189; Boyd and Ramírez, eds., *Bodies of Evidence: The Practice of Queer Oral History* (New York: Oxford University Press, 2012); Kevin P. Murphy, Jennifer L. Pierce, and Larry Knopp, eds. *Queer Twin Cities* (Minneapolis: University of Minnesota Press, 2010); E. Patrick Johnson, *Sweet Tea: Black Gay Men of the South* (University of North Carolina Press, 2011).

26 For a discussion of current projects, such as the "New York City Trans Oral History" project (www.nyctransoralhistory.org), the "Trans Oral History" project (Chicago and Philadelphia [https://www.nyctransoralhistory.org/]), and the "Trans Partner Oral History" project (Toronto and Victoria [www.lgbtqdigitalcollaboratory.org]), see Elspeth Brown, "Trans/Feminist Oral History," *Transgender Studies Quarterly* 2, no. 4 (November 2015): 666–672.

27 Widely cited cross-cultural ethnographic studies include Cruikshank, *The Social Life of Stories*, Cruikshank, *Do Glaciers Listen? Local Knowledge, Colonial Encounters, and Social Imagination* (Vancouver: UBC Press, 2005); Bain Attwood and Fiona Magowan, eds., *Telling Stories: Indigenous History and Memory in Australia and New Zealand* (Crows Nest, NSW: Allen & Unwin, 2001); and the autobiographical text of Guatemalan Indigenous rights activist Menchú: Menchú with Burgos-Debray, *I, Rigoberta Menchú*. Also, there is inclusion of some Indigenous material in such feminist texts as Armitage et al., *Women's Oral History* and her "Stages of Women's Oral History."

28 To provide a brief overview, influential texts in the field that do not explicitly engage Indigenous oral history include Robert Perks and Alistair Thomson, *The Oral History Reader*, 2nd edition (New York: Routledge, 2006); Thomson, "Four Paradigm Transformations in Oral History," *Oral History Review* 34, no. 1 (2007): 49–70; Valerie Yow, *Recording Oral History: A Guide for the Humanities and Social Sciences*, 2nd edition (New York: AltaMira Press, 2005). Newer texts that do so include Abrams, *Oral History Theory* (Abingdon: Routledge, 2010, 2016), 21, 135, 172; and Kristina R. Llewellyn, Alexander Freund, and Nolan Reilly eds., *The Canadian Oral History Reader* (Montréal: McGill-Queen's University Press, 2015), which contains essays by Brian Calliou, Julie Cruikshank, and Winona Wheeler.

29 See Lee Maracle, *Memory Serves: Oratories* (Edmonton: NeWest Press, 2015); Paula Gunn Allan, *The Sacred Hoop: Recovering the Feminine in American Indian Traditions* (Boston: Beacon Press, 1992); Christine Miller and Patricia Churchyk, eds., *Women of the First Nations: Power, Wisdom and Strength* (Winnipeg: University of Manitoba Press, 1996); Aroha Harris, "Modern in a Traditional Way: The Maori Search for Cultural Equilibrium in a Saying, a Song, and a Short Story," in *Huia*

Histories of Maori: Nga Tahuhu Korero, ed. D. Keenan (Wellington: Huia Publishers, 2012), 339–351; Jill Doerfler, Niigaanwewidam James Sinclair, and Heidi Kiiwetinepinesiik Stark, eds., *Centering Anishinaabeg Studies: Understanding the World through Stories* (Winnipeg: Manitoba University Press, 2013); Daniel Heath Justice, *Why Indigenous Literatures Matter* (Waterloo: Wilfrid Laurier Press, 2016); Elsie Paul with Paige Raibmon and Harmony Johnson, *Written as I Remember It: Teachings (Ɂəms taɁaw) from the Life of a Sliammon Elder* (Vancouver: UBC Press, 2014); Leslie A. Robertson and the Kwagu'l Gixsam Clan, *Standing Up With Gaaxstalas* (Vancouver: UBC Press, 2013); George Vizenor, *Survivance: Narratives of the Native Presence* (Lincoln: University of Nebraska Press, 2008). On Madonna Thunderhawk see, for example, *Warrior Women* with Elizabeth Castle and Christina King, accessed 13 October 2017, www.visionmakermedia.org/films/warrior-women.

30 A sample includes Kim Anderson and Bonita Lawrence, eds., *Strong Women Stories: Native Vision and Community Survival* (Toronto: Sumach Press, 2003); Angella Wanhalla, *Matters of the Heart: A History of Interracial Marriage in New Zealand* (Auckland: Auckland University Press, 2013); Mary Jane Logan McCallum, *Indigenous Women, Work, and History* (Winnipeg: University of Manitoba Press, 2014); Audra Simpson, *Mohawk Interruptus: Political Life Across the Borders of Settler States* (Durham: Duke University Press, 2014); Susan M. Hill, *The Clay We Are Made Of: Haudenosaunee Land Tenure on the Grand River* (Winnipeg: University of Manitoba Press, 2017); Lianne Leddy "Poisoning the Serpent: Uranium Exploitation and the Serpent River First Nation, 1953–1988," in *The Natures of Empire and the Empires of Nature,* ed. Karl Hele (Waterloo: Wilfrid Laurier University Press, 2013), 125–147; and references earlier. Mary Jane Logan McCallum and Susan M. Hill discuss the international scope of this important work, citing published and in-progress research on Hawai'i, Guam, New Zealand, and many other locales in their "Our Historiographical Moment: A Conversation about Indigenous Women's History in the Early Twentieth-first Century," in Nancy Janovicek and Carmen Neilson, eds., *Reading Canadian Women's and Gender History* (Toronto: University of Toronto Press, forthcoming). We thank them for generously sharing their important manuscript with us.

31 McCallum and Hill, "Our Historiographical Moment." This piece addresses teaching and mentoring as well as researching and writing Indigenous women's history, and brilliantly examines critical questions related to decolonizing knowledge, reconciliation, and the relationship between the past and present in historical research.

32 These conversations began before we issued a call for papers. On the importance and protocols of relationship-building, see, for instance, Kathleen E. Absolon (Minogiizhigokwe), *Kaandossiwin: How We Come to Know* (Halifax: Fernwood Publishing, 2011); Margaret Kovach, *Indigenous Methodologies: Characteristics, Conversations and Contexts* (Toronto: University of Toronto Press, 2009); Linda Tuhiwai Smith, *Decolonizing Methodologies: Research and Indigenous Peoples,* 2nd edition (London: Zed Books, 2012).

33 A sample of work in oral and public history includes Jacquelyn Dowd Hall et al., *Like a Family: The Making of a Southern Cotton World* (Chapel Hill: University of North Carolina Press, 1987; 2000), which came out of the "Southern Oral History" project at the University of North Carolina at Chapel Hill; Brooklyn Historical Society, www.brooklynhistory.org/; The "September 11, 2001 Oral History" projects located at the Columbia Center for Oral History: http://library.columbia.edu/locations/ccoh/digital/9-11.html; "Groundswell: Oral History for Social Change", www.oralhistoryforsocialchange.org/; "First Story Toronto",

https://firststoryblog.wordpress.com/; "Montréal Life Stories", www.lifestories
montreal.ca/; Ojibway Cultural Foundation, https://ojibwe-cultural-foundation.
myshopify.com/; *The Nipissing Warriors*, directed by Katrina Srigley (2017, Regan
Pictures, North Bay, ON), www.nipissingu.ca/warriors; Glenna Beaucage and
Katrina Srigley, "The Nipissing Warriors," *More Than Just a Game*, Discovery North
Bay, July–August, 2017, permanent location Nbisiing Secondary School, Nipissing
First Nation. All websites accessed on 23 August 2017.

34 Eve Tuck and K. Wayne Yang, "Decolonization is not a metaphor," *Decolonization:
Indigeneity, Education & Society* 1, no. 1 (2012): 1–40. Also see Audra Simpson,
"On Ethnographic Refusal: Indigeneity, 'Voice' and Colonial Citizenship," *Junctures*
9 (December 2007): 67–80; Leanne Betasamosake Simpson, *As We Have Always
Done: Indigenous Freedom through Radical Resistance* (Minneapolis: University of
Minnesota Press, 2017).

35 On the value of recuperative work, see Armitage, "Stages of Women's Oral History,"
and Penny Summerfield, "Oral History as an Autobiographical Practice," *Miranda*
12 (2016): 1–15; on the importance of recuperative work for justice and sovereignty
projects see the essay by Heather Howard in this volume (Chapter 25).

36 A sample of recent work on refugees and exiles includes studies by Al-Ali, Dossa
and others referenced in note 4 and Luisa Passerini's project "Bodies Across Borders:
Oral and Visual Memory in Europe and Beyond (BABE)," accessed 23 August
2017, https://babe.eui.eu/; Nadje Al-Ali and Kahlid Koser, eds., *New Approaches
to Migration?: Transnational Communities and the Transformation of Home*
(London: Routledge, 2002); Steven High, Edward Little, Thi Ry Duong, eds.,
Remembering Mass Violence: Oral History, New Media, and Performance (Toronto:
University of Toronto Press, 2014); High, *Oral History at the Crossroads: Sharing
Life Stories of Survival and Displacement* (Vancouver: UBC Press, 2014); High, ed.,
Beyond Testimony and Trauma: Oral History in the Aftermath of Mass Violence
(Vancouver: UBC Press, 2015).

37 An important exception was Passerini, who early on called for an analytical not
populist oral history, and theorized memory as subjective and informed by personal
and wider cultural myths: "Work, Ideology, and Consensus in Italian Fascism,"
History Workshop Journal 8, no. 1 (October 1979): 82–108; "Women's Personal
Narratives: Myths, Experiences, and Emotions," 189–198.

38 Here, Stacey drew on post-modern ethnography such as James Clifford's
"Introduction: Partial Truths," in *Writing Culture: The Poetics and Poetry of
Ethnography*, eds., James Clifford and George Marcus (Berkeley: University of
California Press, 1985), 1–26, and feminist critical ethnography such as Gordon,
"Writing Culture, Writing Feminism," which also criticized male ethnographers for
appropriating or excluding feminist critical ethnography.

39 Stacey's essay (like Hale's) also drew on feminist critiques of objectivity outside of
post-modernism. The discussion draws on an extensive literature that, besides
Women's Words, includes Armitage et al., *Women's Oral History*; Ann Oakley,
"Interviewing Women: A Contradiction in Terms," and other essays in Roberts,
ed., *Doing Feminist Research*; Geiger "What's So Feminist"; Sangster, "Telling
Our Stories"; Summerfield, *Reconstructing Women's Wartime Lives*; Iacovetta, "Post-
Modern Ethnography"; Sheyfali Saujani, "Empathy and Authority in Oral
Testimony: Feminist Debates, Multicultural Mandates, and Reassessing the
Interviewer and her 'Disagreeable' Subjects," *Histoire sociale/Social History* 45, no.
90 (November 2012): 361–391. See also the chapters written by Cruikshank and
Tatiana Argounova-Low, Jones-Gailani, and others in Anna Sheftel and Stacey
Zembrzycki, eds., *Oral History Off the Record: Toward an Ethnography of Practice*
(New York: Palgrave Macmillan, 2013).

40 See Cathy Caruth, *Unclaimed Experience: Trauma, Narrative and History* (Baltimore: Johns Hopkins University Press, 1996); Kim Lacy Rogers and Selma Leydesdorff, eds., *Trauma: Life Stories of Survivors* (New Brunswick, NJ: Transaction Publishers, 1999); Nanci Dale Adler et al., eds., *Memories of Mass Repression, Narrating Stories in the Aftermath of Atrocity* (New Brunswick, NJ: Transaction, 2009); Selma Leydesdorff, *Surviving the Bosnian Genocide: The Women of Srebrenica Speak* (Bloomington: Indiana University Press, 2011); Henry Greenspan, *On Listening to Holocaust Survivors: Beyond Testimony*, 2nd edition (St. Paul: Paragon House, 2010); Sean Field, *Oral History, Community, and Displacement: Imagining Memories in Post-Apartheid South Africa* (New York: Palgrave Macmillan, 2012); Mark Cave and Stephen M. Sloan, eds., *Listening on the Edge: Oral History in the Aftermath of Crisis* (New York: Oxford University Press, 2014); Erin Jessee, *Negotiating Genocide in Rwanda: The Politics of History* (New York: Palgrave Macmillan, 2017).

41 See Luisa Passerini, *Fascism in Popular Memory: The Cultural Experience of the Turin Working Class*, trans. Robert Lumley and Jude Bloomfield (Cambridge, UK: Cambridge University Press, 1987).

42 For more on Truth and Reconciliation in Canada see: http://nctr.ca/reports.php; in South Africa, see: www.justice.gov.za/trc/, and Field, *Oral History, Community, and Displacement*. Notably, such commissions have also been held in Argentina, Australia, Bolivia, Chile, El Salvador, and Guatemala, to name a few.

43 On this theme, see Yolande Bouka, "Researching Violence in Africa as a Black Woman: Notes from Rwanda," Research in Difficult Settings (2015), accessed 25 August 2017, http://conflictfieldresearch.colgate.edu/wpcontent/uploads/2015/05/Bouka_WorkingPaper-May2015.pdf; Bouka, "Nacibazo, 'No Problem': Moving Beyond the Official Discourse of Post-Genocide Justice in Rwanda," in *Emotional and Ethical Challenges for Field Research in Africa: The Story Behind the Findings*, eds. Susan Thomson, An Ansoms, and Jude Murison (London: Palgrave MacMillan, 2013), 107–122.

44 See Steven High, "Sharing Authority: An Introduction," *Journal of Canadian Studies* 43, no. 1 (Winter 2009): 12–34, and references to publications edited by High et al., in endnote 36.

45 On oral history and performance see Della Pollock, *Remembering Oral History Performance* (New York: Palgrave Macmillan, 2005); Abrams, *Oral History Theory*, 130–152; Edward Little, ed., Special Issue on "Oral History and Performance (Part 1 and 2)," *alt.theatre* 9, nos. 1 and 2 (September 2011 and December 2011): http://alttheatre.ca; Edward Little and Steven High, "Partners in Conversation: A Reflection on the Ethics and Emergent Practice of Oral History Performance," in *History, Memory, Performance*, eds. David Dean, Yana Meerzon, Kathryn Prince (New York: Palgrave Macmillan, 2015), 240–256; Penny Summerfield, "Concluding Thoughts: Performance, the Self, and Women's History," *Women's History Review* 22, no. 2 (2013): 345–52; and the essays by Hourig Attarian, Rachel Van Fossen, and others in High, Little, Duong, eds., *Remembering Mass Violence*.

46 On myths, see the essays by Passerini, Tonkin, and others in Raphael Samuel and Paul Thompson, eds., *The Myths We Live By* (New York: Routledge, 1990) and references in note 37; Alexander Freund and Laura Quilici, "Exploring Myths in Women's Narratives: Italian and German Immigrant Women in Vancouver, 1947–1961," *BC Studies* nos. 105–106 (Spring/Summer 1995): 159–182. On scripts, see, for example, Jill Kerr Conway, *When Memory Speaks: Reflections on Autobiography* (New York: Alfred A. Knopf 1998); Lynn Abrams, "Liberating the Female Self: Epiphanies, Conflict and Coherence in the Life Stories of Post-War British Women," *Social History* 39, 1 (2014): 14–35; Sangster, "Telling Our

Stories"; Saujani, "Empathy and Authority"; Marlene Epp, "The Memory of Violence: Soviet and East European Mennonite Refugees and Rape in the Second World War," *Journal of Women's History* 9, no. 1 (1997): 58–87; Joy Damousi and Paula Hamilton, eds., *A Cultural History of Sound, Memory, and the Senses* (New York: Routledge, 2017); and Abrams' chapter in this volume.

47 On this theme, see Yow, "'Do I Like Them Too Much'"; James, *Doña María's Story*; Lisa M. Tillmann-Healy, "Friendship as Method," *Qualitative Inquiry* 9, no. 5 (2003): 287–319; Anna Sheftel and Stacey Zembrzycki, "Only Human: A Reflection on the Ethical and Methodological Challenges of Working with 'Difficult' Stories," *Oral History Review* 37, no. 2 (Summer–Fall 2010): 191–241.

48 Penny Summerfield's notable work on composure and intersubjective processes includes "Culture and Composure: Creating Narratives of the Gendered Self in Oral History Interviews," *Cultural and Social History* 1 (2004): 65–93.

49 On the broader cultural meanings inherent in oral history narratives and their relation to memory, see Paula Hamilton and Linda Shopes, eds., *Oral History and Public Memories* (Philadelphia: Temple University Press, 2008).

50 For example, Perks and Thomson, eds., *Oral History Readers*; Donald Ritchie, *The Oxford Handbook of Oral History*; Llewellyn, Freund, Reilly, eds., *The Canadian Oral History Reader*.

51 This example is from Linda Shopes, "Beyond Women's Words: Reflections on Feminist Oral History in the Twenty-First Century," 16th Berkshire Conference on the History of Women (Toronto, 2014), 4, which cites Anderson and Jack's chapter in *Women's Words* and Ronald J. Grele, "Movement without Aim: Methodological and Theoretical Problems in Oral History," in *Envelopes of Sound: The Art of Oral History*, 2nd edition (New York: Praeger, 1991), 126–154.

52 For more elaboration, see Michael Frisch, *A Shared Authority: Essays on the Craft and Meaning of Oral and Public History* (Albany: State University of New York Press, 1991); Linda Shopes "Commentary: Sharing Authority," *Oral History Review* 30, no. 1 (2003): 103–110; High, "Sharing Authority: An Introduction," 12–34.

53 Shopes, "Reflections," which cites Frisch, *A Shared Authority*; Alessandro Portelli, *The Death of Luigi Trastulli and Other Stories: Form and Meaning in Oral History* (Albany: State University of New York Press, 1990); Portelli, *The Battle of Valle Giulia: Oral History and the Art of Dialogue* (Madison: University of Wisconsin Press, 1997).

54 Thomson, "Four Paradigm Transformations in Oral History," 70. See also Armitage, "The Stages of Women's Oral History," 181–2; Douglas Boyd, ed., "Special Issue on Oral History in the Digital Age," *Oral History Review* 40, no. 1 (Winter/Spring 2013); Douglas A. Boyd and Mary A. Larson, eds., *Oral History and Digital Humanities: Voice, Access and Engagement* (New York: Palgrave Macmillan, 2014).

55 Sherna Berger Gluck, "Reflecting on the Quantum Leap: Promises and Perils of Oral History on the Web," *Oral History Review* 41, no. 2 (Summer/Fall 2014): 244–256; Gluck, "From California to Kufr Nameh and Back: Reflections on Forty Years of Feminist Oral History," in *Oral History Off the Record*, 39.

56 See Michael Frisch, "Oral History and the Digital Revolution: Toward a Post-Documentary Sensibility," in *The Oral History Reader*, 2nd edition, 102–122; "Three Dimensions and More: Oral History beyond the Paradoxes of Method," in *Handbook of Emergent Methods*, eds. Sharlene Nagy Hess-Biber and Patricia Leavy (New York: Guilford Press, 2008), 221–238.

57 Proprietary and open source tools/software such as InterClipper, Oral History Metadata Synchronizer (OHMS), and Stories Matter. For more on this critique, see Anna Sheftel and Stacey Zembrzycki, "Slowing Down to Listen in the Digital Age: How New Technology Is Changing Oral History Practice," *Oral History Review* 44, no. 1 (Winter Spring 2017): 94–112.

58 Cited in McCallum and Hill, "Our Historiographical Moment," 18.
59 Abrams, *Oral History Theory*, 71.
60 Patricia Monture Angus, *Thunder in My Soul: A Mohawk Woman Speaks* (Halifax, Nova Scotia: Fernwood Publishing, 1995).
61 Shari M. Huhndorf and Cheryl Suzack, "Indigenous Feminism: Theorizing the Issues," in *Indigenous Women and Feminism: Politics, Activism, Culture*, eds. Cheryl Suzack et al. (Vancouver: UBC Press, 2010), 2.
62 Chimamanda Ngozi Adichie, *We Should All Be Feminists* (New York: Anchor Books, 2015), 41; Adichie, *Dear Ijeawele, or A Feminist Manifesto in Fifteen Suggestions* (New York: Alfred Knopf, 2017), 6; bell hooks, *feminism is for everybody: passionate politics* (New York: Routledge, 2015), 45–47.

Section 1

Reflections on women's words

Introduction to Section 1

Reflections on women's words

Linda Shopes

The obvious questions to ask when reading *Beyond Women's Words* are in what ways do the essays go "beyond" the earlier eponymous volume and what do these "beyonds" tell us about changes in feminist oral history, or as the subtitle of the previous volume put it, "the feminist practice of oral history," in the intervening quarter-plus century? The five chapters in this first section suggest some answers, not incidentally because three of them are written by scholars whose work also appeared in the first *Women's Words*.[1] It is to these we turn first.

The section begins appropriately enough with Katherine Borland's reprise of her original *Women's Words* contribution, "That's Not What I Said." In that chapter, she discussed how she and her grandmother, Beatrice Hanson, resolved disagreement over Borland's interpretation of her interview with Hanson, particularly her imposition of a feminist analysis on certain elements of Hanson's story, a perspective and a movement with which Hanson did not identify. The chapter raised important questions about interpretive authority in oral history, and while Borland maintained that oral historians need not have their work "validated by our research collaborators," she did conclude by suggesting that we might "re-envision the fieldwork exchange" to include explicit discussion of meaning.[2] Borland has not changed her mind about this in the intervening years. What has changed, however, is the way she now frames issues of interpretive authority. In line with oral historians' more recent attention to cultural theory, including the work of George Herbert Mead and Mikhail Bakhtin, she argues that social interaction, performed through language—what oral historians sometimes refer to as intersubjectivity—is a continuous process of identity formation; consequently, "[t]he self in narrative becomes not an essence to be uncovered but a matter of narrative positioning in a specific context for a particular end."[3] Interpretive differences are thus not a problem to be solved but intrinsic to the active process of talk. Accordingly, whether or not Hanson was a feminist is not the issue, exploring points of difference is.

The section concludes with Rina Benmayor's chapter about teaching digital storytelling to undergraduates, many the children of Mexican migrants, in a Latina Life Stories class at a California public university. Similar to Borland's work, it both resonates with and differs from themes in her essay in the earlier volume. Though the students and settings are different—in the earlier case, participants in a Spanish-speaking adult literacy program at Hunter College's Center for Puerto Rican Studies in New York City—both chapters consider oral history within a continuum of first-person narrative forms; both affirm that a pedagogy employing these narrative forms can sharpen students' sense of identity and encourage personal empowerment; both link students' work to testimony, or *testimonio* in the Latin American tradition, which seeks to connect the personal to a broader social critique as a step towards change; both locate gender within a range of social identities and structures, assuming rather than interrogating a feminist perspective. As with Borland, where the two chapters differ is in interpretive perspective, also reflecting broader shifts in oral historiography. The earlier piece is situated within Freirian notions of popular education, which aimed at "reciprocity and mutual 'returns'" between researchers and communities of study as a way to disrupt the unequal power relations characteristic of traditional modes of social research, ideas that underlay numerous community-based oral history projects in the 1980s.[4] The current chapter, however, focuses on "the centrality of emotion," as well as the role of voice and image, in the pedagogical practices described.[5] If it is memory that shapes stories, then it is emotion, Benmayor suggests, that unlocks memories.

The third repeat author, Daphne Patai, whose chapter "When is enough enough?" is also the third in this section, reiterates the similar/different dynamic of the previous two. Her earlier piece was a bracing reflection on certain dilemmas of feminist oral history based on her own experience interviewing third world women: attempting to address inequality while operating from a position of privilege; the limits of informed consent, narrator empowerment, and "returning the research" once the researcher goes home to do her work; a tendency towards the emotional seduction of narrators, raising unmet expectations among them; the "fraud" of a "purported solidarity of female identity." For Patai, there is no resolution to these dilemmas. They are embedded in structural inequalities that lie beyond the realm of individual research; one simply carries on as best one can.[6] The current chapter speaks with a sharper contrarian voice and steps outside the feminist frame to critique much of the current oral history enterprise including an excessive focus on identity, often accompanied by inflated claims of "methodological innovation and theoretical sophistication"; a privileging of reflexivity over content; and the subordination of empirical research to political commitments and the conflation of empirical accuracy with narrative truth.[7] There are savvy warnings here, but Patai's work overreaches, belied by Borland's and Benmayor's. For Borland, identity and narrative are intrinsic to an interview's epistemology, not categories that, as Patai suggests, can stand outside it. And Benmayor demonstrates how a carefully developed, methodologically innovative practice focused on identity and grounded in a specific set of circumstances can be non-exploitative and empowering, while also reaching outward to broader theoretical concerns.

But what of the two newcomers to the volume, if not to oral history? In what ways do they go "beyond" the earlier *Women's Words*, and in what ways does it matter? Sanchia deSouza's and Jyothsna Latha Belliappa's "The positionality of narrators and interviewers: Methodological comments on oral history with Anglo-Indian schoolteachers in Bangalore, India," the second chapter in this section, suggests a couple of answers. Admittedly, its problematization of the positionality of interviewers vis-à-vis narrators and related ethical issues echoes themes taken up in the original volume and in feminist oral history more generally. The piece's primary value lies in its subject, which extends beyond the geographic range and social identities of narrators discussed in the original *Women's Words*.[8] And that matters because it speaks to the internationalization of oral history in the last quarter century—and expands the knowledge of readers like me by introducing an unfamiliar female experience. But the authors also note an equally important, more localized value to their interviews with teachers: it is a response to the call of scholars of education in India to address the "insufficient attention paid to teachers' rich perspectives and experiences."[9] Content, in this case, matters.

The final chapter under discussion and the fourth in this section is Kathleen Blee's "Feminist oral histories of racist women," theoretical reflections on her studies of women who are former members of white supremacist groups in the United States including the 1920s Ku Klux Klan and more recent neo-Nazi and white power skinhead groups. As Blee suggests, the very subject of her work falls outside mainstream feminist oral history, with its overwhelming focus on women with whom we presume to share—despite real and acknowledged differences (a la Borland, e.g.)—a certain sisterhood, whose experience we value, even valorize, whose voices we wish to amplify, and whom we wish to restore to the mainstream of history. The subject of Blee's work challenges these assumptions and leads her to identify two analytic tools that advance a feminist approach to her interviews and by extension are more widely applicable to feminist oral history: master status and trauma. The former, a concept from sociology, refers to a status or identity that trumps all others, in her case "racist," leading to an inquiry that tends to skew certain aspects of identity and experience while ignoring others. Combining the category of gender with that of racist thus complicates the story. The latter concept, trauma, which Blee defines as "those experiences that alter a person's (or a societal) identity in deep and seemingly irrevocable ways," is a pathway to understanding women's involvements in racial extremism.[10] Taken together, Blee avers, notions of master status and trauma can help create the analytic space to approach interviews that in their subject matter demand not simply the empathy characteristic of much feminist oral history, but also a critical distance.

How then might these five chapters collectively address the questions posed at the beginning of this Introduction? Certainly older themes and issues continue to resonate with and trouble our work. But what we are also seeing are multiple layers of integration into the ambit of feminist oral history: integration of more diverse subjects, extending the range of our inquiries;

of new theoretical approaches, reflecting broader intellectual developments and giving our work greater depth; and of a more mature, less insistent feminism, assimilating with greater ease into our analytic repertoire. Historians do not predict the future, but what we have here is evidence of a field's and a practice's continuity with its past, expansiveness in its present, and a vitality that suggests optimism for its future.

Notes

1 Sherna Berger Gluck and Daphne Patai, eds., *Women's Words: The Feminist Practice of Oral History* (New York: Routledge, 1991).
2 Katherine Borland, "'That's Not What I Said': Interpretive Conflict in Oral Narrative Research," in *Women's Words*, 63–75; quoted material on 73, 74.
3 Katherine Borland, Chapter 1 of this volume, 33.
4 Rina Benmayor, "Testimony, Action Research, and Empowerment: Puerto Rican Women and Popular Education," in *Women's Words*, 159–174; quoted material on 160.
5 Rina Benmayor, Chapter 5 of this volume, 64.
6 Daphne Patai, "U.S. Academics and Third World Women: Is Ethical Research Possible?" in *Women's Words*, 137–153; quoted material on 144.
7 Daphne Patai, Chapter 3 of this volume, 48.
8 While the original *Women's Words* was exceptional for its time in incorporating work from around the globe (by my calculation, 23 per cent of the chapters were about oral history practiced in non-Western countries, and an additional 15 per cent in Europe) and chapters in the current volume, reflecting the intersectional identities of our age, are harder to categorize, it is nonetheless true that the book in hand reflects a greater range of experiences.
9 Sanchia deSouza and Jyothsna Latha Belliappa, Chapter 2 of this volume, 40.
10 Kathleen Blee, Chapter 4 of this volume, 59.

1 "That's not what I said"

A reprise 25 years on

Katherine Borland

On 4 August 1944, 35-year-old Beatrice Hanson put on a pale, eggshell-colored gabardine dress with big gold buttons down the side, a huge pancake-black hat, and elbow-length gloves, and off she went with her father to see the sulky (harness) races at the Bangor fairgrounds. The events that ensued produced a lively wrangle between father and daughter as they vied to pick the winner, and that night, bubbling over with enthusiasm, Bea recounted the story to her two adolescent daughters. Two days later, Bea wrote to her husband, Frank, who was serving overseas, to tell him about it. Somewhere between 1950 and 1983 she revised the letter slightly and included it in an epistolary novel (never published) about their lives during the war. In 1985, as we passed a racetrack while driving down the New Jersey Turnpike, Bea was reminded of how much she enjoyed horseracing and told me the story. A year later, on 28 December, my sister, her husband, Frank, and I were treated to a highly structured and thoroughly entertaining narrative that I recorded for later transcription and analysis.

My grandmother and I were delighted to be working together—until I sent her a copy of the essay I had written for my graduate class in folklore and performance the following fall. On 22 January 1988, I received a typed, 13-page, single-spaced rebuttal of my feminist interpretation of the story. Insisting that she was not and never had been a feminist, Bea wrote:

> So your interpretation of the story as a female struggle for autonomy within a hostile male environment is entirely YOUR interpretation. You've read into the story what you wished—what pleases YOU (and, I presume, your instructor). That it was never—by any wildest stretch of the imagination—the concern of the originator of the story makes such an interpretation a definite and complete distortion, and in this respect I question its authenticity. The story is no longer MY story at all . . . How far is it permissible to go, in the name of folklore, and still be honest in respect to the original narrative?[1]

This candid critique provided a cautionary tale to feminist researchers who in their enthusiasm for recovering women's perspectives inadvertently appropriated the voices of the very women they sought to champion. In subsequent visits and dialogue, Bea and I were able to come to an understanding of our differences, a process I narrated in *Women's Words*.[2]

I went on to pursue research with people whose identities were not so closely intertwined with my own. But Bea continued to send letters and other writing—her novel and several one-act plays, a genealogical chart, and a recording of a dramatic reading, *To You, With Love*, that she and Frank performed on the Women's Club circuit after their retirement from college teaching. She even got her childhood friend to send a self-made tape of his reminiscences. Both my grandparents welcomed my occasional visits as opportunities to regale me with stories of a long and colorful life together, including Frank's aborted career in Vaudeville and the plots of Bea's prize-winning one-act plays. Rereading Bea's 1988 letter now, I discover that it contains much more than the critique that provided the basis for my methodological intervention in *Women's Words*. On page one, Bea asserts, "But I do believe that the interpretations of any author's work probably often give the work many more facets, many more 'meanings' than the original author ever considered." Like me, she understood that questions of ethics and method are complicated by the contingent, and always provisional, meaning of expressive culture. Bea and Frank are no longer around to correct me if I misrepresent them, so as I revisit the artefacts of their lives, I focus on what these say about the workings of narrative rather than on biographical reconstruction.[3] Even so, life review creeps into many folklore- and oral history-oriented projects because research subjects are likely to regard any representation of their narratives as expressions of self, even if the researcher's project has a different focus.

Researchers and their narrators (or interlocutors) find their footing with one another and define the power relations between themselves in multiple and nuanced ways. Still, I continue to believe that the researcher's confident "I understand you," which emerges partly as a consequence of the rituals of establishing rapport, might well be replaced by the more tentative, "Do we understand each other?" Such a question implies continuing dialogue with narrators after any preliminary attempt at interpretation. It does not require agreement.[4] Recent scholarship has suggested that familiarity can breed a kind of contempt in the interview setting: the closer one's bond to a narrator and the more one knows about the events being narrated, the more difficult it is to listen respectfully without imputing one's own meanings, remembering differently, listening in an "interested" way, or even being wounded by the narrator's words.[5] Certainly, the intimacy my grandmother and I shared may have contributed to my initial inability to respect her difference. However, if our epistemological method, our special form of inquiry into truth, requires the cultivation of an open, nonjudgmental frame of mind to move beyond what we think we already know, we must still acknowledge that telling and listening are intertwined aspects of an interview that is, at base, a social interaction.

Arthur W. Frank calls this stance the hermeneutic approach.[6] However, we can trace the epistemology of deep listening back to the pioneering Progressive Era thinker, Jane Addams. Long appreciated as a social reformer, Addams' contributions to the philosophical movement of American Pragmatism remained underappreciated until the 1990s.[7] She modeled a practice in which she temporarily suspended her own frame of reference to render herself receptive to another's experience. This method recognizes subjective truths as valid forms of knowledge, and advocates for ordinary women's storytelling as a form of empowerment, two ideas that remain relevant to contemporary feminist ethnographic research.[8]

Nevertheless, even a respectful, nondirective listener influences the narratives that are constructed for her by another, because self-representation is an inherently intersubjective process. Intersubjectivity, the mutual fashioning of selves in social interaction, offers another way of thinking about the exchanges between my grandmother and me. Sociologists have long argued that reflexive self-consciousness (the notion that an individual can develop a rich and complex inner life) occurs through interaction with others and through a dynamic interaction with the generalized abstraction that is the social world.[9] This intersubjective dimension of our identities encompasses shared feelings and affects as well as shared thinking.[10] Feminist psychologist Jessica Benjamin describes intersubjectivity as an alternative understanding of the self from that based on the idea of an individual psyche. This is the subjectivity that emerges from the self-in-the-world, a self that is formed by social receptivity and interaction and that recognizes the subjectivities of others rather than seeing others as fantasy extensions of the self's wishes and desires.[11] This notion of identity broadens our understanding of the co-constructed nature of the interview to contemplate the many ways that identity is already deeply co-constructed. Instead of thinking of a person's identity as fixed, we begin to see identity as an ongoing formation, which can shift depending on context and circumstance. The self in narrative becomes not an essence to be uncovered but a matter of narrative positioning in a specific context for a particular end.[12]

According to Mikhail Bakhtin, a philosopher and literary critic, the intersubjective self is formed and can be known only through signs (words, gestures, choice of dress or grooming), which are ideologically saturated and hierarchically layered. In the case of language, the words we use to express ourselves are already loaded with meanings derived from our socio-historical context. For instance, I may speak in a regional dialect that connects me to the time and place of my rearing, even if I no longer live in that region. Moreover, different people may read the *signs* of my dialect differently, depending on their familiarity and associations with my particular (but always socially inflected) form of our shared language.[13]

How do we apply these insights to oral narrative research? Contemporary oral historians and folklorists recognize that the narrative accounts that form the basis of our research are co-created through dialogue, most often questions and answers, and by the assumptions and expectations narrators and researchers bring with them to the interview.[14] Researchers who gather life stories alternately describe the method as a means for narrators to fashion a coherent self out of disparate experiences, a reflexive opportunity for them to re-examine the past to fashion a more mature and agentive self-concept, or as presenting an inherent challenge to a subject's self-composure when the researcher's goals structure the line of questioning.[15] Rather than seeing our interviews as a means for the narrator to gain self-knowledge, as the first two perspectives imply, I suggest that we focus on the researcher as learner. If we embrace the deeply social nature of our identities that intersubjectivity implies, then a focus on incoherence and interpretive dissonance provides both a way to preserve the narrator's distinctive perspectives within our own projects and a way for us, the researchers, to learn from those points of difference.

We might also keep in mind that subjectivities are anything but unitary in everyday practice, and that they transform in response to changing life circumstances and available social scripts. My focus on Bea's narrative self-construction in one story, for instance, violated Bea's sense of her own self-concept understood in a more comprehensive, for-the-record sort of way. Recently, I discovered an interview Bea did with a journalist in the early 1970s about her playwriting. Although she worked as a high school, college, and adult education English teacher, she was passionately involved in amateur theater for most of her life, and wrote several successful one-act plays.[16] The journalist reports that when Bea's husband, Frank, was hired at Montclair State University, Bea stepped down in compliance with an unwritten rule that married couples could not both serve on the faculty. The reporter quotes Bea as saying, "It is a ridiculous situation and should be changed," then comments, "That she goes along with it almost willingly in spite of her resentment against the rule, underscores Mrs. Hanson's guiding belief that 'a woman makes a mistake if she puts her own career first,'" a decidedly double-voiced explanation.[17]

Bearing in mind that narrators can hold conflicting attitudes toward the social roles they inhabit, we can re-examine the physical records we construct through our method. An interview designed to elicit life review is, as Marie-Françoise Chanfrault-Duchet argues, "a ritualized speech act, which results from the conjunction, in the 1970s, of a genre, autobiography, with a new medium, the tape-recorder, within the institutional framework of the social sciences."[18] But it is also an extension of the everyday art of conversation. From the perspective of a folklorist, life review is less about creating a narrative self-portrait where none existed before than about gathering together oft-repeated stories in a new, perhaps more reflective or comprehensive configuration. Recorded interviews, however, materialize and fix one's ordinarily ephemeral conversational self-expression.

The tape-recorder, video camera, or notebook function as signs of a powerful third interlocutor, an absent public who influences how narrators understand and perform the rhetorical task of fashioning accounts of their experience. Researchers often worry about the ways this third interlocutor can produce anxiety and stiffness in the narrator, blocking self-disclosure. In our

1986 tape-recorded sessions, Bea occasionally instructed me to turn off the recorder so that she could remember relevant details and provide an accurate, coherent account. Fully aware of the recorder, Bea still could not know how her narrative would materialize through recording and transcription. In her written response to my interpretation, one-third of her critique addressed the inelegant and incoherent (to her) quality of the transcript:

> Because I know the horse-race story so well, your transcription (or anyone's transcription, at least of the oral version) is bound to be disappointing to me. I miss the *flavor*—the essence that I supposed was mine in telling and writing it.[19] I miss the tension, the suspense that makes the story come alive . . . If you stuck religiously to the tape and what you've set down in the above instance was exactly what I said, and *all* that I said, then I don't see how it even made sense to *you*.[20]

Bea's struggle to reconcile the story, as it existed in her head as compared to how it manifested on paper, highlights the ways in which our research methods produce skeletal representations that lack the "flavor" of not only a living performance, but also a remembered experience. Like the tip of an iceberg, the spoken story presents to a listener words and images uprooted from the context of the narrator's memories and associations. Unlike a written narrative that presumes an absolute distinction between the author and reader, oral narratives leap around, suspending phrases, sketching rather than elaborating, with the usually justified expectation that a listener will silently fill in gaps as needed. To speak of narrative dialogism, then, is not only to recognize the co-production of meaning in the question and answer format of an oral interview. It also connotes how words and images resonate among speakers and listeners in multiple, meaningful ways, how what appear to be monologues are always dialogic, addressed to an actively receptive listener. As a listener accustomed to reading transcripts, I view Bea's focus on the oral narrative of the verbal competition in the grandstand as much more flavorful and interesting than her earlier written version, which focuses more on the drama playing out among the horses and riders. In that earlier written version, however, Bea foregrounds her aspirations for a future with her second husband, Frank, by identifying their marriage with the equine competition on the field. This dimension of meaning is muted in the oral version by the early introduction of the theme of divorce (as opposed to marriage), a circumstance that led me to completely overlook the possibility that the story might resonate with Bea as a symbol of her *second* successful marriage rather than her first failed one.

Cultivating deep listening skills are important ways of moving from a position of knowing/judging to one of learning/appreciating. To understand another's perspective, however, does not require accepting it fully as one's own. Nor do one's own interpretations need to be accepted by one's interlocutors to be defensible. In fact, my own interpretive conflict with Beatrice has led me to greater insight in two related areas. First, I recognize much more clearly the social constraints and opportunities Bea navigated as a woman growing up in the first half of the 20th century, experiences that were very different from my own and that led to a very different sense of self in the world. Second, in the larger body of Bea's recorded stories and reminiscences, I am now much more attuned to those moments when Bea departs from my expected script and speaks differently. I have moved from an engagement with the stories that resonate with me, that confirm my prior understandings of Bea and her world, to productive puzzlement over the pieces that jar, do not fit, or speak differently. Ultimately, for oral narrative research, the issue in "That's not what I said" is not the truth of what happened that day at the racetrack, but in how Bea and I came to an interpretive understanding that was fuller and more nuanced than either of our initial views. It illustrates the generative possibilities of tackling moments of narrative dissonance, of pushing through discomfort to apprehend and explore the worlds we conjure through words.

Notes

1 Letter written by Beatrice Hanson to Katherine Borland, 22 January 1988, 7.
2 Katherine Borland, "'That's Not What I Said': Interpretive Conflict in Oral Narrative Research," in *Women's Words: The Feminist Practice of Oral History*, eds. Sherna Gluck and Daphne Patai (New York: Routledge, 1991), 63–75.
3 See, for example, "Co-narration, Intersubjectivity, and the Listener in Family Storytelling," *Journal of American Folklore* 130 (518): 438–456.
4 See also Elaine Lawless, "'I Was Afraid Someone Like You . . . an Outsider . . . Would Misunderstand': Negotiating Interpretive Differences between Ethnographers and Subjects," *Journal of American Folklore* 105 (1992): 302–314; and my review essay, "Decolonizing Approaches to Feminist Research: The Case of Feminist Ethnography," in *Handbook of Feminist Research: Theory and Praxis*, ed. Sharlene Nagy Hesse-Biber (Thousand Oaks, CA: Sage Publications, 2007), 621–628.
5 Alan Wong, "Listen and Learn: Familiarity and Feeling in the Oral History Interview," in *Oral History Off the Record: Toward an Ethnography of Practice*, eds. Anna Sheftel and Stacey Zembrzycki (New York: Palgrave MacMillan, 2013), 97–112; Martha Norkunas, "The Vulnerable Listener," in *Oral History Off the Record*, 81–96.
6 Arthur W. Frank, *Letting Stories Breathe: A Socio-Narratology* (Chicago: University of Chicago Press, 2010), 94–96.
7 Maurice Hamington, ed. *Feminist Interpretations of Jane Addams* (College Park, PA: Penn State University Press, 2010).
8 For instance, see Addams' analysis of Devil Baby Legends as a means for ordinarily silent and abject elderly women to find voice and authority in her *The Long Road of Women's Memory* (New York: Macmillan, 1916) as well as her autobiographical account, *Twenty Years at Hull House*, ed. Victoria Bissell Brown (New York: Bedford/St. Martins, 1998). For a contemporary discussion of the therapeutic effects of telling one's story to an understanding listener, see Carl Lindahl, "Legends of Hurricane Katrina: The Right to Be Wrong, Survivor-to-Survivor Storytelling, and Healing," *Journal of American Folklore* 125 (2012): 139–176. For an extended discussion of the value of subjective truths, see Alessandro Portelli, *The Battle of Valle Giulia: Oral History and the Art of Dialog* (Madison: University of Wisconsin Press, 1994), 3–23. For a discussion of how personal memories contribute to reconstructing social history, see Joan Sangster, "Politics and Praxis in Canadian Working-Class History," in *Oral History Off the Record*, 59–76.

9 George Herbert Mead, "Thought as Internalized Conversation [1934]," in *Four Sociological Traditions: Selected Readings*, ed. Randall Collins (New York: Oxford University Press, 1994), 293.

10 Eve Kosofsky Sedgwick, *Touching Feeling: Affect, Pedagogy, Performance* (Durham: Duke University Press, 2003); Kathleen Stewart, *Ordinary Affects* (Duke University Press, 2007).

11 Jessica Benjamin, "A Desire of One's Own: Psychoanalytic Feminism and Intersubjective Space," in *The Feminist Philosophy Reader*, eds. Alison Bailey and Chris Cuomo (Boston: McGraw Hill, 2008), 188–203. Benjamin accepts both ideas of the individual psyche and self-in-the-world as useful, complementary constructs for psychoanalysis.

12 Michael Bamberg, "Positioning between Structure and Performance. Oral Versions of Personal Experience: Three Decades of Narrative Analysis," Special Issue of the *Journal of Narrative and Life History* 7 (1987): 335–342.

13 V.N. Volosinov, "Marxism and the Philosophy of Language (1929)," trans. L. Matejka and I.R. Titunik, in *The Bakhtin Reader: Selected Writings of Bakhtin, Medvedev, Voloshinov*, ed. Pam Morris (New York: Edward Arnold), 2009.

14 Lynn Abrams, *Oral History Theory* (New York: Routledge, 2010), 54–77.

15 On coherence, see Charlotte Linde, *Life Stories: The Creation of Coherence* (New York: Oxford University Press, 1993); on self-examination, see Alicia J. Rouverol, "Trying To Be Good: Lessons in Oral History Performance," in *Remembering: Oral History Performance*, ed. Della Pollack (New York: Palgrave MacMillan, 2006), 19–44; on discomposure, see Penny Summerfield, "Dis/composing the Subject: Intersubjectivities in Oral History Research," in *Feminism and Autobiography: Texts, Theories, Methods*, eds. Tess Cosslett, Celia Lury, and Penny Summerfield (New York: Routledge, 2000), 91–106.

16 As a child, Bea played piano for the silent pictures theater in her town and for a dance band when she was a little older. After her 1936 divorce, she worked briefly for the Boston-based American Broadcasting Company as an itinerant director of amateur theater, traveling from town to town, a bag of scripts in one hand and a suitcase full of costumes in the other. She worked her way through normal school cleaning houses, but won an American Society of Composers, Authors, and Publishers award for a one-act play she wrote. The award money allowed her to complete her studies at the University of Maine, where she received her Master's degree. When she taught high school, she directed the school plays and pageants. She continued writing and directing one-act plays with amateur and school groups, and at some point during the 1960s, one of those plays was optioned for Broadway, but it was never produced.

17 Helen C. Smith, "Curtains Are Her Calling," *The Star Ledger* (1971), 41.

18 Marie-Françoise Chanfrault-Duchet, "Textualisation of the Self and Gender Identity in the Life-Story," in *Feminism and Autobiography*, 61–62.

19 Bea refers here to the letter version of the story. At present, I am pursuing these comments in a comparative examination of the written and oral versions of the tale.

20 Letter written by Hanson to Borland, 4.

2 The positionality of narrators and interviewers

Methodological comments on oral history with Anglo-Indian schoolteachers in Bangalore, India

Sanchia deSouza and
Jyothsna Latha Belliappa

> One of our own schoolteachers, she said to me, "Look here, all of you [Anglo-Indian teachers] are going [away]. Then why should we send our children to these schools?"
> I said, "But why, there are other teachers."
> "No, but you'll have something in you'll," she said, "which is completely different. Where's the need for us to send our children if you'll are not there?"
> And another occasion, one of the parents said, "Where are all the skirts gone?" One of the parents said that to me. Where are all the skirts gone?
> Conversation between "Laura" and Sanchia[1]

Many of urban India's educational aspirations in the postcolonial period have centered on the public figure of the Anglo-Indian schoolteacher, an authoritative yet nurturing woman in a skirt with something "completely different" about her that made parents seek out the school where she taught. At the core of our research project on Anglo-Indian women schoolteachers from Bangalore are seventeen life stories involving many hours of conversation. In this chapter, we offer some insights into these illuminating "teaching" narratives but focus in particular on methodology, specifically the theme of positionality in the interview process.

The Anglo-Indian community is a bi-racial Christian ethnic minority with roots in the colonial era. Emerging from the domestic relationships between European men and Indian women, it evolved into a distinct community with a hybrid culture. After Indian independence from British rule in 1947, the community was constitutionally recognized, with Anglo-Indian citizens being defined are those "whose father or male progenitor is of European descent but who is domiciled within India."[2] Their distinguishing features include English as a mother tongue and Eurocentric cultural practices, including Western musical and dance traditions. Anglo-Indian women wear Western attire to distinguish themselves from Indian women and adopt European standards of femininity.[3] Traditions allowing for the social mixing of genders also created a relatively relaxed attitude towards individual choice in matters of love and marriage that is unusual in much of Indian society. The anxiety with which the British and other Indian communities have viewed Anglo-Indians, who face considerable prejudice, has generated long-standing and continuing negative stereotypes. The men are depicted as unreliable, shiftless, and susceptible to alcoholism, for example, and the women as predisposed to loud, licentious, and sexually indiscriminate behavior.[4]

The shifting fortunes of Anglo-Indians also require comment. In the latter half of the 19th century, the British colonial government so preferred Anglo-Indian men (regardless of individual academic achievement) for administrative jobs in the railway, post, and telegraph sector that they came to constitute something of a "railway caste."[5] Considering them loyal on the grounds of their European ancestry but a potentially destabilizing force on account of their racial hybridity, colonial authorities adopted a strategy of ensuring them stable economic status while also constructing them as colonial allies.[6] In the early 20th century, however, changes in government policy, particularly the Montague–Chelmsford Reforms that, following the First World War, opened up administrative jobs to more educated Indians from diverse communities, limited Anglo-Indian men's access to government employment. In response, more Anglo-Indian women entered the workforce to support husbands and children, clustering particularly in teaching, nursing, and secretarial jobs.[7] In Bangalore, many of them sought jobs in European-style schools, especially English-language Christian missionary schools run by Catholic nuns and priests or Protestant clergy. Particularly adept at mobilizing the cultural capital they possessed—ability to teach in English, proficiency in Western traditions of art, music, and theatre, and the relationships formed within the community as a result—to land teaching positions, they comprised a majority of teachers in these minority schools by the 1970s.

The church or school boards that privately manage these schools make decisions on the recruitment of teachers, wages, leave policies, and terms of employment. Funded through student fees and private donations, the schools are affiliated with the Council for the Indian School Certificate Examinations (the Council), which sets curriculum and administers the school-leaving certificate exams taken after class ten (when students are about fifteen years of age).[8] There are no collective bodies to represent the teachers' interests and any form of collective action is strongly discouraged. Relationships between management and staff are deeply hierarchical and governed by a formal, rigid code of conduct based on age and gender. For instance, it is not unusual for management to prescribe a staff dress code with injunctions on the length and fit of clothes.

Our narrators belong to this large group of Anglo-Indian teachers, most of whom have had long careers (30+ years) teaching thousands of students from many different religious and linguistic communities in Bangalore. We calculated that one teacher had touched the lives of more than 20,000 students in her 25-year career. These teachers have thus arguably played a key role in English-language education in Bangalore and therefore in the city's emergence as India's information technology capital and, by extension, in the nation's growth as an economic power.[9]

Here, we address the issue of positionality through a discussion of ethical questions that arose in our interviews with still-serving and retired Anglo-Indian women. As a two-member collaborative team composed of a senior researcher, Jyothsna Belliappa, and a junior one, Sanchia deSouza, we usually interviewed the schoolteachers individually, engaging in a one-on-one discussion. We used a life story approach to elicit teachers' memories of their careers and to locate their experiences in the changes that have occurred in Bangalore's English-language school system over the past 50 years. (We also conducted additional interviews with members of the Bangalore Anglo-Indian community and wider education community.) In our core interviews with seventeen teachers between 47 and 77 years of age, we found that gender identity, community membership, and faith tended to influence narrators' accounts of professional life.

Following the feminist principle of locating interviewers' subjectivities, we note the initial motivations that guided our research questions. Both of us, though not Anglo-Indian ourselves, have been taught by Anglo-Indian teachers. Additionally, we have direct experience of the teaching profession: Sanchia's mother was a school teacher while Jyothsna was previously one. Before our collaboration, we had been working separately in the field, gathering oral histories from teachers and students from two different schools for separate public history projects. We decided to collaborate because we thought it would better allow us to address gaps in the research and literature on Indian education—namely, the insufficient attention paid to teachers' rich perspectives and experiences. By focusing on women from a marginalized ethnic and religious minority within Indian society, and how they are experiencing marginalization by neo-liberal educational regimes, we endeavoured to bring an intersectional perspective to research on teachers and teaching.[10]

Private conversation, public performance

The oral history interview frequently involves an intimate conversation between interviewer and narrator, but with a sense of privacy that is largely an illusion, given that the interview is intended in part or whole for an archive or for publication. We used the snowball method to recruit narrators, asking friends and community members to put us in contact with those who might be interested in speaking with us. We promised privacy, as much as possible, and pledged to use pseudonyms in all publications and avoid any mention of schools. Given that many teachers obtained their jobs through their communal relationships—or their social capital—they often find themselves in a rather delicate position. They cannot afford to annoy the school management, which might include the powerful members of their community or church who played a role in their hiring and who will continue to influence the terms of their employment. Consequently, ensuring confidentiality and anonymity was particularly important.

If the oral history interview is a private conversation, it also takes on the character of a public performance, albeit with a largely invisible public that is represented by the interviewer. Feminist oral historians argue that the interviewer plays a role in co-constructing the narrative that emerges through the questions asked, the interjections made, the manner in which they listen or respond to the narrator, and the ways in which authority is shared.[11] Issues of self-representation and the power differential that can characterize relations between narrators and researchers are thereby significant to the creation of narratives throughout the interview.

Our narrators' understanding of performance in the interview was centered on the recording. Indeed, our promises to switch off the recorder if they wanted to share anything "off the record" elicited such a high level of trust that we began to question just how much power we had. At any rate, it became clear to us that our power was based on how much they trusted us. For reasons we explain in more detail below, their trust in us was very strong and based on their view that we shared much in common with them. This, in turn, raised a related issue: whether the creation of intimacy exploits narrators. Feminist researcher Janet Finch effectively articulated the problem when she reflected on the dynamics of interviewing clergymen's wives in England in the 1980s when she herself was a clergyman's wife. "I have also emerged from interviews with the feeling that my interviewees need to know how to protect themselves from people like me," she writes, adding: "They have often revealed very private parts of their lives in return for what must be, in the last resort, very flimsy guarantees of confidentiality: my verbal assurances ... that I would make any public references to them anonymous and disguised."[12]

In our project, we attempted to mitigate such power imbalances by offering to share transcripts with our narrators, which they appreciated. We also offered to provide drafts of anything we might publish, though most were not interested in reading this material. In the initial stages of our research, we attempted to use written confidentiality agreements (signed by researcher and narrator), which are common in Western contexts, but found that they tended to erode trust rather than establish it in Indian settings. Two teachers who signed consent forms indicated that they were unsure what sorts of "rights" over their narratives would be signed away for our use.

Prefaces and self-disclosure

We have fully respected every teacher's request to keep a section(s) of their interviews private. Our observational notes on our meetings with them, particularly before and after the actual interview, are illuminating and form part of the conceptual framework for our analysis. In our respective efforts to gain access to, and build rapport with, our narrators, both of us tended to invoke the concept of "sameness" in ways that led our narrators to relate to us in what we describe as "teacher/aunt" mode. For example, Jyothsna's previous experience as a school teacher and Sanchia's identity as Goan resonated with the women in particular ways. Specifically, Goan Catholics, who are a product of Goa's past status as a Portuguese colony, possess a hybrid cultural identity that is similar to that of Anglo-Indians. Now viewed as highly Westernized, Goan Catholics have been subject to the same gendered stereotypes that plague Anglo-Indians. Further, highly Westernized Goan women in urban India have followed a similar employment trajectory to that of Anglo-Indian women— teaching, secretarial work, and nursing—though it occurred later in the 20th century between 1940 and 1980.

The sense of "sameness" that helped us gain our narrators' trust was not simply imposed by us but instead co-constructed in conjunction with our narrators. Our narrators had few if any qualms about questioning us about our personal lives and motives before beginning the recorded interview portion of our meeting. Sanchia, as a younger woman from a community with an ethos of Christianity and hybridity similar to that espoused by Anglo-Indians, found herself in a position of vulnerability and power. The sameness invoked in conversation led narrators to adopt a role that can best be described as both teacher and aunt. For instance, they frequently addressed her as "my girl"— a phrase typically used to indicate the speaker's seniority in a familial or community context. Some women shared sensitive information about their lives in undertones. Many did not hesitate to ask Sanchia probing questions about her personal life and her position on marriage, motherhood, and other issues. They also asked about her status—whether she was single or married— and her relationships with parents and siblings. They offered pointed advice, such as "you better hurry up and have children if you want to." The dynamics were similar to those described by Jieyu Liu, who conducted interviews in China with women who were at least one generation older than herself. According to Liu, the position she held as the junior woman—the learner, the daughter—was valuable in terms of creating closeness and rapport with the women and obtaining deeply textured accounts. Our experience bears out her emphasis on the importance of creating research relationships within the framework of social norms based on gender, age, and seniority on both ethical and academic grounds.[13]

That the narrators did not ask Sanchia whether they shared the same faith, and Sanchia's own silence on the matter, also deserves comment. Sanchia's surname "deSouza" immediately marks her as Catholic by descent in India, and probably by faith as well. Sanchia is not a practicing Catholic, but, knowing that a young person's decision to move away from religion can provoke strong reactions in older people whose faith is so integral to their lives, she avoided discussing her stand on religion. It seems likely that the narrators' identification of her as Goan Catholic and therefore a fellow Christian, along with the opportunities they had to question Sanchia about her personal life, increased their level of comfort when it came to carrying out the interview. It may well have enabled them to share with her controversial opinions or painful personal details that are usually withheld from strangers, such as criticisms of the church and alcoholism in the family. The status that interviewer and narrator shared as members of a marginalized and occasionally stigmatized minority very likely encouraged the frank admission regarding alcoholism.

A judicious use of self-disclosure, then, can be an important tool in feminist oral history research, one that can contribute towards further developing the narrative being told in the interview. To offer another example of the value of judicious self-disclosure, this one involving Jyothsna, we begin with the following exchange:

> LAURA: It's important to correct spelling, grammar—doing corrections helps you get to know your children. You learn what they know, what mistakes they make. You correct their errors—you know where they tend to go wrong. Then you come to know their background from the way they write, whether the parents are taking an interest in their work. . . . Nowadays teachers don't correct! You leave the spelling and the punctuation just like it is! . . . How can a teacher put her signature on a book with so many spelling mistakes and punctuation mistakes?
> JYOTHSNA: And you come to know their personalities—
> LAURA: Yes! From all their little compositions. Children love to talk and they love to tell you all their stories. What happened at home and what mother said and what father said. We never finished with the school at three o'clock. We brought home corrections and we had extra spelling. I joined [school's name] in 1977 and I had 77 children. They gave us a helper who could do the corrections. But I didn't like that—because the helper was not that particular with corrections. I think they've done away with that.

Having been a primary school teacher, Jyothsna identified with some of Laura's motives for keeping up with "corrections" (marking and grading). In this exchange, Laura seems encouraged by Jyothsna's comment to articulate her sense of pride in carrying out this work. Although Jyothsna has, on some occasions, effectively drawn on this teaching experience to create familiarity with narrators either before or during the interview, she is also acutely aware that the context in which she taught, at a 21st-century international school with a more egalitarian work culture, differed significantly from narrators' experiences. For this reason, and because she was hesitant to take away "airtime" from the narrator, she avoided making regular references to her own experiences.

Personal myth-making

As Luisa Passerini long ago observed, narrators tend to draw on personal myths in interviews, sharing narratives that include conflict, crisis, and resolution, and sometimes even triumph, as they position themselves as the heroes of their narratives. Such individual myth-making in narratives of rebellion carries great symbolic value, offering a means of resisting a social reality oppressive to women, even if rebellious features might be exaggerated to create a certain effect.[14] In our project, we have seen elements of this myth-making, though the women sometimes found themselves in situations where they risked much to challenge the school management's authority. Interestingly, Georgiana spoke of having "the heart of a pilot and paratrooper" before explaining how she made the choice to be a teacher:

> I couldn't imagine myself sitting at a desk [as a stenographer] . . . I wanted to be out with children and I felt being in the open air was far better than being confined. And I didn't like being a nurse. I didn't have so much empathy in me at that particular time to feel sad for those who were sick, you know. I was lively and I wanted to be out with children. That's how I went in to be a teacher. No regrets.

Ruth explained that she was constantly in conflict with school management in part because "I wasn't such an easy person that took everything they said lying down. I argued back. I was always arguing about the salary being very low," she said, but also added: "They had a lot of regard for me." In support of the latter claim, she explained how she was given a position of responsibility by management, recruiting teachers. In her narrative, then, she is both formidable and worthy of respect (higher-level positions) precisely because of her obstinate character.

In another narrative in which a heroic challenge of authority wins the day, Rosemary described her school's disapproval of her decision to sell encyclopaedias to augment her income, and how she defended her behavior:

> I got into trouble with Sister (the principal) over that. She said, "You're not supposed to take up another job." I said, "I didn't know that." There was no written rule like that. So she said, "You'll have to stop this." And then, I don't know from where I got the courage, I said, "Sister, you sisters teach us to go out into the world and take care of ourselves, you know, not be a burden to others, to stand on our feet. And what am I doing, I am working hard to see that my two sons finish their education. And that is the reason. I'm not doing it to build a house or to get rich." She says, "No, no, no, you'll have to stop it." I said, "Well sister, I'm sorry to tell you this, but I cannot stop it." And I walked out of there.

Significantly, while Rosemary's narrative highlights her defiance, it only briefly hints at the real risks involved. As she disclosed elsewhere in her interview, her family was dependent upon her income to pay school fees, so losing her job would have been disastrous. Her presence of mind in using the school's own principles to make a case in her favor allowed her to challenge both the principal and the management's claim to have control over her activities.

The description of her dramatic exit conveys her sense of having taken complete control of the situation.

Meek dictators

As researchers, we were surprised by how several of the teachers who narrated the kind of confident, even defiant, narratives just cited ended the interview process once we switched off the recorder. After the performance part was over, the dynamic shifted again to a footing in which we, the researchers, were placed in a position of relatively greater power. Most of our narrators had attained a Teacher Training Certificate (TTC) educational level following high school graduation. As post-graduate degree holders working in the field of education, we, as interviewers, were constantly aware of our privilege and reflected on it throughout the process. Our narrators occasionally invoked this marker of prestige (higher levels of formal education) and our employment in tertiary education to suggest that we had more expertise as educators than them. Sanchia was initially startled, for example, when Rosemary apologized for some of her teaching methods, even asking Sanchia, "Is that all right, what I did?" Her uncertainty possibly arose from her experience of having had several colleagues and superiors challenge her teaching methods over the years, incidents that she narrated in their conversation.

An educationist and historian of education in India, Krishna Kumar has well captured the position of Indian teachers, historically speaking, with the term "the meek dictator," meaning that they enjoy a high degree of prestige and authority in the classroom among students (and in an earlier time, with parents), but are disempowered by administrators and school management. In Kumar's view, this disempowerment derives from the way the colonial education system took away teachers' power to decide a curriculum—something that village-based teachers under the pre-colonial indigenous systems had possessed—and thus the sort of knowledge they could impart.[15]

Trained teachers enjoy a certain prestige as members of a "noble profession" that both cares for and educates the younger generation, yet this same responsibility also generates societal suspicions of them and how they do their jobs. Thus, we would extend the concept of the "meek dictator" to encompass the limited empowerment teachers experience in their roles, being constantly monitored and controlled by school management and the principal and, via them, by parents. When we first approached teachers and school administrators for interviews, several expressed concern that we might be journalists out to "expose" their schools (they later explained in interviews that there had recently been some negative media reports). We would argue that this position of meek dictatorship also shaped the dynamic of our interviews. The performance aspect of the interview—a space in which the teachers could be said to be teaching us about their lives—brought out their sense of authority, but the enmeshed meekness and diffidence also came out during other aspects of the process.

Finally, given the sensitivity of the community to the prejudices they have experienced, both historically and in the present, we had to face suspicions about why outsiders like us were interested in the Anglo-Indian community and how we were going to represent it. Such concerns also affected some teachers' willingness to be identified, since they did not want to be known as having spoken negatively about their school or community. Given this condition, we have been forced to leave out fascinating stories of defiance because the description of the incidents would immediately expose our narrators' identities. Out of concern for their welfare, we have used pseudonyms for everyone, even though some expressed a willingness to be identified. This begs the question of whether we have attributed too little authority and power to our narrators and emphasized their disempowerment too much—a difficult question to answer.

Conclusion

In reflecting on our methodology, we have highlighted some of the intriguing shifts in power dynamics that can characterize the formal and informal interview process. Our focus on a community doubly marginal in Indian society—Anglo-Indian women who are schoolteachers—brought to light some of the ways in which the professional, community, and personal positionality of both researchers and narrators have to be carefully negotiated, but also showed that these remain difficult to pin down. Given the kind of authoritarian systems and gender relations through which the Anglo-Indian women schoolteachers we interviewed have lived their professional and personal lives, we found that they were rarely called upon to speak about themselves. Many approached the "task" of recounting their experiences and achievements with some diffidence ("I cannot praise myself," said one) but seemed to enjoy it once we established initial rapport. Our interview process and the resulting narratives revealed that in the simultaneously public and private setting of classroom and interview, these teachers constantly moved between diffidence and authority as they navigated a changing educational and social milieu. We, as feminist oral historians, show our desire to protect (and maybe inadvertently over-protect) teachers and enable their speaking through choosing which stories to share publically and through our own careful self-disclosure in the interview process. The challenge of balancing such ethical considerations with an analysis of the narratives themselves, and how they reflect myth-making and our narrators' self-representational desires, is an ongoing one.

Notes

1 All names used are pseudonyms, as agreed to in discussions with the teachers.
2 Government of India, Constitution of India, art. 366 (b) (1950). This official use of the term "Anglo-Indian" for a mixed-race political constituency differs from the way it was used in most colonial-era literature, where it referred to British people who had spent significant time in India but were not necessarily mixed race.

There are some ambiguities in how the current community defines its identity and disagreement over whether the term should include Portuguese-descendants (Goan or East Indian community members).

3 Lionel Caplan, *Children of Colonialism: Anglo-Indians in a Postcolonial World* (Oxford: Berg, 2001).

4 Caplan, 63–66, 77–78; Alison Blunt, *Domicile and Diaspora: Anglo-Indian Women and the Spatial Politics of Home* (Oxford: Blackwell, 2005), 15–16; Geetanjali Gangoli, "Sexuality, Sensuality and Belonging: Representations of the 'Anglo-Indian' and the 'Western' Woman in Hindi Cinema," in *Bollyworld, Popular Indian Cinema through a Transnational Lens*, eds. Raminder Kaur and Ajay J. Sinha (New Delhi: Sage, 2005), 143–162.

5 Marian Aguiar, *Tracking Modernity: India's Railway and the Culture of Mobility* (Minneapolis: University of Minnesota Press, 2011), 21–23.

6 See Adrian Carton, *Mixed-Race and Modernity in Colonial India: Changing Concepts of Hybridity Across Empires* (London: Routledge, 2012), on the development of the category of race amidst the changing political structures of colonial India.

7 Caplan, 27–31.

8 While the Council requires schools to follow government guidelines on wages, it has limited resources to monitor their implementation; anecdotal evidence suggests some schools try to avoid strict compliance.

9 M.K. Raghavendra, "Local Resistance to Global Bangalore: Reading Minority Indian Cinema," in *Popular Culture in a Globalized India*, eds. K. Moti Gokulsing and Wimal Dissanayake (London/New York: Routledge, 2009), 17–19, for a succinct discussion of the history of language in Bangalore and its connection with globalization.

10 Poonam Batra, "Voice and Agency of Teachers: Missing Link in National Curriculum Framework," *Economic and Political Weekly* 40, no. 40 (2005): 4347–4356; Nandini Manjrekar, "Women School Teachers in New Times: Some Preliminary Reflections," *Indian Journal of Gender Studies* 20, no. 2 (2013): 335–356.

11 See Ann Oakley, "Interviewing Women: A Contradiction in Terms," Helen Roberts ed., *Doing Feminist Research* 30, no. 6 (1981): 1; Gayle Letherby, "Feminist Methodology," in *The SAGE Handbook of Innovation in Social Research Methods*, eds. Malcolm Williams and Paul Vogt (London: Sage Publications, 2011), 62–79; Katherine Borland, "That's Not What I Said: Interpretive Conflict in Oral Narrative Research," in *Women's Words: The Feminist Practice of Oral History*, eds. Sherna Berger Gluck and Daphne Patai (New York: Routledge, 1991), 63–75; Michael Frisch, *A Shared Authority: Essays on the Craft and Meaning of Oral and Public History* (New York: SUNY Press, 1990); Steven High, "Sharing Authority: An Introduction," *Journal of Canadian Studies* 43, no. 1 (2009): 12–34; Linda Shopes, "Commentary: Sharing Authority," *Oral History Review* 30, no. 1 (2003): 104.

12 Janet Finch, "'It's Great to Have Someone to Talk To': Ethics and Politics of Interviewing Women," in *Social Research: Philosophy, Politics and Practice*, ed. Martyn Hammersley, (London/Thousand Oaks, New Delhi: Sage, 1993), 170.

13 Jieyu Liu, "Researching Chinese Women's Lives: 'Insider' Research and Life History Interviewing," *Oral History* 34, no. 1 (2006): 43–52.

14 Luisa Passerini, "Women's Personal Narratives: Myths, Experiences and Emotions," in *Interpreting Women's Lives: Feminist Theory and Personal Narrative*, ed. Personal Narratives Group (Bloomington: Indiana University Press, 1989), 189–197.

15 Krishna Kumar, *Political Agenda of Education: A Study of Colonialist and Nationalist Ideas* (New Delhi: Sage, 1991).

3 When is enough enough?

Daphne Patai

For more than twenty years I have noticed that current books and manuscripts in the field of oral history routinely claim to raise new methodological issues in the context of their particular projects. So, too, do many conference papers, as if the advent of each new subject necessarily raises unique methodological problems not previously considered. Despite this rhetoric, in practice the only novelty in oral history for some time has been the focus on ever more specific identity groups and ever more detailed articulations of the various aspects of identity. Why, then, do authors pretend otherwise? An obvious explanation is that academic work both demands and thrives on supposed methodological innovation and theoretical sophistication.

Oral history researchers have by now spent many years thoroughly going over the problems: the complexities of the interview situation, the role of the interviewer in what can be (but is not always) a dense personal interaction, the relative merits of insider versus outsider status, the elements of time and space, the role of language, the need to make decisions at every stage of the process, the debates over the resulting product, the uncertainties of interpretation. It would seem that we have by now exhausted self-reflexivity and ethical awareness, talk of collectivity and return, uncovering "silenced" voices, and claims to occupy the political and moral high ground.

Mulling over these matters, I have come to wonder for how much longer we can till the same soil, always unearthing familiar pebbles and rocks that we strain to treat as startling new discoveries. Perhaps this is unavoidable when academic demands for methodological awareness continue unabated. There is scant reward for saying: The object (or subject) of my study may be new, but new themes or identity groups by no means necessarily entail new method-ological problems or issues, however much we wish to believe the contrary. In addition, each new generation of researchers tends to read current or recent versions of work in their field while too often ignoring older research, leading to lack of awareness of how familiar both their research concerns and solutions may be. The central questions that frame my discussion here, then, are: Must claims for constant theoretical or methodological innovation be made if oral history is to continue to have some validity? Is there really anything new under the oral history sun?

Other scholars with substantial experience in this field are evidently beginning to feel the same impatience. In a 2014 essay in the *Oral History Review*, Linda Shopes, a leading oral historian, wrote of her fatigue with the "clumsy imposition" of theory on interesting oral history projects that do not require such justification.[1] Extending that argument a year later, she explained that in her twelve years as co-editor of Palgrave Macmillan's *Studies in Oral History* series, she grew weary of projects "in which presumed theoretical ideas—themselves often expressed in turgid and obfuscating language—strained to connect to the interviews at hand even as they overpowered what were, in fact, often quite informative, thoughtful, and eloquent narratives."[2] This is a reasonable response to the growing disjuncture between the inherent interest of many projects and the theoretical and methodological claims, usually astonishingly thin and distinctly familiar, with which scholars surround their work.

A related focus has been on ethical dilemmas in conducting oral history work. After my own absorption in these problems in the 1980s, I began to realize the limited utility of such explorations and concluded that, however committed one might be to proper practices, in the most fundamental sense the ethical issues separating researchers and researched had very limited solutions.[3] In the end, we simply had to decide whether or not our research (imperfect as it always is) was worth pursuing. In a 1994 essay on what I called the "nouveau solipsism," I suggested that ultimately it is the work itself, not our ceaseless reflections on ourselves and the "process," that is of value.[4] This perception was stimulated by the ever more egregious self-involvement of scholars whose research subjects actually deserved better. A case in point at the time was anthropologist Ruth Behar's *Translated Woman: Crossing the Border with Esperanza's Story*, in which she averred that her own struggle to get tenure at a North American university was not all that different from Esperanza's struggles as a street peddler in Mexico City.[5]

Leaving aside such fantasies, other dubious propositions are frequently asserted by scholars. In a 2015 article, Shopes refers to the "broadly subversive nature of so much of our work" in oral history, a familiar claim made in recent decades by scholars in many different fields, eager to assert the political significance of their work.[6] Subversive of what, one may well ask, and for what purposes? The politics of the scholar, like those of the speaker in an oral history interview, are not necessarily "subversive." To the contrary, in today's academy, leftist politics are the norm, as if scholarship had no intrinsic value and must be defended in some other terms. Challenges to the status quo, however, have become the status quo. Transgression is long gone, though its vocabulary lingers on.

The insistence on "subversion," like the pretense that "our" research necessarily promotes (or should promote) progressive goals, confuses the aspirations (often self-aggrandizing) of researchers with the specific demands of sound scholarship. Interestingly, in the same essay, Shopes also makes clear her commitment to empirical research as a necessary component of oral history work. In other words, nothing she writes suggests she believes truth and accuracy should be sacrificed to our love of "subversion" or to our political commitments. Furthermore, perhaps demonstrating that little is new in the field of oral history, Shopes discusses a variety of problems (ethical and practical) that arise as conflicts develop between narrator and researcher over control of a project and of its interpretation.

But these, too, are familiar themes. Katherine Borland's essay in *Women's Words*, for example, dealt ably with such a disagreement over interpretation.[7] And, well before her, other scholars revealed their own stake in arguments regarding control and credit in oral history work. Nearly 40 years ago, the historian Nell Irvin Painter frankly recounted the conflict she had with Hosea Hudson over whose name should appear on the book she created from his narrative of his life as a Communist organizer in the southern United States starting in the 1930s.[8] Or, to take a more drastic case, the French scholar Philippe Lejeune cited the disquieting attitude of writer Adélaïde Blasquez toward Gaston Lucas, the subject of her 1976 book.[9] Not only, it turned out, had Blasquez destroyed the tapes of her interviews with Lucas, but when Lejeune, invited by Blasquez's publisher to do an interview with her, suggested that Lucas, too, should be interviewed, Blasquez replied that Lucas had nothing of value to say regarding her work. He existed, she maintained, only as a character that she, through her art, had created in the book.[10]

Perhaps because oral history is so plainly dependent on willing narrators, who may indeed never before have had their stories recorded, its practitioners may be especially vulnerable to extravagant pronouncements of its unique role in the world. One oral historian active in Brazil has actually argued that the primordial objective of the "discipline" of oral history (seen as inherently supportive of leftist goals) is to formulate political arguments.[11] But oral history need not and should not be defended on the questionable grounds that it supports particular political commitments. No research tool in itself has political valence, though the use we make of it may well do so. And when it does, this in fact raises the possibility that problems of bias might cloud the researcher's judgment and distort the work. To insist, as is frequently done, that all research is politically motivated is an easy, and unconvincing, retort, against which I have written for some time.[12] It confuses the content and the context of research. This is why Linda Shopes, like many other scholars, is right in insisting on the importance of empirical research. Granted, this is a pre-postmodern stance—and it should be applauded as such. In practice, even those who, on the one hand, state that reality is just a verbal construct, on the other rapidly abandon that stance when it comes to defending the accuracy of their own pronouncements, or when writing about the suffering, exploitation, and oppression that they accept as the objective reality of their subjects' experiences.[13] Few would bother doing oral history if they thought the stories they gathered were no different from fictional narration—which, yes, contains a "kind of" truth, but not necessarily truth about the actual world, historical events, or even individual perceptions and experiences.

One cannot have it both ways. Passion and political commitments are inherently neither honest nor admirable; they are not necessarily good guides to understanding the world, however deeply felt. And narratives, no matter how convincing, are not automatically either true or accurate. We see this clearly in the spate of supposedly autobiographical books that have been exposed as fake—that is, as fiction.[14] Denunciations of fraud have also arisen in relation to the race and ethnicity of public figures in recent years, as apparent in public reactions to revelations regarding Rachel Dolezal, a white activist who claimed to be black and rose to be president of the Spokane, Washington, chapter of the National Association for the Advancement of Colored People (NAACP). Or, to take another recent case, Massachusetts Senator Elizabeth Warren, who claims, without evidence, to have Native American heritage and was lauded by Harvard Law School as an example of their commitment to hiring minority women. Where sexual identity is concerned, by contrast, self-designation is now widely accepted and is rapidly becoming an orthodoxy, though not always without controversy (as in, for example, Smith College's announcement in 2015 that it would accept applications from people born male who "identify as female," and in the "transgender bathroom wars" of early 2016). In other words, we are living through a time of extraordinary confusion about if and how to gauge the validity of individuals' statements about their "identity."

Problems of authenticity arise in relation not only to claims to identity, of course, but to the very content of oral narratives, which, like other accounts, oral and written, may contain deep distortions, even lies, as happened with Nobel Peace Prize winner Rigoberta Menchú. Her famous *testimonio*—the term used primarily for the oral history narratives of Latin American leftists—of her life as a Guatemalan political activist promoting Indigenous peoples' rights, was highly praised and celebrated for years. But then anthropologist David Stoll published his research showing that Rigoberta had fabricated certain important and oft-cited aspects of her life story, relating to her education, her brother's death, and the key conflict in which her family was embroiled.[15] A heated controversy ensued, in which Stoll was angrily denounced as if he were an apologist for the Guatemalan dictatorship, as if this resolved the empirical questions raised by his work. Attacks on Stoll were often buttressed by questions about what motivated him to do his research in the first place.

Once her lies were exposed, Rigoberta's shifting explanations—first blaming Elisabeth Burgos, who recorded and published her story, then affirming that her narrative was "my truth"—did not help matters. Nor did the immediate defense of her by numerous academics, who argued that the actual truth of her account was insignificant in view of the "larger truth" about the Guatemalan military.[16] Such sophistry, however, undermines the very cause a narrator's distortions and lies may have been created to support. In reality, any struggle for justice and human rights must depend on accurate representations of events and experiences. Claims to victimhood should not automatically be granted a privileged status—especially in today's world in which such claims have turned into a valuable commodity, readily brought into play.

To say that what might have happened is no different than what did happen has become a familiar reaction to questionable and even patently false allegations of crimes and perceived offenses against women and minorities.[17] Adopting such a stance, however, means entering into a slippery world in which everything is subjected to politics. Once the distinction between fact and fiction dissolves, everyone can enter into the game, which will eventually self-destruct. In the realm of fiction, the South may have won the Civil War, Hitler perhaps was killed in his youth or emerged victorious in World War II, and Communism prevailed throughout Europe into the 21st century. Such fictional scenarios abound, and are known as "allohistory"—that is "other," "alternative," or "counterfactual" history, what might have happened as opposed to what actually transpired. But in the realm of fact, something very different took place, even if we might argue about particular events and their interpretation.

The work of discerning the world and trying to interpret it is multifaceted and never ending, true, but we cannot just make things up as we go along, with no foundation, simply because it better serves some immediate purpose. Bridges built without respect for physical principles will collapse. Among the real-world consequences of conflating fact with politically motivated fictions is the debasement of learning and education in general, which cannot survive if subjected to political tests. This is obviously true in scientific and technical fields, and also in the humanities and social sciences. Oral history is a form of narrative, and this is important to understand, but it is not merely narrative, indistinguishable from fiction. The "history" part of the term "oral history" actually carries some weight.

Since the 1991 publication of *Women's Words*, an enormous amount of research in oral history has appeared, particularly devoted to identity groups considered marginalized, silenced, or simply ignored. Many publishers and journals constantly seek out work utilizing oral history, and numerous courses and programs devoted to it exist. But the more institutionalized a field becomes, the more desperate the continuing claims for its newness and unique relevance sound. The main change in oral history, as in many other fields, has involved newly emerging identity groups, which have become a prized category. Though certainly researchers must be able to adapt to different situations, there is no evidence beyond the rhetorical that the identity of either researcher or narrator entails a particular ethics, methodology, and/or a specific political ideology. Nor do I think the "intersectional analysis," popularized by Women's Studies and designed to recognize multiple oppressions, resolves any of these issues.

Scholars, it seems to me, have responsibilities as scholars that can only be subordinated to politics at some peril. Contrary to currently fashionable allegations, the value of scholarship has to do with the integrity and thoroughness of the research and not with its underlying political commitments. For when we argue about the substance and value of oral history work, we invariably do so with reference to something outside of "narrative" and "identity"—vastly overused words these days. The history of intentionally politicized research and knowledge claims is well documented and hardly provides an inspiring model. As one political scientist said to me in an interview, there's "stuff" out there in the world that we must deal with.

Perhaps it is an appropriate awareness of the "stuff," the life of the world, to which our words refer and relate, that explains the recent surge in books on the subjects of trauma and crisis.[18] In these books there is typically less angst about the researcher's role, less solipsism. While methodological issues are raised, it is revealing that the more popular the book, the less likely it is to focus on methodological and theoretical concerns.[19] Still, the researchers' politics may intrude, at times to the detriment of the work.[20] Historical and other kinds of research are absolutely crucial for these projects, if they are not to be relegated to the category of fiction or fraud, as is a critical awareness of the problems associated with memory, both individual and collective. But the excessive self-reflection, methodological obsessions, and political declarations typical of much feminist oral history, and continued in queer oral history and other identity-focused research, at times strike a discordant note. Of course, when researchers write primarily for other researchers, they should expect those other researchers, if they are familiar with the field, to be skeptical about claims to innovation that are by now shopworn.

Apart from the numerous works on trauma and crisis in recent years, a significant body of research has developed in fields that shed important light on oral history, given its key elements of speaking, remembering, and listening. Especially suggestive is recent work in neurobiology, psychology, and philosophy, which have illuminated both the neurological and existential aspects of memory, consciousness, and the sense of self.[21] These do not, however, replace the more empirical research oral historians still need to undertake to contextualize, understand, and interpret the oral narratives they gather. But they do take us far beyond the constant emphasis, decades old by now, on the interaction between researcher and narrator (though "intersubjectivity" continues to be a hot topic), the solipsism of the tirelessly self-reflexive scholar, and the ceaseless cultivation of identity politics.

New technologies may allow us to gather such stories in particularly compelling ways, and to use them in venues that go beyond the written text—all of which have led to their own issues and problems. But these are part of the oral historian's path, well-trodden by now and not requiring constant reinvention merely because it is group X or Y that has come into focus. As demonstrated by Jorge Luis Borges's delightful fictional creation of the *Heavenly Emporium of Benevolent Knowledge*, a new taxonomy may well be a fascinating way of re-categorizing and apprehending things in the world, and, indeed, of showing the arbitrariness of (some) conventional categories, but it remains, nonetheless, an instance of taxonomy, not a reordering of the world.[22]

The allure of oral history, its fascination as a tool for researchers, and as a unique experience for readers and spectators, continues unimpeded. Identity groups founded on victim status come and go, whether as the focus of projects or as manifestations of the researcher's own assertion of self. Like new themes and objects of oral history research, however, they very seldom raise fundamentally new methodological issues. In the end, having gone through extensive permutations and ruminations, we are back with the basics: a teller, a story, and a listener.

Notes

1 Linda Shopes, "'Insights and Oversights': Reflections on the Documentary Tradition and the Theoretical Turn in Oral History," *Oral History Review* 41, no. 2 (Summer/Fall 2014): 257–268.

2 Linda Shopes, "After the Interview Ends: Moving Oral History Out of the Archives and Into Publication," *Oral History Review* 42, no. 2 (Summer/Fall 2015): 300–310.

3 See Daphne Patai, "Ethical Problems of Personal Narratives, or, Who Should Eat the Last Piece of Cake," *International Journal of Oral History* 8, no. 1 (February 1987): 5–27.

4 Daphne Patai, "Sick and Tired of Scholars' Nouveau Solipsism," *Chronicle of Higher Education* (1994): A52.

5 Ruth Behar, *Translated Woman: Crossing the Border with Esperanza's Story* (Boston: Beacon Press, 1993).

6 Shopes, "After the Interview," 309.

7 Katherine Borland, "'That's Not What I Said': Interpretive Conflict in Oral Narrative Research," in *Women's Words: The Feminist Practice of Oral History*, eds. Sherna Berger Gluck and Daphne Patai (New York: Routledge, 1992), 63–76.

8 Nell Irvin Painter, *The Narrative of Hosea Hudson: His Life as a Negro Communist in the South* (Cambridge: Harvard University Press, 1979).

9 Adélaïde Blasquez, *Gaston Lucas, serrurier: Chronique de l'anti-héros* (Paris: Plon, Terre Humaine, 1976).

10 Paul John Eakin, Foreword to *On Autobiography*, by Philippe Lejeune, trans. Katherine Leary (Minneapolis: University of Minnesota Press, 1989), xvii–xix.

11 José Carlos Sebe Bom Meihy, *Manual de História Oral* (São Paulo: Edições Loyola, 1996; 5th edition, 2005), 274. Meihy's claims for oral history are grandiose. Particularly as practiced in Brazil, he argues, it is a kind of superdiscipline that uniquely challenges the status quo, is subversive, supports affirmative action and social inclusion, promotes democracy, and so on. It is not surprising that he also advocates "transcreating" (a term borrowed from translation theory) the text—that is, changing the speaker's words so as to better capture his/her essence, which the "oralista" (Meihy's term for the oral history practitioner) presumably understands far better than the speaker.

12 See Daphne Patai, "When Method Becomes Power," in *Power and Method: Political Activism and Educational Research*, ed. Andrew Gitlin (New York: Routledge, 1994), 61–73. In the years since this essay was published, methodolatry seems to have gained even more traction in academic research, perhaps because taping a story and then turning it into a text can be easily criticized as far too simple and lacking in academic rigor.

13 See Alan B. Spitzer, "The Debate Over the Wartime Writings of Paul de Man: The Language of Setting the Record Straight," in *Theory's Empire: An Anthology of Dissent*, eds. Daphne Patai and Will Corral (New York: Columbia University Press, 2005), 271–286, demonstrating that even the most avid postmodernists switch tacks and insist on "setting the record straight" when they feel misrepresented or misunderstood by others, which ought to be a logical impossibility for them.

14 See Forrest [Asa] Carter, *The Education of Little Tree* (New York: Delacorte Press, 1976); Misha Defonseca, *Misha: A Memoire of the Holocaust Years* (Boston: Mt. Ivy Press, 1997); Norma Khouri, *Forbidden Love* (London and New York: Doubleday, 2003). See Paul John Eakin, Chapter 1, "Talking about Ourselves: The Rules of the Game," in *Living Autobiographically: How We Create Identity in Narrative* (Ithaca, NY: Cornell University Press, 2008), for an important discussion of such texts.

15 David Stoll, *Rigoberta Menchú and the Story of All Poor Guatemalans* (New York: Westview, 1999).

16 Daphne Patai, "Whose Truth? Iconicity and Accuracy in the World of Testimonial Literature," in *The Rigoberta Menchú Controversy*, ed. Arturo Arias (Minneapolis: University of Minnesota Press, 2001), 270–287. The vast majority of essays in this book defend Rigoberta and attack Stoll and those who took his work seriously.

17 See the Tawana Brawley case and other alleged hate crimes, or the instantly believed charges of rape at Duke University, the University of Virginia, and numerous other examples of causes célèbres that turned out to be lies.

18 See Sarah Helm, *If This Is a Woman. Inside Ravensbrück: Hitler's Concentration Camp for Women* (London: Little, Brown, 2015), which utilizes a vast array of material, including her own interviews; and Steven High, ed., *Beyond Testimony and Trauma: Oral History in the Aftermath of Mass Violence* (Vancouver: UBC Press, 2015), which attempts a more holistic approach to survivor testimony. Its emphasis on narrators as collaborators rather than "objects" of study is, however, familiar.

19 Svetlana Alexievich, *Voices from Chernobyl*, trans. Keith Gessen (Normal, Ill: Dalkey Archive Press, 2006), for example, says nothing whatsoever about methodology.

20 For example, some of the essays in Mark Cave and Stephen M. Sloan, eds., *Listening on the Edge: Oral History in the Aftermath of Crisis* (New York: Oxford University Press, 2014), while not delving greatly into methodological issues, at times reveal all too clearly the researchers' biases (as in the essays about the 1994 Cuban rafter exodus and Muslims in post-9/11 America), not helped by the difficulty the reader has in discerning whether these biases reside in what was asked and/or what is presented to the reader.

21 See Antonio R. Damasio, *The Feeling of What Happens: Body and Emotion in the Making of Consciousness* (New York: Harcourt Brace, 1999); Raymond Tallis, *The Knowing Animal: A Philosophical Inquiry into Knowledge and Truth* (Edinburgh: Edinburgh University Press, 2005); Daniel L. Schacter, *Searching for Memory: The Brain, the Mind, and the Past* (New York: Basic Books, 1996); Eric R. Kandel, *In Search of Memory: The Emergence of a New Science of Mind* (New York: Norton, 2006); David Morris and Kym Maclaren, eds., *Time, Memory, Institution: Merleau-Ponty's New Ontology of Self* (Athens: Ohio University Press, 2015); and journals such as Sage's *Memory Studies*, founded in 2008.

22 Jorge Luis Borges, "John Wilkins' Analytical Language," trans. Eliot Weinberger, in *Borges: Selected Non-Fictions*, ed. Eliot Weinberger (New York: Viking Penguin, 1999), 229–232.

4 Feminist oral histories of racist women

Kathleen Blee

It is now commonplace to note the optimistic premise of feminist oral history. Early formulations assumed that eliciting stories was a means of sharing authority between researcher and researched, that telling stories empowered narrators who might otherwise have few opportunities to tell their life story with an (implied) audience beyond their own social networks, and that both outcomes advanced feminist scholarship and politics.[1] For scholarship, feminist oral history promised to elicit broader and more contextualized and meaningful information about ordinary people. Politically, it offered a way to recover and center the experiences, thoughts, and histories of marginalized persons: women as well as the poor, racial, ethnic, and religious minorities, LGBTQ+ people, those with different abilities and disabilities, the "undocumented," and many others. As part of this broader project, feminist oral historians recovered both private and public stories, including those of domestic violence, workplace harassment, neighborhood-based collective action, and non-commercial artistic endeavors. The scholarly and political promises of feminist oral history have been fulfilled in numerous studies that make visible the lives of women and marginalized men whose struggles for recognition and dignity would otherwise have been lost to history. Its mission was less clear, however, with respect to unsympathetic subjects, who lacked dignity, or did not give voice to socially valuable insights. It was especially murky when the narrators were actively engaged in efforts to harm or deny others social rights and resources.

In this chapter, I reflect on the implications for feminist oral history of two studies of former members of white supremacist groups in the United States. For one, I interviewed elderly women in the 1980s who were members of the 1920s Ku Klux Klan, perhaps the largest explicitly racist political movement in American history, with at least three million men and a half million women determined to defend white, Protestant supremacism and undermine the economic, political, and social positions of Jews, Catholics, non-whites, and immigrants. For the second project, I interviewed women in the 2000s and 2010s who belonged to white supremacist groups in the 1990s and 2000s, such as neo-Nazi, Ku Klux Klan, and white power skinhead groups. These groups were hostile to Jews, all people of color, and the US federal government, which they considered to be Jewish-dominated or ZOG (Zionist Occupation

Government, to suggest that invisible Jewish conspirators secretly control the state). The women I interviewed in both projects had left racist activism, so they recalled their involvement from their perspective as former members.[2]

Initially, I assumed that both sets of women would be doubly distanced from racist activism, as former members of racist groups and as former believers in racist ideologies. The interviews revealed the fallacy of this assumption: neither group had fully rejected the beliefs of their former racist groups. Most of those active in the 1920s Klan had left the organization only because it collapsed precipitously at the end of the decade. Most of those active in the late 20th century took active steps to leave racist groups, but often continued to accept their ideology. In some of these cases, exit was prompted by non-ideological concerns, such as the viability of the group or personal conflicts with members or leaders.[3]

Interviews with racist women are examples of "awkward" research that does not fit well into the ordinary assumptions of scholarship. Elsewhere, I have outlined the ethical and methodological challenges posed by studying people and groups that differ significantly from the progressive activists and movements usually examined by feminist oral historians. These include ethical concerns about providing publicity for political agendas that seek to restrict social justice, human rights, or social equality, and the ethical responsibilities of scholars who study people and groups that advocate violence toward others.[4] The challenges are also methodological: How can feminist scholars present rich and accurate oral histories of people and social worlds that are difficult to fully access or understand? This chapter moves the discussion towards possible solutions. By reflecting on insights and missed opportunities in my studies of 1920s Klanswomen and contemporary female racist activists, I outline two concepts that may serve as analytic tools for feminist oral histories of exceedingly offensive narrators: master status and trauma.

Master status

Sociologists have long described a status that overpowers all others as a "master status."[5] Gender is an example of a master status, as it both creates expectations for how a person will think, act, and speak, and sidelines attention to other statuses that might create contrary expectations. A woman medical doctor, for example, is generally expected to exhibit stereotypically "female-traits," rather than stereotypically "doctor-traits." Similarly, the racial status of an African American mathematician is generally highly visible, whereas a white mathematician's race would rarely command attention.

Feminist oral history is sensitive to the problems of master status. As pioneer practitioners noted, women's experiences do not surface fully when scholars interpret narratives through a master-status lens, whether the working class, Holocaust survivors, or African American civil rights activists.[6] But gender itself can be a master status, obscuring the multiple and often conflicting identities and statuses of race, social class, nationality, and sexuality that shape oral narratives, along with the actions, motivations, ideas, and personal agendas of narrators.[7]

Master status complicates the process of oral history by creating expectations for what is relevant to explore in the interview and what is less salient. This is certainly true when working with racist activists, since racial extremism is both highly stigmatized and widely regarded as a master status.[8] Seeing someone as a "racist" sets expectations for what they are thinking and what motivates their actions, overshadowing other aspects of their lives. It pulls the interview and analysis in a pre-set direction, toward instances of racism at the expense of everything else. When a white supremacist man recounts a story of attacking his African American neighbor, there can be little incentive to push the narrator to discuss his motives, as they seem to flow clearly from his racist identity. But this may obscure the complicated layers of motivation that fuel racial violence. Further explanation might reveal his sexual entanglements with the neighbor, a property dispute, or simply an alcohol-fuelled battle among friends. Similarly, in studies of hate crimes, the search for evidence of a motive that is covered in hate-crime statutes can swamp the search for other motives.[9]

A feminist oral history approach provides a partial remedy to the problem by pushing one to search for gender subtexts within the master status of "racist" through direct evidence of gendered perspectives and attention to silences in the text.[10] In the narratives of 1920s Klanswomen, for example, I found that women joined the Klan to advance their gendered interests as (white Protestant) women as well as their racial/religious interests as white Protestants—a complicated intertwining of gender and racial politics. In the interviews with women racists of the late 20th century, I found evidence of despair that was strikingly different than the bravado and exhilaration recounted by their male racist counterparts. Women, but rarely men, were negative about the quality of leaders and interpersonal dynamics within their groups. Indeed, they rarely wanted their children, especially daughters, to devote their lives to racist extremism even if they wanted them to hold racist beliefs.[11]

I was not able to fully move beyond the lens of master status when analyzing the narratives of racist women, so other aspects of their experiences remained elusive. In interviews, my narrators spoke extensively about sexuality and friendships, problems with alcohol or anger issues, and worries about their future. While each topic was a chance to understand these women in a more comprehensive way, I rarely followed up except to explore how these experiences fit into their racist commitments, such as how sexual conflicts led to racial ideas. I missed the chance to understand how their involvement in white supremacism was inflected by other status categories, such as being heterosexual, middle class, a child, or a victim. Looking back, a deeper recognition of the power inherent in the analytic lens of master status could have alerted me to be broader in my scope, to ask questions, and push my analysis beyond the simple explanation of racism. My narrators' identities, ideas, and aspirations were clearly tied to racial extremism, but this does not explain all they were.

Trauma

A second conceptual tool of value to feminist oral histories of racist women is trauma, those experiences that alter a person's (or a societal) identity in deep and seemingly irrevocable ways.[12] Feminist principles of empathy and rapport in interviewing, and sensitivity to gendered social reality in interpretation, position scholars to understand the multiple layers of recounted trauma, which may be revealed by silence and reluctance to describe experiences as much as by direct testimony.[13]

By employing a feminist approach when interviewing racist women, I uncovered many complex accounts of trauma experienced before, during, and sometimes after women's time in racial extremism. Many indicated that they joined racist groups because of earlier incidents of personal trauma, such as an assault by a non-white person. Others described motivating traumas instead as an ideological shock induced by learning that much of what they had believed was wrong: they recounted, for instance, the trauma of hearing the racist doctrine that an invisible cabal of Jews controls the world. Further, racist women drew on traumatic stories to describe how their lives became more embedded in racist extremism, and thus increasingly dominated by hate, violence, and social marginality. They told stories of being excluded from family circles, losing jobs, and involvement in criminal activities. Recalling the end of their time in racial extremism, they even narrated the process of exiting a racist group as occasioning trauma. Walking away made them vulnerable to retaliation by former comrades, sanction by law enforcement, and ostracism from racist family and friends.

Trauma is not a constant theme among racist women, a finding that reveals much about the relationship of racial extremism to the wider society in which it is embedded. Klanswomen in the 1920s, for example, rarely made reference to trauma when relaying the process of joining the Klan as Klan communities did not differ significantly from white society in many localities. Indeed, early 20th century, white US Protestant majority populations broadly assumed their superiority over non-whites, immigrants, and Catholics. However, these 1920s Klanswomen did raise the issue of trauma in a different, and unexpected, context. They claimed to be wounded by what they perceived as the unfairly negative characterization of their Klan by subsequent generations that required them to hide their involvement from their children and grandchildren. They insisted that the Klan, not the African Americans, Catholics, and Jews it attacked, was the real victim of history. All of these women left the Klan at some point in the 1920s as its chapters folded and the national Klan ceased to exist by 1930. But if they experienced any sense of trauma in leaving, it was not legible in their narratives. No woman I interviewed would discuss her experience of leaving the Klan in any detail, although exiting was almost certainly emotionally difficult given that the organization collapsed in a firestorm of sexual and financial scandals.

By contrast, women who were involved in racist extremism in the late 20th century were much more apt to narrate a story of trauma that extended across the full process of entering, participating in, and leaving racist groups. Almost every woman I interviewed about her time in white power skinhead, neo-Nazi, Ku Klux Klan, or white supremacist groups in the 1990s and 2000s talked about the traumatic events that led her into racial extremism, including abuse by parents, bullying by peers, and sexual assault. While important to note the widespread accounts of trauma that preceded entry into racist groups, we must also be cautious in interpreting the meanings of this trauma. Radically separated from mainstream society, contemporary racist groups exist on the political and social fringes or virtually underground. Being a member of such a group thus requires a foundational shift in identity and lifeway for all but the very few who grow up in racial extremist families or communities. When a former member is asked to account for her decision to make such a dramatic change, she will likely describe dramatic and traumatic episodes as causal events. Traumatic events may well have led these women into racial extremism, but the widespread incidents of trauma experienced by women who did not go that route suggests that trauma is not the sole precipitating factor.

More revealing are the accounts of trauma experienced while women are in racist groups or leaving them. Organized racism is a hidden world, carefully shielded from the surveillance of police and anti-racist organizations. In such communities, abusive behavior toward women and girls, which includes sexual assault and losing their ability to make choices about their work, education, or personal lives, can be difficult to detect or stop. Leaving these groups can also involve trauma, from attacks from former comrades to negative reactions of those who discover their racist pasts.

Trauma can be a useful conceptual tool for mapping the fundamental reorientation of one's sense of self and the world that is required to cross the divide from mainstream to racial zealot—a shift from someone who may have racist attitudes to someone who fully embraces the agendas of Nazism, is convinced that a Jewish conspiracy controls the world, and works to expel non-whites from the US But the concept can also be misleading. When racist women narrate a story about the traumatic reorientation of their lives and identities as they move from mainstream into racist groups, they imply a vast difference between the world of organized racism and the rest of white-dominated society. Certainly, there are significant differences between the two but it is important not to overstate the ideological gulf between them. Despite an overall trend toward acceptance of racial equality in the US, there remains an overlap between the white supremacist ideas of racist groups and the everyday racist understandings of many white Americans.[14]

Conclusion

Oral history narratives are deeply woven into the cultural understandings of the societies in which they are produced.[15] Feminist oral historians have rightfully been attentive to issues that arise when the cultural worlds of scholars and narrators overlap, as exemplified by Judith Stacey's early warning of the danger of exploitation in feminist methods that depend on empathetic connection.[16] The issues that come to the fore when working with people whose politics, ideas, or agendas are radically opposed to our own—and who pose a threat to the principles of justice, equity, and democracy—are less well studied even though our distance from these narrators may better position us to analyze rather than simply accept their accounts.[17]

Interpreting oral histories of racist women requires feminist oral historians to stand both inside and outside their narratives. It demands both an empathetic understanding and a critical, skeptical stance. The concepts of master status and trauma can be useful tools in this endeavor as they place feminist scholars in a reflexive space that simultaneously respects and pushes back against the narratives of racist women. Master statuses shape how others interpret words, actions, and life. For feminist oral historians, the concept of master status provides a caution against interpretation that too easily assigns overwhelming significance to the most obvious status of a narrator, such as their racial activism. Similarly, accounts of trauma are powerful moments in oral history narratives but these must be analyzed with care so as to avoid overly simplistic interpretations of the complex, causal pathways that define people's lives.

Notes

1 Sherna Berger Gluck and Daphne Patai, eds., *Women's Words: The Feminist Practice of Oral History* (New York: Routledge, 1991).
2 Kathleen Blee, *Women of the Klan: Racism and Gender in the 1920s* (Berkeley: University of California Press, 1991); *Inside Organized Racism: Women in the Hate Movement* (Berkeley: University of California Press, 2002); "Personal Effects from Far-Right Activism," in *The Consequences of Social Movements: People, Policies, and Institutions*, eds. Lorenzo Bosi, Marco Giugni, and Katrin Uba (New York: Oxford University Press, 2016), 66–84.
3 Blee, *Women of the Klan*; Blee, "Personal Effects"; David Chalmers, *Hooded Americanism: The History of the Ku Klux Klan* (Durham, NC: Duke University Press, 1987).
4 Francesca Polletta, "Mobilization Forum: Awkward Movements," *Mobilization: An International Journal* 11 (2006): 475–500; Kathleen Blee, "Evidence, Empathy and Ethics: Lessons from Oral Histories of the Klan," *Journal of American History* 80, no. 2 (1993): 596–606; Blee, "Methods, Interpretation, and Ethics in the Study of White Supremacist Perpetrators," *Conflict and Society: Advances in Research* 1 (2015): 9–22; Blee and Ashley Currier, "Ethics Beyond the IRB," *Qualitative Sociology* 34 (2011): 401–433; Blee and Timothy Vining, "Risks and Ethics of Social Movement Research in a Changing Political Climate," *Research in Social Movements, Conflict and Change* 30 (2010): 43–70.
5 Everett Cherrington Hughes, "Dilemmas and Contradictions of Status," *American Journal of Sociology* 50, no. 5 (1945): 353–359.
6 See *Women's Words*.
7 Karen Olson and Linda Shopes, "Crossing Boundaries, Building Bridges: Doing Oral History among Working-Class Women and Men," in *Women's Words*, 189–204; Liz Stanley, "Whites Writing: Letters and Documents of Life in a QLR Project," in *Documents of Life Revisited: Narrative and Biographical Methods for a 21st Century Critical Humanism*, ed. Liz Stanley (Surrey, UK: Ashgate Publishing Ltd., 2013), 59–73.

 8 Mitch Berbrier, "Making Minorities: Cultural Space, Stigma Transformation Frames, and the Categorical Status Claims of Deaf, Gay, and White Supremacist Activists in Late Twentieth Century America," *Sociological Forum* 17, no. 4 (2002): 553–591.

 9 Lu-in Wang, "The Complexities of 'Hate,'" *Ohio State Law Journal* 60 (1999): 799–900.

10 Kathryn Anderson and Dana C. Jack, "Learning to Listen: Interview Techniques and Analyses," in *Women's Words*, 11–26.

11 Blee, *Inside Organized Racism.*

12 Lynn Abrams, *Oral History Theory* (New York: Routledge, 2010); Jeffrey Alexander, "Toward a Theory of Cultural Trauma," in *Cultural Trauma and Collective Identity*, eds. Jeffrey C. Alexander et al. (Berkeley: University of California Press, 2004), 1–30.

13 Gadi BenEzer, "Trauma Signals in Life Stories," in *Trauma and Life Stories: International Perspectives*, eds. Kim L. Rogers, Selma Leydesorff, and Graham Dawson (New York: Routledge, 1999), 29–44; Berhard Giesen, "The Trauma of Perpetrators: The Holocaust as the Traumatic Reference of German National Identity," in *Cultural Trauma and Collective Identity*, 112–154; Selma Leydesorff et al., "Introduction: Trauma and Life Stories," in *Trauma and Life Stories*, 1–26.

14 Blee, *Inside Organized Racism.*

15 Abrams, *Oral History Theory;* Nancy Janovicek, "'If You'd Told Me You Wanted to Talk About the '60s, I Wouldn't Have Called You Back': Reflections on Collective Memory and the Practice of Oral History," in *Oral History Off the Record: Toward an Ethnography of Practice*, eds. Anna Sheftel and Stacey Zembrzycki (New York: Palgrave Macmillan 2013), 185–199; Pamela Sugiman, "I Can Hear Lois Now: Corrections to My Story of the Internment of Japanese Canadians—'For the Record,'" in Ibid., 149–168.

16 Judith Stacey, "Can There Be Feminist Ethnography?" in *Women's Words*, 111–120.

17 Erin Jessee, "The Limits of Oral History: Ethics and Methodology Amid Highly Politicized Research Settings," *The Oral History Review* 38, no. 2 (2011): 287–307; "Rwandan Women No More: Female Genocidaires in the Aftermath of the 1994 Rwandan Genocide," *Conflict and Society: Advances in Research* 1, no. 1 (2015): 60–80. Also Erin F. Johnston, "'I Was Always This Way . . .': Rhetorics of Continuity in Narratives of Conversion," *Sociological Forum* 28, no. 3 (2013): 549–573.

5 Emotion and pedagogy

Teaching digital storytelling in the millennial classroom

Rina Benmayor

"The beauty and power of a tale told to an empathetic listener," writes prominent feminist anthropologist Ruth Behar, "is at the heart of the most meaningful scholarship."[1] It is also at the heart of my most meaningful teaching. Oral histories, life stories, and *testimonios* have the power to transform students, and the classroom more generally, into a unique space of empathetic learning, creativity, and personal empowerment.[2] This was my experience working as an oral historian with the El Barrio Popular Education Program in East Harlem, which recorded older Latina women's life histories as part of an action-research project of educational empowerment. Writing about that project in *Women's Words*, I argued that the acts of telling and writing one's life story were key components to an empowerment process; that the classroom nurtured collective awareness of cultural rights; and that this awareness had the potential to translate into collective claims and action.[3]

Over the past fifteen years, I have witnessed this same transformative power in a different educational context, this time teaching my undergraduate digital storytelling course called "Latina Life Stories" at a California public university where a significant number of students are the daughters and sons of migrant Mexican farmworkers.[4] I have written extensively about this class, analyzing pedagogical strategies, student learning, and the value of digital *testimonios* as a "signature pedagogy" for Latino Studies.[5] Here, I consider the role of emotion and feeling in my digital storytelling classroom, assessing its value for a critical feminist pedagogy with transformative potential. Digital storytelling (which I first encountered in the late 1990s) is used in various contexts, including in community heritage projects, schools, awareness-raising social projects, and in tandem with oral history.[6] I saw in the short digital movie format a rich active-learning tool for teaching Latina literature, which is so firmly grounded in the autobiographical narrative.

Emotion is at the core of memory, and hence all storytelling. My approach to teaching digital life storytelling includes pedagogies that engage emotions and are rooted in foundational feminist concepts and practices: that the personal is political; subjectivity and identity involve complex intersections of race, class, gender, and other social identities in analysis; discourses and narratives are shaped in memory through positionality and emotion; breaking silences requires vulnerability and safety; and storytelling has the potential to be empowering, both individually and collectively. While epistemological concern with emotions has long been central to feminist studies, in the last decade the interconnection between emotions, memory, and subjectivity has generated renewed interest among cultural historians.[7] In oral history, emotion and affect are fundamental methodological concerns, of course, and much, including a number of chapters in this collection, has been written on their centrality to understanding Holocaust and trauma narratives in particular.[8] However, the "emotional turn" in teaching oral history and life storytelling has not been explored.

I am well aware of the dangers of blurring boundaries between oral history, a fundamentally dialogic process between two interlocutors, and life storytelling which can be created in an interview context but also in private, as an individual creation.[9] The digital stories I work with have oral dimensions but they have not been produced by dialogic interviews. They are self-narrations, stories of personal experience, voiced orally in dialogic spaces, then written as dramatic scripts, recorded in oral performance by the narrator in their own voice, and turned into short movies that include visual and sometimes musical texts. Orality is a part of the process. Aurality, the telling of stories in the narrator's own voice, gives meaning and power to those stories.

The digital stories my students produce are *testimonios*; I use the Spanish term "*testimonio*" to signal an intentional act of bearing witness and testifying. The stories my students tell are primarily personal, but they have collective referents to a social or cultural injustice or celebrate accomplishments forged under difficult circumstances. They are emotion stories that explore meaningful moments in students' lives, most of whom are Latinas, with a handful of Latinos, other students of color, and white students. Their stories address issues of migration and assimilation, the gendered and racialized body, racism, sexism, and homophobia, ethnic and cultural identity, mixed race heritage, education, family and community, and individual life challenges and achievements. They reveal that so-called millennial students care deeply about social issues and their relationships to others. While some sign up for "Latina Life Stories" because it fulfills several requirements or it fits their schedules, Latina/os tend to be drawn to the class because it directly addresses their own cultural and lived experiences.

Every student holds within them a story that needs to be told, and the class facilitates that telling. But how that telling is situated matters. Taking cues from autobiographical writings of contemporary Latinas, students' *testimonios* are not merely emotive tellings.[10] Also deeply oppositional, they speak back to people and forces that oppress, marginalize, and devalue their lives. Student *testimonios* are also propositional, articulating new ways of understanding struggles and conflicts, which will benefit others like them, and especially members of younger generations. In what follows, I reflect on the centrality of emotion in the creative process that organizes the course and detail some of the pedagogical strategies involved. For a fuller appreciation of what transpires, readers are encouraged to first view some of the videotaped stories and a short video about the course (links are provided in the notes).[11]

Texts of emotion

"Latina Life Stories" is structured to activate what Spanish Basque oral historian Miren Llona calls "enclaves of memory," deep emotional experiences that are seared in memory and that in turn construct subjectivity.[12] In my course, a number of activities trigger these enclaves, beginning with the course readings, which include autobiographical and theoretical writings by Latinas of diverse national/cultural origins, born or raised and living in the United States. Since the 1980s, Latina writers have not only produced a rich body of literature based in personal experience narratives, but also contributed key theories and concepts that are now widely used in the humanities and social sciences. Narrating her lived and psychic experience as a Chicana in the "borderlands" of South Texas, Gloria Anzaldúa's path-breaking book, *Borderlands: La Frontera*, theorized a new mestiza consciousness through theoretical inter-sections of colonialism, ethnicity, race, class, gender, myth, and sexuality.[13] Thirty years later, her work continues to inspire students. Contemporaneously, Chicana poet, playwright, and essayist Cherríe Moraga linked personal narrative to bodily emotion as a source of critical knowledge, in what she called doing "theory in the flesh."[14] Others, like Puerto Rican poets Aurora Levins Morales and Rosario Morales, explored the embodiment of hybridity through histories of migrations, mixed ethnic heritages, and feminist politics.[15] The texts of these and many other Latina writers model the move from emotional memory to building social theory. They are what Luisa Passerini calls texts of emotion, which are socially constructed through both normative and "outlaw" discourses of emotion.[16] Because these are culturally grounded stories of personal experience, students find the readings deeply engaging. They recognize in them their own experiences and, more importantly, they stir feelings that are deeply rooted in their memories.

Pedagogies of emotion: Getting to story

The course has two major assignments: to create and produce a digital *testimonio*, namely a three-minute digital movie that combines an original story script, performed and recorded in the author's voice, with a visual treatment and perhaps music; and to write a final paper reflecting on and theorizing the story in connection with course themes and concepts. Getting to the story involves several weeks of preparation, during which students dis-cuss the readings, listen to, watch, and analyze digital *testimonios* produced in previous semesters, do "memory writes," and hold story circles. Described below, each of these activities engages emotions and emotional memory in particular ways.

Memory writes: Each class session begins with five minutes of free journaling, which I call a "memory write" about a personal experience. These memory writes are related to class themes such as migration, gender roles, racism, discrimination, the body, or heritage identity. This personal journal space allows students to access intimate emotional memories without the pressure of disclosure. Many of them take up the invitation to share their memory writes, thereby giving public voice to personal experiences and feelings. These students set the tone for the class because their memories spark among the other students recognition of commonalities. Since each student in the class feels the vulnerability of personal disclosure, their responses to these shared memories are caring and supportive. Memory writes may evolve into digital stories, but the real importance of this exercise is empathetic—to spark a bonding process based on careful listening and mutual respect of commonalities and differences.

Critiquing *testimonios*: Part of each class is devoted to viewing digital *testimonios* produced by students in previous years, which serves to generate constructive critiques of form—which elements (dramatic dimensions of the story, effectiveness of the performance, choice and treatment of visual images) worked particularly well and which did not. These critiques also spark reactions to the content of the stories being told. Given that these are stories produced by peers, students can more readily relate to them and this brings forth intense responses to the situations and feelings recounted.

Story circles: In the more intimate space of a small story circle, students discuss readings and begin to break their own silences, recounting their pasts and exploring possible story topics. Story circles are usually composed of groups of three, but sometimes the entire class becomes one large circle (the course is capped at 26 students). These circles enable feedback to be given and serve as testing grounds for the story that each student will eventually make into their movie.

All of these exercises create spaces for personal disclosure that transform the classroom into a safe storytelling environment. In her final reflection paper, student Ana Elías-Morales commented about students' willingness to take the risk of sharing their intimate experiences and feelings and, in doing so, transform what might have been an ordinary class discussion into something much more meaningful. She stated:

> Sharing my stories in class was liberating; hearing stories from others . . . was inspiring . . . Reading their drafts and helping them figure out what to write about was not only revealing, but made me see many of them with new eyes . . . We all have so many stories to tell, but it's up to each of us to share them and either let them consume us, or empower us.[17]

Perhaps because these accounts are personal, emotionally compelling truths, they provoke mindful listening, respect, compassion, and empathy. Vulnerability opens the way for solidarity across differences. As naïve as it may sound, I have never witnessed in this class the vitriolic interactions that can erupt among students around issues of race, politics, and privilege. As Herminia Cervantes expressed it:

> Listening to their stories and comments made my story better and it helped me get comfortable with sharing my story because my classmates never judged me in a bad way. They were always there to give me suggestions and listen to what I had to say.[18]

Perhaps since this class is about students' own trajectories, they see it as a space for positive emotional work.

Significantly, the next stage—producing a script (maximum one-and-a-half pages double spaced), recording it, and making the digital movie—is not merely technical work. Carrying it out can be equally powerful and challenging from an affective standpoint.

Performing story

The heart of a digital story is voice. The story, in this case, moves from oral sharing to written script. Once the script is ready, the next step is to perform it as an oral telling.[19] This step is doubly emotive, both voicing memoried feelings and embodying the performance. To record their stories, students brave the heat and confinement of a sound booth and my dramatic direction. While they may have practiced their scripts at home to the wall, the moment of recording is still laden with fear. Now the narrator stands before the microphone, script pinned to the booth wall, trying to imagine their intended audience on the other side. To help make this transition back into an oral mode, the story is printed out in poetic format, rather than as a written paragraph, with line breaks that mark natural speech and breath patterns. It usually takes three takes to "get it right," *telling* the story, rather than reading it, achieving the right pace, rhythm, emphasis, pitch, and tone.

Performing is stressful on multiple levels, but it is usually here that the core emotion of the story tumbles out. The narrators try hard not to "lose it," but often do. Speaking about difficult life experiences brings tears to my students' eyes, causing their voices to crack; happier stories invite laughter and volume. In speaking about her experience, Ana Elías-Morales stated: "The first indication that this story was very personal was in my first attempts to record it in the sound booth; I cried. I felt as though my mom was speaking through me."[20] Ultimately, emotion carries the story and makes it "real."

Producing story

The emotive power of digital media, like film, lies in the marriage of story, image and sound. As Passerini notes, "new texts . . . no longer concern orality

Figure 5.1 Screen shots from *Fighting for My History* by Kristen La Follette

but visuality." Visuality, she argues, "is crucial to studying emotions that might never be articulated in words," requiring different decoding strategies as well as, I must note, different encoding strategies.[21] Take, for example, the following images. Kristen La Follette inscribed herself into archival photographs of her paternal ancestor, the radical socialist and statesman Robert La Follette, aka "Fighting Bob." Her goal was to convey how Robert, as she called him, and his politics continue to inspire her today.[22] Her digital manipulations of the images signified an emotional strategy. In the first, she rendered her horse in living color and led it beyond the frame of the archival photograph; in the second, she placed herself on the wagon alongside but also slightly in front of her ancestor. In explaining these subtle manipulations, she stated: "I did this to reclaim my space into my own history, and to show that I ally with my ancestors. It felt good to see myself in family pictures where my identity had been missing before."[23]

Emotion and political activism are the catalysts here. The digital manipulation creates an independent visual drama that supports the story, but can also symbolically stand on its own. Visually, Kristen affirmed the legacy of political struggle for social justice that drives her.

Music and soundscapes also set mood and signal the dramatic and emotive dimensions of a story. Copyright and fair use laws restrict students' ability to use music from their favorite playlists. They are encouraged to explore instrumentals from public access websites. They also find a piece of music that complements the rhythm, mood, and story's emotional shifts between major and minor keys. Some opt to use copyrighted music at the beginning and end of the story, and perhaps at an appropriate interval in the story, so as to not exceed the allowable percentage of fair use. Others commission original scores from musician friends. Many spend hours searching for the right piece or constructing their own soundscapes to emotionally "nail" the story. Ana Elías-Morales declared:

I knew that it had to be a melody that would capture the essence of my mom and also maintain a constant rhythm . . . I accidentally found the music and knew when I heard it that it was the right one! . . . It is a lovely piece of music called *Mimbre y escarcha*, and enhanced my story perfectly.[24]

Nonetheless, the use of music is optional. What matters in the end is the performative voice that tells the story.

Theorizing story

The final paper assignment asks students to connect their story to the concepts learned throughout the semester and to reflect on its meaning. In other words, they are required to theorize their story and explain and evaluate their creative processes. Theorizing is the most difficult task, as it requires stepping outside the narrative to foreground ideas rather than feelings, although the two are obviously linked. I actually believe that emotion is at the core of all critical reflection, catalyzing the move from the individual to the social, in short, a "theorizing from the flesh," to use Cherríe Moraga's language.[25] Liliana Cabrera-Murillo's *testimonio*, "Dancing into *Mi Cultura*," articulates how she experienced this shift, as she sought to find her place within both her Mexican heritage and what she calls her "privilege" as a fourth-generation, middle-class Latina. It was in Gloria Anzaldúa's concept of borderlands consciousness that Liliana discovered a space of belonging.[26] She wrote:

For so long I was desperately seeking to name my experience. [. . .] I had to find a way to claim an identity that embraced a rich Mexican heritage as well as a fourth generation citizen experience. [. . .] It now seems ironic that the name that I've found to identify my experience [new mestiza consciousness] . . . requires me to embrace a comfort in ambiguity. With this new paradigm available to me, I have learned to use the privilege of my education . . . aware of the oppressions, the systems that support the breeding of future oppressors, and [discover] a new position for me to join the resistance against them.[27]

The emotive language—"desperately seeking," "embraced," "comfort," "aware"—illustrates the intensely affective dimension of her conceptual discovery. Passerini speaks of how "emotions can shape a new self."[28] As Liliana's reflection suggests, theorizing one's narrative articulates that transformative move from feeling to gaining a new understanding of one's place in the world.

Coming to this awareness of new discourses on identity and consciousness is tremendously empowering. Digital storytelling in itself is not a form of social activism. But for students like Ana, Kristen, and Liliana, it can lead there. Finding in Latina feminist theory and *testimonio* a way to name individual and collective struggles situates students as cultural and social actors in history.

The class readings offer new discourses of identity, belonging, and fights for equality. The digital *testimonio* provides a space in which students can give voice to their own identity struggles and triumphs, inscribing themselves as thinkers and authors in their own right. This, in my view, opens the door to forms of activism as millennial students contemplate future roles in their communities and the larger society. The *testimonio* is not just a storied representation of an individual's lived past, but becomes a personal statement, a glimpse into who that individual is and the kind of person they may become.

Presenting story

The digital *testimonio* is an artifact. It is as tangible as a published book. The in-class and public screenings provide immediate audiences, but in many cases the stories are also copied onto discs and presented to parents as gifts or shared through social media.

The in-class screening is a particularly important transformational moment. Although students have bonded in the class and know quite a bit about one another by this time, each *testimonio* seen on the big screen brings a deeper level of understanding and insight into their classmates' histories and personae. As Jacquelyn Gallardo said: "Watching everyone's video was very emotional and I feel like I've gotten to know each one of them on a deeper level because they let me in to a part of their life" [sic].[29]

The *testimonios* are received with respect and appreciation, not only for the experiences they recount, but also for the creative production involved. While the classroom has become a safe sharing space, the public screening creates a new moment of vulnerability as well as one of great pride. As Gallardo noted,

Figure 5.2 2014 Festival poster

it was an unveiling of intimacy, personal history, innermost feelings, and creativity to complete strangers, but also to family and friends: "Seeing people crying, especially my mother[,] made me realize how important these stories are. My mother later told me how proud she was of me for growing as a person . . ."[30] The full emotional import of the whole process is not entirely felt until this moment. As the Kleenex box circulates among the audience, tears, hugs, and proud smiles mark the conclusion of the festival and the course. Since final papers are not due until after the public screening, they allow the student to reflect on that final process as well.

Conclusion

I call "Latina Life Stories" my "heart" class because that is where the stories come from and, in turn, create a deeply felt experience. In this regard, the class might well fit into Alexander Freund's critique of the storytelling boom as a neoliberal emotion industry of confessional, self-help, survival, and triumph life narratives.[31] But while my course creates a space that privileges emotion and emotional knowledge, with pedagogical strategies that intentionally kindle affective memory, it is also an intensely political space and project. Storytelling is situational and life stories mean different things in different contexts to different people, depending on whether you are the listener, the teller, or the critic. The act and process of creating a story—in this case a digital *testimonio*— can be deeply self-liberating to the individual, but it can also produce new cultural discourses and pathways to social action that have implications for a larger collectivity. The process of having the authors or "tellers" provide their own interpretations of their stories gives special insight into what these new discourses might be. For Latino students and all students who live in "othered" spaces, many of them the first generation in their families to attend college, speaking back to power and proposing new relational discourses, identities, and cultural constructs through their narratives matters to them personally. They carry these stories as well as a greater appreciation of them as they make their way in the world, and interact with others in their cultural communities. To quote José Garza: "For it is classes like this that ignite my desire to become a writer, a teacher, and a better human being."[32]

Notes

1 Ruth Behar, Jacket endorsement to *Memory, Subjectivities, and Representation: Approaches to Oral History in Latin America, Portugal, and Spain*, eds. Rina Benmayor, María Eugenia Cardenal de la Nuez, and Pilar Domínguez Prats (New York: Palgrave MacMillan, 2016).
2 Among Spanish speakers and American Latinas, the term "*testimonio*" is widely used to designate personal narratives that bear witness, that testify. Latina Feminist Group, *Telling to Live: Latina Feminist Testimonios* (Durham: Duke University Press, 2001). In the class, we use "*testimonio*" rather than "life story"; in writing my use of each term is contextual. I use "digital storytelling" when speaking generically and "*testimonio*" to signal the type of stories my students produce.

3 Rina Benmayor, "Testimony, Action Research, and Empowerment: Puerto Rican Women and Popular Education," in *Women's Words: The Feminist Practice of Oral History*, eds. Sherna B. Gluck and Daphne Patai (New York: Routledge, 1991), 159–174.

4 California State University, Monterey Bay was inaugurated in 1995, as the 21st campus of the California State University system. Located on the Central Coast and on the edge of the Salinas Valley, it is a Hispanic-serving institution, with 30 per cent of the student body largely of migrant Mexican families. I was part of the university's founding faculty and taught "Latina Life Stories" every year from 1995 until retirement in 2011.

5 Rina Benmayor, "Digital Testimonio as a Signature Pedagogy for Latin@ Studies," *Equity and Excellence in Education* 45, no. 3 (Summer 2012): 507–524; "Theorizing through Digital Stories: The Art of 'Writing Back' and 'Writing For,'" *The Academic Commons*, last modified 7 January 2009, https://fysc2015.files.wordpress.com/2015/09/benmayor.pdf; "Digital Storytelling as a Signature Pedagogy in the New Humanities," *Arts and Humanities in Higher Education* 7, no. 2 (June 2008): 188–205.

6 See Joe Lambert, *Digital Storytelling: Capturing Lives, Creating Community*, 4th revised edition (New York: Taylor & Francis, 2012); the South African Sonke Gender Justice uses digital stories to raise awareness around HIV/AIDs, gender equality, and human rights: www.genderjustice.org.za/; Concordia University's Centre for Oral History and Digital Storytelling: http://storytelling.concordia.ca/.

7 See Luisa Passerini, "Connecting Emotions. Contributions from Cultural History," accessed 5 October 2017, www.nnet.gr/historein/historeinfiles/histvolumes/hist08/historein8-passerini.pdf; Miren Llona, "The Healing Effect of Discourses: Body, Emotions, and Gender Subjectivity in Basque Nationalism," in *Memory, Subjectivities, and Representation*, 77–92.

8 See the chapters by Theresa de Langis, Stéphane Martelly, Hillary Hiner, and Hourig Attarian et al. in this collection as well as Shoshana Felman and Dori Laub, *Testimony: Crises of Witnessing in Literature, Psychoanalysis, and History* (New York: Routledge, 1991); Kim Lacy Rogers, Selma Leydesdorff, and Graham Dawson, eds., *Trauma: Life Stories of Survivors* (Piscataway, New Jersey: Transaction Publishers, 2004); Alistair Thomson, "Anzac Memories Revisited: Trauma, Memory, and Oral History," *Oral History Review* 42, no. 1 (Winter/Spring 2015): 1–29.

9 Alexander Freund, "Under Storytelling's Spell? Oral History in a Neoliberal Age," *Oral History Review* 42, no. 1 (Winter/Spring 2015): 96–132, in which he makes a case for the danger of conflating storytelling and oral history.

10 Latina autobiographical writers we read in the course include: Gloria Anzaldúa, Norma Cantú, Sandra Cisneros, Teresa Marrero, Cherríe Moraga, Aurora Levins Morales, Rosario Morales, Judith Ortiz Cofer, and the Latina Feminist Group.

11 See, for instance, Ana Elías-Morales, "Letter to my Family," www.youtube.com/watch?v=NXQQaKaiH18; Liliana Cabrera-Murillo, "Dancing into Mi Cultura," www.youtube.com/watch?v=h6oynUJhXxA&feature=youtu.be; José A. Garza, "Welcome to the Family," www.youtube.com/watch?v=j0AQOe15Blg&feature=youtu.be. To view a video about the course itself, go to: "U-Stories: Latina Life Stories," www.youtube.com/watch?v=bLbh2gw8EsA.

12 Llona, 80.

13 Gloria Anzaldúa, *Borderlands, La Frontera: The New Mestiza* (San Francisco: Aunt Lute Press, 1999).

14 Cherríe Moraga, no title, in *This Bridge Called My Back: Writings of Radical Women of Color*, eds. Cherríe Moraga and Gloria Anzaldúa (New York: Kitchen Table, Women of Color Press, 1983), 23.

15 Aurora Levins Morales and Rosario Morales, *Getting Home Alive* (Ithaca: Firebrand Books, 1986).
16 Passerini, 118. Also see Alison M. Jaggar, "Love and Knowledge: Emotions in Feminist Epistemology," in *Gender/Body/Knowledge*, eds. Alison M. Jaggar and Susan R. Bordo (New Brunswick: Rutgers University Press, 1992).
17 Ana Elías-Morales, "Revelations of my Identity," 6 May 2008, 6.
18 Herminia Cervantes, "Theorizing Story," 13 December 2012, n.p.
19 Digital *testimonio* scripts are generally one-and-a-half pages in length, double-spaced. They go through multiple drafts, attending to length, the dramatic arc of the story, and the use of spoken rather than written language.
20 Elías-Morales, 5.
21 Passerini, 122.
22 Kristen La Follette, *Fighting for My History* (2005), last modified 16 August 2016, https://youtu.be/m0d5u0iKkUs.
23 Kristen La Follette, "A Reframed Identity," 14 May 2005, 10.
24 Elías-Morales, 5.
25 Moraga, no title, 23.
26 Anzaldúa.
27 Liliana Cabrera, "Dancing into *Mi Cultura*," Spring 2004, 8–9.
28 Passerini, 120.
29 Jacquelyn Gallardo, final paper; no title, 30 November 2012, 7.
30 Gallardo, 7.
31 Freund.
32 José A. Garza, "Welcome to the Family," 5 May 2010, 9.

Section 2

Doing feminist oral history then and now

Introduction to Section 2
Doing feminist oral history then and now

Penny Summerfield

As feminist oral historians, we frequently want to share our enthusiasm with the women we interview. Through an oral history conversation about feminism in the past and the present, we hope to deepen our understanding of principles, practices, hopes, and dreams that are important to us, as well as to enlarge feminist historiography. Imagining that the stories we are hearing belong within a memory frame furnished by feminist ideas, we expect a positive response. The concept of feminism, however, does not always reverberate with our narrators. Far from facilitating memory stories, it can sometimes inhibit them.

These insights are explored and developed in two of the chapters in this section. Lynn Abrams describes interviews with women who confidently and fluently told stories of asserting their independence and grasping opportunities as young women in the 1950s and 60s, but whose composure fell apart when asked to comment on their relationship with feminism. Lianne C. Leddy was more circumspect in her interviews with Indigenous women in northern Ontario. But when she asked one of her interview partners, tentatively, if she felt the word "feminism" applied to her, she received an abrupt "no" in reply.

Both Abrams and Leddy explore why the term "feminism" has negative effects on women's narratives. Abrams sees it partly in terms of life course: her narrators came of age before the international Women's Liberation Movement took off, and were mostly married with young children by the early 1970s, when they sought to meet their needs for support without a conscious resort to "feminism." However, her question produced not just confused, but defensive and guilty answers, as if she was subjecting her narrators to a test. Just what "feminism" meant, to interviewer, narrators, and within public culture more generally, was at issue, but did not have a place within the interview frame.

Leddy's knowledge of feminism's meaning for Indigenous women in Canada gave her prior warning of the possibility of negative responses. She writes that the recent feminist movement was not inclusive of Indigenous women, while early 20th century feminism was actively antagonistic, criticizing Indigenous mothering practices and adopting eugenicist approaches. With such a heritage it is hardly surprising that her older narrators were wary of the term. Nevertheless, as with Abrams' interviews, it was not hard for Leddy to interpret the views and activities of many of her narrators as consistent with feminism. In her case, women's stories of standing up against colonial legislation that inflicted unequal and discriminatory treatment of Indigenous women who "married out" of their community, was one such example.

The frankness with which these historians write about the dilemma of the "f-word" is itself a fitting legacy of the kind of reflexive practice that *Women's Words* encouraged us to adopt. It helps us to deepen our engagement with the ideal of shared authority, and the flattening of hierarchies in the research relationship, which historians such as Kristina Minister discussed.[1] It increases our awareness of the power of public discourse and of the long reach of historical experience in the lives of those we research. It underlines the concomitant demands on us to explore particularly potent words and concepts with our narrators, rather than unwittingly allowing them to unsettle the dialog.

Valerie Korinek writes that she was aware of the possibility of freezing conversations with her narrators by communicating terminology and assumptions that alienated them. She therefore tried to leave her own queer feminist commitments at the door when interviewing women who lived as lesbians in Saskatchewan, Canada, in the second half of the 20th century. She wanted to appear balanced, judicious, and open, but knew that some narrators recognized where her activist sympathies lay. She writes that many objected to the term "queer," others to "lesbian." It was not that such terms presented a baffling challenge—the women knew to what they referred. It was as if she was tapping into a feisty determination to resist categorization. More troubling than these interchanges about specific terms, however, was the silence of women who would not be interviewed. Korinek was aware, from the testimony of lesbian activists, that there were many more whose preference for privacy and discretion sealed their lips. In spite of all her efforts, she managed to get only one such covert lesbian to speak to her, who then, frustratingly, embargoed most of the interview.

Why is it sometimes so hard for us, as oral historians, to persuade those whose experiences and viewpoints we are keen to understand, to speak? Research in the UK bears out the methodological problems of queer oral history to which Korinek refers. Rebecca Jennings found it impossible to recruit lesbians of the 1950s and 60s to talk to her, and so used the Hall-Carpenter Oral History Archive instead.[2] After extensive efforts, for which she was rewarded with homophobic hate mail, Emma Vickers recruited just ten gay men to interview about their experiences in the armed forces in World War II.[3] In both cases, the narrators were activists, with a stake in particular types of queer history. Tapping the memories of activists is, of course, of vital importance and is, in itself, not always easy. Even when adopting the techniques of "slow scholarship" that allow time for trust to build, it can be hard to persuade any women, burdened as we are by cultural constructions that diminish our value, to participate in projects. Oral histories of activists, however, feed a sub-cultural story that gains dominance, and which in itself, as Elizabeth Lapovsky Kennedy has pointed out, excludes and marginalizes those whose lives do not fit the narrative.[4] Korinek determinedly points to the complexities that glimpses of "the silent majority" bring to notions of LGBTQ+ communities. And she hopes that the testimony of the noisy, through its revisionist capacities, will eventually persuade the silent to speak.

Ponni Arasu and Uma Chakravarti's chapter, based on Arasu's interviews with Chakravarti, a leading Indian academic and an oral historian in her own right, is all about activism. Chakravarti has no problem identifying as a feminist. Much of the discussion focuses on the intersectionality of her feminism with her concerns for human rights and an end to discrimination not only by gender, but also by caste and class. Chakravarti's life history brings into focus a major shift in the definition of feminism in India. The 1970s and 80s was the period in which activists such as her emphasized the need to center campaigns on women's bodies, particularly their vulnerability to rape and sexual violence, and thus to base feminist politics on gender difference, rather than on a simplistic understanding of equal rights.[5] While Arasu's conversations with Chakravarti suggest that an expanding women's movement aligned itself with this approach, they also bring out divisions between feminists. Some were resistant to the concept of "state impunity"—that is, the idea that the state, through the police, condoned (or even encouraged) sexual violence against poor, low status women. Arasu brings out Chakravarti's conversion to "fact finding" as a feminist methodology that enabled her to address such doubts within as well as outside the movement. Chakravarti speaks movingly about how the collection of evidence about atrocities, through oral history, became vital to campaigns to expose and end outrages. In these days of seeing oral histories as texts to decode rather than data to analyze, such testimony is a poignant reminder not to dismiss "fact finding" too readily as mere "positivism."

Nadje Al-Ali's overview of her oral history work with women on the recent history of Iraq focuses on memories of particular crises and periods, and what they meant for widely diverse communities of Iraqi women. As in Arasu and Chakravarti's article, the dominant and disturbing theme is sexual violence against women. After the relative advantages for women of the early decades of the Ba'th regime, policies focused on women's bodies turned the tide against women. Al-Ali quotes testimonies that recount the banning of contraception during the war with Iran, as well as ethnic discrimination against Kurdish women who were coerced into Arab marriages and raped and murdered as part of the state's policy of Arabization. International sanctions, imposed by the United Nations, were no solution for women: in response, Iraqi society became more conservative, and levels of criminal violence rose, increasing women's fear of assault. It is to Al-Ali's credit that, through "slow scholarship," she facilitated such narratives. Her piece raises, as does Chakravarti's "fact finding" approach, the ethical issue of how an oral historian can interview women about such horrors without re-traumatizing them.

These five chapters extend the explorations of *Women's Words*, both methodologically and substantively, raising new and challenging questions about the feminist practice of oral history. The issues that stand out concern our uses of historically laden terminology, the challenge of confronting silence, the political value of "fact finding," and the importance of uncovering traumatic histories without inflicting further harm on those who bravely narrate them.

Notes

1   Kristina Minister, "A Feminist Frame for the Oral History Interview," in *Women's Words: The Feminist Practice of Oral History*, eds. Sherna Berger Gluck and Daphne Patai (New York: Routledge, 1991), 27–41.
2   Rebecca Jennings, *Tomboys and Bachelor Girls: A Lesbian History of Post-War Britain* (Manchester: Manchester University Press, 2007).
3   Emma Vickers, *Queen and Country: Same Sex Desire in the British Armed Forces 1939–45* (Manchester: Manchester University Press, 2013).
4   Elizabeth Lapovsky Kennedy, "Telling Tales: Oral History and the Construction of Pre-Stonewall Lesbian History," *Radical History Review* 62 (1995): 58–79.
5   See, for example, Annie Devenish, "Performing the Political Self: A Study of Identity Making and Self Representation in the Autobiographies of India's First Generation of Parliamentary Women," *Women's History Review* 22, no. 2 (2013): 280–294.

6 Talking about feminism
Reconciling fragmented narratives with the feminist research frame

Lynn Abrams

LYNN: Well, kind of to finish up I was going to ask you about feminism.
SHIRLEY: About, sorry?
LYNN: Feminism.
SHIRLEY: Oh yes.

Interview with Shirley, 2010

For women in the Western world, the quest for the autonomous self is closely bound up with the advent of feminism of the so-called second wave.[1] The notion of the essentialist self, contained within the biological/reproductive body of woman, has been seen as particularly debilitating to a woman's ability to create a unique, differentiated personhood or subjectivity that draws on her authentic experience. Women's liberation from this framework has thus been a key component of feminist writing and campaigning. Driven by a commitment to "research by, about, and for women," the concept that women's experiences could be legitimated by listening to their stories, and using them to inform understandings of women's position in society, became a plank of the emancipation struggle and ongoing project of feminist scholarship.[2] It is a circular reinforcing process—each voice or story contributes to an alternative historical narrative for other women, who then feel freer to narrate their own subjective experiences liberated from dominant norms and expectations. Given the recent outpouring of research on feminist activism, which tends to privilege the voices of those who can clearly situate themselves within the organized movement, opening up a discussion about the meaning of feminism to those who watched it from the sidelines is both timely and important.[3] Talking about feminism in all its manifestations both with those who positively identify with the movement and those who had little or no active association with it produces a range of memory narratives that broaden and deepen understandings of the past as it was lived and interpreted. It also reminds us that feminist oral history should be open to counter and alternative narratives.

Women's Words elaborated and complicated the feminist oral history project by urging oral historians to interrogate their research practices and dig deeper into the structures of meaning embedded in women's narratives. This chapter considers both the dynamics of the interview in the moment and the subsequent analysis of what the narrator means. In doing so, it addresses what appears to be an inconsistency in women's memory stories with respect to content and composure. The interviews in question were conducted with British women of the so-called "transition generation," those born in the 1940s who matured to adulthood in the 1950s and 1960s, and who bridged the gap between the war and domesticity and the advent of the women's liberation movement. In these interviews, there emerged a jarring and disconcerting contradiction between, on the one hand, narratives relating to what might be termed "autonomy journeys" or even "liberation narratives" told within a "coherence system" (a narrative device used to frame a life story to achieve continuity and to make it understandable to the listener) that accepted the precepts of equality of opportunity, choice, and freedom (in effect, a feminist script), and, on the other, the respondents' discomposure when feminism was introduced into the room.[4]

In this chapter, I consider what happens and what it means when a feminist research practice seemingly shuts down rather than liberates women's voices.[5] Why do life narratives that hitherto have been coherent and self-realizing, stutter and fragment in the encounter with a concept—feminism—that forms the foundation or framework for the life stories in the first place? For some of my narrators, the introduction of feminism (either as a set of beliefs or as manifestations of the seventies-era women's movement) into the conversation— often towards the end of the interview—prompted discomposure, fragmented narratives, and, in some cases, doubt about the self they had hitherto presented with such confidence. I suggest that for this generation of women, particularly those with little or no active encounter with the organized women's move- ment, feminism provides a framework of meaning for the life story as told to a feminist scholar with explicit interest in their lives as women. However, they lacked the language and the set of referents (to feminist practices and feminist culture), which would allow them to associate with and celebrate feminism in a generalized sense. As a result, my questions often induced an epistemological reaction; the interview became a test, and a burden, rather than a conversation.

The production of memory stories, especially in relation to personal narra- tives, can require significant psychological and emotional investment. It can open up psychological fissures, prompting re-evaluation (sometimes for the first time) and revelation. Life stories are constantly being revised through self- narration over the life course in daily interactions, but the life-story interview provides a rare opportunity to articulate that self in a highly coherent fashion. In the interview, the power of the researcher can also induce discomposure, which may be disconcerting for both parties. Penny Summerfield argues that "in the name of returning to women their 'honest voices,' feminist oral history is particularly likely to produce discomposure." This may occur as a result of a disjuncture between the research frame and the memory frame or on account of the feminist desire to reveal interiority (understood here as authentic subjectivity), thereby exposing the contradictions in women's lives between, for example, conformity to generalized gender norms and negotiation with or resistance to those norms.[6] In my oral history project, the respondent whose composed narrative was suddenly called into doubt through the f-word was confronted by the gap between feeling and doing. In other words, her narrativization of her life enveloped within the coherence system of feminism, broadly defined, was undercut by her failure to evidence a feminist life through certain self-imposed (or publicly available) manifestations of "feminism," such as reading certain books or campaigning on certain issues.

Scholars who have interviewed women *actively* engaged in the postwar women's movement, and who positively identify as feminists, have noted that feminism (its key tenets and as a structure) provides the framework for their narrators' life stories. This is a group that self-consciously, then and now, aligned beliefs with identity. Their feminist consciousness and active involvement drive a self-narrative that positions feminism as a pivotal moment— a rupture, "feminist awakening" or "zero hour"—which then frames everything that happens next.[7] We see this pattern in the narrative of a speaker at a Scottish witness workshop on feminist lives who spoke about feminism marking a major shift in her life story, anchored by some of the best-known activities and publications associated with the movement:

> And then when I went to university—and this is of course where I was fortunate—I met people and read books that gave names to these things that said there are such things as patriarchy, there is sexism, there is oppression. So it gave me the language and the kind of framework to understand what all these kind of amorphous feelings and anger and resentment were about. So that's where I got involved a bit more formally. When I went to university in Lancaster [I was] in the Women's Liberation Movement, and it was mainly through a consciousness-raising group, a CR group, does anybody else . . .? Yes [*laughter*]. And, I have to say that, my involvement there was very skimpy, but . . . the reason I want to mention it is, it did lay a lot of good foundations and bad foundations for what happened in the future. The good foundations were the understanding that I've just referred to, that, you know, because we would read books, we would look at *Our Bodies Ourselves*, and all these texts, we'd talk about Shulamith Firestone and all these people, and ideas, you remember it, and look at *Hidden From History*, that, it was fantastic, it was exciting.[8]

Others used metaphors such as "scales falling from eyes," whereby participation in a CR group or a Women's Liberation Movement campaigning organization revealed a new reality. Those who self-identified as feminists had a common language and set of cultural reference points (an epistemology) not available to those without an intimate relationship with the women's movement. Ruth, for instance, who had been active in left politics when she moved to Canada, spoke about Take-Back-the-Night marches and campaigning for an

Everywoman clinic.[9] Helen, who became a feminist academic, easily listed key feminist texts of the period that she expected I would recognize:

> [B]ut I certainly remember reading Juliet . . . I was in college with Juliet Mitchell, and Juliet wrote for *New Left Review* to which I was a subscriber in those days; um, she wrote something called *The Longest Revolution*— you must know it? And I remember reading that and thinking yes, that's very right on and then she wrote something in *Black Dwarf* . . . which was also something to do with women's liberation and then when we went to Vancouver in 1970 I remember reading Kate Millett on the plane, so I was kind of . . . and of course Betty Friedan which come out in '67 and there was a book by a woman called Hannah Gavron called *Captive Wife*.[10]

In such cases, feminism (often understood as sets of relationships, organizational affiliations, and an engagement with ideas and action) provides the validating or framing device for decisions made and paths taken thereafter. Moreover, these narratives were shaped by memories, networks, and friendships that originated in the 1970s and 80s and continue to sustain a shared culture. In so far as they exhibit distinctive characteristics, feminist narratives might be described as feminographies—biographies that center on feminist precepts and actions. Communication scholars Kristin Langellier and Eric Peterson offer insight into understanding feminographies.[11] In their analysis of everyday storytelling practices, they describe illness narratives or pathographies (biographical narratives that focus on illness and disease and its effects on an individual's life) as a distinctive genre—"a modern adventure story constructed around recovery and healing." For example, breast cancer narratives illustrate how illness as lived experience is translated into stories that serve to reclaim the body (and the self) from medical or diagnostic histories. Conscious feminist narratives also exhibit particular features in terms of content and structure; they serve as testimonials to a belief in a set of fundamental principles, which reaffirm the narrator's self-identification as a feminist and sustain the discursive narrative for posterity. In short, feminographies validate feminist life stories through shared references to practices and common understandings. Such narratives can also be exclusive, denying those who did not share in the practices the possibility of belonging to the same narrative community.

The majority of women in the 1970s and 80s were not active in the feminist movement but, as I have argued elsewhere, a generational shift took place in the postwar decades as daughters distinguished themselves from their mothers, materially and morally.[12] They founded lives upon a liberationist practice, but rarely (or at least not consciously) upon liberationist ideology and movements. Leaving behind the model of the female self that prioritized self-control, self-denial, and respectability over self-expression, they adopted ways of being that embraced self-fulfilment and self-realization through travel, education, career trajectories, moral decisions, and self-fashioning. They did not require political feminism to achieve this self-actualization. But in narrating their life stories, they drew upon the language and frameworks made commonplace by feminist discourse, which created a template enabling them to speak about their personal experiences in ways that legitimated their choices, whether that meant choosing to terminate a pregnancy, travel or work overseas, or not marry an unsuitable partner.[13] Yet, despite living feminist lives in the sense of subscribing to such principles as women's rights and autonomy, a number of my respondents were reluctant or unable to fuse their own life stories with the more generalized discursive field. Feminism was interpreted, variously, and usually implicitly, as a set of precepts, behaviors, and beliefs rather than a roadmap for life.

Caroline, for instance, after recounting a life story that encompassed university and a career in journalism, responded in the following way when asked to comment on her relationship with feminism:

> I'm very ashamed of this question, Lynn, because I think I let it all pass me by, I definitely was aware of it, I didn't disapprove of it or particularly approve of it. I think I was terribly selfish because things had gone so well for me, I had a job I hadn't had to fight for, I had a salary which I have no idea if it was on a par with the male equivalents. It seemed like riches to me after quite a, well, a very straitened time as a student. Em, no I think I was far more revelling in the sense of independence that I had without stopping to think about it on a bigger scale and I wish I had now, looking back, I wish that I'd been more politically aware and had realized that women, a lot of women, did have to fight for [it]. But I didn't I'm afraid, it was rumbling away in the background.[14]

The image of feminism "rumbling away in the background" is an appropriate metaphor that conforms to the notion that self-identity is constructed over the life course whereby external events or institutions are only salient when they intrude, negatively or positively, on self-development.[15] In Caroline's case, it was not feminism, either as an ideology or manifested in the women's movement, which shaped the self she had come to inhabit and project. Prompted to reflect on her relationship with feminism in the context of an interview with someone she identified as a feminist scholar, she produced a reflective and self-accusatory response that she later re-affirmed: "I just feel looking back I was so blinkered and self-centered not taking an interest in [the women's movement] . . . I read those books like Marilyn French and it all seemed to be happening on a different planet."[16]

My questions about feminism usually came towards the end of a life-history interview, which covered most milestones in my respondents' lives; they were also framed within a research project investigating the apparent shift from moral conservatism to women's liberation in postwar Britain. At the time, I thought it a logical question to ask given that most of my narrators would have been in their late 20s and early 30s when Britain's women's movement was taking off and most had completed some form of higher education and embarked on a professional career. Even if born a little early to be actively

involved or engaged in the formative years of the women's liberation movement (most were married with children at that time), I imagined they would
have been aware of the movement and might have engaged with its ideas or
campaigns, either as individuals or as members of other groups. Thus, I was
not really prepared for the discomposure that mention of the women's
movement and feminism occasioned. For Lorraine, who studied at art school,
travelled abroad, and then married in 1963, subsequently accompanying her
husband to the Sudan, my mention of the f-word prompted uncertainty in
her response:

> LYNN: Can I ask you maybe finally about feminism because by the time
> you came back and you were here, late 60s, early 70s—the beginning
> of the feminist movement—were you conscious of that at all? You are
> obviously conscious of it in retrospect from the answers you are giving
> me.
>
> LORRAINE: Yes. I actually find that quite a difficult question because there
> are so many different angles. I mean one of the things I remember, I
> don't know if this is anything to do with feminism or not, in the
> university they started a women's group, right, so we all went along
> and it was sub-divided into book groups or baking groups or child-
> minding groups. That was incredibly useful in that we had a baby-
> sitting—this isn't very feminist at all . . . And I remember there were
> quite a few women who had had careers and were still involved with
> teaching and such. One of them said come along and give a talk on
> female circumcision in the Sudan, and I gave a talk on that and there
> was quite a lot of discussion on things like that, but I'm not sure that
> we actually did very much about it. We just talked about it, so I would
> say therefore that some people may have done something but I don't
> know if we did, really. Um, I find it difficult now to think back on
> what exactly [*pause*]. I mean the idea of equal pay for equal work
> seems to be such an unquestionable right and it was not the case then.
> It still isn't working, so I think I took it as read, it was just a given
> that, so, how would you describe what feminism was? I mean we all
> read; yes, we all read the books and things.[17]

Lorraine struggled to fit her experiences into a framework that was ill-defined
or, worse, one she thought I had defined without spelling it out. The women's
group attached to her husband's university was primarily a support group for
the wives and partners of male academics. The timing of its founding suggests
a feminist influence, but as she started describing its activities Lorraine became
uncertain about whether it *counted* as feminist. Similarly, she downgraded
talking about issues like female circumcision (female genital mutilation or
FGM) because no action was taken following her presentation. In the interview
context, activities which my narrator might have interpreted for herself as
"feminist" or connected to the woman question were suddenly relegated

as not particularly feminist (or not feminist enough) while other activities, such as reading the "books and things," were given a higher status in a self-imposed hierarchy. In fact, "books and things" were frequently mentioned by respondents as totems of feminism in this period—Germaine Greer's *The Female Eunuch* especially (it was published in the UK in 1970) and novels such as Marilyn French's *The Women's Room*. Kathleen, who had been active in the National Housewives' Register (NHR, renamed the National Women's Register, NWR, in 1987)—a grassroots organization established in 1960 by women who wanted to be more than "housebound mothers"—recalled one of her NHR friends encouraging the group to read feminist texts:

> KATHLEEN: Germaine Greer, yes, that was one book we did discuss at NWR.
> LYNN: Did you, *The Female Eunuch*? Did you discuss the other one? Did you look at Betty Friedan's . . .
> KATHLEEN: No, and there was another lady—Susie . . .
> LYNN: Orbach
> KATHLEEN: Yes, I remember reading . . .
> LYNN: *Fat Is a Feminist Issue?*
> KATHLEEN: Yes, that's right.
> LYNN: Right, so you did read some feminist things?
> KATHLEEN: Yes we did because this lady, Christine was her name, in our group, was very into that; she was an ex-teacher and I think she kept feminism very much alive in Wickford and Billericay [small towns in the south-east of England]. [*Laughter.*] So we weren't allowed to slip . . . I think maybe she didn't want us to slip backwards into sort of um just a mother nurturing, caring sort of environment.[18]

However, since the books are a well-known symbol of the movement, a respondent like Kathleen might have mentioned them to indicate an ability to engage my question, to show she had been aware of feminist currents, rather than as evidence of active engagement. Rosemary similarly castigated herself for not having read Greer's seminal text: "Did I read stuff on purpose? No. I tend to read novels and I'm ashamed to say I have never read *The Female Eunuch*, I should have, shouldn't I, but I haven't."[19]

I came to the conclusion that my questions were inducing unease in my narrators and that, far from facilitating their narrative selves, I was unintentionally closing them down. Pam, who struggled to talk about herself as a child, referred to herself in the third person when describing her formative years growing up in a religious culture that constrained her options. Thereafter, however, she produced a confident and coherent narrative in the first person, which conformed to what we might describe as an autonomous identity. After relaying how she rejected what had been expected of her—marriage to a local man and work in the local denominational school—and left Scotland for a job in Spain, Pam took control of the interview.[20] Now she inhabited the self she

recognized and felt comfortable in. At my mention of feminism, however, she
again struggled to articulate herself:

> LYNN: I am going to ask . . . were you aware at all of feminism, or any of
> that sort of activity, around the late 60s, early 70s?
>
> PAM: Belatedly, yes. I missed the beginning of it, um, I only began to be
> aware of it almost in retrospect I think, um . . .
>
> LYNN: What would have that been, I mean what would you have been
> . . . what issues would you have become conscious of or was it not
> like that?
>
> PAM: [*Very long pause*] I am trying to think, um I think I became more
> aware of historical things that were wrong rather than the things that
> were happening currently, things like the generation before mine—as
> soon as you got married you gave your job up, you had no options
> and that began to mean something to me, or the reading I was doing
> it became—obviously "What?" so I think I was more aware of what
> it used to be like, began to make the question about what it was like
> now. First of all, it is much better now but no, wait a minute . . . it
> was a gradual . . . does that make sense?
>
> LYNN: Yeh, yeh, well the marriage bar wouldn't have, I mean that was
> still in place until the 50s for married women . . .
>
> PAM: It was still very much there and so [*pause*] I can't remember now
> why, I must have been reading something, um, when this happened,
> and put things into a context and then beginning to realize that there
> were things going on now and "Oh, oh yes, I didn't realize that that
> was an injustice or a . . ." [*pause*] it's a bit vague, but things like
> changing to his name was just so . . . you just did, no one questioned
> it and then people began to question it—"Why would you, why?"
> And you think, "Yes, why would you?"[21]

What accounts for this hesitant and rather disjointed response? Why, having
told life stories that easily fit a feminist frame of female advancement and independent choice, did so many of my narrators flounder when asked to recall the
advent of feminism in Britain? Why did they exhibit signs of guilt or shame or
anxiety? Jane's response was typical. When asked if she was aware of feminism,
she hesitated, as if being tested, then said: "Yes, vaguely, but you'll have to
trigger me though, to see if I even . . ." When I replied, "I am trying not to
trigger you [*laughter*]," she added, "I don't even know if I have got the
timescales right you see."[22] The intersubjectivities present within the interview
may provide part of the explanation. These women knew I was a senior female
academic researching women's history; some knew me personally and may
have ascribed to me certain feminist beliefs or presumptions about what
constitutes feminism. This made them anxious. It is common for narrators to
endeavor to please, perhaps especially among women. It was important to
them to be able to answer my questions, hence the feelings of inadequacy or

guilt exhibited by those who had lived lives paying little attention to the struggles others were undertaking on their behalf, or at not having been sufficiently engaged by the issues (not reading the "right" books), or aware of their own oppression. Another possible explanation is the popular media discourse on second-wave feminism that, in the UK at least, still sometimes portrays the women's liberation movement using negative stereotypes of radical ideologues. Listening in stereo, as Anderson and Jack urged us to do, would have alerted me to the tension inherent in my injunction to my narrators to talk about feminism.[23]

My question also prompted a second kind of response whereby narrators sought to align their own life experiences with what they believed was my agenda by focusing on everyday activities and experiences that could count as feminist. Scholars have characterized some of the 60s-era women's organizations as unfeminist or at least not having engaged in critical reflection on gender relations. To my narrators, however, involvement in the NHR, the pre-school playgroups movement, the National Childbirth Trust (NCT) and the Campaign for Nuclear Disarmament (CND) was evidence of awareness of and active engagement with equality issues and movements that mobilized women to work for change that would improve their lives and those of others.[24] Carole, who experienced blatant sexism in her job with the police, became involved with the NHR when she moved to a town in another part of the country. The NHR was not explicitly feminist. Indeed, it adopted a broadly neutral stance on most women's issues and many of its members would probably have agreed with the comments of a woman who wrote that: "I think it's played an important part in helping women grow in confidence and ability. We may not be radical feminists but we are active and involved–and that's what it's all about." But Carole understood her involvement in the organization as feminist on the grounds that "talking to other women" about issues was important "because if you were a housewife you were seen to be the dross."[25] Sally, who founded a branch in rural Scotland, where there were few opportunities for women to get together ("you know, it wasn't like a lot of my friends ... were in consciousness-raising groups by then") similarly credited the NHR with introducing her to feminist thinking on an everyday level:

[W]ithin the Women's Register there was feminism at the level of sheer equality with men, we ought to be equal, we oughtn't to be put down, you know, and a lot of them were experiencing difficulties within the marriage because they wanted to be freer than their husbands had been brought up for their wives to be, and there were often battles going on, you know? Go to these conferences and "oh how great, not to have to cook a meal" and to leave the children, it was so difficult to find someone to look after them, or "get my husband to do it" or "I'll have to get back early because he can't do it on a Sunday night, he has to go to ..." that sort of thing.[26]

Another narrator, Jane, described the National Childbirth Trust, which worked
to counter the medicalization of childbirth by providing women with advice
and support, as the place where she "was aware of women being in control."[27]
Ann, who became a mature university student in the 1970s while raising small
children, was one of the few who said, "I was aware, yes, I was aware of the
feminist movement." But for her it was CND rather than explicitly feminist
organizations that enabled her to answer my question:

> I remember being involved with Parents for Survival, that was part of the
> CND movement, but I was involved in CND in London, but the Parents
> for Survival must have been in Glasgow. Parents used to go off with all
> the weans [children] in their buggies. My children have memories of so
> many demonstrations in their buggies: "Oh no not another demonstration
> mum."[28]

It was easier, though, for narrators to retrospectively acknowledge their own
support for broad equality issues such as maternity leave and equal pay. The
interview gave them the opportunity to share and express undisguised
resentment at the discriminatory treatment they received in various everyday
contexts. Carole was outraged—at the time and again in the interview—at
being treated as her husband's possession in the 1970s when she

> wanted to buy a pushchair for number two son and they wouldn't give
> me credit, because even though we had a joint bank account my husband
> had to sign the form; and also when I got the coil fitted (contraceptive
> IUD), he had to give his written permission.[29]

Shirley, who trained and practiced as a doctor, also recalled that in the early
1970s feminism was relevant to her life:

> Oh yes, very much so I think, yes, I remember feeling very strongly that
> I had the right to work especially when I had my first child and I could
> tell that my mum and my mother-in-law were kind of mmmmmm
> [*inaudible*] going back to work you know. It was very, very . . . I found
> it really important, it was a principle um and I say, equal rights and you
> know the injustices that were in the system I felt really angry about it.[30]

Revealing later in our conversation that, when she married in the 1960s, she
had refused to allow her father to give her away in church, Shirley said: "[Y]ou'll
laugh about this, but I refused to let my dad give me away at my wedding."[31]
Why did she think I would laugh? Because I would judge it as a rather feeble
feminist act? In contrast with those narrators who struggled to identify a book
they had read or a campaign with which they had identified as "counting" as
feminist, Shirley's account of her struggle to maintain her medical career when
her children were young, and in the face of an unaccommodating system in

general medical practice, was an authentic and heartfelt feminist narrative. What we might describe as everyday feminism—the choices made to pursue a path in life that contravened prevailing norms, as did Shirley, and Frances, who divorced her husband despite parental disapproval—better describes these women's relationship with a set of beliefs that they integrated into their own thinking. Admitting to having led a charmed life until leaving university, Frances found herself in an unhappy marriage in the early 1960s and determined to extricate herself from it. Although patronized by her father's lawyer—"He said 'There, there, dear don't worry, it'll all work out,' pat, pat on the head"— she saw it through. "I guess that is the big change in me," she told me, "because there was no way anyone was going to talk me out of it."[32]

In some cases, the mention of feminism and the truncated discussion it prompted brought the interview to a premature end. The discomposure in these instances was not especially fruitful. It was as if my question had cast doubt on the self that, at some emotional cost to them, they had presented. Never intending to mute and disempower my narrators, I reconsidered my own practice. Here, however, it bears noting that those women who spoke of feminist lives or feminographies, which effectively intertwined the personal and the political in a way that an academic would understand, were academics themselves, conversant with articulations that linked experience, consciousness, and action. They were also more inclined to understand feminism in capacious rather than narrow terms. Frances, who worked in science research and then retrained as a child psychologist when her children were older, responded in this way:

> LYNN: Well I was just going to ask you about feminism really. You said you were aware of reading stuff and so on—were you aware of the movement as such?
>
> FRANCES: Yes, yes, I was. I was very aware of friends who were suffering from being second-class citizens. I wasn't active unless perhaps you'd call it active [*pause*]. It was always in my mind in my work because there was a lot of family work as well and so it became very clear where the problems were of that nature and I don't know if this is relevant but what I found fascinating was when jobs were hard and men were losing their jobs, and women could earn some money by cleaning in schools morning and evening, etc., either it seemed, it sometimes seemed black and white which clearly nothing is, either things worked out and the men took their kids to nursery or the men just went under and the whole thing was awful. They lost their identities but that's perhaps not a feminist issue but it relates to balance in households and gender roles, and how strong women can be when they have to— they just take on the lot, you know, plus depressed husbands.[33]

For this smaller group of women, feminism was part of the self, embedded in the way they had lived their lives, not something that could be separated out

from everyday life. In contrast to feminist narratives that, closely tied to involvement in the women's liberation movement, hinge upon moments of epiphany
or rupture which in turn instigate significant life changes, the everyday life
stories of women who predated the women's movement or who, in their
words, let it pass them by, adhere to a different kind of script. Their script
contains more implicit signs of an everyday lived feminism exhibited in life
choices and personal responsibility. Sandra, who grew up in a family of female
schoolteachers and for whom the value of education was central to how she
conceived of her life, eventually taught feminist theory at university. Feminism
for her did not need to be exhibited or proved to me through membership to
organizations or involvement in campaigns. Rather, feminism was something
imbricated in her life narrative that was characterized by self-determination.
Here Sandra is speaking at the end of our interview about how her education
underpinned her life course:

> And particularly, well those two people, the priest and the English
> teacher, who just said, you know, Eastbourne is a small place, look out
> and look at Australia, and look at the past and think about what Milton's
> doing in *Paradise Lost*, you know um and think about it as an issue,
> not as something you've got to learn [*inaudible*] of. *Paradise Lost*, you
> know, is about freedom and in a way it's a good thing to be chucked out
> of Eden and be responsible for and you know, she always managed to
> make it have something to do with our own sense of ourselves and our
> own morality.[34]

As a scholar of literature, Sandra neatly summed up the feminist life as one
that embraced self-determination, freedom of the individual, and self-realization.

Drawing largely on oral history research, the production of histories of 20th
century feminism serves to recreate and reinforce ways of speaking about
feminism and the women's movement that privilege those who played an
active role; Valerie Korinek makes the same observation about writing LGBTQ+
histories.[35] Those women who can fluently and knowledgably speak about CR
groups and reading Juliet Mitchell (as opposed to the more widely known and
read *The Female Eunuch*) have a set of ready-made references, which anchor
their stories in an interview with a feminist researcher. Like the breast cancer
narratives referred to earlier, feminist narratives assume their own pathology.
Those outside this narrative culture may not have the language and syntax to
speak about something that has had a more diffuse but no less formative
impact on their lives. Ultimately, the loss of composure in those who struggled
to respond suggests fruitful areas of inquiry about how we might talk about
feminism in a way that opens up rather than closes down conversations. When
Caroline said near the end of our interview, "I'm afraid this is where I feel I'm
not very useful to you because none of it [feminism] impinged at all," she
could not have been more wrong.[36]

Notes

1 For a more detailed discussion see Lynn Abrams, "Liberating the Female Self: Epiphanies, Conflict and Coherence in the Life Stories of Post-War British Women," *Social History* 39, no. 1 (2014): 14–35.
2 Sherna Berger Gluck and Daphne Patai, eds., *Women's Words: The Feminist Practice of Oral History* (London: Routledge, 1991), 2.
3 A good example of such research is the "Sisterhood and After" collection of oral histories with British women who were active in the 1970s era feminist movement: www.bl.uk/sisterhood.
4 See Charlotte Linde, *Life Stories: The Creation of Coherence* (Oxford: Oxford University Press, 1993).
5 The author conducted all interviews cited here, using a life-course format, between 2009 and 2013. Narrators were born between 1939 and 1949 and hail from the British Isles, though some now reside overseas. The majority had careers or held professional jobs, including in teaching, health services, and journalism. At the time of interview, all were or had been married, most had adult children, and all but one were retired or partially retired from their careers though many were still working.
6 Penny Summerfield, "Dis/composing the Subject: Intersubjectivities in Oral History," in *Feminism and Autobiography: Texts, Theories, Methods*, eds. Tess Cosslett, Celia Lury, Penny Summerfield (London: Routledge, 2000), 91–106.
7 On rupture in feminist narratives, see Luisa Passerini, *Autobiography of a Generation: Italy 1968* (Middletown, Connecticut: Wesleyan University Press, 1996); Maud Anne Bracke, *Women and the Reinvention of the Political. Feminism in Italy, 1968–1983* (London: Routledge, 2014), 24 and 209.
8 Glasgow Women's Library: Witness at Scottish Women's Liberation Movement Workshop (transcript), Edinburgh 2009. The texts she was referring to are: The Boston Women's Health Book Collective, *Our Bodies, Our Selves: A Book By and For Women* (1976)—a British edition was published in 1978; Shulamith Firestone, *The Dialectic of Sex: the Case for Feminist Revolution* (1979); Sheila Rowbotham, *Hidden From History: 300 Years of Women's Oppression and How to Fight Against It* (1973).
9 Interview with Ruth (all narrator names are pseudonyms), 2011.
10 Interview with Helen, 2011. The texts she referred to include: Juliet Mitchell, *Women: the Longest Revolution: Essays on Feminism, Literature and Psychoanalysis* (1984); Betty Friedan, *The Feminine Mystique* (1963); Hannah Gavron, *The Captive Wife: Conflicts of Housebound Mothers* (1963).
11 Kristin M. Langellier and Eric E. Peterson, *Storytelling in Daily Life: Performing Narrative* (Philadelphia: Temple University Press, 2004), 189.
12 Lynn Abrams, "Mothers and Daughters: Negotiating the Discourse on the 'Good Woman' in 1950s and 1960s Britain," in *The Sixties and Beyond: De-Christianization in North America and Western Europe, 1945–2000*, eds. Nancie Christie and Michael Gauvreau (Toronto: University of Toronto Press, 2013), 60–83.
13 I discuss this in terms of narrative practices in Abrams, "Liberating the Female Self," 14–35.
14 Interview with Caroline, 2009.
15 Anthony Giddens, *Modernity and Self-Identity: Self and Society in the Late Modern Age* (Cambridge: Polity Press, 1991), 75–76.
16 Interview with Caroline. Here she refers to Marilyn French, *The Women's Room* (1977).
17 Interview with Lorraine, 2010.
18 Interview with Kathleen, 2011. Susie Orbach's *Fat is a Feminist Issue* was first published in 1978.

19 Interview with Rosemary, 2011.
20 For a more extensive analysis of Pam's narrative, see Abrams, "Liberating the Female Self."
21 Interview with Pam, 2010.
22 Interview with Jane, 2009.
23 Kathryn Anderson and Dana C. Jack, "Learning to Listen: Interview Techniques and Analyses," in *Women's Words*, 11–26.
24 Most critical in this respect is Elaine Wilson, *Only Half Way to Paradise: Women in Post-war Britain 1945–1968* (London, Routledge, 1980).
25 Interview with Carole, 2011. LSE, Women's Library, 5/NWR/3/5: unidentified newspaper cutting—"Gill Vine."
26 Interview with Sally, 2013.
27 Interview with Jane, 2009.
28 Interview with Ann, 2009.
29 Interview with Carole, 2011.
30 Interview with Shirley, 2010.
31 Interview with Shirley, 2010.
32 Interview with Frances, 2011.
33 Interview with Frances, 2011.
34 Interview with Sandra, 2009.
35 See Korinek's essay, Chapter 9 in this volume.
36 Interview with Caroline, 2009.

7 "Are you only interviewing women for this?"

Indigenous feminism and oral history[1]

Lianne C. Leddy

When I approached one Anishinaabe Elder at Serpent River First Nation (SRFN) in spring 2014 as part of a historical project on Indigenous women's activism in the post-1945 period, her immediate response got to the heart of Indigenous notions of gender complementarity.[2] "Are you only interviewing women for this?" she asked in a way that made clear the correct answer was "No." I assured her that I was interviewing both men and women Elders about their experiences as youth and young adults in the community.[3] In keeping with her understanding of Anishinaabe womanhood, a community story could not be adequately told without the voices of women and men, irrespective of the fact that colonial policies have impacted them differently.[4]

This chapter uses the idea of gender complementarity in oral history interviews with Anishinaabe knowledge holders to consider issues relating to the definition of Indigenous feminism(s), which includes exploring whether Elders saw Indigenous women's actions as feminist (or not) and examining the complex interplay between colonialism, feminism, and gender. My own position is that of an Anishinaabe kwe researcher: I am a citizen of Serpent River First Nation (SRFN) in Northern Ontario, Canada, and I grew up in nearby Elliot Lake. My mother is from SRFN and my father, a miner from an Irish-Canadian family, was raised in Elliot Lake. My previous work on the impact of Cold War-era uranium mining at Elliot Lake on SRFN examined watershed pollution and damage caused by an acid plant on the reserve. My current project started with an interest in the Indian Homemakers' Club—an on-reserve organization formed by the Department of Indian Affairs to "teach" Indigenous women homemaking—and its activities in the postwar period.[5] My use of archival and oral history sources to explore how women ran these clubs within their respective communities prompted deeper reflection on the interview experiences themselves.[6] A volume that seeks to decolonize feminist oral history must take Indigenous worldviews into account, both in theory and practice. To that end, this chapter draws on four interviews—two with men and two with women— conducted at SRFN to explore stories of politics and community, and how colonialism, gender, and "feminism" intersect with and shape them.

An analysis of the various viewpoints on Indigenous feminism, and whether feminism as constructed by whitestream feminism adequately captures

Indigenous perspectives, requires a discussion of Indigenous gender roles.[7] To take Joyce Green's definition,

> The characteristic of feminism—be it socialist, maternal, radical, liberal, Aboriginal, or ecofeminist—is that it takes gender seriously as a social organizing process and, within the context of patriarchal societies, seeks to identify the ways in which women are subordinated to men and how women can be emancipated from this subordination.[8]

Green also argues that, regardless of how our pre-colonial societies were organized, and what roles or status Indigenous women enjoyed before contact, dispossession and legislation like the Indian Act—as well as settler racism—have contributed to the subordination of Indigenous women in contemporary communities.

Notwithstanding this important consideration, historians such as Jean Barman have also identified Indigenous women at the "cusp of contact" acting in ways that we would now describe as feminist.[9] In other words, if feminism is by its very nature activist in the face of patriarchy, how can scholars and Indigenous peoples explain the fact that even in societies that held women in high regard, women exerted feminist actions and words? Could it also be that feminism is a 20th-century label that does not adequately capture the lived experiences of Indigenous women at different points in time? Cree and Métis scholar Verna St. Denis has reflected on her re-evaluation of feminism throughout her career, noting that feminism itself has undergone significant changes as a movement. Arguing against viewing feminism as stagnant or monolithic, St. Denis explains that,

> [The] past four decades, and the debates, schisms and differing viewpoints among Western feminisms are often not acknowledged by those Aboriginal women scholars who, in viewing feminism as a static form of analysis and focusing on a liberal agenda, argue that feminism is not relevant to Aboriginal women and their communities.[10]

Of course, the feminist movement's exclusion of Indigenous peoples goes back much further to the Western iteration of maternal feminism at the turn of the last century, with its inclusion of eugenicist elements that took aim at Indigenous mothering (and Indigeneity as a whole) as well as the child-rearing methods of poor, immigrant, or so-called immoral women.[11] Feminism and Indigeneity were therefore sometimes at odds—a pattern that, for many of us, continues today despite the evolution of these terms and their changes over time.

Not surprisingly, these academic discussions and historical dynamics continue to play out in interview and community contexts, with significant consequences for Indigenous women. For instance, those who identify as feminist or work for gender equality within their communities risk being critiqued as not "traditional enough" or, as Janet Silman found, disregarded as "'white-washed women's libbers' who [are] undermining their Indian heritage."[12] The Indian Act has a long history of gender discrimination, whereby Indian status (a legal definition of persons registered under the Indian Act) for an Indigenous woman was dependent on her relationship to a man: first her father and then her husband.[13] "Marrying-out," as it was called, meant that women who married non-Status Indian men lost their status, and the Indigenous rights and community services that went with it—even the right to live in those communities and to legally belong to them as members of a First Nation. As more women protested these forms of discrimination, they faced criticism from friends and family for putting gender equality before the larger (and presumably more important) project of decolonization. This conflict was particularly pronounced during the 1970s and 1980s, when what became called "second wave" whitestream feminism gained traction just as Indigenous women across the country engaged in a struggle for equality under the Indian Act.[14] As Joanne Barker observes, the response of Indigenous political leaders, almost exclusively male, to Indigenous women's activism—namely, that once decolonization took place they would take care of the women—was also self-interested:

> Indian women's assertions of their rights to everything from reserve housing and employment to full participation in band governance and national politics were an attempt to reclaim a particular kind of tradition that valued women's "separate but equal" place in Indian communities and politics. This countered the assertion of many Indian men, particularly those in band government and national Indian organizations, who wanted to claim a tradition that justified the exclusion of Indian women and the negation of gender issues within sovereignty politics. Men who wanted, in other words, to affirm the privileges of men in reserve, band, and national politics.[15]

Indigenous women's struggles to achieve equality under the Indian Act faced challenges not only from the country's settler legislative and judicial bodies, but also from Indigenous leaders. In collaboration with Janet Silman, women from the Tobique First Nation elucidated these conflicts within First Nations communities, as have women I have interviewed in my own work.[16]

One of the significant legislative victories won by Indigenous feminists during this period was Bill C-31 (1985), which restored Indian Status to women who had "married out" as well as their children—a form of legal identity that shaped community and self-perceptions as well as rights.[17] Marella Schofield (MS), who lost her status when she married a non-Indigenous man and then later regained her status in the 1980s, recounted her memories of that time when I asked her about it during our conversation in May 2014. Her reflection takes into account the strong kinship patterns that are the foundation of our communities, but also that "marrying-out" had profound effects on how other people saw her. Ultimately, she explains, the strong kinship systems on reserves helped to mitigate the changes and funding problems that Bill C-31 brought.

> MARELLA: It did have an effect because it was sorta like you're not Indian anymore. . . . And out in the other society you're Indian. So you're torn between two: one you're Indian and the other you're not. And it's still almost seen the same way today. 'Cause when I hear some people and they say, "she's French" and "she's Polish now" because they married Polish people or French people, you now are known as French, but you're not.
>
> LIANNE: Right.
>
> MARELLA : You're Native. You know you never, just because you married that person, that don't make you French. Or that doesn't make you German or Polish or anything. You're still that, but there's that division that's there of: you're French, you know. And they'll still say, "Oh, she's Polish now" or "She's French now." You say, "No, I changed my name but I didn't change my nationality!" [*Laughter.*] I'm still Native! You know. And that same thing with your children. Like, politically, the Native people here said okay, we don't want them to come home and whatever. So we in turn said now if your daughter marries a white person and your grandchildren . . . are you going to refuse them?
>
> LIANNE: Um hm.
>
> MARELLA : Because it affects you, too. Not only me. It affects you. And if your grandchildren marry someone else, now they're gonna be refused. So how is that going to affect you? You can't bring them to the reserve because you wrote in policy that there are no white people allowed on the reserve. But your relatives, your siblings married. So you have to think on both sides. So there was a big controversy over that, that policy of letting the white girls—the Natives that married the white people—come back on the reserve.
>
> LIANNE: Do you—was there any kind of meetings that people had to go to?
>
> MARELLA : I think, yeah. There were, I didn't have to go, well, I didn't live here. I had moved away. But, they had meetings about, of what they were going to do with the Native girls that married into the white society.[18]

When I asked Marella whether or not many women moved back to the community after the Bill C-31 amendments, she said it was difficult for women and their children to do so. The reinstatement of more than 100,000 people plus future children not yet born meant that underfunded First Nations were put under even more economic stress. But she also noted that kinship connections often eased disagreements among community members over women's reinstatement of rights under the Indian Act or people returning home. As the following exchange indicates, the fact many families are related, and many leaders and community members had family members affected by Bill C-31, helped to mitigate some conflicts.

> LIANNE : Yeah. So, did you find that a lot of people moved back here after that, though?
> MARELLA : Um.
> LIANNE : Or was it not necessarily the case?
> MARELLA : No, it wasn't. Because I think we weren't really accepted. Yes, they didn't like the white society moving in, but because we're all closely related nobody really wanted to say anything because it was their relative.
> LIANNE : Hm.
> MARELLA : When you look at the whole reserves. Most of the reserves are the same you know. They're all related.
> LIANNE : Yeah. A couple of big families.
> MARELLA : Yeah. All big families, and they're related so really can't— don't—want to say too much because they have children that might marry out there too.[19]

Marella was not alone. An Elder who prefers to remain unnamed also recalled her experience of "marrying-out," saying:

> Yes, I lost my status when I married because I married a white person. And, but I gained it—got it back when I came back to the reserve, eh. Yeah, we did. We did, if you married someone off . . . a white person, you lost your status and you're going out there and you're on your own! [*Laughter.*] Yeah. Yeah. But now, today, it's different. They can get their status now, which is good.[20]

This Elder's emphasis on "you're on your own" is reflected in Kathleen Jamieson's comparison of the gendered nature of enfranchisement for men and women. According to her statistical analysis of the period 1965–1975, approximately 5 per cent of voluntary enfranchisement under the provisions of the Indian Act encompassed both men and women, while 95 per cent of enfranchisement came as a result of the Act's "marrying-out" policy. For those women and children, enfranchisement (i.e., becoming Canadian citizens) was overwhelmingly compulsory.[21] By contrast, Indigenous men wishing to be enfranchised had to demonstrate good character, education, and self-sufficiency. No such test existed for women who "married out" because the federal government considered their marriages to men without Indian status as sufficient requirement for assimilation.[22]

Such blatant gender discrimination inspired legal challenges and activism across Canada and internationally. It framed a story of feminism (although not necessarily named as such) in my own family history. My mother was one of the women reinstated under Bill C-31, along with my younger sister and me.

We were children at the time. I do not remember these debates, although I later became aware of the story as a teenager and university student. At this stage, I questioned how feminism (as it was usually defined in the Western sense) applied to this story, because it was never defined this way in my family history. Gender discrimination was at the heart of it, certainly, and there was an intense awareness that it was unfair legislation; however, the answer to it (as I understood it) was not feminist activism, but Indigenous women working to address inequality at the community level. It was about women, not necessarily about feminism. Given this personal history, I sought to understand what women at the time thought about women's community contributions and their relationship (if any) to feminism.

As in the literature, and in Lynn Abrams' chapter in this volume (Chapter 6), my participants did not easily connect with feminism. Perhaps these discussions could be more appropriately called reflections and remembrances of Indigenous women's roles in the community, with some people explicitly identifying actions as feminist, while others simply considered them a natural part of their roles as Anishinaabe kwewak. While I really wanted to ask about feminism—both the term itself and the acts associated with it—I was unsure how to raise the topic in my interviews. Aware from casual conversations that it could be a problematic term, the matter came up in my interview with Marella.

> LIANNE: Yeah . . . One question I did have. It's the other one I'm curious to know. There are a lot of differences in the way that Aboriginal women, the way we think of our roles and feminism.
>
> MARELLA: Right.
>
> LIANNE: Or if feminism is even a word that applies. I'm just curious what your thoughts are. What does feminism mean to you? Do you think that it applies to you or the women in your family?
>
> MARELLA: No.
>
> LIANNE: No.
>
> MARELLA: No, not really. Women are women and they do their role to what they know and what they were taught.
>
> LIANNE: Yeah.
>
> MARELLA: And to be feminist, I don't know.
>
> LIANNE: I doesn't . . . no . . .
>
> MARELLA: No, I'm a woman! [*Laughter.*]
>
> LIANNE: Yeah.
>
> MARELLA: That's it! And a strong woman, you know. I feel I'm a strong woman, and doing what we did when we were younger made us strong as a group.[23]

Marella's words reinforced what I had suspected: not all Indigenous women, regardless of how involved they are in activism in their communities, see the word "feminism" as appropriate. Of course, many do, including me, and discussions surrounding restorative justice and domestic violence underscore the need to include feminist perspectives. Still, Marella's words and my own stumblings underscore the challenge of labelling.[24] What Bonita Lawrence said about Indigenous womanhood and feminism in her conversation with Kim Anderson in *A Recognition of Being* resonates: "I find myself arguing anti-colonialism to feminism and feminism to traditionalists."[25] While some Indigenous women embrace "feminism" as a label, others, like Marella, see their community roles as women as sufficient to identify their strength. This does not mean that women's activism is unnecessary in our communities, but rather that there is work to be done to decolonize feminist discourse and reassert women's roles in our urban and reserve communities.

An understanding of Anishinaabe and more broadly Indigenous gender roles reflected around the world can move us beyond Western discussions of feminism and gender. Maori scholar Makere Stewart-Harawira writes about the force of Indigenous feminism against imperialism by positioning herself as a grandmother:

> And because it is my privilege to be the grandmother of six wonderful people, I further use this space to call for the voice of the grandmothers to be powerfully raised against systems of being that are founded in greed, consumptions and corruption as they impel our world yet further into the abyss of genocide and destruction, and to demonstrate in its place a political ontology of compassion, love and spirit as the only possible remedy, the only way forward.[26]

Other scholars have noted the importance of mothering in Indigenous feminism, and as extensions of that, the roles of Indigenous women in caring for Elders and children, and indeed for our communities as a whole.[27] Consider this exchange about food:

> ELDER: And [the Elder] used to make, you know, on the stove, she used to cut up, slice up potatoes and she'd put it on the stove, and when we came down from singing with the guitar and we were just saying goodnight, she'd call us in and she'd give us some of those potatoes that were burnt on the stove. [*Laughter.*] We really enjoyed that! It wasn't anything much, but we sure appreciated it. . . . And we used to get those wild potatoes and we'd take off the ends and just wash them in that creek and then eat them. Oh, they were good, you know? We had, in a way we had all healthy food. We had it from the garden; we had all the wild stuff. Every time somebody was sick, they'd go in the bush and look for their medicines and give it to you and you were better, you know.
>
> LIANNE : Yeah.
>
> ELDER: I says it's a lost art, really, because you got a sore stomach, "Oh, gotta go in the bush," Grandma says, and she makes a tea and then

we drink it and then we're fine. Anything. And everything. Whatever problems you had, you just went to the old folks and they got the medicines and we were better. But today, we hardly know what the medicines are about. That's what I was saying when they had the health fair. I says, "Well, you know," I says, "You've got everything here that's for the health fair, . . . but you haven't got the Native you know all the herbs from the bush." I says "That should have been set up there." I says, "Because that was way back when that was what we used to use and we don't know it."

LIANNE : No.

ELDER: Not now. Like, very little know it. And the ones that know it, like it was a past thing that people used to say it with their minds, you know, keep it in their minds and not write it down. Because if you write it down it was of no value.

LIANNE : Okay.

ELDER: But that's why they pass it on with speaking it out to their family. That's how they're supposed to bring up their family, and it eventually faded away. Whereas the parents used to say . . . it's like if you have deer meat or moose meat and you sell it, it's . . . You're not supposed to do that as Native people. You're supposed to give it, share it. So and that's what we used to do. When we had moose, we'd share the meat. Or a deer, or whatever, we shared. And that was the way we lived.[28]

This Elder found continuity in her own youth and the traditional teachings of the Anishinaabek about food, including sharing, hospitality, and community responsibility. Food and medicinal knowledge are intertwined, to be transmitted orally, and protected in community by members tasked with keeping it safe or sharing it when appropriate. As an Anishinaabe kwe, the Elder transmitted the land-based knowledge in our interview through Anishinaabek ways using her words and actions.

My narrators taught me that women participated in politics in various ways in the post-1945 period, providing a rich and necessary revision to our historical knowledge about Indigenous women. Typically, historical narratives focus on the political activities of Indigenous men, advancements in Indian Affairs policies, the federal franchise in 1960, and enhanced degrees of self-government. With few exceptions, we know little about the role of Indigenous women in these changes.[29] Marella shared with me childhood stories about women's political activism:

MARELLA : Like the Agneses were working with the Chief, which was Bill Meawasige. So his wife, and her friend. And when there would be meetings, their meetings would be at the house but the women would be there also. Not just the men.

LIANNE : Oh, okay. Like chief and council meetings, or . . .?

MARELLA : Well, I guess you could . . . because there was really no council.

LIANNE : Oh okay yeah.

MARELLA : But it was the chief, and so. And the Indian Affairs people would come and have their meeting with the chief. I remember because I was a little girl and I used to sit under the table at Mrs. Meawasige's house and listen to them but I was only young. I didn't really pay too much attention at that time but . . . [*Laughter.*] No, they would have a big meeting.

LIANNE : Okay.

MARELLA : At Bill's House.

LIANNE : Okay.

MARELLA : And they would talk about whatever needs to be talked about to be done for the reserve.

LIANNE : Um hm.

MARELLA : You know for the people.

LIANNE : Yeah.

MARELLA : All the Indian Agents would be there and all the yeah. That type of stuff. . . .

LIANNE : And would the women, if they were at these meetings, would they talk at these meetings?

MARELLA : Yes, they would.

LIANNE : And they would speak up?

MARELLA : Yeah.

LIANNE : Okay. Yeah.

MARELLA : Because they were part of it. Like, I don't think people realize that they were. That the—his wife and her friend—they were part of the Indian Agents and speaking up and how to run. It wasn't only Bill. Plus he had some councillors as it started going on. But they would have the meeting and they would be there.

LIANNE : Wow.

MARELLA : It's not like . . . Like, people think they weren't there, there was no people. No women allowed. But no, they were there. I know they were there because I was there. . . . [*Laughter.*] So nobody could tell me they weren't there because they were. 'Cause I was there. I say, I sat under the table while they were holding their meetings. You know, so, yeah. I remember those.[30]

Marella's memory of Chief and Council meetings highlights the political roles of women in the community, something that Band Council resolutions and Indian Agent correspondence from the time do not reveal. Furthermore, they point to the need to listen to men's and women's stories. As I documented in my work on the Homemakers' Club, the Indian Act did not allow for Anishinaabe kwewak to vote or run for office in reserve elections until 1951. Given that the women described above were either legally excluded from band politics or new to it, their involvement in these political discussions, their "speaking up" with powerful voices, drew instead on deeply rooted Anishinaabe traditions of gender complementarity.[31] While the Indian Act made Chief and Council male-dominated spheres, Marella's recollection reminds us that Anishinaabe kwewak had important and continuing governance roles.

Heeding the Elder's advice that opens this chapter, I also interviewed men about their experiences of growing up and being young adults in the community. When I asked Frank Lewis about women's political and community roles, he first honestly admitted that: "What I'm telling you right now, I'm not too familiar with the women. I know men, some men's [groups]—I used to belong to mostly."[32] Later in his interview, however, he emphasized Anishinaabe kwewak activism within the community, citing women's efforts to organize and fundraise for playground equipment and activities for children.[33] Gendered ideas of complementarity that sit outside Western gender binaries but nest comfortably within the Anishinaabek worldview shaped Frank's interview in other ways as well. This is particularly evident in his memories of the sulphuric acid plant that operated in SRFN from 1957 to 1963 as part of the Cold War uranium industry. He starts by recalling landing work at the plant:

> That was when I when I started work then. Before that, I was—let me tell you—my dad used to trap and we used to cut pulp. That's all we ever did in my life. Before that, before the acid plant came in. And then it started to change. I noticed the band here—the people themselves—most of them, you know. Not all of us worked at the plant. Just a bunch. Oh, maybe five or ten or something like that. That's all there was—that worked from here. But the change the way at home, at my place, we changed. The kids, you know, had food on the table. But I'm not saying we didn't have no food before, but we had wild meat and that's all we ever ate. But before and after that, it changed. And you could tell on the reserve that people that worked there, it all changed. It wasn't the same. And I used to play lots of ball. A lot of ball.[34]

It was clear that my question to Frank about his life in the 1950s and 1960s prompted memories of male youth in the community that tied together baseball and work at the Cutler Acid plant. A few minutes later, he returned to the topic of wage-earning, explaining the dangerous nature of plant work, and remembering lives now gone.

> FRANK: Yeah, and another thing I was gonna say about that . . . about when I worked at the plant. I'm just gonna change subjects there.
> LIANNE : Yeah.
> FRANK : When I worked at the plant the guys that I work with now, they're all gone. Every one of them. I don't know why, I don't know why it happened. It could be they all died of cancer.
> LIANNE : Um Hm. . . .

FRANK : [Driving a local route] That's what I was doing at the big plant here. But those boys I'm talking about, they all worked inside the plant. And I used to see them coming out at five o'clock, four o'clock. Gagging away, you know. Coughing, coughing. And I don't know, maybe that's the cause of it, I don't know.

LIANNE : Yeah. Oh, I'm sorry to hear that.

FRANK : Yeah, but getting back to playing ball, there. And those boys that I'm talking about, they're all gone over there now. Every one of them is pretty near laying in that graveyard that's there you know.[35]

Leisure activities, like baseball, stand out in Frank's memories of this time, as did his role in working at the plant. He also went on to describe the work he and others did as employees of SRFN to reclaim pow wow traditions, a form of anti-colonial activism. Frank's memories emphasize change in the roles of men, especially between his father's generation and his own and the importance of activism to identity reclamation.

Orval Commanda similarly focused on community roles and wage-earning both at the mines at Elliot Lake and in labour positions in Southern Ontario. When I asked him about community life, he recalled, "Well, in the 50s and the 60s I remember everybody worked, even the young ones, as soon as they started walking and could do something, you know. Either wash dishes, or carry wood, you know."[36] At the outset of our interview, Commanda emphasized that every person contributed to the wellbeing of the household. He continued to talk about work as he described working in Toronto after finishing school and then in mining at Elliot Lake. He then described the leisure activities in the community, including playing pool and baseball, attending dances, and working in recreation for SRFN.[37]

Through a discussion of interviews with Elders in my community, this chapter thereby contributes to a dialogue about Indigenous feminism and gender complementarity; it seeks to understand and recount Indigenous histories through Indigenous worldviews. Together, the stories of these four Elders emphasize life transitions, community activism, family connections, and the challenges of colonialism. The emphasis on wage-earning and community involvement in Frank and Orval's stories complement the memories of the women Elders who focused on their roles in family and community. Listening well to storytellers, especially when using an unstructured interview format, also means that knowledge holders can tell the stories that mean the most to them. Frank, for instance, stated outright that he did not feel it appropriate to share specific women's stories, but wanted instead to focus on his life experiences. Orval talked about gender balance in his own household growing up, where everyone had responsibilities. All four interviews highlight gender differences, but through a framework of complementarity rather than division. These Elders' stories also point to the impact of colonialism in politics and the economy. The Indian Act loomed large in the memories of the women, while mine work, both the better standard of living and the risky nature of the job, was a major theme for the men. Ultimately, the environmental impact of uranium mining also played a major role in the political activism of the men and women that I interviewed. Having heeded the direction from an Elder to reshape my original community project so that I listened to the voices of men as well as women, I engaged in interviews that made it clear that a complete story of activism and community in SRFN necessitated such an approach. The different things that Elders told me reflected their individuality and gifts as community members, but also their own gendered experiences.

Notes

1 I say "miigwetch" to the Elders who shared their recollections of growing up in Serpent River First Nation (SRFN) with me: Marella Schofield, Frank Lewis, Orval Commanda, and an Elder who wishes to remain unnamed. I thank Janice Gamble, who spread the word at Elder Tea, and helped shape the interview questions and shared them in advance. I acknowledge the support of a SSHRC Insight Development Grant.
2 Anonymous, interview with author, SRFN, 21 May 2014. Unless otherwise noted, the interviews were conducted by me. I have respected this Elder's wish not to be identified, but acknowledge that, typically, we honor the expertise of Indigenous knowledge holders by identifying them. Note that I have informed consent to use the names of other narrators. For an overview of complementarity and decolonization in Indigenous gender studies, see Leah Sneider, "Complementary Relationships: A Review of Indigenous Gender Studies," in *Indigenous Men and Masculinities: Legacies, Identities, Regeneration*, eds. Kim Anderson and Robert Alexander Innes (Winnipeg: University of Manitoba Press, 2015), 62–79.
3 Indigenous communities and nations are gender diverse and include two spirit peoples; however, the Elders interviewed for this project identified as women and men.
4 For more on Indigenous men's experiences see Kim Anderson and Robert Alexander Innes, eds., *Indigenous Men and Masculinities: Legacies, Identities, Regeneration* (Winnipeg: University of Manitoba Press, 2015).
5 On SRFN's relationship to the uranium industry see Lianne C. Leddy, "Cold War Colonialism: Serpent River First Nation and Uranium Mining, 1953–1988," (PhD diss., Wilfrid Laurier University, 2011); "Interviewing Nookomis and Other Reflections of an Indigenous Historian," *Oral History Forum d'histoire orale* 30 (Special Issue 2010): 1–18; "Poisoning the Serpent: Uranium Exploitation and the Serpent River First Nation, 1953–1988," in *The Nature of Empires and the Empires of Nature*, ed. Karl Hele (Waterloo: Wilfrid Laurier University Press, 2013), 125–147. Community-based histories include Lorraine Reckmans, Keith Lewis, and Anabel Dwyer, eds., *This is My Homeland: Stories of the Effects of Nuclear Industries by People of the Serpent River First Nation and the North Shore of Lake Huron* (Serpent River First Nation, 2003); Janice Gamble and Elder Tea, *Connected to the Land: Stories from the Serpent's Band* (Serpent River First Nation, 2013).
6 Lianne C. Leddy, "Mostly Just a Social Gathering: Anishinaabe Kwewak and the Indian Homemakers' Club, 1945–1960," in *Aboriginal History: A Reader*, 2nd edition, eds. Kristin Burnett and Geoff Read (Toronto: Oxford University Press, 2016), 352–363; Katherine Magee, "For Home and Country: Education, Activism and Agency in Alberta Native Homemakers' Clubs, 1942–1970," *Native Studies Review* 18, no. 2 (2009): 27–49; Aroha Harris and Mary Jane Logan McCallum, "'Assaulting the Ears of Government': The Indian Homemakers' Club and the Maori Women's Welfare League in their Formative Years," in *Indigenous Women and Work: From Labour to Activism*, ed. Carol Williams (Urbana: University of Illinois Press, 2012), 225–239.

7 Here I use the term as described in Maile Arvin, Eve Tuck, and Angie Morrill, "Decolonizing Feminism: Challenging Connections Between Settler Colonialism and Heteropatriarchy," *Feminist Formations* 25, no. 1 (Spring 2013): 8–34.

8 Joyce Green, "Taking Account of Aboriginal Feminism," in *Making Space for Indigenous Feminism*, ed. Joyce Green (Black Point, NS and Winnipeg, MB: Fernwood, 2007), 21.

9 Jean Barman, "Indigenous Women and Feminism on the Cusp of Contact," in *Indigenous Women and Feminism: Politics, Activism, Culture*, eds. Cheryl Suzack, Shari M. Huhndorf, Jeanne Perreault, and Jean Barman (Vancouver: University of British Columbia Press, 2010), 92–108.

10 Verna St. Denis, "Feminism is for Everybody: Aboriginal Women, Feminism, and Diversity," in *Making Space*, 37.

11 Mariana Valverde, *The Age of Light, Soap, and Water: Moral Reform in English Canada, 1885–1925*, 2nd edition (University of Toronto Press, 2008), 60–61; Karen Stote, *An Act of Genocide: Colonialism and the Sterilization of Aboriginal Women* (Blackpoint, NS and Winnipeg, MB: Fernwood, 2015), 21–27. Angus MacLaren estimates that in Alberta, "Indians and Métis, who represented only 2.5 per cent of Alberta's population, accounted for over 25 per cent of those sterilized." See *Our Own Master Race: Eugenics in Canada, 1885–1945* (Toronto: Oxford University Press, 1990), 160.

12 Janet Silman, *Enough is Enough: Aboriginal Women Speak Out* (Toronto: Women's Press, 1987), 13. Also see Heather A. Howard in this volume (Chapter 25).

13 A piece of Canadian federal legislation that has been in effect since 1876, the Indian Act has defined who is an "Indian" based on blood quota, and defines the rights and citizenship limitations of status Indians in Canada. For more details, see Indigenous and Northern Affairs Canada, accessed 15 August 2016, http://laws-lois.justice.gc.ca/eng/acts/i-5/.

14 While scholars have paid more attention to this period, and to now well-known women like Mary Two-Axe Earley, Jeannette Corbiere-Lavell, Sandra Lovelace, and Yvonne Bedard, Indigenous women have been active in this area since the 19th century.

15 Joanne Barker, "Gender, Sovereignty, and the Discourse of Rights in Native Women's Activism," *Meridians* 7, no. 1 (2006): 148.

16 Silman, 1987.

17 Katrina Srigley's work with Anishinaabe kwewak women in Northern Ontario has outlined the politics of Indigenous identity and the power of reclamation following Bill C-31: "'I am a proud Anishinaabekwe': Issues of Identity and Status in Northern Ontario after Bill C-31," in *Finding a Way to the Heart: Feminist Writings on Aboriginal and Women's History in Canada*, eds. Jarvis Brownlie and Valerie Korinek (University of Manitoba Press, 2012), 241–266.

18 Marella Schofield, interview, SRFN, 16 May 2014.

19 Schofield, interview.

20 Elder, interview.

21 Kathleen Jamieson, *Indian Women and the Law in Canada: Citizens Minus* (Ottawa: Minister of Supply and Services Canada, 1978), 63–64.

22 Jamieson, 63.

23 Schofield, interview. On Indigenous women and community strength, see Kim Anderson and Bonita Lawrence, eds., *Strong Women Stories: Native Vision and Community Survival* (Toronto: Sumach Press, 2003).

24 See Kim Anderson, *A Recognition of Being: Reconstructing Native Womanhood* (Toronto: Sumach Press, 2000); Kim Anderson, "Affirmations of an Indigenous Feminist," in *Indigenous Women and Feminism*, 81–91. On sexual violence and restorative justice, see Tina Beads with Rauna Kuokkanen, "Aboriginal Feminist

Action on Violence Against Women," in *Making Space*; Andrea Smith, *Conquest: Sexual Violence and American Indian Genocide* (Durham: Duke University Press, 2005).

25 Anderson, *A Recognition of Being*, 275.

26 Makere Stewart-Harawira, "Practicing Indigenous Feminism: Resistance to Imperialism," in *Making Space*, 127.

27 Jeannette Corbiere and D. Memee Lavell-Harvard, eds., *Until Our Hearts Are on the Ground: Aboriginal Mothering, Oppression, Resistance and Rebirth* (Toronto: Demeter Press, 2006); Kim Anderson and D. Memee Lavell-Harvard, *Mothers of the Nations: Indigenous Mothering as Global Resistance, Reclaiming, and Recovery* (Bradford: Demeter Press, 2014).

28 Elder, interview.

29 On Elsie Knott, Canada's first female Indian Act Chief, see Cora Voyageur, *Firekeepers of the Twenty-First Century* (Montréal and Kingston: McGill-Queen's University Press, 2008).

30 Schofield, interview.

31 Leddy, "Mostly Just a Social Gathering," 356.

32 Frank Lewis, interview, SRFN, 16 May 2014.

33 Lewis, interview.

34 Lewis, interview.

35 Lewis, interview.

36 Orval Commanda, interview, SRFN, 19 May 2014.

37 Commanda, interview.

8 Living, archiving, and reflecting on feminism and activism in India

An oral history with Uma Chakravarti[1]

Ponni Arasu and Uma Chakravarti

Uma Chakravarti is a distinguished historian of India who has produced groundbreaking scholarship on Buddhism, caste, and gender as well as being a leading figure in the Indian women's movement. A long-time civil rights activist, she has written extensively on contemporary issues. More recently, she has been documenting the history of feminist activism in India through an oral archive of videotaped interviews and through film-making. Her *Fragments of a Past* (2010) on the activist Mythily Sivaraman powerfully explores the themes of personal and historical memory. A feminist "foremother" who both makes history and archives it in various forms, Uma herself is an ideal oral history subject. As a considerably younger Indian queer feminist activist and theater practitioner researching the Indian women's movement, I have been interviewing Uma. For me, Uma is a respected scholar, inspiring activist, beloved elder, and friend of more than fifteen years. Documenting her life history is at its core a form of activist oral history. I carry out this project, only fragments of which appear here, conscious of my role as a feminist activist of my generation who, like Uma, has chosen to be politically involved in multiple ways and across different social and political movements. This, then, is about doing oral history that can inform and sustain cross-generational and contemporary forms of feminist activism.[2]

Drawing on two lengthy interviews, this chapter highlights three intertwined themes in Uma's narrative: her politicization within the context of traumatic events that exposed the stark limitations of the post-Independence Indian state, the multivalent character of her activism, and a political praxis that simultaneously fostered movement building and the archiving of those movements.[3] This oral history also constitutes a critical archive that slides temporally. Notwithstanding the age difference, Uma's and my continuous involvement in feminist and civil rights activism, research, and art-making makes us contemporaries. That our conversations are influenced as much by that relationship as our inter-generational one reflects our membership in an Indian feminist culture that is rooted in respectful but non-hierarchical and irreverent cross-generational relationships and solidarities. As I document and analyze Uma's life, I also *do*[4] my own history—that of the women's and civil rights movements, of feminist historical research, and feminist archiving practices. In its dance across time, this oral history is additionally grounded in history, enabling us to collapse time and envision futures of feminisms, individually and collectively. It makes for a vibrant politics whose unfettered imagination is *grounded* in its history but is *not bound* by it.[5]

Teachers' movement, civil rights, women's rights

When I first asked Uma to tell me about her work in the civil rights movement and the women's movement and how she saw the connection between that and her academic work, she responded: "My own trajectory was that I was in the teachers' movement before I went into the civil rights movement in the late 1970s and early 1980s. And it is only from the civil rights movement that I go on into the women's movement."[6]

During the interviews, Uma recalled—usually with little or no prompting from me—episodes in her transformation from a young left-oriented but not yet activist lecturer at Miranda House, the premier woman's college at Delhi University, into an activist scholar involved in the movement for democratic rights and then the women's movement. As she recalled through vividly told stories that cannot be fully reproduced here, Uma possessed "a broad democratic sympathy for people's movements and for radical change" when she was hired at Miranda House in 1966. From a year spent living in a village in Rajasthan state with her sociologist husband Anand in 1964, she learned from personal experience about "the stark workings" of caste and gender in rural communities. She recalled being assigned a male "fictive relation" to act as her "protector" because "it was well known that husbands troubled their wives!" She remembered the "furor" that broke out in their village over news that Anand had not only "gone into" a settlement of Dalits—who belong to the lowest of castes (formerly called Untouchables)—but broke food taboos by drinking their milk. Her memory of witnessing the restrictive practice of purdah (women's seclusion) was conveyed through the juxtaposition of two contradictory images: the "bizarre" moving-screen effect created by the women who, to stay covered in public, walked alongside a white sheet; and the opposite one of women stripping off the fancy "tinseled" garments donned for a festival, exposing their bodies but protecting their outfits from the rain.[7] But her transformation into activist really occurred in the political context in Delhi in the late 1960s and early 1970s, overlapping her career at Miranda House. As the following excerpt illustrates, her narrative is punctuated by memories that evoke the heady atmosphere of the era:

> If I look back on my early years as a teacher of history at Miranda House between 1967 and 1975—really the starting point of my intellectual and political growth—I think I was fully absorbed with what was going on

with students who are either in my class or hanging around the corridors and catching you as you pass by.[8] One day a young student told me about her family, a molestation which she can't tell others about. This relationship with students is building up, as I am fairly young, and we have a lively relationship in class—we talk about all sorts of things whether it's formally in the course or not! . . . And I think we all are broadly sympathetic to the unresolved questions of the national movement—post-independence failures and the land question that the Naxalites had raised.[9] In fact, the slogan "*yeh azadi jhooti hai, desh ki janta bhooki hai*" ("this freedom is false, the people of the country are hungry still") had been a slogan among the left from 1947 onwards, but it was much sharper in 1967 as that was twenty years after independence and yet sharp inequalities had remained.[10] The land grab movement of the socialists had taken place in the early 1960s, so the land question is strikingly on the mental horizon, and when the students were going underground, or living in the villages, to help conscientize the peasants, we shared their idealism. Roma Mitra, my senior colleague, a socialist, was fully into politics and . . . I am talking to her about Indian politics and its contradictions. One girl in my college also went underground and caused quite a stir . . . In 1974, a close family member returned from England all radicalized, parked his bags with us [she and Anand], and went on to do various other things . . . So the movement was all around us.[11]

Uma's narrative, of her growing involvement in the radical teachers' movement at Delhi University, which she remembered as "a very, very active" campus already in the late 60s, even if "we were then armchair discussants," underscores a critical theme of her narrative: the *fluid and mutually reinforcing* links between the personal, the intellectual, and the political:

We had the Delhi University Discussion Society (DUDS!), in which the left played a big role. The university teachers started it, including the legendary political science teacher Randhir Singh. While normally the students would try and escape from attending classes, his would be full with no room to even stand outside in the corridors. He taught the stodgy syllabus he was given, "From Plato to Rousseau," but taught it all via Marx, which was not given to him to teach because he was a communist. I also remember reading the radical piece by Mythily Sivaraman on the killings of Dalit agricultural laborers in Venmani, Tamilnadu in 1969. There were a lot of sympathetic ML [Marxist-Leninist] types at Delhi, NRIs [non-resident Indians] monitoring and supporting democratic activities, producing publications. I read a piece by Mythily and was very struck by it. This was even before the horrible and casteist judgment came, which let off the killers on the grounds that gentlemen farmers would not kill![12] The ML movement that sent off people like the labor historian Dilip Simeon underground, into the villages, had its resonance even in Miranda House. We had a student who was quite actively engaged with the Naxalites. The MH auditorium was sometimes used by outside [activists] and by [left] students and teachers in the university. We would have plays which were very leftist and quite interesting. People like Maya Rao and Anuradha Kapoor, both of whom became significant theater people, were in MH, transforming the theater scene in the college quite dramatically. In Delhi, you had a very active, almost volatile, students' movement with a strong socialist component [that] was closely linked to the Lohiates, who spearheaded a very important movement at that stage for teaching and evaluation in Hindi (as opposed to exclusively in English) in the university . . .[13]

In the 1970s, there was a major case of violence against peasants in Bihar in a village of Santhals, an Indigenous community that has fought for their rights to the lands they had cultivated for generations as tenants. In the accounts of this case, we got to know about the way women are complicit in reproducing class and caste inequality. A group of men from the dominant Rajput community, local landlords, fired into *tola* (a settlement) wherein fourteen to fifteen Santhal women and children were killed in a dispute over their rights as sharecroppers. The attack itself had been preceded by the women of the Rajput households challenging their menfolk, saying: "What kind of men are you? You can't even 'police' these characters, keep them under control." It was the second major killing following an agrarian dispute in post-independence India. All around us, agrarian relationships became crucial to our understanding of society. So was caste, although in lived practice, we had not had caste experiences as it was *invisibilized* to many urban people, especially if they married across caste, as we [Uma and Anand] had done . . .[14]

And in 1971, the Bangladesh war happened. Nandita Haksar, who became a courageous human rights lawyer, was a student of mine . . . She dragged me to a demonstration on Bangladesh, and then we give blood. I faint after it. She gets up and marches off quite energetically—quite hilarious it was. We [MH teachers] share this bond with students, who were actually very active and *engaged* politically. A democratic teacher couldn't stand outside of what they were doing . . . questioning and resistance, the microcosm of the university reflecting the macrocosm of India . . . The Delhi University Teachers Association was also especially active. So you had this sense of there being a discussion space in the university. In these years before the Emergency [1975–1977], the state was increasingly being regarded as lacking legitimacy. It had failed to deliver on its promises, radical transformation had not taken place; you could actually sense this disappointment and disillusionment with "Independence": political independence but nothing more.[15]

As our conversation developed, I asked Uma to reflect on her emergence as a feminist. In response, she noted an early campaign against a beauty contest, but also that this, like other actions helping to lay the groundwork for a post-Independence women's movement, was quickly overtaken by The Emergency period (discussed below). She also stressed that for her feminist consciousness grew in tandem with other forms of political activism:

The 70s—1974 perhaps—some discussions of feminism were already happening in Miranda House . . . Nandita Haksar, whom I see as a very important feminist, was also a very strong civil rights activist. I don't think people saw themselves as divided [into separate movements]. Civil and democratic rights and feminist issues were going on simultaneously in the lives of many of us women. I often said, when I am in the civil rights camp, I go plead the cause of gender. And when you're sitting in the women's movement, you talk about civil rights and the repressive state . . . You have a foot in both camps—you can't actually separate them, I think . . .

The Miss Miranda contest generated some critical questioning around questions of gender in a sort of pre-formulated sense, thinking around patriarchy . . . without calling it patriarchy maybe at that stage. The woman's question was being articulated as an independent axis even though they were not giving it that language I think. It's the time when Urvashi Butalia [co-founder of the women's press Kali For Women] and Nandita Haksar were students at Miranda House . . . They got involved in thinking about stereotyping women into objects: canons of beauty were being questioned. One of the issues was, "Are you saying that the woman who works on the roadside, stone-quarry worker, whatever, who was part of the rhetoric of the national movement, is not beautiful? My mother, who is aging and has lines on her face, she's not beautiful?" Interestingly, the divide was between the trendy English-speaking honors students versus the "behenjis," the provincial, Hindi speakers . . . who [provided] the grassroots support for abolishing Miss Miranda . . . as a very elite, rubbishy contest that should just be dumped. And it was successfully done . . .

However, that was a history that got aborted during the Emergency because *that* crisis was of a totally different order. So the women's question may have surfaced in different parts spontaneously and got sidetracked by the larger issue of the whole nation going under a repressive regime. Later, I think, there were various kinds of interventions that had to be made. But for me in Delhi, the cathartic moment [in raising her feminist consciousness] was following the Emergency . . . If you go back to the early writings in the feminist journal *Manushi*, you might find an interesting piece written by the *Manushi* collective which was quite brilliant; it said that women don't need an emergency, they're in a permanent emergency. They don't have a right to speak, they don't have a right to mobility; they don't have a right to all the things that were challenged during 1975 to 1977. Controlled and under surveillance all the time, so what is the big deal! The article was almost mocking the Emergency; it is not that they weren't involved with resisting the Emergency, but . . . it was quite an interesting [feminist] formulation. I often use it in sessions with students, with groups of people.[16]

Uma's recollection of early feminist rumblings led her to immediately recollect the Emergency Period (1975–1977). Like many from her generation of Indian leftists, the highly repressive era ushered in by Prime Minister Indira Gandhi's unilateral declaration of a state of national emergency, one that witnessed the suspension of elections and civil liberties and a mass sterilization campaign, was tremendously important to Uma's narrative of politicization. As the following excerpt suggests, the intertwined themes of personal and political outrages and traumas profoundly inform her memory of these years. Indeed, it is in these passages of her narrative when Uma appears at her most vulnerable. The Emergency is a founding moment: as the scale of the horror of the repression sunk in, her resolve also thickened, making her determined to "keep going," both personally and politically. The interplay of emotion and intention that deeply informs Uma's life story is evidenced here in her memory of the founding of key civil rights organizations in the aftermath of The Emergency:

The Emergency became a cathartic moment in our lives, and increasingly so at Delhi University, because a large number of teachers were picked up and put in jail. The press was censored. It's quite an extraordinary moment. A number of those arrested at Delhi University were supposedly right-wingers, but the university was the heart of the place where dissent was being articulated in multiple ways. The fact that the university space was actually lost to us as a place of debate was deeply felt by us. All elections to any university body came to an end. Student elections ended and instead you had nominated student bodies. The [apolitical] festival culture, which I *abhorred* as a teacher, can be traced back to the Emergency and post-Emergency—cultural festivals [replacing] the [earlier] political debates.[17]

It was a *terrible* time. I remember feeling in a state of permanent, complete depression. I mean, what have we come to? You couldn't speak in class because of this panic rumor of informers and so on. After a while, I think we got so furious with this induced state of fear that we began challenging it. My students and I were being just anarchically subversive, sitting in the class saying whatever we wanted because we couldn't allow our lives to be completely taken over . . . And then of course the Emergency inexplicably came to its own logical—or illogical—end.

Demonstrations were so common in those days; one had gone to hundreds of demonstrations before and after the Emergency. But one of the best demonstrations was at the end of the Emergency, when thousands of people from Delhi University came out for this march through the campus. Then a *big* meeting was held at 35 Ferozeshah Road—the big auditorium that was the scene of so many amazing meetings, but is now a horrible car park that has physically erased so much history. I can still remember that meeting—that auditorium jam-packed with thousands of people. Some people had come from Bombay University, which had experienced the Emergency in very powerful ways: the students from the Department of Sociology had spent time in jail. So there was this big civil rights meeting, and then the PUCL [People's Union for Civil Liberties] and PUDR [the Delhi-based People's Union for Democratic Rights] was formed at that stage.

Sudesh Vaid [a civil rights activist] . . . was there. We had been active in challenging the Delhi University Amendment Bill, which . . . said that [the authorities] could throw out a teacher for "good and sufficient reason" to be defined later on by ordinance. They didn't even have to press charges against the teacher . . . For two months, we held a very militant campaign and, finally, that bill was allowed to lapse . . . But the Emergency came thereafter and that was for the whole nation! Everybody who vaguely had an ounce of democratic sentiment in them was at that big meeting. And we were all then part of PUCL and PUDR: at that time, it was the [combined] PUCL&DR, and that's how it began. Over a period of time, fact-finding was one way we would participate in civil rights work. We used the university space to hold meetings . . . Anand Patwardhan's 1978 documentary *Prisoners of Conscience* was shown in Miranda House.[18] I was on study leave, but had organized it. And the principal said, "Uma, you should just settle down and do your research work." She was basically telling me, don't be involved in "politics," but this was the kind of atmosphere that we had at that stage . . .

As a feminist who has researched the topic of sexual violence, I am well aware of the role that cases of custodial rape (rape perpetrated by state agents such as the police and security forces) have played in feminist mobilizations in India.[19] This prompted me to ask Uma why *she* thought the Mathura case—the 1972 rape of a Dalit girl by two policemen in a police station in the Chandrapur district of Maharashtra, and the legal case that dragged on into the early 1980s—became "a trigger for a new phase of the women's movement in post-Independence India." Uma's reply captures the outrage that followed the Supreme Court's acquittal of the accused on the grounds that the girl was "habituated" to sexual intercourse. Interpreting the mere presence of a torn hymen as constituting voluntary consent on the girl's part, the court determined that, under such circumstances, only sexual intercourse, not rape, could be proved. The subsequent protests eventually led to some amendments in India's rape law. Uma's recollection of this controversial case underscores the overlapping analyses and activisms in which she grounded her feminist politics. Her utter contempt for the courts' use of the "two fingers" virginity test (checking for the presence of an intact hymen) to determine rape cases is as palpable on the page as it was in our interview:

It became the trigger to start examining issues of women's right to not be subjected to violence and sexual violence, that's the backdrop. Because the Indian women's movement was at that point strongly influenced by the left—a lot of the early autonomous women's movement had come out of the left—their anger was about women's issues not being given their due . . . and their not being regarded as capable of creating theory, or even actually holding an argument . . . the classic situation of women not being regarded as anything more than cadres, or supporters. Also, in a sense, class oppression is the wider backdrop, in which you look at the vulnerable, marginal woman, and rape is regarded as . . . an institutional form of dominance. That's also very much there in the post-Emergency period and this acts as a flashpoint for a large-scale mobilization. There's also a generation of women who are coming back to [political activism after the Emergency], who are truly different from the generation of their mothers [who were politicized in the earlier anti-colonial, nationalist context]. The [younger women] became politicized between 1969 and 1979; they've had ten years of thinking, and in between has come the terrible Emergency . . . The fact that the most marginal in this period are, or could be, the Adivasi [Indigenous] women is what triggers the mobilization around Mathura.

We must also put together the context of encounter killings, where young people were picked up, taken to a forest, and then shot in cold blood—that happened to ML movement cadres— and the issue of custodial rape. So, now, you have a different understanding of the state and, therefore, when you think about rape or sexual violence, you're not going to think about it simply in the context of the middle-class woman who's protected by her class and caste. You will see as outrageous the violation of the most marginal sections of society. And, then, because the judgment articulated this in the grossest of those terms, it allows you to conceptualize, very powerfully at that moment, the nature of the institutionalized form of violence [against women] perpetrated by state agencies.

This [thinking] is also happening in the West, but also something to consider in the subcontinental context as state power is particularly brutal here; the poor and the vulnerable are squashed completely . . . It is most creative on [the feminists'] part to not "look at" sexual violence per se in public spaces, but to turn it into something which is custodial rape. That's the extraordinary move they're making because they're actually talking about the *thana*, the police station, as a place where a woman would be most vulnerable. And who is going to get raped there except the poorest and most marginal? So, in that sense, I think the women's movement in India, despite the criticism of the Dalit movement and Dalit feminists, has been actually fairly close to the Indigenous soil from which it has sprung, at least in its initial phase. It has not looked for theory from outside. We have responded to situations, have been able to see women in disaggregated terms even though we may have claimed a sort of universal "sisterhood"

. . . and said all women are subjected to rape.[20] I think the specific issues have been very strongly determined by the nature of the contradictions in our society, and, therefore, custodial rape [of a marginalized woman] was the trigger for thinking about sexual violence . . .

The Nagpur women's movement first picks up the Mathura case. Seema Sakhare, who was in Nagpur, is a lawyer, and she's monitoring that case to start with. And then after the Supreme Court judgment, there is the outrage experienced by the lawyers in Delhi, who write the 1979 Open Letter to the Chief Justice of India[21] [protesting the concept of consent used]. And then the Open Letter was converted into a petition . . . so the Supreme Court sort of reviewed that judgment but upheld it. That was really outrageous. But while that happened, there was so much public pressure that had been generated and mounted on the streets, even in Delhi.

See, the civil rights movement has come into existence by then . . . so there is a playing out of the forces that come together, creating that moment of resistance. And that's why the police *thana* is so central . . . it is the space of the state, it's so called institutional apparatus, which is the very site of the actual violation. So people may say it or not, but that's underpinning the sense of outrage that is generated. And there's equal outrage against the judges, who are such morons that they don't have a sense of the context. They're actually dumping these stupid middle-class norms upon this girl because she had a boyfriend and she was supposed to be a chaste woman to get the protection of the courts! And in every damn situation of the Indian criminal legal system, they'll do that rubbishy two-finger test. And [if] two fingers easily pass, that means the woman/girl is habituated to sex. This habitualé category is an important part of the thinking of the Indian legal system at that time. And it's outrageous. So I think I can't see this as anything but a post-Emergency moment. Remember that the Emergency is that big bad thing that has happened, which has actually stripped the state of its legitimacy . . . The encounter killings, the Tarkunde Commission which highlighted these killings, has happened. So it's a moment that we should factor into the writing of the Mathura story. We shouldn't just declare it linearly—that there was the Open Letter, then boom, the women's movement is born! In reality, it was a much more complicated moment.

Keen to explore further the complex and overlapping relationship between the civil rights and women's movements, I asked Uma why the 1984 *Inside Family*, the main fact-finding report on dowry murders (women were burnt to death for not bringing a dowry to the marriage) was written by members of the civil rights organization PUDR, and not by a women's group.[22] In response, Uma recalled how fact-finding missions, the tool of human rights activists, became central to feminist mobilizations in India in the 1980s, with Sudesh Vaid, a feminist civil rights activist first playing a key role. Uma also expressed her frustration over the inability of the women's movement to develop a stronger critique of custodial rape at this time, something she attributes to an "over-investment" in the nation state.[23]

> Let's remember that the only real and proper documentation is happening through the connection of a woman activist, Sudesh Vaid, who has got half a foot in the women's movement and one-and-one-half feet in the democratic rights movement. Fact-finding or fact-reporting is a notion that is coming from democratic rights groups, not from women's groups . . . While the reports are being done we are also formulating *conceptually* our understanding of custodial state violence. Even so, the army, especially its role in the Northeast, was not being looked into, in terms of custodial rape. It's a very strange moment in the history of the Indian women's movement, limited by its inability to understand that there is a parallel and more heightened way in which custodial rape has been happening in other areas. How will we look at the army man who is there to "protect" the territory under his control, but in reality is actually unleashing this kind of violence upon women?
>
> In the late 1980s, the Oinam [fact-finding] Report came. Oinam is in the Ukhrul district in Manipur, where security forces (Assam Rifles) attacked the Naga villages. There were accounts of sexual violence and disappearances.[24] The Oinam Report is the beginning of women's groups going out and doing fact-finding in the conflict-ridden Northeast, and it was put together by Nandita Haksar. By then she had her law degree, and it is the first time an all-women's team is going for fact-finding. They found so much direct evidence of the army's atrocities, and yet two members on the team did not sign the report, [saying] "How can we indict the army which protects us?" So, the notion of custodial violence does not [lead them] to question the national security apparatus. I have held that the Indian women's movement has been overinvested in the idea of the nation state. Only a few of us can say that we pushed the idea of custodial violence to other areas where there were struggles for self-determination, especially in the Northeast and Jammu and Kashmir, since the birth of the nation in 1947–48.[25]

Since Uma's recollections of the multiple sites on which she enacted her politics in these years downplayed her scholarship, I asked about "logistics"— a question significant to activist academics, but particularly those who are women. How did she juggle the demands of political and scholarly work, the latter of which involved reading Buddhist texts in Pali (a classical language) for her first academic book? Knowing, too, that activism and scholarship often exist as separate and mutually inaccessible worlds, the relations between them deeply hierarchized, I also asked how she managed to "disseminate" her scholarly research among activists as well as scholars. This prompted an exchange that sheds further light on Uma's intertwined self-identify as a historian/activist.

UMA: I think, fairly early on, to write on gender was linked up to the fact that it had to be accessible. In all my writing thereafter I have had this debt, this compulsion that it has to be understandable. Also, as a person, I am not someone who goes into some convoluted language. I am a historian. The archive or the text is my material . . . it is something that I read from, read off from, read into, and extract. But always it has to have this rootedness in terms of how am I analyzing it, bringing it up, and how people will respond to it . . .

I'll give you an example of the Ramayana piece that I took to a conference in Warangal in 1982.[26] At this conference, there was lively discussion on texts and how they change over time. Outside the formal conference, I did an evening session on that paper with the women activists of the Chattisgarh Mukti Morcha in Hindi so that they can understand.[27] And we get a very interesting reaction because the women partly identify with Sita but . . . the oppression of Sita is also over the top as far as they are concerned . . . But they are very interested in changes in the narrative line over many texts across a number of centuries and get the political point that texts are not static. My activism . . . has something to do with my persona. I am not someone who can actually compartmentalize much . . . You are responding to the challenge of your times. So it is one way in which you live. You are in the teachers' movement, the civil rights movement, whatever. And you go for fact-finding and to demonstrations and then back to the classroom!

PONNI: In the process of living like this, do you think there is a certain sustained-ness to involvement in different things?

UMA: There were few options for someone like me: first, the Emergency happened, and then the follow-up of the Emergency. Then 1984 happens, the killings of Sikhs.[28] That is a dramatic moment, a shift. This idea of a distinct academic self and a political self, or feminist self . . . is nonsensical. The civil rights movement in the late 70s and early 80s fully occupies me. The first fact-finding that I ever did was for the PUDR in 1983, when we went off to investigate the tragedy of the coal miners, a people's mine run as a cooperative by marginalized indigenous people of the Saharjori area in Bihar that faced state violence.[29]

I travelled to Bihar and spent a long time there and it became an incredible experience, because while we are fact-finding into the state's actions against the coal miners we are told that . . . we have to investigate an agrarian struggle in Jahanabad for *Gairmazarua*, the common lands, launched by those who were landless. There had been an assault on a village and people had been beaten up . . . And I meet Harnandan, a Dalit agricultural laborer who takes a shine to me because I am this woman who has walked a long way to do this fact-finding along with Subba Rao, who is very active in the PUDR and had been in jail during the Emergency. And because he thinks I can't now walk back, he commandeers a cycle rickshaw which he doesn't know how to drive, puts me into it, and off we go to end up in a ditch. I can see and hear him even now . . . but have never met him again.[30]

A very specific example of the intertwined nature of Uma's political and scholarly life is that her first two books, one an activist-based oral history, *The Delhi Riots: Three Days in the Life of a Nation* (1987), and the other, a scholarly study based on ancient texts, *Social Dimensions of Early Buddhism* (1987), came out at the same time.[31] The former became the subject of an energetic exchange. It was triggered by my asking Uma about the effort to document the stories of the survivors of the 1984 carnage against the Sikhs in Delhi. I asked specifically about this project because it has struck me as an especially potent moment when her role as historian, archivist, and civil rights and feminist activist all came together, a defining moment when historical/archival rigor was being employed for explicitly activist purposes. In reflecting on the politically dangerous work of carefully documenting the brutality of the violence (4000 Sikhs were killed in Delhi and Kanpur mainly) and state impunity (exemption from punishment) through oral histories, Uma reflected on the principle of creating an archive of the massacre and on how that history interacts with the present. I began by asking what happened to the recordings:

UMA: The recordings are still sitting with me. I hid them at the time because we were being targeted for the work we were doing. I had to actually hide them somewhere. But I recovered them and I still have people's testimonies on those tapes. The bulk of them were transcribed. Some were unpublished because it just became too much. And we put our own money into the publishing . . . We published the interviews exactly as they were!

PONNI: Transcribed?

UMA: Transcribed, including the oohs and the aahs [*laughter*] and we were criticized for that. But we wanted *the feel* of the interview to come through rather than to turn it into a sanitized version of the actual interaction that was happening between us.

PONNI: In English?

UMA: I translated all the Punjabi ones [into English].

PONNI: Your Punjabi was that good?

UMA: It was quite good.[32] My students too got involved in the transcription. So we had this 1000-page manuscript which finally came out as a 650-page book. One decision that we took was to publish the interviews as they were and we would not mediate the voices of the people. It was meant to be an archive, a published archive, not a book written by us which *interpreted* the experiences of people. All we did was write a long contextualizing introduction . . . that covers

Operation Blue Star . . . and the Sikh question, and up to the moment of the violence and how some of us got involved at that point.[33]

That [involvement] also meant that I have never gone off the 1984 question; it comes up in certain ways even today. Every time you take a taxi and you have a Sikh taxi driver you actually get into this conversation: "So where were you in '84?" and they start telling you. The most amazing thing about the unexpectedness of archiving is my recent experience related to 1984. As you know, I've been making a film on women political prisoners. And since 2013, I have been trying to get to this extraordinary woman, Nirpreet Kaur, who was 16 or 17 when her father was killed and she saw [it]. She named the killers. She was hounded for that and went on to become a militant herself. She ended up in jail. And now I get to know that she is my taxi driver's sister—how extraordinary and wonderful is that?!

So, when she next came to Delhi from Punjab she seemed to be much more open to me, and we started the interview, and she's quite a storyteller. I did one interview with her and she went on and on and we only started with the Partition. So I said, okay, now we have to do another one. And we did another and we aren't anywhere near done! The oral history archive, Women in Resistance Movements, continues to be compiled and will feed into the ongoing film-based work. That's the current project and it has a long way to go![34]

Having become a film-maker at the age of 67, Uma's current project on documenting the lives of women involved in movement politics who have been jailed for their political work is her third documentary, and her second to draw on interviews with activist women. Originally meant to be Uma's last film, the project has expanded so significantly—she has now filmed about 40 women— that she has planned to make three separate films set in 1949, 1967–77, and the contemporary moment. In describing the documentary archive, which is in her home on many hard drives, she noted that "my youngest protagonist is about 26–27 and the oldest is 94. The material is amazing: a combination of courage, laughter, camaraderie, and poignancy as women recall their past.[35]

As Uma edits footage and builds storylines and working scripts, only the stark reality of limited funds interrupts the project. Meanwhile, she notes, "two of my protagonists have died and I have become the official memorializer for their memorial meetings as I am the only person who captured them on camera." In her continuing work as oral historian/film-maker, she uses yet another medium for enacting the principle of using historical/archival tools for political activism.

Conclusion

Uma's narrative of personal and political transformation overlaps with many of the significant moments in the history of democratic and civil rights as well as women's rights movements in India. Her narrative embodies a culture free of boundaries (between activism, scholarship, art, legal practice, and other realms) that has been inherited by subsequent generations of activists who, like me, choose to be politically involved in myriad capacities. It also highlights founding moments of thinking through major issues such as sexual violence, state impunity, and the nation state framework. Similarly, it maps the history of important political practices such as fact-finding reports and feminist movement-building work, which has involved a critical and rigorous documenting/archiving of movements. Moreover, Uma's stories about multiple forms of work invoke issues, oppressions, and resistance that persist and come back to haunt her, as they do many activists across time and space.[36] It is therefore not surprising that Nirpreet Kaur, who was a teenager when Uma and other feminists produced perhaps the first extensive oral archive of a massacre, is now part of Uma's current project on women political prisoners, a project that is also about writing histories of women's political activism in the context of state repression and impunity. And thus the cycle, of repression and oppression, but also of hope, unwavering commitment to resistance and change, and sheer political grit, continues.

Notes

1 We wish to acknowledge Franca Iacovetta's role in facilitating the writing of this chapter. It can be resolutely declared that if not for Franca's patience and direct work on the organization and language of the chapter this work would not have been done. Her vision and trust in the contribution this narrative can make to this volume and to thinking through feminist oral history, in general, is the inspiration for this chapter.

2 On oral history as activism, see, for example, Sherna Berger Gluck, "Advocacy Oral History: Palestinian Women in Resistance," in *Women's Words: The Feminist Practice of Oral History*, eds. Sherna Berger Gluck and Daphne Patai (New York: Routledge, 1991) and the chapter by Sarah Loose with Amy Starecheski in this volume. Important Indian feminist oral history texts include: K. Lalita, *"We Were Making History—": Life Stories of Women in the Telangana Armed Struggle* (New Delhi: Kali for Women, 1989); Urmila Pawar, Meenakshi Moon and Wandana Sonalkar, *We Also Made History: Women in the Ambedkarite Movement* (New Delhi: Zubaan Books, 2014); Ritu Menon, *Making a Difference: Memoirs from the Women's Movement in India* (New Delhi: Women Unlimited, 2011).

3 I interviewed Uma in Delhi on 23 July 2011 and 1 January 2017.

4 Here I use the term "do" to broadly indicate an open-ended interspersed web of tasks that are part of history making. This involves various kinds of documenting, layers of questioning, reflecting and critical thinking. It involves contextualizing history in the past, present and future in its method as much as in its content. My conversation with Uma and the "doing" of this history with her is an attempt to make such a history(ies).

5 These themes matter greatly to historians of postcolonial societies and influence me deeply as a feminist historian. Varied articulations of multilayered concepts of time that also influence me include: Velcheru Narayana Rao, David Shulman, Sanjay Subrahmanyam *Textures of Time: Writing History in South India 1600–1800* (Delhi:

Permanent Black, 2001); Donna Haraway, "Situated Knowledges: The Science Question in Feminism as a Site of Discourse on the Privilege of Partial Perspective," *Feminist Studies* 14, no. 3 (1988): 575–599; Doreen Massey *Space, Place and Gender* (Minneapolis: University of Minnesota, 1994); Jacqui Alexander, *Pedagogies of Crossing: Meditations on Feminism, Sexual Politics, Memory and the Sacred* (Durham: Duke University Press, 2006); Jacqui Alexander and Chandra Talpade Mohanty, eds., *Feminist Genealogies, Colonial Legacies, Democratic Futures* (New York: Routledge, 1977).
6 Interview with Uma (hereafter Interview), 23 July 2011.
7 Interview, 23 July 2011.
8 I have respected Uma's mixed use of past and present tenses when describing past events.
9 Deriving their name from the village of Naxalbari in Bengal, which saw an early, armed Marxist-Leninist rebellion of landless laborers and waged workers against landowners, the movement exists in many parts of India. The Naxalites are engaged in armed rebellion against the state and upper-caste landed gentry over "unfair wages, unequal land ownership and caste violence." Dilip Simeon, "Permanent Spring," *India Seminar* (2010), www.india-seminar.com/2010/607/607_dilip_simeon.htm.
10 This is the date of the initial Naxalite rebellion.
11 Interview, 23 July 2011.
12 The Madras High Court Judgment acquitted the accused—local upper-caste feudal landlords—in the burning and killing of 42 Dalit farmers, including women, children, and elders in Kilvenmani village, Thanjavur District, Tamilnadu. Mythili Sivaraman was centrally involved in the protest campaign: "Gentlemen Killers of Kilvenmani," *Economic and Political Weekly* 8, no. 21 (1973): 926–928.
13 Language was a significant matter of debate following independence; it took many forms, including prioritizing Indigenous languages over a sole focus on English in education, and non-Hindi speakers protesting the imposition of Hindi as the "national language." Uma is referring to the demand for instruction in Hindi in higher education to enable students across social backgrounds to have access to education beyond high school.
14 Uma is of the highest caste, Brahmin, and Anand, while not of the lowest caste, is from a Non-Brahmin lower caste. As per brahminical rules, theirs is the most reprehensible of inter-caste marriages and the children of such a union are deemed untouchable. If the hierarchy was reversed, and the husband was upper caste, the children might still have some "salvation" and would inherit the father's caste.
15 Interview, 23 July 2011.
16 Interview, 23 July 2011.
17 Heavily sponsored by companies, these festivals involved colleges competing over skills such as dance, music, theater, and debating, and were/are decidedly apolitical.
18 A courageous act, the film documents a traumatic period in which more than 100,000 people were arrested without charge and imprisoned without trial: *Prisoners of Conscience*, directed by Anand Patwardhan (1978), http://patwardhan.com/?page_id=222.
19 Ponni Arasu and Priya Thangarajah, "Queer Women and Habeas Corpus in India: The Love that Blinds the Law," *Indian Journal of Gender Studies* 19, no. 3 (2012): 413–435; Ponni Arasu and Priya Thangarajah, "Queer Women and the Law in India," in *Law like Love: Queer Perspectives on Law*, eds. Arvind Narrain and Alok Gupta (New Delhi: Yoda Press, 2011), 325–337.
20 As Uma's reference to Dalit feminists suggests, feminists in India, as elsewhere, have and still debate the idea of "universal sisterhood." Just as differences based on class,

race, and citizenship status have informed Western debates, Indian debates have grappled with differences based on caste, class, region, language, and issues of sexualities, gender identities, and subjectivities.

21 http://pldindia.org/wp-content/uploads/2013/03/Open-Letter-to-CJI-in-the-Mathura-Rape-Case.pdf.

22 People's Union for Democratic Rights, *Inside the Family: A Report on Democratic Rights of Women* (March 1984).

23 Interview, 1 January 2017.

24 In 1983, the incident led to a case in which the Supreme Court gave compensation to two widows whose husbands were killed in the army operations at Oinam, Manipur.

25 Uma is referencing the Kashmir fact-finding reports in which she participated: *Grim Realities* (2001) and *Shopian: Manufacturing a Suitable Story—A Case Watch* (2009); both of these documented state violence against civilians in these disputed regions. Uma's consistent public stand on Kashmir is significant. This region never belonged to the Indian nation state willingly from Independence onwards, but has remained contested territory amongst the erstwhile ruling kings of Kashmir, various militant groups fighting for self-determination, and successive Indian and Pakistani governments. A warzone from the inception of independent India, Kashmir has witnessed a display of nationalist militaristic power from India and Pakistan and a struggle for freedoms and self-determination by many different groups. Indian feminists have criticized and lobbied against laws that violate human rights and attacks on civilians, especially women, by armed forces, but even within such relatively radical politics, most still find it awkward or unimaginable to publicly acknowledge or consciously know that many in Kashmir never have been and still do not want to be "Indian." Uma and the few other feminists who have taken a stand on Kashmir are exceptional in rejecting the default idea of the nation state as that which governs an "undivided" national territory. This politics is also based on listening carefully to a plethora of Kashmiri voices, particularly women, and the complex realities, truths, and resistance politics contained therein.

26 Interview, 1 January 2017. A reference to Uma's analysis of the ancient epic poem, which is the story of King Rama's heroic exploits but also that of his wife Sita's sufferings after he abandoned her.

27 This is a union of workers and peasants in Chattisgarh very active in the 1980s and 1990s.

28 The Indian Congress Party directed the mobs in response to the assassination of Indira Gandhi by her Sikh bodyguards.

29 When India nationalized the mines, their mine became illegal and they were denied official worker status and the right to incorporate. They continued to mine and faced state violence nevertheless: "Abandoned Miners of Santhal Parganas," *Economic and Political Weekly* 18, no. 40 (1983): 1690–1692.

30 Interview, 1 January 2017.

31 Uma Chakravarti and Nandita Haksar, *The Delhi Riots: Three Days in the Life of a Nation* (New Delhi: Lancer International, 1987); Uma Chakravarti, *The Social Dimensions of Early Buddhism* (Oxford University Press, 1987).

32 The report was published in English to enable circulation in state and media circles and among political progressives (whose shared language is English). The testimonies were in a mixture of Hindi and Punjabi, the two languages spoken by Sikh Punjabi persons in Delhi. Originally Tamil, but also a native speaker of Hindi, Uma communicates in Punjabi too.

33 Operation Blue Star, June 1984: the army attacked the Golden Temple at Amritsar, revered by Sikhs as the holiest of their shrines, to "flush" out the militants holed

in there; it preceded the assassination of Indira Gandhi (31 October 1984) and the pogrom against the Sikhs in early November 1984. The Sikhs have yet to recover from their sense of betrayal over both events, especially as justice has eluded the survivors of the November carnage.

34 Interview, 1 January 2017.
35 Email exchange, 3 March 2017.
36 A theme common among South Asian activists, it also looms large in the 30-plus interviews I have conducted with feminists in India and Sri Lanka.

9 Locating lesbians, finding "gay women," writing queer histories

Reflections on oral histories, identity, and community memory[1]

Valerie J. Korinek

In July 2003, I had the privilege of interviewing "Dorothy," a 75-year-old self-proclaimed gay woman. During a nearly three-hour conversation about her life history and her perceptions of gay and lesbian life and history in Saskatoon, we had several fascinating exchanges about sexual behavior, culture, identity, life courses, politics, and class. Adamant that she was a "gay woman," not a lesbian, Dorothy said the latter is a "harsh word" that "a lot of older women do not like," adding that "we don't like dyke" either, as it is "even harsher than lesbian."[2] When I responded to her claim that dislike of these terms was a generational one by saying that, perhaps, it was a class thing, she retorted, "My father worked for the railway yard; we're middle class." I have written about Dorothy (born in 1928) before, describing her insights, her motorcycle trip to Edmonton with her first lover, her subsequent early marriage, and her position as the "original lesbian" involved in Saskatoon gay and lesbian activism.[3] In her interview, Dorothy gave a feisty, engaging performance for my benefit, while I, allergic to cats, struggled to breath as one of her long-haired cats sat happily perched beside me the entire time. On the audiotape, we both sound like raspy elderly ladies. While I shudder to think how, for the want of an inhaler, I failed to ask more follow-up questions (or at least to speak more audibly), this interview brought into sharp focus key challenges I faced in dealing with the oral histories I collected.

Like other oral historians who have explicitly addressed their emotional responses to narrators, I found myself torn between admiration for Dorothy and conflicted appraisal of some of her analysis.[4] Assessing her life history was a challenge. A charming raconteur who regaled me with stories about growing up and living in Saskatoon, she clearly took pride in having been ahead of her time and in becoming an early leader within the lesbian and gay community. But there were also flashes of anger and bitterness, memories of poignant losses, local homophobia, social exclusions, and class tensions that disrupted the jaunty tone she strove to strike. Like many of my male narrators, Dorothy's memories focused on activism and colorful exploits. When she died, in

November 2010, her obituary revealed many details she had not shared, including the fact that she was a "well-known and much loved social activist" whose support for the Cooperative Commonwealth Federation (CCF) and later New Democratic Party (NDP) had put her "on the front lines of the battle to establish universal health care."[5] Astonishingly, Dorothy never told me about this activism. She had a determined script, about gay activism, that she believed I wanted to hear and from which she did not deviate.

Dorothy's interview belongs to a handful of remarkably rich interviews that opened a veritable Pandora's Box of issues related to the methodological challenges of researching and writing LGBTQ+ histories drawn primarily from oral interviews and life stories. These interviews were conducted as part of a larger queer history, *Prairie Fairies: A History of Queer Communities and People in Western Canada, 1930–1985* (*PF*), which is also based on extensive research into primary materials in regional, university, and community archives across western Canada. Of the 82 interviews that inform *PF*, I conducted 30 of them in Winnipeg, Saskatoon, Regina, Calgary, Edmonton, Ottawa, and Toronto. The rest come from three community oral history projects in Winnipeg.[6] *PF* historicizes the emergence of gay and lesbian organizations, communities, social activity, and activism. It was purposefully designed as a "queer" history so as to provide a more inclusive framework that moved beyond the binaries of gay and straight, "out" and closeted, and thus better captured daily life in small and mid-sized prairie cities.[7] This decision was also necessitated by the fact that *PF* includes the era prior to 1969 (or pre-Stonewall) before "coming out" and identifying openly as a member of sexual minority communities was possible. Furthermore, even after 1970, when open identification as lesbian or gay was increasingly common (particularly for younger people), there remained sizeable numbers of people who continued to act "discreetly." They were not comfortable with these more politicized identities or the reality that jobs, families, and social networks might be at risk if they revealed their sexual orientation. *PF* is also a queer history in the sense that it employs a "queer view" of the prairies that purposefully decenters and challenges the hetero-normative historiography of the prairie west with its emphasis on family settlement, agriculture, Indigenous-settler relations, and the Great Depression.[8]

This chapter grapples with questions related to assessing consciousness and identity formation, focusing in particular on the methodological and theoretical challenges historians face when historicizing women who loved, lived, or had sex with women. A key issue was that of voice. Who speaks for communities? Who chooses to share their stories and be visible? The power to speak, and to have one's histories recorded, is an important one. After many years of working with these collections, and analyzing their meanings, I remain troubled by the power of silence and of those who refused to speak for a host of reasons. How do we write fully rendered histories given such layers of self-selection, censorship, or silence? How do we balance those narrators who were openly engaged in politics and gay and lesbian communities from those who were discrete and more insular? Do we write about the shadow communities of women who refused to speak, but were spoken about by all the informants? As Horacio N. Roque Ramírez and Nan Alamilla Boyd note, "The fact that we do not all occupy the same historical time period and its attendant politics of identity in relation to sexual consciousness makes queer oral histories methodologically tricky."[9] It is that trickiness that is at the heart of this chapter.

Setting the stage

Historians of sexuality have made extensive use of oral history interviews because initially there were very few archived cultural, legal, or social documents from which to reconstruct worlds that their inhabitants intentionally kept covert. Fully illustrating the radical possibilities of interviews for sexualities history, John D'Emilio's 1983 *Sexual Politics, Sexual Communities*, which used oral histories to write a history of homophile activism in the 1950s and 60s, was therefore quite groundbreaking given that it interviewed homophile activists and, in the process, made use of their private caches of papers, letters, and cultural ephemera. Public historian Alan Bérubé's landmark *Coming Out Under Fire* (1990), which explored the experiences of gay and lesbian service personnel during World War II, also underscored the value of interviews for writing revisionist histories.[10] Thus, while *Women's Words* was highly influential among feminist oral historians, the absence of material devoted to queer oral history practices meant that it did not play a central role for sexualities scholars.

The first book to self-reflexively comment on oral history practices within sexuality studies was Elizabeth Lapovsky Kennedy and Madeleine Davis' award-winning monograph *Boots of Leather, Slippers of Gold* (1993). Many of us are indebted to the painstakingly detailed and nuanced portrait the authors provided of Buffalo's working-class lesbian bar culture in the 1950s and 60s. That volume, and Kennedy's subsequent articles, offered the earliest, and still valuable, insights into the methodological challenges such histories posed. Kennedy enumerated the time-consuming and highly politicized work of locating queer informants and the care and skills required to establish trusting relationships. She demonstrated how to frame an analysis that respected the racial, gendered, materialist, and regional contexts in which the narrators operated.[11]

Given the centrality of oral history methodology to histories of sexuality, it is perhaps surprising that, with the important exception of Ann Cvetkovich's *An Archive of Feelings* (2003), on queer ethnography, and a smattering of other articles, it was not until the publication in 2012 of Horacio N. Roque Ramírez and Nan Alamilla Boyd's edited collection *Bodies of Evidence: The Practice of Queer Oral History* that sustained discussion of the methodological challenges related to oral history narratives, informants, and practices emerged within the field.[12] More recently, trans activists and scholars have also begun to grapple with issues surrounding the ethics of interviewing, privacy, and historical legacy within the context of major trans oral history projects.

One of these ambitious initiatives, the "Transgender Oral History" project, which is part of the University of Minnesota's Jean Nickolaus Tretter Collection, also looks "west." It aims to collect interviews with 200–300 trans women, men, and gender non-binary individuals to write a history of trans lives in the Midwest.[13]

Bodies of Evidence is a foundational text that clearly delineates the "overtly political function and liberating qualities" of queer oral history. It highlights the "particular set of ethical, political and academic challenges" that practitioners of queer oral histories must navigate as well as the challenges faced by our narrators, such as "heavy social stigmatization", "state policing of queer behaviors and public expressions," and traumatic experiences involving the medical system, religious institutions, or family and friends.[14] Boyd and Ramírez stress, too, that it is only recently that scholars have been able to research and write histories of queer sex and genders "without risk of academic sanction or public reprisal," though I would caution that this optimistic assessment may not apply to all students, scholars, or practitioners. "Doing" queer oral history may still limit job opportunities or, at the very least, prompt others to make assumptions about a researcher's sexuality, politics, and identity issues—something from which other academics working with oral history research may well be spared.[15]

Locating lesbians and finding gay women

Determined to write a feminist queer history of western women's and men's same-sex, gay, lesbian, and queer experiences, the first methodological challenge I faced was locating sufficient numbers of women willing to participate in my interviews. In the end, there were equal numbers of people who identified as women and men in my narrator pool, but those simple statistics obscure just how difficult it was to find women to interview and, conversely, how eager gay men were to share their life histories. Since most everyone "knew" of someone I should contact, I did not lack for suggestions of women to interview. But those suggestions, and my willingness to cast a wide net, were not enough. Women were far more reticent than men to put themselves forward. They did not view their lives as worthy of academic interest. Many were not sure they met the criteria of "lesbian" if they had not been exclusively identified as one since their early adult years. Some just chose to stay private. Even so, everyone who declined said they could not wait for the book to be written so they could read it!

I now realize that one of my major challenges involved terminology. I sought out "gays and lesbians," or "queer" subjects, but a number of my narrators did not identify as lesbian or gay. Despite the wide adoption of "queer" within academic and contemporary LGBTQ+ circles, everyone disliked the term intensely. There was a strong generational resistance to reclaiming this term. As Marion Alexander (born 1934) bluntly informed me, "I hate that word. I am not queer. I am a plain ordinary person."[16] This discomfort with labels and identities—which Lynn Abrams similarly detected among some of her British narrators when she tried to get them to discuss the f-word (feminism)—should certainly be borne in mind when taking on any oral history project.[17]

One's role in the community also significantly influenced who was willing to speak. Not all my oral histories were of "leaders" or rebels; indeed, most were "ordinary women" who had lived extraordinary, and often difficult, lives. I heard tales of psychiatric institutionalization, of lost children and families, and promotions denied. A large number of my narrators were cautious about revealing their sexual orientation publicly. Few came from cold calls or media publicity; most were referrals from community leaders or other narrators. I personally knew only two of my narrators before I began the interviews. What made me successful, ultimately, was persistence and time. These interviews were conducted over the course of a few years, and towards the end of the archival research, by which time I had built up sufficient trust among people in Saskatchewan. My public presentations had also generated enough interest in the project to make people think it worthwhile to volunteer their time to participate. This "slow scholarship" was only possible because I have a tenured faculty position.[18]

While my larger study intentionally includes an equal number of gay male and lesbian narrators, here I have concentrated primarily on lesbian narratives. My decision to do so is not based on some essentialist notion of feminism, but rather because it was with this cohort that I experienced my greatest challenges, including with respect to recruiting participants. It was also this cohort of narrators that challenged my notion of who does and does not "belong" in a queer community and queer urban histories. The gay men I interviewed also came from a range of age groups, and they too had varied experiences within their particular city context, but they were much easier to locate and interview. Furthermore, never once did one of them express surprise at being asked to contribute an interview, nor did they second-guess the value of telling their respective life histories. They also took a big tent view of the gay communities within their cities, willingly offering other contacts and seldom judging the value of recording other narrator's histories. The marked difference between the two pools of narrators was both unexpected and, for the purposes of this article, academically interesting.

In the end, I was the truly grateful beneficiary of many people's willingness to tell very honest, personal stories that were at times affirming of their life decisions to live as lesbians and gays but, at other times, contained heart-breaking memories.[19] Some lesbians had never really socialized with other lesbians beyond their partners, while community members vilified others for being "too activist." There were men who identified as gay but had never had sex with other men as well as men who had never divulged their real name to sexual partners and had never had long-term lovers, let alone relationships. There were men and women who had held leadership positions, either professionally or politically, but spoke in bitter tones about how isolated and lonely those positions had made them. Taken together, these memories defy easy categorization or analysis, precluding any reductive rendering of "identity" or "communities." Regardless of the tenor of the interviews, a handful of which were very dark, all of my narrators claimed pride in their survival and in their choices to forge different paths. These "happy endings" were affixed to many a challenging life history, reflecting a person's determination to convince me, and perhaps themselves, that it was all worth it. After all, I was there, in the service of history, recording their stories for "posterity."[20]

Activists versus ordinary people

The narratives contain equally strong views for and against activism that were often expressed in terms of feminism and gay/lesbian activism versus "being ordinary people." "Selena" (born 1937) explained how she supported feminism, particularly notions of equality and equal pay for women and men, but took issue with "extreme feminism." She was equally offended by "extreme activism" that she viewed as "pressure to get you out and become an aggressive activist," adding: "I was really quite offended by the way they treated me in the sense that either you are or you aren't . . . And they tried to make me feel guilty."[21]

Selena's interview, like Dorothy's, provides a rare firsthand account of a group of Saskatoon lesbians who are otherwise conspicuously absent from my oral histories. Successful professionals, many of these women worked on campus as administrative staff, though a few were academics. Their private lives revolved around their long-term partnerships with other women. Couples owned homes together. The women travelled, played sports, and socialized in groups of ten to twenty women, but seldom attended a gay or lesbian event (some recalled one couple at a women's dance), club, or social. If Selena's recollection that there were two or three such lesbian circles, organized around sports, culture, or professional interests, is true, then I am missing a sizeable cohort of Saskatoon women who lived with and loved other women.

While respectful of my narrators, and aiming to frame their life experiences within appropriate contexts, and to "check [my] presumptions about the nature of sexual identities, love and loss," I still struggled with Selena's interview.[22] All of my other Saskatoon narrators mentioned these campus lesbians, usually in strongly critical terms. For example, Marion scoffed at their misplaced belief that they had "pulled the wool over people's eyes."[23] Liz (born 1948), a well-known lesbian activist in Edmonton, was equally critical of a similar, albeit younger, group of professional lesbians:

> A lot of them live very middle class lives, but they are not feminists . . . they don't have much political awareness . . . They wear rings and they go to house parties and they pull the curtains and I see most of them once a year at a barbecue . . . I remember one woman saying that her partner . . . a retired nurse needed hearing aids and [she] wouldn't let her partner submit the claim for healthcare benefits because somebody might figure out that they were lesbians that way . . . I don't even know where to begin with that.[24]

When asked what differentiated her from that group, Liz admitted: "I have never quite figured it out. You know it cost me a lot over the years; I have suffered more for it within the women's community for being out . . . I don't know what it is."[25] These tensions within the interviews speak to the tremendous variability in how prairie lesbians strategically organized their lives, a variability that is easily reduced to age, educational attainment, or class.

I tried to find and create spaces for those discrete middle-class lesbians to talk with me, but very few did. Those who did speak addressed the toll that silence had wrought. Significantly, the activists said the same about being outspoken. Each "side" felt they had suffered from exclusionary tactics—politically or socially—and both looked to me, the historian, to validate those experiences. During the interviews with the campus lesbians, I listened carefully, being scrupulous not to judge or intrude with my own stories, and asked follow-up questions. As a younger feminist and openly queer historian from Toronto who was generations removed from the stories being told, I was a complete outsider to this group. At times, I sound perplexed as they explain various scenarios. No doubt, some of them accurately summed up where my sympathies lay, while others likely found me completely clueless about "prairie life." At all times, I sought to prioritize my narrators' life histories, though of course my own research questions, theoretical framing, and politics also affected the project.[26]

Inclusivity versus exclusivity

I greatly appreciated Selena's willingness to be interviewed, though the interview itself was self-censored and guarded, if not as scripted as Dorothy's. While valuable, her life history mainly details her own experiences and does not offer a broader view of the various women with whom she socialized for decades.[27] My ethics protocol for the interviews enabled narrators to opt out of questions or withdraw their answers and to choose an alias. Laughing, Selena chose an alias meant to throw people off track as it was such an incongruous name for her. Between what she deemed confidential and later wanted removed, much of this crucial interview is not usable. Nor are the revealing off-the-record comments made after the end of the formal interview.[28]

Other Saskatoon lesbians did volunteer information about the campus lesbians, though they expressed bitter regret over the group's exclusionary practices. For them, not being invited to lesbian social events in a small city where many people knew about each other smacked of classism. They thought too that the campus lesbians had conveyed the impression that they considered open discussion or identification as a lesbian was déclassé. As Dorothy glibly observed, "They wouldn't say they were gay if they were in bed together."[29] When asked whether they should be in my book, she said both that "they are not part of the community" and "they are an interesting aspect of gay life I think." Pushed to explain her comments, Dorothy mused over "the fact that everybody in town knows their little secret and yet they don't seem to want to acknowledge that in any way," making it clear she felt they ought to have acknowledged and taken pride in their successful long-term relationships. Selena, however, was emphatic that her sexual orientation, and identification as a lesbian, was a private matter, saying that no one had a right to label her or her "private" life unless she gave them permission.

In seeking to "map" lesbian identities and communities, I faced the methodological challenge of deciding whether these privatized lesbians, who lived quietly with a lover for decades, and seldom participated openly in queer activities, belonged in a history of the queer west. I decided they did as they provided a window into a fascinating history that also revealed how friends, coworkers, and neighbors helped them lead a discreet lesbian life. For a city of Saskatoon's size, this history offers a graphic example of the prairie ethos of "live and let live." The discrete group had good jobs and, on the face of it, social respect. They lived openly with female partners for decades, but did not flaunt their sexuality. Straight colleagues and neighbors realized they were not merely roommates, but chose to play along, remaining quiet and sometimes even protecting them from having their "private" lives exposed.

Understandably, the lesbian and gay activist narrators who had borne the brunt of open disclosure—in the form of lost jobs, lost families, and economic marginality—felt little sympathy for those who, having chosen differently, also appeared to have suffered less. But the silent did pay a price. A male narrator from Regina, Leonard (born 1943) said that he "always compartmentalized [his] life," keeping his sexual orientation a secret: "I had my life with work, I had my home life and I had my gay life."[30] Pushed further, "Leonard" offered a strikingly tone deaf assessment of why some early Saskatoon activists could be more open than he was in Regina: "There were a few people like Dorothy [who] didn't really care; she had been married and had two kids and they knew and she didn't care." He said the same about activist Gens Hellquist.[31] Having interviewed Hellquist (born 1946), I knew that was not the case. Hellquist, whose activist career in Saskatoon stretched to nearly 45 years, took pride in his foundational role in Saskatoon's queer community. He was also angry about the backlash, both economic and social, that accompanied his decision not to live a compartmentalized life.[32] These tensions reflect the dramatic changes in the early 1970s, "after gay liberation and lesbian feminism demanded visibility for identities and communities that had previously existed underground. LGBT politics became centrally organized around a politics of coming out, of declaring one's sexual identity clearly and unequivocally."[33] The tensions among my narrators are evidence of how the persistence of older models of queer community organization that involved discretion and class-based notions of privacy confounded gay and lesbian activists and complicated research intended to reveal the breadth of queer life within prairie cities.[34]

Conclusion

Having had the privilege of meeting and recording the life histories of queer elders, many of them now deceased, I have worked assiduously to capture their multilayered memories of having lived and loved as lesbians, gay women, and gay men in the prairie west between 1930 and 1985. As a professional historian, I grappled with the challenges of interpretation through careful attention to historical context as well as relevant archival material. In retrospect, the challenge of interviewing queer people on my own campus, in my home community and across generations, was further complicated by my reluctance to be more invasive than I was for fear that any sign of aggressive questioning would immediately freeze my pool of narrators.[35]

As much as oral histories enable the writing of a broader, more diverse range of social historical experiences, they also bring unique challenges. Those who bravely step forward to be interviewed help structure the histories we can write. Only so much can be made of silence, absence, or discretion. In a study like mine, it skews the sample towards activists, community-builders, and Euro-Canadian "mavericks."[36] Aiming for "gender balance" with my narrators was also challenging because of the reticence of potential lesbian narrators, the reasons of which are familiar to women's and feminist historians as well as sexualities historians. In the case of the latter, issues related to insider/outsider status within a given city or community, and an ongoing desire for privacy, can loom especially large.

It is equally important to be cognizant of the tensions within a group of narrators, whose experiences are highly individualistic and personal. As Elise Chenier observes in this volume (Chapter 23), using oral history sources to write history now is a different process than one aimed at collecting oral narratives for "posterity."[37] In light of the kind of political, gender, racial, and class divisions my project revealed, I caution against writing "community" histories that feature the important activist narrators, and their memories of activism, to the extent of excluding those who chose not to be so public. In my study, I have included the "silent majority" because their stories tell us about the alternative queer spaces that were created while also recognizing that "internal stratification" remains an ongoing issue with our LGBTTQ communities.[38] Their inclusion also demonstrates the complexity of living queer lives long after the shift to more open, identity-based politics. Ultimately, though, it is the talkers in my study who triumph. Their voices are strong, their stories resonate, and their histories predominate. It was their willingness to share their life histories that contributed significantly to the writing of a revisionist western Canadian history that, I hope, will open up more spaces and research, and stimulate further discussions about the place of queer people in the prairie west. Future researchers might find inroads into the silent majority but, for now, as they say in the west, "You've got to dance with the one that brung you."

Notes

1   I thank Elizabeth Lapovsky Kennedy, Marcia Gallo, Marc Stein, and Elise Chenier for their feedback on an earlier version of this paper.

2 "Dorothy" (alias), interview with V.J. Korinek, 8 July 2003. Unlike the other aliases used in this chapter, Dorothy's choice of an alias (chosen because she thought it highly incongruous) does not keep her "anonymous" since Saskatoon residents of a particular vintage or bent will guess her identity. But I am respecting her wishes.

3 See V.J. Korinek, "The most openly gay person for at least a thousand miles," *Canadian Historical* Review 84, no. 4 (December 2003): 517–550.

4 An excellent early example is Valerie Yow, "Do I Like Them Too Much?": Effects of the Oral History Interview on the Interviewer and Vice Versa," *Oral History Review* 24, no. 1 (Summer 1997): 55–79.

5 "Dorothy," Obituary, *The Star Phoenix*, 13 November 2010.

6 For more details, see V.J. Korinek, "'We're the Girls of the Pansy Parade': Historicizing Winnipeg's Queer Subcultures, 1930s–1970s," *Histoire sociale / Social History* 45, no. 89 (May 2012): 125–127; Provincial Archives of Manitoba (PAM), Manitoba Gay Lesbian Archives Committee, C1861–1903, 1990, copies of 33 cassette tapes (25 hours) C1869–70. In 2002, I was granted access to these tapes by the archivists at PAM and at the Rainbow Resource Centre (RRC) in Winnipeg, Manitoba, which then held the originals. The original interviews are now part of the University of Manitoba Archives and Special Collections, Winnipeg Gay and Lesbian Archives Collection (A.08–67, A.09–28).

7 For a recent discussion of the difference between gay and lesbian social historical approaches and queer historicism, see Colin R. Johnson, *Just Queer Folks: Gender and Sexuality in America* (Philadelphia: Temple University Press, 2013). Examples of queer approaches that have come to define the field include John Howard, *Men Like That: A Southern Queer* History (Chicago: University of Chicago Press, 1999); Nan Alamilla Boyd, *Wide-Open Town: A History of Queer San Francisco to 1965* (Berkeley: University of California Press, 2003); Matt Holbrook, *Queer London: Perils and Pleasures in the Sexual Metropolis, 1918–1957* (Chicago: University of Chicago Press, 2005).

8 For elaboration on this theme, see V.J. Korinek, "A Queer Eye View of the Prairies: Reorienting Western Canadian Histories," in *The West and Beyond: New Perspectives on an Imagined Region*, eds. Alvin Finkel, Sarah Carter, Peter Fortna (Edmonton: Athabasca University Press, 2010), 278–296.

9 Horacio N. Roque Ramírez and Nan Alamilla Boyd, "Introduction—Close Encounters: The Body and Knowledge in Queer Oral History," in *Bodies of Evidence: The Practice of Queer Oral History*, eds. Nan Alamilla Boyd and Horacio N. Roque Ramírez (New York: Oxford University Press, 2012), 13.

10 John D'Emilio, *Sexual Politics, Sexual Communities: The Making of a Homosexual Minority in the U.S. 1940–1970* (Chicago: University of Chicago Press, 1983); Alan Bérubé, *Coming Out Under Fire: The History of Gay Men and Women During World War II* (New York: Free Press, 1990). See also George Chauncey, *Gay New York: Gender, Urban Culture and the Making of the Gay Male World, 1890–1940* (New York: Basic Books, 1994); Alan Bérubé, *My Desire for History: Essays in Gay, Community and Labour History*, eds. John D'Emilio and Estelle B. Freedman (Chapel Hill: University of North Carolina Press, 2011).

11 Elizabeth Lapovsky Kennedy and Madeleine Davis, *Boots of Leather, Slippers of Gold: The History of a Lesbian Community* (New York: Routledge, 1993); Elizabeth Lapovsky Kennedy, "Telling Tales: Oral History and the Construction of Pre-Stonewall Lesbian Identity," in *The Oral History Reader*, 2nd edition, eds. Robert Perks and Alistair Thomson (New York: Routledge, 1998), 271–282.

12 Ann Cvetkovich, *An Archive of Feelings: Trauma, Sexuality and Lesbian Public Cultures* (Durham: Duke University Press, 2003); Boyd and Ramírez, *Bodies of Evidence*.

136   *Valerie J. Korinek*

13 "Transgender Oral History" project, University of Minnesota Libraries, Jean Nickolaus Tretter Collection in GLBT Studies: https://umedia.lib.umn.edu/taxonomy/term/946. For other examples, see Elsbeth Brown, "Trans/Feminist Oral History," *Transgender Studies Quarterly* 2, no. 4 (November 2015): 666–672.
14 Ramírez and Boyd, 11.
15 See Becki L. Ross, "Preface: Beginnings, Backlash and Brazenness," in *Burlesque West: Showgirls, Sex and Sin in Postwar Vancouver* (Vancouver: University of British Columbia Press, 2009), xiii–xix; Marc Stein, "Crossing Borders: Memories, Dreams, Fantasies and Nightmares of the History Job Market," *Left History* 9, no. 2 (2004): 121–139.
16 Marion Alexander, interview with author, 26 August 2003.
17 See Lynn Abrams' chapter in this volume (Chapter 6).
18 Alison Mountz et al., "All for Slow Scholarship and Slow Scholarship for all," *University Affairs/Affaires Universitaires*, 9 May 2016.
19 Like historians who have cried in the archives, oral historians are also exposed to harrowing material: Antoinette Burton, *Archive Stories: Facts, Fictions and the Writing of History* (Atlanta: Duke University Press, 2006) and (on lesbian oral histories and trauma) Cvetkovich, *An Archive of Feelings*, 205–238.
20 Eric C. Wat, "Thanks for the Memories: A Narrator Asks an Oral Historian for Validation," in *Bodies of Evidence*, 253–267.
21 "Selena" (alias), interview with author, Saskatoon, 8 September 2003.
22 Marcia M. Gallo, "Dancing with Stella, Los Angeles Daughters of Bilitis Pioneer," in *Bodies of Evidence*, 218.
23 Marion Alexander, interview with author, 26 August 2003.
24 Elizabeth Massiah (real name used with permission), interview with author, Edmonton, Alberta, 13 September 2003.
25 Massiah, interview.
26 On this theme, see, for example, Anna Sheftel and Stacey Zembrzycki, "Only Human: A Reflection on the Ethical and Methodological Challenges of Working with 'Difficult' Stories," *Oral History Review* 37, no. 2 (2010): 191–214.
27 "Selena," interview.
28 On the value of analyzing such material, see, for example, Nadia Jones-Gailani, "Feminist Oral History and Assessing the Dueling Narratives of Iraqi Women in Diaspora," in *Sisters or Strangers: Immigrant, Ethnic and Racialized Women in Canadian History*, eds. M. Epp and F. Iacovetta, 2nd edition (Toronto: University of Toronto Press, 2016), 584–602.
29 "Dorothy," interview.
30 "Leonard" (alias), interview with author, Regina, 28 July 2003.
31 "Leonard, interview.
32 Gens Hellquist (real name used with permission), interview with author, Saskatoon, 17 December 2002.
33 Daniel Rivers, "Queer Family Stories: Learning from Oral Histories with Lesbian Mothers and Gay Fathers from the Pre-Stonewall Era," in *Bodies of Evidence*, 69.
34 Kennedy, "Telling Tales," 274, reports that middle-class lesbians of an "earlier period" (pre-World War II) did not announce or discuss their lesbianism, but, clearly, the practice continued.
35 Cvetkovich, *Archive of Feeling*, 189–201.
36 Aritha van Herk, *Mavericks: An Incorrigible History of Alberta* (Toronto: Viking, 2001).
37 See Elise Chenier's chapter in this volume (Chapter 23); "Twin Cities GLBT Oral History" project, *Queer Twin Cities* (Minneapolis: University of Minneapolis Press, 2010).
38 Ramírez and Boyd, 14.

10 Memory, history, and contestations in present-day Iraq

Nadje Al-Ali

About a year after the US-led invasion of Iraq in March 2003, I was approached by Zed Press to write a book about Iraqi women in the present situation. It was certainly an interesting and challenging proposal. But after thinking about it for a while, I refused, feeling strongly that a general Western readership would not be able to grasp the full extent to which women are losing out in the present period without being familiar with the broader historical context. I could see how a description and analysis of what was happening to women in the post-Saddam Hussein era could all too easily be misconstrued in terms of culture, tradition, or religion, raising familiar questions like: "Isn't this just another instance of a Muslim country oppressing its women?" The idea for my 2007 book *Iraqi Women: Untold Stories from 1948 to the Present* emerged from this context.[1]

My previous work had challenged the idea of Muslim and Middle Eastern women being passive victims. I had carried out research on Egyptian feminists who had been mobilizing since the turn of the 20th century, initially as part of a struggle for independence against the British colonial presence, and then turned to work on the impact of dictatorship and economic sanctions on women and gender relations in Iraq.[2] Influenced by feminist scholars such as Deniz Kandiyoti, Lila Abu-Lughod, Avtar Brah, and Chandra Mohanty, I found a home in transnational feminist politics that not only challenged the simplistic binaries of traditional versus modern, and Western versus Eastern, but also combined insights from poststructuralist theory with materialist approaches.[3] Attention to political economy seemed inevitable given the complex material realities that provided the background and shaped the range of Iraqi women's experiences.

The book was as much about the past—about how history is constructed and how it is used—as it was about the present. In the context of the aftermath of the 2003 invasion, the escalating violence and sectarian tensions, and contestations about power and national identity, history has become a very important and powerful tool. Contesting narratives about what happened in the past relate directly to different attitudes towards the present and visions about the future of the new Iraq. They relate to claims about rights, resources, and power. More crucially, the different accounts of the past lay down the parameters of what it means to be Iraqi, and who is to be included and excluded. History justifies and contains both narratives of unity and narratives of divisions and sectarianism.

My starting point has been the experiences, life stories, and oral histories of Iraqi women, interwoven with more conventional published histories as well as my own anecdotes, experiences, and observations. Trying to put together a complex puzzle, juggling different personal experiences, narratives, and official accounts is not a mere narrative technique. Processes of construction and selection have already begun at the level of the women's own narratives. Memories, whether individual or collective, are not static and frozen in time; they are alive, rooted in the present as much as in the past, and linked to aspirations as much as actual experiences.

Memory is also subject to change and is both selective and fluid. History and memory are not merely about the past but dialectically linked to the present. Individual memories are complex constructions based on personal experiences, worldviews—political, religious, and ethical—and collective narratives. In my work, the women's stories, accounts, and experiences are their own and certainly not devoid of particularities, personalities, and idiosyncrasies. Yet, the stories are also reflective of wider narratives positioning an individual in terms of her gender, class, political orientation, ethnicity, religious affiliation, and places of origin and residence.

Throughout my own work, I have tried to present varying narratives, sometimes more congruent, sometimes contesting. It was obvious throughout the process of meeting and interviewing women that certain forms of knowledge and experiences were being privileged over others: at the very least, a woman's own personal experience was often privileged over those of others. But often, collective memories and histories creep into these personal accounts. Although there is a difference between remembering a personal experience and interpreting it, memories are often constructed in the context of interpreting, analyzing, and making sense of particular situations, events, and developments. I have sought to keep a balance between presenting different accounts and contesting narratives and intervening as the author with my own views and interpretations.

For me, one of the biggest challenges in writing about Iraqi women has been to recognize that experience, memory, and truth do not necessarily overlap, that there might be multiple truths about an event without diminishing either the significance of memory or the importance of finding out what "really" happened in terms of political developments, repression, wars, and social changes. The question is how to acknowledge the validity of contesting subjective truths without falling into the postmodern trap of nihilistic relativism. The Iraqi women I interviewed experienced specific historical moments differently based on their social class, place of location, political affiliation, and ethnic and religious backgrounds, but also their individual experiences and personalities contributed to variations in narratives and interpretations about certain events and developments. Despite or because of this complexity, I felt it was important for me as the researcher and author to intervene and construct a narrative of events, structural inequalities, or human rights atrocities. The regime of Saddam Hussein, for example, systematically discriminated against Kurds and engaged in human rights atrocities against Kurdish populations in the North. It was important to stress this fact even if not every Kurdish woman felt it equally or if an Arab Iraqi woman might deny these atrocities in her narrative. "Everything goes" is not good enough when recounting stories of repression, suffering, torture, flight, and attempts to remain alive when violence reigns. It is also not good enough in a context where distortions, partial truths, outright lies, and propaganda have serious and far-reaching implications for people living inside Iraq.

In my work, I point to differences on the level of experiences and memory among women, but I am also trying to delineate a series of different trends and developments that have affected everyone, even if in distinct ways, as well as aiming to provide a historical context to the current crisis and chaos. I have worked both as an academic and as an activist to document the various ways in which Iraqi women and gender relations have been changing in the context of political repression under the Ba'th regime. The secular socialist-oriented and Arab nationalist Ba'th party came to power in Iraq in 1968, with Saddam Hussein becoming President in 1979 until his ousting in 2003. During the Ba'th regime's 35-year-reign, the country became a militarized dictatorship that went through different stages in terms of women's roles, gender norms, and gender relations. In the first decade, in the context of an economic boom after the oil crisis in the early 1970s, women were very much encouraged to obtain an education and participate in the labor force. During the 1980s, the eight-year long war with Iran (1980–1988) pushed women even further into the labor force and the public sector, but regime rhetoric changed as women's reproductive roles became more significant in the context of the war. From 1990 to the end of the regime, economic sanctions, following Iraq's invasion of Kuwait in August 1990, devastated Iraqi society and led to a conservative shift in gender norms as well as gender policies as the state was no longer able to provide generous childcare and working benefits.

In the aftermath of the 2003 invasion of Iraq, I built on this earlier work, and extended the historical frame to include the period before the Ba'th regime (1968–2003), but also looked back to the transition from monarchy to republic (the late 1940s through the revolution of 1958 to the early 1960s). I tried to deepen my understanding by interviewing over 250 Iraqi women in Erbil, Sulimaniya, Amman, London, Detroit, and San Diego. Most of these women were from the capital, Baghdad, but I also spoke to women from other major cities and towns, such as Basra, Najaf, Karbala, Mosul, Babylon, Kirkuk, Irbil, Sulimaniya, and Dohuk.[4]

Through my Iraqi networks in London, I managed to get in contact with Iraqi women in the various diasporic places I visited, but also inside Iraqi Kurdistan. In Detroit, my father helped me get in touch with former neighbors who kindly hosted me and introduced me to other Iraqis. Throughout my research, my Iraqi roots and connections helped to open doors, but also served as a hindrance given that the nature of conflict meant that many Iraqis were suspicious of someone not being of the same ethnic and religious background or political persuasion. Being half German and an academic helped to mitigate some of the negative perceptions towards certain kinds of Iraqis. Yet, with many women, it took many sessions of tea drinking and shared conversations before they started to open up and trust me. In the process, they learnt as much about me and my life as I learnt about theirs.

Conventional accounts of Iraqi history provide a linear chronological account of the political, social, and economic changes that Iraqi women have experienced from the late 1940s to the present day. Instead, I have tried to show how different women have experienced specific historical periods. And difference, one of my central arguments, is not necessarily defined in ethnic and religious terms—that is, whether a woman is Shi'i, Sunni, Kurd, or Christian, for example. It is important to emphasize that these are relatively new paradigms for classifying Iraqis. Until very recently, difference was experienced largely in relation to social class, place of residence, urban or rural identity, professional background, political orientation, and generation. This is not to argue, however, that sectarian sentiments or tensions did not exist, and that all problems started with the 2003 invasion, especially in light of Saddam Hussein's divide and rule tactics and systematic repression of the Iraqi Kurdish and Shi'i populations.

After Saddam Hussein's 1979 assumption of the presidency, divide and rule tactics increased the polarizing of sectarian divisions inside Iraq. There is no doubt that Kurds and Shi'i bore the brunt of the atrocities committed by the regime, as exemplified by the anti-Kurd *Anfal* campaign, which included chemical attacks against the Kurds in the 1980s, the deportations of Shi'is in the late 1970s and throughout the 1980s, and the brutal repression of the uprisings of Kurds in the north and Shi'i in the south after the 1991 Gulf War. Yet, Sunni Arabs in political opposition parties and, increasingly, even within the Ba'th party were also subjected to arrests, torture, and executions, as were members of other minorities such as Chaldeans, Assyrians, Turkmen, and Mandeans if they were part of opposition groups or, at least, suspected to be so.

At the same time, the accounts of Iraqi women reveal that an urban middle class identity, especially the more cosmopolitan Baghdadi identity, continued to subsume ethnic and religious differences even throughout the period of the sanctions. In other words, a middle class Shi'i family in Baghdad had more in common with its Sunni Arab and Kurdish middle class neighbors in mixed neighborhoods than the impoverished Shi'is living in Madina al-Thawra (renamed Saddam city and now called Sadr city), or the majority of Shi'is in the south. Indeed, Baghdadi families have frequently been multi-religious and multi-ethnic and mixed marriages among urban Baghdadi middle classes were quite common. Since the late 1970s, differences along the lines of secular and Islamist political positions started to assume greater significance and influenced women's experiences of the regime. Members or sympathizers of the Islamist

Shi'i *Da'wa* party, for example, were targeted not so much because of their religious affiliation but because of their opposition to the regime and their aim to establish an Islamic state.

Changing women and gender relations

Although most of the women I interviewed were of urban background, their narratives and historical documents give evidence of the sharp disjuncture between urban and rural lives during the 1950s and 1960s. Women in the countryside did not benefit from the expanding education system in the last years of the monarchy (Feisal II) and in the post-revolutionary period following the 1958 coup under President Abdelkarim Qassim. Urban women benefited from the innovative and dynamic cultural and intellectual movements and events that made the period exhilarating and inspiring for the older women I interviewed. The other immense rupture existed between social classes, with the majority of girls and women belonging to impoverished classes with no access to education or adequate health care facilities. The revolutionary changes and relatively liberal social values and norms experienced by educated middle and upper middle class women stood in harsh contrast to the tribal and traditional patriarchal values shaping the lives of the majority of Iraqi women at the time.

Without ever wanting to diminish the magnitude of the crimes and atrocities committed by the Ba'th regime, my research suggests that a closer and more nuanced analysis is needed to comprehend the various ways the former state impacted women, gender relations, and society more generally. This is not only because state policies towards women were complex and often contradictory, but also because the Ba'th regime itself radically changed both its rhetoric and policies towards women in response to changing economic, social, and political conditions on the ground. However, limited and driven by pragmatic considerations, the regime's initial policies of pushing women into the public sphere, especially in the educational system and the labor force, certainly had an impact on the position of women in society and on relations between men and women. This was particularly the case within the expanding urban middle classes but even women of other socio-economic backgrounds benefited from literacy programs, improved health care, and welfare provisions. Many middle class Shi'i, Sunni, Kurdish, and Christian women concurred in their appreciation of the achievements of the early Ba'th in education, modernization of infrastructures, and welfare provisions. However, the memories of those who were politically active in opposition to the regime are filled with accounts of political repression, mass arrests, torture, and executions. Yet, even some of those women who had experienced arrests or political persecution, spoke about some of the gains women made during the early period of the Ba'th regime. Samia H., for example, who had been imprisoned and tortured in the late 1970s due to her political affiliation and activism linked to the Iraqi communist party told me:

The regime was oppressive from day one. No opposition was tolerated. We communists were persecuted, imprisoned, and systematically tortured. I hated the regime. But looking back I have to say that many Iraqi women benefited from the government's push to educate women, and to include them in the workforce. The regime was also good in providing the infrastructure that allowed women to have families and work at the same time.

From 1968 to the late 1980s, the Iraqi state attempted to shift patriarchal power away from fathers, husbands, brothers, sons, and uncles to make itself the main patriarch and patron of the country. Many middle class men and women welcomed the relatively progressive social policies of the state, which continued while the economy prospered. Yet, among the more religious and conservative forces in Iraqi society such as tribal leaders and Islamists, there was considerable resentment at the state's attempt to interfere in people's traditions and sense of propriety. The limitations of "state feminism"—that is, the easy reversal of progressive reforms and changes imposed from above— became apparent as conditions on the ground changed. The historically ambivalent position towards women as educated workers on the one hand and mothers of future citizens on the other was acutely apparent during the Iran–Iraq war, when Iraqi women were expected to be "superwomen." They had to contribute in even greater numbers to swell the ranks of the depleted labor force, the civil service, and all public institutions while men fought at the front. At the same time, women were pressured to produce more children—ideally five, according to Saddam Hussein—and contribute to the war effort by providing future generations of Iraqi soldiers. Aliya N., who was working as a university lecturer in the 1980s, told me the following during an interview in Amman:

> The government really changed its tone in the 1980s. We were still working and you could see women everywhere, given that most men were at the front fighting. But unlike the 1970s, we became mainly reproducers of children during the war with Iran. We were all told to produce future soldiers. Contraception was made illegal and so was abortion. I found it difficult to juggle my work and responsibilities at home. Fortunately, my husband managed to escape much of the fighting as he had a heart condition. But many of my friends and family lost their loved ones during the Iran–Iraq war.

The regime used women to demarcate boundaries between communities and carry the heavy burden of honor in a society that was becoming more and more militarized. Increasingly, their bodies became the site of nationalist policies and battles. Iraqi men were encouraged to divorce their "Iranian" wives during the war with Iran. On the other hand, Iraqi Arab men were encouraged to marry Kurdish women as part of the regime's Arabization policies in the north. Kurdish women in the north of the country experienced terrible atrocities at the hands of the regime and its soldiers, most notably chemical attacks during the Al-Anfal campaign in the late 1980s. At the same time, Islamist, Kurdish nationalist, communist, and other women affiliated with political opposition were tortured and sexually abused—the latter a form of gendered state violence that, as the chapters by Theresa de Langis and Hillary Hiner illustrate for the dictatorial regimes in Cambodia and Chile, is aimed particularly at women. This type of violence serves not only to humiliate them but also to "dishonor" their male relatives. A Kurdish activist shared the following:

> These were some of the worst times I remember. Many Kurdish women were forced to marry Arab men, so that their children would become Arab. Our neighbor's daughter ended up marrying an Arab. But even worse, we Kurds suffered from the chemical attacks during the Anfal campaign. During that time, the regime's soldiers raped many of our women. Some were killed, others traumatized for life.

After the 1991 Gulf War, following the invasion of Kuwait in August 1990, and the uprisings by Kurds in the North and Shi'a in the South in 1991 following the war in 1991, there was a radical shift from Saddam Hussein's previous policies of centralization and suppression of tribal powers. Weakened by another war and a deteriorating economy, one of Saddam Hussein's strategies to maintain power was to encourage tribalism and revive the power of loyal tribal leaders. Central to the cooption of tribal leaders and a bargaining chip to obtain loyalty was the issue of women and women's rights. The regime accepted tribal practices and customs, such as so-called "honor" killings in return for loyalty.

There is a tendency to write out of history the devastating impact of the most comprehensive sanctions system ever imposed on a country. Sanctions were upheld after the liberation of Kuwait through the United Nation's Security Council Cease Fire Resolution SCR 687 (3 April 1991), which linked the lifting of sanctions to various conditions: recognizing the sovereignty and territorial boundaries of Kuwait; agreeing to the payment of war reparations (estimated at over US$100 billion); ending the regime's repression of its own citizens; eliminating weapons of mass destruction, monitored by a United Nation's Special Committee (UNSCOM); and the releasing of Kuwaiti prisoners. Although sanctions were officially intended to contain Saddam Hussein's power and to control his regional and domestic abuses of human rights, it was not the Iraqi regime but the majority of the Iraqi population that had to pay a heavy price. "A price worth paying," in the famous words of the former US foreign secretary Madeleine Albright, when asked on national television in May 1996 what she thought about the fact that 500,000 Iraqi children had died as a result of sanctions.[5] Hala G. remembered the sanctions period as follows:

Sanctions changed us a lot. First there was no money anymore for the state to pay our salaries. I was a teacher, and had to quit my job as it became too expensive for me to pay for transportation, which used to be free before. Also childcare used to be provided by the state before the sanctions. So I ended up staying at home, trying to help with the education of my children and trying to keep them safe. For the first time, we experienced criminals breaking into our homes. We had to sell all our books and most of the furniture to make ends meet. If it was not for the government's monthly food rations we would have starved. But it was not only that we became poorer and that all the services like healthcare deteriorated. Something happened to us Iraqis. Society became much more conservative and criminality rose drastically.

Far from wanting to suggest that everything was fine prior to the sanctions period, the narratives of the women I spoke with made it clear that dramatic changes related to women's position in society, social values, and living conditions were characteristic of the 1990s. Seen against the current situation in post-2003 Iraq, the changes and developments triggered by sanctions and changing state policies provide the most immediate context and background to the current situation. It is a measure of the desperate straits to which the country has been reduced over the past four years that many Iraqi women now refer even to the sanctions period in nostalgic terms and compare it favorably with the current situation.

Accounts of the more recent past since the 2003 invasion and the subsequent occupation are polarized as well in terms of experiences and assessment of the situation, but accounts have also shifted radically over the years. Initially, many of my Shi'a and Kurdish narrators recounted the post-invasion developments in terms of a shift from authoritarian dictatorship to democracy and freedom, while many of my Sunni Arab narrators were far more critical. However, with time, most of the Iraqi women with whom I spoke, whatever religious or ethnic background, point to the many challenges Iraqi women have faced since 2003, most crucially the lack of security and increases in various forms of gender-based violence. The list is long: domestic violence, verbal and physical intimidation, sexual harassment, rape, forced marriages, child marriages, trafficking, and forced prostitution. These more recent oral histories have created another series of challenges for me as a feminist researcher who is based in the Global North. In what follows, I share my reflections about the conundrum of addressing systematic inequalities and forms of gender-based violence without falling into the trap of either culturalizing developments in Iraq or glossing over the agency and complicity of local actors.

How to speak about gender-based violence?

However seriously we take the task of feminist knowledge production, using oral histories methods and life stories to make narrators participants and subjects as opposed to merely objects of our research, we, as researchers, do the selecting, interpreting, framing, writing, and narrating. Like other authors in this volume, I stress the importance of recognizing our respective and often shifting positionalities when we frame and retell the stories, experiences, and traumas of the people we study and with whom we work.

In a recently published article on sexual violence in Iraq, I bemoaned the various ways that violence has been instrumentalized historically and in the current context, noting that

> sexual and gendered violence is not merely employed as a racist and othering discourse by imperialist powers, and right-wing constituencies in the West, but discourses about sexual violence have emerged at every single moment of political and sectarian tension in modern Iraq as a central polarizing and political device amongst politicians and activists.[6]

I pointed as well to the importance of historicizing gender-based violence to escape the "presentism" and myopic views that absolve a wide range of perpetrators, but also historical complicities and silences, as evident in contemporary representations of gender-based violence in Iraq.

In other words, it is not all about *Daesh* (IS). The UK and US occupation, various Iraqi governments and their militia, insurgents and Shi'a sectarian groups, armed gangs, and individual family members have all been perpetrators of the most vile forms of gender-based and sexual violence in Iraq, ranging from domestic violence, verbal and physical intimidation, sexual harassment, rape, forced marriage, trafficking, forced prostitution, female genital mutilation, and honor-based crimes, including killings.[7] Iraqi and Kurdish feminist activists, who have been at the forefront of struggling against gender-based, as well as other forms, of violence linked to authoritarianism and sectarianism, note that international outrage about ISIS' kidnapping, enslavement, forced marriages, rapes, and torture of Ezidi women has translated neither into adequate material and political support nor into asylum rights. Similarly, those same feminists underscore that gender-based violence and other forms of atrocities are also committed by Shi'a militia against Arab Sunnis.[8]

In recent years, I have increasingly recognized my own pitfalls and difficulties in talking about gender-based violence in Iraq. Refraining from contributing to either the taboo and silencing of sexual and wider gender-based violence within domestic Iraqi politics on the one hand, or the sensationalizing and essentialist culturalist discourses so common in Western media and popular discourses on the other, has been challenging. In this chapter, I have tried to reflect on the habitually impossible task of finding nuanced and genuinely intersectional ways to talk about gender-based violence. I have argued that, in practice, the tension is often reduced to explanatory frameworks that firmly root violence within neo-colonial, imperialist, and neo-liberal policies (particularly those linked to the US and Israel). In other instances, it restrictively references national and local cultures and local manifestations of patriarchy as sources of gender-based inequalities and forms of oppression. However, as I have argued previously, I urge scholars to refrain from applying simplistic and dichotomous frames of analysis and narratives and to engage with the complex interplay of international, transnational, regional, and local power structures and systems of inequalities. Even if our narrators might blame it all on US imperialism or local culture, not too dissimilar from some of the media and policy accounts, we need to resist engaging in oral histories as if violence, inequalities, and traumas have mono-causal roots.[9]

Notes

1 This chapter is based on Nadje Al-Ali, *Iraqi Women: Untold Stories from 1948 to the Present* (London: Zed Books, 2007) as well as subsequent research and reflections.
2 This work was published as Nadje Al-Ali, *Secularism, Gender and the State in the Middle East: The Egyptian Women's Movement* (Cambridge: Cambridge University Press, 2000).
3 Chandra Mohanty, "Under Western Eyes: Feminist Scholarship and Colonial Discourses," in *Third World Women and the Politics of Feminism*, eds. Chandra Mohanty, Ann Russo, and Lourdes Torres (Indiana University Press, 1991); Chandra Mohanty, *Feminism Without Borders: Decolonizing Theory, Practicing Solidarity* (Durham and London: Duke University Press, 2003); Lila Abu-Lughod, "Do Muslim Women Really Need Saving? Anthropological Reflections on Cultural Relativism and Its Others," *American Anthropological Association* 104, no. 3 (2002): 783–790; Lila Abu-Lughod, *Writing Women's Words: Bedouin Stories* (Berkeley: University of California Press, 2008); Lila Abu-Lughod, *Local Contexts of Islamism in Popular Media* (Leiden: Amsterdam University Press, 2006); Deniz Kandiyoti, *Major Issues on the Status of Women in Turkey: Approaches and Priorities* (Ankara: The Association, 1980); Deniz Kandiyoti and Ayse Saktanber, *Fragments of Culture: The Everyday of Modern Turkey* (London and New York: I.B Tauris, 2002).
4 Nadje Al-Ali and Nicola Pratt, *Women and War in the Middle East Transnational Perspectives* (London: Zed Books, 2009); Al-Ali, *Iraqi Women.*
5 One of the most reliable studies on sanctions in Iraq is the report by Richard Garfield, *Morbidity and Mortality Among Iraqi Children from 1990 through 1998: Assessing the Impact of the Gulf War and Economic Sanctions* (New York: Columbia University, 1999). Garfield, an expert on the impact of sanctions on public health, conducted a comparative analysis of the more than 24 major studies that analyzed malnutrition and mortality figures in Iraq during the 1990s. He estimated the most likely number of excess deaths among children under five years of age from 1990 through March 1998 to be 227,000. Garfield's analysis showed that child mortality rates were double those of the previous decade. He has recently recalculated his numbers, based on the additional findings of another study by Mohamed M. Ali and Iqbal H. Shah, "Sanctions and Childhood Mortality in Iraq," *The Lancet* 355, no. 9218 (May 2000): 1851–1857, to arrive at an estimate of approximately 350,000 through 2000. Most of these deaths are associated with sanctions, according to Garfield, but some are also attributable to the Gulf War, which destroyed eighteen of twenty electricity-generating plants and disabled vital water-pumping and sanitation systems. Untreated sewage flowed into rivers used for drinking water, resulting in a rapid spread of infectious diseases. For further information, see also David Cortright, "A Hard Look at Iraq's Sanctions," *The Nation*, last modified 3 December 2001, www.thenation.com/article/hard-look-iraq-sanctions/.

6 Nadje Al-Ali, "Sexual Violence in Iraq: Challenges for Transnational Feminist Politics," *European Journal of Women's Studies* (2016): 1–18.
7 Al-Ali, "Sexual Violence in Iraq."
8 Nadje Al-Ali, "How to Talk about Gender-Based Violence?," *Kohl: A Journal for Body and Gender* 1, no. 2 (2016): 8–11.
9 Al-Ali, "Sexual Violence in Iraq"; Al-Ali, "Gender-Based Violence?"

Section 3

Decentering and decolonizing in feminist oral history

Introduction to Section 3
Decentering and decolonizing in feminist oral history

Nan Alamilla Boyd

The chapters in this third section document the ways that Western imperial violence has left a path of gendered destruction in its wake. They center the voices of narrators and address stories of wartime trauma and survival. Almost uniformly, the authors of these chapters assert that trauma is survived through human interaction and connection, through breaking silence and, as Theresa de Langis makes clear, "speaking private memory to public power."[1] Questions of feminism and oral history methods are explicitly addressed but decentered as speculative analysis about histories of sexual violence, which move gendered survival to the foreground. Interpersonal communication through storytelling, witnessing, and testifying are methods of survival rather than mechanisms for the production of data. Memory politics are pushed to the side in favor of, as Stéphane Martelly concludes, "allowing us to think in an opaque and broken way about opaque and broken things."[2]

Western epistemologies and methods of knowledge production embrace the value of scientific methods, and Western feminist oral history methods push back, asserting the value of subjective and multiple truths while empowering women's voices. As Sue Anderson, Jaimee Hamilton, and Lorina L. Barker note in their piece, oral history emerged as a new field of study in Western contexts in response to the 1960s civil rights and anti-colonial movements, but the oral transmission of knowledge through yarning and *Dadirri*, Australian Indigenous practices of knowledge transmission through storytelling and deep listening, have long embraced the values that feminist oral history practitioners embrace. Together, they assert that contemporary feminist oral history projects, both recorded and unrecorded, are a *revival* or adaption of Indigenous practices rather than an innovative, new practice. Key aspects of yarning include respect and reciprocity as stories are re-told and re-enacted. Aboriginal knowledge production is secured through deep listening and reflection rather than citation or documentation. While embracing feminism, the academic utility of oral history methods is discarded in favor of everyday or community-based knowledge production.

These insights—the rejection of Western epistemologies in favor of community-based or deeply local ontologies—emerge in multiple ways and with uncanny regularity through this section of *Beyond Women's Words*. Theresa de Langis' chapter, for instance, describes how the "Cambodian Women's Oral History" project (CWOHP) collected 126 hours of publicly available testimonies of sexual violence during the Khmer Rouge's genocidal regime in late-1970s Cambodia. De Langis focuses on the special ethical considerations that must be taken into account when collecting stories of sexual and gender-based violence under conditions of mass atrocity; she highlights the "stakes of disclosure" and the "potential treacherousness" of the interviewer and narrator relationship. For example, the Tuol Seng Genocide Museum's archive in Phnom Phen, which houses the CWOHP interviews, also preserves the forced confessions of thousands of prisoners who were tortured by the Khmer Rouge. De Langis reminds readers that while the act of remembering may function as a method of contemporary political redress, it has also served as a central disciplinary technology for mass atrocity and genocide. To this end, she asks: What is the difference between Khmer Rouge interrogators and contemporary researchers who evaluate the veracity of women's memories of sexual violence? In response, but also to defuse the fetishization of trauma stories, de Langis develops a method of ethical engagement that attempts to minimize risks for narrators who have experienced sexual and gender-based violence, which involves taking herself almost completely out of the picture. Narrators decide the location, who is present, and which memories will be made public or kept confidential. Narrators also communicate with and through young Khmer research assistants rather than de Langis, an outsider who does not speak the local language. Counseling, self-care, check-ins, and post-interview debriefings became necessary for both narrators and assistants. Most importantly, de Langis describes a process that prioritizes narrators' healing over the production of truth:

> Is the memory true? Is it verifiable? Is it accurate after decades of contortion and neglect? While these questions are central to an adjudicative process seeking formal justice, from a feminist oral history perspective, they seem secondary to the act of speaking what was previously unspeakable.[3]

In the end, data collection and the politics of truth-telling are decentered in favor of a collective and deeply local method of ethical engagement that supports cross-generational witnessing of women's heretofore silenced stories of survival.

Hillary Hiner's meditation on wartime sexual violence, torture, and memory politics in Chile echoes and extends many of de Langis' concerns. In Latin America, oral history repositories often function as tools of political repudiation, exemplified by what Hiner calls *nunca mas* politics: shedding light on the mechanics of violence during periods of state terrorism so these practices will never again be deployed. Hiner, like de Langis, compares state-sponsored oral history methods to those she practices as part of a feminist oral history project of Chilean women. Her approach speaks to the ethical care of survivors who, by participating in highly political testimonies, risk being re-traumatized by memory politics. Importantly, Hiner also highlights the stories of queer and trans women who have been ignored or silenced by state-based memory projects.

Similarly, Stéphane Martelly questions the relationship between authorial centers and margins in her observations as a scholar who worked within the "Montréal Life Stories" project, which collected the stories of Montréalers who identify as displaced peoples and are situated within communities of refugees and exiles. For her part, Martelly focuses on interviews conducted with *Les femmes endeuillées de La Maison d'Haïti*, a post-earthquake grieving group of Montréal-based Haitian women. In the process of conducting interviews and, later, facilitating a creative writing group, Martelly notices a discursive shift brought on by resistant narrators. Again, questions of violence and survival are foregrounded. In this case, a non-linear form of narrative develops as the project's methodological concept of "shared authority" morphs into a multivalent form of expression that defies individual authority: narrators chose an anonymous group-speak, which shattered the form of the interview: "The interviewers were not interviewing anymore, as the women were asking most of the questions to us and each other."[4] More importantly, "the subject was not defined and singular anymore, as it was . . . plural in voice" and "the narration itself ceased to be linear," becoming fragmented and overlapping.[5] Strikingly, narrators refused to be filmed or identified. What emerged through a process of uneasy collaboration was a new mechanism that defied and rejected normative methods of data collection in order to offer strength and care. Martelly observes that "a knowledge of uncertainty, a knowledge of resonance instead of reason . . . began to appear as a distinct possibility."[6] Narrators transformed both the form and function of the oral history project. They pushed back against Western epistemological concerns, especially the utility of the archival project, to construct a collaborative non-narrative that displaces the authority of linear individual life stories in favor of collective healing.

The contribution of Grace Akello echoes these concerns. In a piercing analysis, she centers wartime trauma and survival from an intersubjective perspective; Akello is an anthropologist who employs an ethnographic approach in studying the impact of violence on children in northern Uganda. In contrast to Western feminist concerns with self-reflexivity and positionality, her personal history as a child survivor of poverty and violence raises questions of transference and over-identification, which cause Akello to challenge her own social science methods:

> If ethnography is in its concise sense "writing about people," then how do I classify a study where the researcher and the respondents compose a narrative depicting a weaving together of their joint past and present experiences in an intersubjective space?[7]

Akello researches the healthcare complaints and requests of children displaced by war and living in child-headed households. As she becomes conscious of her "embodied experiences" of empathy and identification with some of the children who participate in her research, she acknowledges that her own embodied fears and history of trauma impact her research findings in ways that pull at the edges of "truth." However, in the process, something valuable has been uncovered. Following Luisa Passerini, Akello speculates that memory functions as a mechanism of subconscious desire. Alongside other authors in the section, she rejects the deep-rooted binary between researcher and researched and explores the profound possibilities of knowledge produced through empathy, care, and collective storytelling. These are not scientific methods but, rather, methods for collective grief and recovery.

Notes

1   Theresa de Langis, Chapter 11 of this volume, 155.
2   Stéphane Martelly, Chapter 13 of this volume, 190.
3   Theresa de Langis, Chapter 11 of this volume, 166.
4   Stéphane Martelly, Chapter 13 of this volume, 188–189.
5   Stéphane Martelly, Chapter 13 of this volume, 189.
6   Stéphane Martelly, Chapter 13 of this volume, 189.
7   Grace Akello, Chapter 14 of this volume, 196.

11 Speaking private memory to public power

Oral history and breaking the silence on sexual and gender-based violence during the Khmer Rouge genocide

Theresa de Langis

Conflict-related sexual violence has come to be recognized as one of the most horrific weapons of war, an instrument of terror usually targeted against women, but that affects entire societies. This chapter focuses on an independent self-funded research initiative, the "Cambodian Women's Oral History" project (CWOHP), conducted between 2012 and 2016.[1] The collection of 21 life-story narratives is among the first cohesive set of publically accessible oral histories that relay the distinct experiences of women in armed conflict and mass atrocity scenarios, a growing area of interest in international relations and security studies.[2] Particularly noteworthy is the candid ways that narrators detail accounts of sexual and gender-based violence committed largely with impunity during the brutal Khmer Rouge regime. Collectively, the narratives represent a watershed moment, dispelling a long-held belief that sexual crimes were not a distinct element of the Cambodian atrocity, and that women would not tell their stories. Without the existence and preservation of these life stories, this aspect of the Khmer Rouge's brutal history may have faded into oblivion.

I am a 52-year-old white woman from the United States living full-time in Phnom Penh as a college professor, an independent researcher, and an international technical expert on women's human rights in conflict and post-conflict scenarios. As a feminist who believes that women are the best experts on their own experiences, and that their stories, too often silenced, must be given public space for articulation, I conceived CWOHP as both a political *and* an ethical project. Guided by the critical principles and insights detailed in *Women's Words*, my project worked from the premise that, in aiming for non-oppression, its processes and products would seek to avoid, if not disrupt, the perpetuation of exploitation of women.[3] Like the Chilean memory projects discussed by Hillary Hiner in this volume (Chapter 15), the CWOHP aims to contribute to a nascent body of oral history projects by critical feminist scholars working on issues of sexual violence in conflict scenarios, gender, and memory.[4] Such projects forefront issues of oppression and power, both as embedded within the narrative itself and as existing between interviewer and narrator. Eschewing positivism, they not only attempt to break hierarchies, but also supplant appropriation with reclamation of suppressed women's voices and histories, even political identities, as narrators situate their lives for the first time in relation to a national historical narrative of protracted conflict and genocide.

I wrote this chapter while preparing the Khmer language files of the CWOHP collection for deposit into the Tuol Sleng Genocide Museum, in Phnom Penh, Cambodia. As Judith Stacey observes, feminist inquiry is radically self-reflective, and vigilant to the "structural inequalities in research and . . . the irreconcilability of Otherness."[5] The moment of deposit of files similarly prompts assessment of the processes and products of the oral history endeavor. My reflections here are guided by the following questions: What are the ethical considerations involved when collecting testimonies of conflict and mass atrocity involving sexual and gender-based violence? How does oral history make space for women to "talk back" to the conditions of their oppression and exploitation? What difference do such accounts make and what unique perspectives arise regarding the impact of atrocity when women speak private memory to public power?

Prologue: Confessions

I am sitting at a desk in one of the many decrepit buildings at the Tuol Sleng Genocide Museum in the heart of Cambodia's capital city, Phnom Penh. The museum preserves the notorious secret prison and interrogation center, code-named S-21, which became a house of horrors under the totalitarian regime of Democratic Kampuchea, more commonly known as the Khmer Rouge regime, which controlled Cambodia between 1975 and 1979.[6] An estimated one-quarter of the population—upwards of two million people—is thought to have perished as a result of ultra-Maoist policies aimed at creating a "pure" collectivist agrarian utopia. Whole cities were forcibly evacuated and an entire population was mobilized to toil in the rice fields and in primitive irrigation construction sites. Private property was abolished, as were the private family, personal loyalties, and private life. Slave-like conditions stripped many thousands of people of basic human rights; starvation, disease, overwork, torture, and execution prevailed.

Any infraction of the rigid Khmer Rouge regulations—pilfering grains of rice, mourning a loved one's death, wearing glasses, or even reading—was considered political betrayal to the regime, warranting harsh punishment or death. S-21, converted from a high school campus, was the regime's principal interrogation and torture facility and the central hub for hundreds of death camps throughout the countryside. An estimated 15,000 "enemy traitors" entered its gates. Only a handful survived. A policy of "destroying the weeds by killing the roots" meant whole families were arrested and held at S-21. Some of the survivors were barely toddlers when Vietnamese forces entered the city in 1979, sending Khmer Rouge supporters fleeing back to the jungle.

I have taken up a six-month residency at the museum to prepare for the deposit into the museum archives of the Khmer files of the CWOHP, thereby fulfilling my commitment to the narrators and to a code of ethics that behooves the oral historian to find the most appropriate repository in which to preserve and make accessible such documents. The Tuol Sleng Genocide Museum is a memory site of national and indeed international significance. Founded in 1980, months after the fall of the Pol Pot regime, the museum is well known for its macabre presentation of the arrival of Vietnamese soldiers who came to "liberate" the country with a vanguard of Khmer Rouge defectors. They occupied the country for the next ten years. An eerie paralysis hangs there, as even today, torture rooms and miniscule holding cells are preserved. Near life-sized photos of victims' remains in the contorted shape in which they were first found are displayed, and wall upon wall of prisoner mug shots, taken as part of the registration process, gaze like specters beyond death. Although the vast majority of Cambodian fatalities occurred in rural areas, the museum is commonly identified as *the* "museum of the Cambodian nightmare."[7] Visited annually by tens of thousands of individuals and renowned scholars from around the world, its archive is registered on UNESCO's Memory of the World roster. The museum seems the most appropriate home for the CWOHP and its stories.

A few days into my residency, I realize the place is haunted. I am under (self) interrogation. This moment of deposit does indeed provoke self-reflection and radical exposure on my part. In dredging up these memories, I ask myself, what did we generate, at what level of quality, and to what end? As I check translations against transcripts against audio and video recordings, I fear that once the papers are deposited, no matter how meticulously organized and neatly archived, my limitations in managing the chaos of the interview and its results will be on permanent display. If the stakes of disclosure are disquieting for me, the potential costs are excruciatingly severe for the narrators.

As a feminist oral historian, I know that "the inequality and potential treacherousness" of the relationship between interviewer and narrator is "inescapable."[8] Indeed, just beyond the shared wall of my office lies the Tuol Sleng archive, where the CWOHP papers are headed. The archive preserves forced confessions of 4,000-plus prisoners, largely fabricated through extreme torture, documenting the "awesome cruelty of the regime toward its citizens" and serving as partial evidence of the crimes against humanity committed here.[9] According to David Chandler, the very practice of forcing prisoners to recount false and self-incriminating testimonies—some of the transcripts produced are close to 100 pages—made S-21 a "total institution."[10] Here, memory, the act of remembering, was exploited as a central element of the prison's disciplinary technology of oppression and control. In meticulously producing and preparing these documents, and then preserving them long after the confessors' execution, did the regime not also seek to exert power over the past, solidifying its hegemony over the unforgiving reality of the then-present?

I am haunted by the uncanny resemblances between the process that produced the Khmer Rouge confessions and the process by which oral historians write sympathetic oral histories. Both interviewers and interrogators use controlled conversations to illicit life stories and then transcribe and painstakingly preserve them as historical documents. I was no torturer, but did I not prod my narrators to revisit scenes of trauma and tragedy? Who was I— an American whose nation's political legacy was intertwined with the Khmer Rouge takeover of Cambodia—to be collecting stories about these atrocities? Was I not also wielding power over agonizing memories of sexual crimes that had been repressed for more than three decades? Was that evidence, those intimate details of violation, not coming "under my investigation and scrutiny" to be exposed as "spectacles" of sexual offenses, with survivors reduced to narrators and their recorded stories to "documentary sources."[11]

My process, informed by feminism as both social movement and critical inquiry, intentionally sought to produce a countervailing voice to the discussion—and denial—surrounding sexual violence under the Khmer Rouge regime. Given the restrictions, both normative and institutional, that silenced these memories, the project also sought to create spaces in which women could share their experiences of sexual abuse. Their discourse has been overwhelmed by the proceedings of the Extraordinary Chambers in the Courts of Cambodia (ECCC), known as the Khmer Rouge tribunal, which has been adjudicating crimes alleged against senior-level surviving leaders of the regime. Feminists have long critiqued the ECCC for its reluctant, narrow, and partial treatment of reported sexual crimes committed under the regime. As with other such tribunals, those proceedings also necessarily interrogate the veracity of human-memory-as-evidence and (over)determine the subject as the victim of a crime, leaving survivors feeling unheard and undervalued.[12] For sexual violence survivors, who are often framed as complicit, manipulative, and prevaricators, engaging with formal judicial systems is always risky, but all the more so with a tribunal that is thrust into the international spotlight.[13]

I choose feminist oral history as my method precisely to record the "muted channels of women's experience" and to foreground subjectivity in mapping social experience.[14] Even while documenting women's oppression, I saw the narrators as agents of change and sought to avoid robbing them of their intrinsic value as human beings by fetishizing their trauma or re-fetishizing sexual violation as a quintessential crime against women.[15] The life-story approach highlighted the context and their choices, however limited. I expected the women's stories to depart from the dominant discourse; once publically declared, these stories, I also hoped, would disrupt, not echo, the status quo.

Following decades of widespread refusal to acknowledge pervasive sexual violence during the Khmer Rouge period, the CWOHP narrators recounted an astonishing range of sexual violence as part of their experience of the atrocity, including abusive forced marriage, rape within forced marriage, forced pregnancy, sexual slavery, rape prior to execution, rape as torture, mass rape, gang rape, and rape with the object of sexual mutilation.[16] Narrators came from throughout the country, and spoke from their positions as civilians, Khmer Rouge cadre, Indigenous people, transgendered, and religious minorities. Knowing they had long been told that their stories did not matter or were not true, I aimed to demonstrate to CWOHP narrators my confidence in their stories and my conviction in their value.

While not always aware of my full intentions, in hindsight, I was aspiring to collect "anti-confessions" as an antidote to the Khmer Rouge atrocity and violent manipulation of memory. S-21, with its forced confessions, was a house of lies. Today, for many Cambodians, it is a "sinister place full of ghosts and strange happenings," a crime site "perpetuating silence about the past" and "facilitating passive victimhood."[17] The CWOHP narratives are powerfully provocative in such a context. Inspired by the demands of survivors and motivated by their desire to collectively shatter the silence, shame, and blame imposed on sexual violence victims, the narratives speak private memory to public power in calling for justice and an end to impunity for the full scope of Khmer Rouge sexualized crimes. The confessions next door inscribe vicious deceits, but the CWOHP narratives speak back with defiantly courageous impertinence.

Process: Private memory to public power

The CWOHP is positioned on an advocacy continuum that catalyzed in 2011 at the first Cambodian Women's Hearing (CWH) on Sexual Violence under the Khmer Rouge. I co-facilitated the event, which was convened by the local human rights organizations, the "Cambodian Defenders" project (CDP), and the Transcultural Psychosocial Organization of Cambodia (TPO). The hearing created a non-judicial truth-telling platform for victims and witnesses to publically "testify" about widespread sexual crimes under the regime. It reflected a tradition of feminist story-based advocacy and was part of a global movement to provide alternative truth-telling forums in cases where formal judicial mechanisms prove unable or unwilling to bring justice particularly to survivors of gender-based crimes committed during armed conflict and under repressive regimes.[18] The CWH was a response to the ongoing ECCC proceedings and their exclusion from the public record of rampant sexual violence.[19]

In garnering international attention, the CWH promoted public acknowledgement of, and reduced social stigma related to, decades-long silenced sexual crimes. Subsequent hearings held in 2012 and 2013 generated recommendations that included calls to document and preserve survivor stories for international exposure to younger generations. A sense of urgency reigned as the victims were aging. At the time, I was working as a consultant on women, peace, and security issues in the Asia-Pacific region, based in Phnom Penh. Through this work, I launched an oral history project to record the life stories of women survivors, with broad geographical representation.

In preparation, I attended specialized trainings and conversed extensively with important oral history mentors.[20] I understood that I would be collecting a specific "genre" of testimony that asks survivors for an invocation of the "destruction" of atrocity, and that such stories could only unfold with ample time, through a process that moved from information gathering to shared decision making.[21] I trained myself on the obligations involved in collecting stories of atrocity, especially the need to minimize risks for those dealing with the aftermath of sexual violence, and applied my experience in protection and prevention advocacy in Afghanistan and the United States. I also maintained relationships with the organization and partners hosting the CWH, and with women testifiers receiving legal assistance and psychosocial support. I conducted two focus groups with survivors through TPO to design the project and validate its oral history approach. An online web presence (http://cambodian womensoralhistory.com/) would show excerpts of narratives and videos selected in conversation with the narrators. In both focus groups, the women insisted that the oral histories include women's stories only, though all participants welcomed both men and women on the research team.[22] Aspiring to a shared decision-making methodology, I largely self-funded the project to remain independent, hence responsive solely to the narrators and the process. Funding restrictions kept the project small (a maximum of 24 interviews) but I designed a low-cost platform that local activists could replicate.[23]

The collection team comprised a small group of assistants, primarily recent Khmer university graduates with varying English-language abilities. We trained

Figure 11.1 Nam Mon and her husband watch the interview excerpt on
         http://cambodianwomensoralhistory.com/ in Kampong Cham, 12
         September 2013. Credit: Theresa de Langis

ourselves and everyone else involved in the project (including the tuk-tuk and taxi drivers) on confidentiality procedures (paid assistants and volunteers signed confidentiality and risk mitigation agreements) and ethical codes of conduct for post-conflict data collection of sexual violence information. Blending multiple disciplines, we committed to a conflict-sensitive and survivor-centered collection of testimonies for public historical preservation, and we prioritized mitigating the risk of re-traumatizing and/or retaliation against narrators. Since recording the stories was their idea, I began the interview process with eight of the CWH participants. The fact that these women had previously testified publically reduced potential risks and anxiety. As the project grew, the single stipulation for participation (outside of identifying as a woman) was that narrators had already shared their stories with family and community members. To assure they had a safety net of support beyond the interview itself, all the narrators were introduced to me through local intermediary organizations.

In most cases, the interviews took place in women's traditional Khmer homes. Scattered across the remote countryside, the houses have palm-leaf walls, thatched roofs, scant electricity, no indoor plumbing, and little to no privacy. My team from Phnom Penh and I were shocked by the level of poverty that existed even after an influx of billions of dollars of international aid. Still, we agreed that paying the narrators was not a good idea (participation was completely voluntary), even though many participants, even elderly women, sacrificed a day's income to participate in the interview. The interviews, recorded by tablet audio and video to capture ambient sounds, lasted roughly six hours, over one or two sultry Cambodian days. We tried to keep our footprint light, carrying in water and snacks, and leaving for the traditional two-hour lunch break and mid-day nap so narrators could relax in peace. Each interview began with a two-stage, 30-minute consent process: a pre-interview request for permission to record, then a post-interview request for permission to use, deposit, and make the interview publicly accessible. Most narrators well understood the consent process. Many became impatient with it, saying that after decades of shame they were determined to publicly name and claim the atrocities under their own names.[24] Our 3G phones helped explain the risks of public disclosure in an Internet age. My expertise as a human rights practitioner helped me discuss the safety plans that would take effect if the interview re-triggered trauma or provoked reprisal from perpetrators who continue to live in the community, some of whom are in positions of power. I continually had to brace myself to respect the risks that narrators were willing to take. Given the narrators' low level of literacy, we recorded the reading and clarification of the informed consent form, which we signed for them, and then gave them hard copies in Khmer and English, as well as bilingual business cards.

A system of silent, simultaneous translation minimized recorded voices except the narrator's. I asked guiding questions through an interpreter while a translator took summary notes in English. Ultimate authority over the interview rested with the narrator. She chose the location, break times, who would be present, and which memories would be either made public or kept confidential. I answered all questions related to the process, my life, and my experiences. The guiding questions requested an historical narration, from first-life memories, through life stages, to the present-day conditions of their lives.[25]

We staged interview "missions to the field" (as my Khmer assistants called them) that lasted about five days, during which we collected multiple narratives.

Figure 11.2 Prak Yoeun stands in front of her house in Kampong Speu, 14 December 2013. Credit: Theresa de Langis

We then took breaks for transcription and translation and for me to take on new consultancies to maintain funding. The process was utterly draining and humbling for all, individually and collectively. Counseling, self-care, check-ins, and deep post-interview debriefings helped maintain the team's emotional, mental, and professional health. Together, we repeatedly clarified our objectives. We were not investigating crimes or diagnosing trauma disorders, for example, so referred such cases to the experts. We never probed to the extent that narrators felt compelled to divulge something they did not want to share. We did not try to influence the order in which events were relayed or to contain repetition. We did constantly negotiate translations and interpretations.[26] Because I am a white foreign professor, the women treated me with deference. However, the lags in interpretation and translation meant that I often lost track of the line of questioning—and any sense that I was the "expert." The greatest feminist lesson I learned was that of profound humility. I learned to relinquish control of the "research scene," and to trust that the chaos was somehow generative. Over the course of the interviews, I became increasingly quiet. Without constant translation, the interview evolved into an intergenerational dialogue between the project's young Khmer assistants and the narrator.

The CWOHP collected 126 hours of interviews for eventual deposit in the Tuol Sleng Genocide Museum's archive. These stories, once in jeopardy of

Figure 11.3 Prak Yoeun is interviewed by You Sotheary, lead research assistant for the CWOHP, in Kampong Speu, on 14 December 2013. Credit: Theresa de Langis

being lost from the public record, have already begun to proliferate, opening new narrative space and possibility for collective remembrance of a long-neglected part of the atrocity. In March 2016, the museum held a public exhibit featuring CWOHP narratives and announced the collection's deposit. Some narrators were there, as was the Minister of Culture and Fine Arts, who oversees the museum. In her speech, the Minister not only publicly acknow-ledged these long-hidden crimes, but also poignantly shared her own experience of multiple escapes from a forced marriage ordered by the regime. The narratives will serve as a basis for a Khmer classical opera. The ECCC endorsed the opera, an effort to change cultural norms through the use of a beloved art form, as an official, if only symbolic, judicial reparation for survivors of forced marri-age—pending conviction. Coming full circle in the long arc of an advocacy continuum, in 2015, the ECCC initiated new sexual crime investigations for the remainder of their cases. The courageous women who offered their testimonies of sexual violence during the regime, claiming public power by reclaiming private memory, have forever changed how we tell the history of the Khmer Rouge atrocity. Their actions are gendering and transforming the political contours of Cambodian national identity in a way that puts women's human rights at its core. In eradicating the amnesia of brutality against women, in all of its forms, in conflict and in peace, these women's bravery is part of a global story that touches all of us.

Last words: Women's voices speak back

The stories recorded through the CWOHP demand a rigorous and multivalent form of listening that attends to trauma while opening space for the narrative agency of suppressed subjects. If feminist approaches to oral history enable a shift away from "scientific interviewing" and the search for "verified facts," they also validate the importance of ceding control to engage in the simple act of "believing [in] the interchange."[27] They honor the narrator by being "totally present, committed and attuned listener[s]," where even analysis is "suspended or subordinated to the process of listening."[28] Such listening—in sustained suspension—is not easy. Yet, it is essential.

Careful listening to the subjective female life experiences relayed by our CWOHP women narrators revealed a "counter narrative" reverberating in the cracks of a dominant master narrative that excluded them.[29] As the following excerpt from narrator Lash Vanna illustrates, the women confronted a master narrative that did not consider them credible sources:

> The ECCC officials came here and held a meeting, and someone asked, "Who experienced rape during the Khmer Rouge?" I was too ashamed to answer in front of so many people. But I told others secretly that I was raped during that time [of the] regime. Someone from the ECCC overheard and asked, "Is it true?" I said, "Yes, I was raped." He replied, "Do you have evidence?"[30]

The CWOHP narratives are as relevant to questions of justice as they are to security studies based on partial accountings of armed conflicts. They speak volumes in their provocation of the Khmer Rouge's state-sanctioned master narrative, its silences and ellipses. They teach us about the many silences, some imposed, others adopted—or re-positioned—in a struggle for survival. They offer insight into how mass atrocity is intricately connected to the control of voice and the public display of identity—issues that matter to feminist oral historians. Speaking to these themes, narrator Mon Vun said:

> If we knew the truth [about the rape], we'd be killed faster than the victim. ... We were silent. That night I said, "I feel such pity for Din. She was raped and killed by the Khmer Rouge cadre." The others responded, "Please be silent! Don't talk about this! The spies can hear us!" I thought the world had turned upside-down. I wanted everyone to know the truth, that she had been raped by four cadres, who then cut out her gallbladder and killed her. We worked together. We slept near each other. We saw. But no one talked about it. The Khmer Rouge was a dictatorship, and their power was everywhere.[31]

Even today, many consider accounts of Khmer Rouge-era rape as "shameful stories." This shame and silence perpetuates the blaming of victims and impunity for perpetrators. The Khmer Rouge's violent, hegemonic control over memory and what constituted the "truth" was reinforced by the restrictive cultural and gender codes of Cambodian society that both pre-dated and outlasted the regime. Such structural and cultural inequities mean that women benefit much less than men from the peace dividend of national healing and reconciliation in post-conflict societies. Many of the CWOHP narrators pointed out how the social stigma related to their rapes was as severe as the crime itself, and far outlasted it. Lash Vanna explained:

> If a person was raped, she could not tell anyone. It was a shameful story. The value of a woman depends at that place [with virginity]. Even after the Khmer Rouge was finished, how could we tell our stories? We did not want to be judged by others as bad women because the Khmer Rouge enemy had raped us.[32]

Yet, the stories lingered, often in whispers. Knowledge of the sexual violence during the regime was preserved in the power of rumor, gossip, informal chatter—women's localized talk. As Prak Yoeun remembered:

> During the Khmer Rouge time, we heard about rapes from mouth to mouth as we were forced to work, eat, and sleep collectively. We knew what [the District commander] did, but we dared not say it out loud. He was a high-ranking cadre and a chief.[33]

Within such a context, the process of (re)claiming private memory through public story, whereby the narrator controls and owns the story, is politically powerful as well as personally recuperative and transformative. Net Savoeun shared:

> Previously, I had felt secretly ashamed in front of other people. After I shared my story [with a psychosocial support organization], I didn't mind anymore sharing openly with the villagers. They must have all along known the real truth—that, when we were called to be killed or punished, the women also were raped. I am an old woman now, and no one discriminated against me for telling this story. In fact, my neighbors admire me for speaking out.[34]

A recognition of the women's stories provides a more comprehensive and accurate account of Khmer Rouge atrocities. They shed light on how it operated within a system of multivalent gender oppression and on how women managed to exert agency even in the most inhumanely oppressive of circumstances. Because memory in mass atrocity is rigidly controlled, and memory of sexual violence deeply suppressed, keeping alive the memories of sexual violence victims is both a form of human tribute and an act of radical resistance. As Sok Samith shared:

> My family thinks it is useless to remember that the past is the past, and even the ECCC is a show put on for foreigners. But I think, I survived, and I have a right and responsibility to share my story. Especially Mrs. Ouk's story, because it has never been revealed and she was my friend, she helped me survive. A Khmer Rouge chief raped her until she became pregnant, and then she was put in jail, tortured and killed. Not many people will say this story out loud. Only I know the truth, so I must find the courage to tell it. If I remain silent, the story will die with me. If I speak out, then Ouk can claim her human dignity as someone who once existed.[35]

Is the memory true? Is it verifiable? Is it accurate after decades of contortion and neglect? While these questions are central to an adjudicative process seeking formal justice, from a feminist oral history perspective, they seem secondary to the act of speaking what was previously unspeakable. At least, it opens the question of whether the recuperative power of the whispered story spoken aloud exceeds the retributive aims of official adjudications, such as those at the ECCC, especially when retribution only serves to re-inscribe the subordinate status of women and normalize the violence against her, in peace and in armed conflict. Feminist oral history, in opening space for women to talk back to the conditions of their own oppression, changes the story for all of us. It transforms our efforts at justice and peace—but only if we are ready to listen, suspending certainty for the sake of narrative discovery. Here, Mon Vun gets the last word:

The ECCC said they will not include rape in the trial because women didn't speak out about it. Well, we were ashamed to talk about that story. I attended the Women's Hearing in 2011. I was inspired by the women who spoke out that day. I had always wanted to share what happened to me, but I didn't have the confidence. Now I want the world to know about what happened to me. The perpetrators are out of prison because we let shame keep us from telling the whole truth.[36]

Notes

1 My deepest gratitude to the women of the CWOHP, the Cambodian Defenders Project, Open Society Asia Justice Initiative, and donors to the crowd-funding Kickstarter campaign for supporting this largely self-funded project.
2 Morten Bergsmo, Alf Butenschon Skre, and Elisabeth J. Wood, eds., *Understanding and Proving International Sex Crimes* (Beijing: Torkel Opsahl Academic EPublisher, 2012); Laura J. Shepard, ed., *Gender Matters in Global Politics* (New York: Routledge, 2010); Annick T.R. Wibben, *Feminist Security Studies: A Narrative Approach* (London: Routledge, 2011).
3 Sherna Berger Gluck and Daphne Patai, eds., *Women's Words: The Feminist Practice of Oral History* (New York: Routledge, 1991). Also see Shulamit Reinharz, *Feminist Methods in Social Research* (New York: Oxford University Press, 1992), 27; G.C. Spivak, "Can the Subaltern Speak?" in *Colonial Discourse and Postcolonial Theory Reader*, eds. Patrick Williams and Laura Chrisman (Hemel Hempstead: Harvester, 1993), 66–111.
4 Besides Hiner's chapter in this volume, this literature includes Hillary Hiner, "They Dance Alone: Gender in the Chilean Transition to Democracy," *Anamesa* 3, no. 1 (2005): 3–21; Marlene Epp, "The Memory of Violence: Soviet and East European Mennonite Refugees and Rape in the Second World War," *Journal of Women's History* 9, no. 1 (1997): 58–87; Selma Leydesdorff, *Surviving the Bosnian Genocide: The Women of Srebrenica Speak Out*, trans. Kay Richardson (Bloomington: Indiana University Press, 2011); and Luisa Passerini, especially in *Gender and Memory: International Yearbook of Oral History and Life Stories, Volume IV*, eds. Selma Leydesdorff, Luisa Passerini, and Paul Thompson (Oxford: Oxford University Press, 1996).
5 Judith Stacey, "Can There Be a Feminist Ethnography?" in *Women's Words*, 116.
6 Elizabeth Becker, *When the War Was Over: Cambodia and the Khmer Rouge Revolution* (New York: Public Affairs Press, 1998).
7 David Chandler, *Voices from S-21: Terror and History in Pol Pot's Secret Prison* (Berkeley: University of California Press, 1999), 5.
8 Stacey, 113.
9 Chandler, 49.
10 Chandler, 15, 47.
11 Henry Greenspan et al., "Engaging Survivors: Assessing 'Testimony' and 'Trauma' as Foundational Concepts," in *Daupin: Studies on the Holocaust* (The Institute for Holocaust Research at the University of Haifa, 2014), 192.
12 Greenspan et al., 195.
13 Monica Eileen Patterson, "The Ethical Murk of Using Oral Historical Research in South Africa," in *Oral History Off the Record: Toward an Ethnography of Practice*, eds. Anna Sheftel and Stacey Zembrzycki (New York: Palgrave MacMillan, 2013), 201–218.
14 Kathryn Anderson and Dana C. Jack, "Learning to Listen: Interview Techniques and Analyses," in *Women's Words*, 20; Reinharz, 28.

15 Sherna Berger Gluck, "Advocacy Oral History: Palestinian Women in Resistance," in *Women's Words*, 205. See also Shahrzad Arshadi et al. in this volume (Chapter 20) on "re-witnessing" via oral history without "sensationalizing or deepening existing wounds."

16 Michael Vickery's arguments that women were never safer from sexual abuse than during the Khmer Rouge regime, in *Cambodia: 1975–1982* (Seattle: University of Washington Press, 2000).

17 Kristina Chhim, *Perspectives Series Research Report: "Pacifying Vindictiveness by not Being Vindictive": Do Memory Initiatives in Cambodia Have a Role in Addressing Questions of Impunity?* (The Netherlands: Impunity Watch, 2012), vii.

18 Dianne Otto, "Impunity in a Different Register: People's Tribunals and Questions of Judgment, Law and Responsibility," in *Impunity and Human Rights*, eds. Ken Davis, Karen Engle, and Zinaida Miller (Cambridge: Cambridge University Press, 2015), 291–328.

19 I served as a co-facilitator and a practitioner specialist on women, peace, and security issues: Theresa de Langis, "A Missed Opportunity, a Last Hope? Prosecuting Sexual Crimes under the Khmer Rouge Regime," *Cambodia Law and Policy Journal* 2 (2014): 40. See also *Report on the Proceedings on the 2011 Women's Hearing on Sexual Violence Under the Khmer Rouge Regime* (Phnom Penh: Cambodia Defenders Project, May 2012), accessed 10 August 2016, http://gbvkr.org/wp-content/uploads/2013/01/Report-on-2011-Womens-Hearing_Phnom-Penh.pdf.

20 These included the Intensive Course on Truth, Memory, and Justice convened by the International Center for Transitional Justice in Barcelona, Spain, in 2009, and the Summer Institute at Columbia University with the Center for Oral History, entitled "What is Remembered: Life Story Approaches to Human Rights Contexts," in 2012. The research team's training included reading and then signing off on a copy of the World Health Organization's *Ethical and Safety Recommendations for Researching, Documenting and Monitoring Sexual Violence in Emergencies*, 2007, accessed 8 October 2017, www.who.int/gender/documents/OMS_Ethics&Safety 10Aug07.pdf, and "Principles and Standards of the Oral History Association," found in Donald A. Ritchie's *Doing Oral History: A Practical Guide*, 2nd edition (Oxford: Oxford University Press, 2003), 252–255.

21 Greenspan et al., 191. See also Kim Lacy Rogers and Selma Leydesdorff, with Graham Dawson, eds., *Trauma and Life Stories: International Perspectives* (London: Routledge, 1999).

22 Special gratitude is extended to Sotheary You, who worked with me throughout the duration of the project. Thanks also to the visionary leadership of Chhay Visoth, Director of the Tuol Sleng Genocide Museum, for understanding the importance of the CWOHP files.

23 The lead research assistant documenting the life stories of Cambodian women human rights defenders has replicated the methodology: http://lwhrd.org/about/.

24 Narrators could choose to use their full identity, an alias, or remain anonymous. Of the 21 narrators, only one participated under an assumed name.

25 The first question was always: "What is the very first thing you can remember from childhood?" I commonly had to ask narrators to dwell longer on childhood before jumping to the Khmer Rouge period, which clearly demonstrated how the genocide, which last four years, dominated their memory and overshadowed other aspects of identity and resilience. I asked specifically about experiencing or witnessing sexual violence if the topic did not arise spontaneously.

26 Nadia Jones-Gailani, "Third Parties in 'Third Spaces': Reflecting on the Role of the Translator in Oral History Interviews with Iraqi Diasporic Women," in *Oral History Off the Record*, 171.

27 Anderson and Jack, 28.

28 Greenspan et al., 199; Anderson and Jack, 15.
29 Jones-Gailani, 171.
30 Narrator #10, interviewed by author, CWOHP, Sihanoukville, 14 December 2014.
31 Narrator #8, interviewed by author, CWOHP, Siem Reap, 11 September 2013.
32 Narrator #10, interview.
33 Narrator #11, interviewed by author and You Sotheary, CWOHP, Kampong Speu, 14 December 2014.
34 Narrator #12, interviewed by author, CWOHP, Svay Rieng, 31 May 2014.
35 Narrator #2, interviewed by author, CWOHP, Phnom Penh, 26 January 2013.
36 Narrator #8, interview.

12 Yarning up oral history
An Indigenous feminist analysis

*Sue Anderson, Jaimee Hamilton,
and Lorina L. Barker*

Yarning, a form of storytelling, is a significant feature of knowledge transmission within Australian Indigenous cultures, particularly between women and children. Children learn through yarning and observation of their environment. A yarning culture practiced for tens of thousands of years has ensured that the art of listening and telling was, and continues to be, embedded within the Australian Aboriginal female psyche. Oral history methodologies hold many commonalities with the yarning that is so deeply rooted in Indigenous culture. For example, both involve a narrative shared between people in an intimate environment and the protocols of trust, reciprocity, and respect. In this chapter, we explore the relationship between Indigenous yarning and oral history theory and practice through the lived experience of Indigenous and non-Indigenous women.[1]

But first it is important to explain the difference in meaning of the terms "yarning" and "oral history" for Indigenous and Western cultures, as the two are often conflated, leading to confusion. Oral history has been variously defined as "information about a historical event or period that is told to you by people who experienced it," a "field of study and a method of gathering, preserving and interpreting the voices and memories of people, communities, and participants in past events," and "the collection and study of historical information using tape recordings of interviews with people having personal knowledge of past events."[2] The Cambridge Dictionary does not require the recording of the information, the United States Oral History Association sees recording as optional, and the Oxford English Dictionary considers it mandatory. Recording is an inherent part of what we consider oral history to be today, an argument to which we return later.

Yarning, on the other hand, has been defined as "an Indigenous style of conversation and storytelling also known as narrative," a "process of making meaning, communicating and passing on history and knowledge," and "a special way of relating and connecting with . . . culture." A definition of yarning that describes it as "a conversational process that involves the sharing of stories and the development of knowledge" notes that "it prioritizes Indigenous ways of communicating, in that it is culturally prescribed, cooperative, and respectful."[3] Here, we use the term "yarning" in the Indigenous sense to indicate the passing on of important knowledge. We do not relate this term to casual conversation or storytelling (usually between males) that has become part of the stereotypical Australian persona.[4] Nor do we draw any parallels with the "yarning" associated with sailors, bad language, and sea shanties.[5] Our belief that yarning is a culturally inherent form of communication that privileges Indigenous ways of knowing, being, and doing also underpins our evaluation of contemporary oral history, not just in the Australian Indigenous context, but globally.[6]

In regards to Australian Indigenous methodologies, Aileen Moreton-Robinson points out: "We are involved in a constant battle to authorise Indigenous knowledges and methodologies as legitimate and valued components of research."[7] Over the past ten to fifteen years, Australian Indigenous academics have worked hard to gain important recognition for the validity of yarning as a reliable methodological approach to qualitative research, though the literature devoted to it remains small. Nevertheless, yarning in an Australian Indigenous context has its roots firmly entrenched in Indigenous standpoint theory, "the position that," as Moreton-Robinson explains, Indigenous women's standpoint "generates problematics informed by our knowledges and experiences."[8]

Our central argument is that oral history has arisen as a field of study out of a realization of the value that yarning has had in representing the primary means of knowledge transmission among Indigenous peoples. Because women are traditionally the educators of children, yarning in Australian Indigenous cultures has also been seen as the domain of women.[9] For example, Aunty June Barker explained how female Elders on the Brewarrina Aboriginal Station, "The Old Mission," during the 1930s found ways to teach children about Country, culture, and language.[10] As she explains, the "small children always went with the women" to the river, where both girls and boys listened to the stories and swam together, up until a boy reached a certain age.[11] Similarly, Antikirinja/Yunkunytjatjara woman Mona Ngitji Ngitji Tur told Sue Anderson that her life as a young child living in her desert country "was very, very good because even though . . . my family lived on the cattle station, they would take us hunting for bush tucker, and sometimes the men would go out hunting for kangaroo and emu while the women went out for the small game." She recalled how her mother, grandmothers, and aunties

> started teaching us about our Wapar, our Dreaming, and that would happen all the time when we were going out with the Elders and also every night before we went to sleep we were told our Wapar so that we could remember the adventures and travels of our ancestral beings.[12]

After the 1788 European invasion of Australia, and the subsequent introduction of the patriarchal social model, the role of Indigenous women in knowledge transmission was subsumed by Western gender roles, lowering it in status in comparison to the written work of mainly white, middle-class men. In the text that follows, we discuss how this development came about, reflect on how formal oral history practice was revived (rather than how it began) as a "new" field, and consider how Western values were placed upon it.

Orality in Indigenous and Western social settings

Oral traditions

For millennia, prior to the European colonization of Australia, the country's Indigenous peoples lived a rich cultural life. Indigenous people are traditionally oral societies and the holistic nature of Indigenous cultures and lifeways has long been recognized.[13] It was premised upon the principle that "everything living is family," so that connection with Country embodies spiritual, psychic, emotional, and physical attachment. So, too, are the various cultural expressions of this belonging inter-related.[14] As Meriam/Wuthathi lawyer Terri Janke observes:

> The many stories, songs, dances, paintings and other forms of cultural expression define the relationships between the land, the people, plants and animals. Arts and cultural expression are therefore important aspects of Indigenous cultural knowledge, power, identity and spirituality.[15]

While gendered roles still exist in more traditional communities, there is no hierarchical privileging of one gender over others; rather, each is autonomous. Some have noted that Indigenous Australian cultures represent the "apogee of egalitarianism."[16] Storytelling is integral to, and a sacred part of, cultural practice, and stories are considered true; that is, they are real and indeed did happen.[17] These stories connect groups to each other and people to all living things in the natural and spirit worlds. For example, the Dreaming stories in Australian and many other Indigenous cultures form the reference point for all of a community's social structures and behaviors. Further, as Julie Cruikshank and Tatiana Argounova-Low note, for Indigenous communities, knowledge is grounded in traditional stories that belong to everyone, not just an individual, and the collective is stressed in all aspects of life.[18] They also note that these stories situate oneself "in dialogue with society," and inform the telling of life stories. Indigenous people maintain and continue to practice the oral traditions of storytelling through the process of yarning in one's own cultural setting or as an Indigenous research methodology.

Western concepts

When Europeans arrived in Australia they brought with them a very different worldview and set of social constructs. Some have described them as "funda-mentally different" or even "antithetic" to Australian Indigenous epistem-ologies.[19] Westerners brought with them Enlightenment thinking that valued the "scientific" and the individual rather than the collective. They brought, too, a belief in Social Darwinism (survival of the fittest) and a hierarchical system of inferiority and superiority that placed white-skinned people at the top and Aboriginal people at the bottom of the "chain of being." The European colonizers also brought a class system. Portraying themselves as superior beings (in the Social Darwinian sense), they cast Indigenous Australians as "primitive" and lacking in culture and sophistication; they also believed that Aboriginal and Torres Strait Islander peoples were a "dying race."[20]

Additionally, Westerners brought a society that privileged written over oral knowledge and a patriarchal social structure according to which women's roles were "limited" to the domestic sphere while men's were in the public realm. This way of thinking placed Indigenous women—and their role as storytellers and educators—at the bottom of the status ladder. Moreton-Robinson has written extensively on how Australian Indigenous women have had to navigate being both Indigenous and female. She states: "Our lives are always shaped by the omnipresence of patriarchal white sovereignty and its continual denial of our sovereignty."[21] If Western women were marginalized under patriarchy, then Indigenous women were trebly marginalized by virtue of their "race," gender, and class.[22] So, too, were their oral histories.

The one similarity that stands out for the purpose of this chapter is that in both worlds, women have historically been the educators of children through interactive storytelling. Both Indigenous and Western women's roles (and particularly their stories) have also been relegated by patriarchy to the realm of the fanciful and unimportant. Through the process of colonization, Western androcentric epistemologies silenced Indigenous women's voices, along with those of their male counterparts, and ignored their roles and positions. As Lynore Geia et al. explain, knowledge systems with "exclusionary research practices have silenced [Indigenous people] and rendered their stories invisible."[23] Women's roles are pivotal to the healthy development of any culture and should be nurtured and recognized for their social significance. So what is the role of yarning today?

Importance of yarning in contemporary contexts

Yarning is a lived experience of a story and the key elements of it are respect and reciprocity, whereby the listener is tasked with the responsibility of transferring the knowledge onto the next generation. Children re-enact and re-tell the stories on Country and, in doing so, experience the knowledge and truth of the story.

These stories are re-told and re-enacted in place through a dynamic and fluid process triggered by the environment. When swimming at the river or walking in the bush, children are cautioned to always be aware of, and adhere to, cultural protocols and practices. For example, children know how to avoid mischievous and harmful spirit beings by walking through natural passageways. Sighting such features in the environment triggers the re-enactment of the story, and then the knowledge and experience is transferred from the older girls onto their younger charges (both male and female).

As Palyku women Gladys Idjirrimoonya Milroy and Jill Milroy argue, yarning is Indigenous people's birthright:

> For Aboriginal people, the land is full of stories, and we are born from our Mother the land into these stories. The old people tell us stories that nurture and sustain us through life into old age, so that we can tell children the stories they will need to sustain them. The great life-story cycle has been that way for millennia. It is the birthright of all Aboriginal children to be born into the *right* story.[24]

Indigenous people use the terms "yarn" and "yarning" on a daily basis, but, as scholars have observed, the practice "is more than just a light process and an exchange; it encompasses elements of respect, protocol and engagement in individuals' relationships with each other [and] establishes relationality and determines accountability."[25] According to Greg Lehman, the concept of "truth," considered integral to yarning, is based on the premise that one knows "the truth" of any piece of knowledge through experience. Sharing an experience and negotiating its meaning collectively determines "truth." To know "the truth" is to experience a narrator's knowledge, to feel the emotions of the story, to envision the story, and to become one with the story.[26]

Bessarab and Ng'andu explain that yarning is a relaxed style of communication where all participants go on a collective journey together and many topics may be explored, all while experiencing the "truth." Although Lehman is a man, he gathered his understandings and relationships with yarning and the "truth" from his matriarchal Elders—his grandmother and mother—which enabled him to learn how to experience the truth of any yarn.

Another crucial element of yarning is *Dadirri* (deep listening). The yarn cannot take place without speakers and listeners (usually a person is both) because both engage in deep contemplation of what is being transmitted. Following from this, the "truth" is then sought by absorbing and locating the knowledge within the collective spirit. A fuller definition of *Dadirri* is "a special quality, a unique gift of the Aboriginal people."

> [It] is inner deep listening and quiet still awareness. *Dadirri* recognises the deep spring that is inside us. It is something like what you call contemplation. The contemplative way of *Dadirri* spreads over our whole life. It renews us and brings us peace. It makes us feel whole again. In our Aboriginal way we learnt to listen from our earliest times. We could not live good and useful lives unless we listen. We are not threatened by silence. We are completely at home in it. Our Aboriginal way has taught us to be still and wait. We do not try to hurry things up. We let them flow their natural course—like the seasons.[27]

Yarning and *Dadirri* bind people together and nurture spiritual wellbeing through the expression of life experiences. As a result, knowledge may be passed on by absorption, experience, and deep listening rather than through a Western notion of pedagogy, which associates learning from stories with a fictional or non-fictional plot separated into beginning, middle, and end. In her book *Toni Morrison and Motherhood: A Politics of the Heart*, Andrea O'Reilly explains Morrison's use of the term "ancient properties" as "black women who are these cultural bearers" who ensure connections to the motherline, to black culture, and history.[28] It was also through the matrilineal line that Linda Tuhiwai Smith, a Maori academic, was nurtured and developed "a sense of place."[29]

Further, yarning has recently been identified as both a means for decolonization and a research method.[30] Given the close association between women and yarning, it is also not surprising that women have explored its use as an Indigenist tool, which is slowly becoming accepted as a *bona fide* qualitative research methodology in Western academic contexts.

To record or not to record?

The re-evaluation of yarning, both as an important cultural mechanism and a research method, requires us to explore its implications for the future of oral history recording. For some Indigenous Australian communities, making an enduring record is not a priority. The stories themselves are, after all, the recording. And what is the point of recorded interviews that languish in an archive and are not accessed by the people for whom they are intended? One of the fallacies regarding the work of recording by Western academics employing Western epistemologies is that the communities themselves want the recordings. On the other hand, many Elders who have recorded their stories did so for the future generations, to leave a lasting record of the history, knowledge, and cultural practices of their groups. For example, Barker's great-grandfather, Jimmie Barker, made over 100 recordings especially for this purpose, which resulted in the publication of *The Two Worlds of Jimmie Barker*.[31] While different forms of multimedia technology can make oral histories accessible to many communities, those people living particularly in rural and remote communities have little or no access to the Internet or other forms of multimedia technology. The issue of privilege and access remains for communities who are not aware of the resources available to them and where to find them.

The relationship of communities to recordings is unsurprisingly complex and context-dependent. For some Indigenous oral historians, advancing technology can create a heightened desire to record people's memories, stories, and experiences because it offers an easier means of doing so, and also a way of making the "research data" immediately accessible. For example, Barker has used oral history recordings to create a lasting record of her grandmother's ancient lore, life, and experiences by filming her family's return to the Country and the stories that came with it.[32] Another Indigenous academic, Elfie Shiosaki, used oral history recordings to trace the history of her activist Aboriginal forebears. Brenda Gifford, a professional musician, has researched the history of Indigenous activist music through interviews with Aboriginal musicians.[33] These acts are deeply embedded in relationship and context, particularly Indigenous notions of gifting stories.

A "new" field of study and a feminist influence

While we suggest that women in Indigenous and Western cultures share a commonality as educators through storytelling, we also believe that, just as yarning has adapted to modern imperatives, so has oral history recording. Oral history began to take shape in the Western world as a "new" field of study in the 1960s and 1970s in recognition of the skewed nature of the historical record that favored the famous and the elite. The primary aim was to preserve stories that would otherwise not be heard—those of the marginalized, oppressed, and uneducated. It is well established that there is a direct relationship between this development and second wave feminism throughout the Western world.

Feminism began as a white, Western endeavor before being challenged by African American feminists such as bell hooks, Toni Morrison, and Gwendolyn Etter-Lewis, for failing to represent the experiences of women of color.[34] A Google Scholar search shows that Indigenous women around the globe have since embraced feminism.[35] However, Australian Indigenous women have not been so quick to join the fray. Larissa Behrendt suggests that a key reason for this is that they are first and foremost politically aligned with Indigenous men in their fight for justice and to end racism. She says that for Indigenous women to suddenly align themselves with non-Indigenous feminists would be to align themselves with women who are both oppressed by men and the oppressors of Indigenous peoples. As she explains, "For white women, sexism is the enemy. For black women, racism is just as insidious."[36] Similarly, Bronwyn Fredericks has dismissed feminism as resulting in

> the denial and sidelining of Aboriginal sovereignty and in the further oppression and marginalization of Aboriginal women. Moreover, strategies employed by non-indigenous feminists can result in the maintenance of white women's values and privileges within the dominant patriarchal white society.[37]

Ironically, it was an Indigenous male who first promoted a feminist model to further the cause of Indigenous Australians. Basing his methodology on the feminist shift to "place the feminine experience at the centre of feminist research," Lester-Irabinna Rigney called for a similar approach to Indigenist research. In opposition to the standpoints adopted by Behrendt and Fredericks (see earlier), Rigney also noted the way feminism "adapts, borrows, and modifies significant research to advance their struggle, which need not originate from female researchers" to advocate for Indigenous-centered research that does not deny critical research by non-Indigenous Australians, but rather requires the researcher to be responsible to Indigenous communities and their struggle.[38]

Nevertheless, storytelling has been central to the feminist movement. As Sherna Berger Gluck notes, "personal disclosure [is] a political act," and it was this notion that fuelled the 1970s feminist movement.[39] Further, Gluck and Daphne Patai's *Women's Words* attests to oral historians' contribution to feminist debates and the ways feminism has since been applied to the field. Indeed, it was feminist oral historians, by means of a framework of reflexivity, inclusivity, and an analysis of social inter-relations, who embraced the debate on what Michael Frisch famously labelled "a shared authority."[40]

Women's Words initiated a critical discourse that led us to challenge many previously unaddressed issues. As Koni Benson and Richa Nagar observe, this discourse, together with postcolonial theory, made oral historians

> extremely cautious about oral/life history and ethnography as both representation and as data, about shifting matrices of power relations in/outside the "field" and about not imposing their own meanings and organizations onto "other" people or places, or events of the past.[41]

Indigenous women, like their male counterparts, are drawing on thousands of years of cultural knowledge, history, and law to decolonize oral history and apply an Indigenous research framework of cultural conventions.

Furthermore, when we look at the beginnings of oral history in Australia, we notice that the most prestigious award conferred by Oral History Australia is the biennial Hazel de Berg Award for Excellence in Oral History. The award is named after the person who prompted the National Library of Australia to establish its oral history collection. The National Library website describes de Berg as the "pioneer of oral history in Australia."[42] Over a period of 27 years, de Berg recorded oral histories with 1,290 Australians born between 1865 and 1953. In line with our argument that oral history was born out of yarning, we assert that it is no coincidence that Hazel de Berg was a woman.[43]

The National Library's oral history collection is the largest in the country with over 45,000 hours of recordings, increasing by about 1,000 hours each year. It is not possible to ascertain what percentage of the contributing interviewers are women, but given that the majority of members of Oral History Australia are women, it is reasonable to assume that women predominate. This is not to trivialize the role men play in recording oral histories, but rather to emphasize the proliferation of female practitioners in the field. Men's contribution to oral history has been significant, as evidenced by valuable contributions by such scholars as Frisch, Alessandro Portelli, Alistair Thomson, Paul Thompson, Donald Ritchie, and Steven High. It may be a legacy of patriarchy or discipline norms that help explain why we do not refer more often to the work of feminists such as Gluck, Patai, Lorraine Sitzia, Linda

Shopes, Paula Hamilton, and Rina Benmayor—not to mention the editors of this volume. More attention to female authors might lead us to challenge more of our concepts and methodologies and to think about the interrelationships embedded in methodologies integral to Indigenous communities.

The life history model

Only recently have women begun to question the life history template that is the basis of most contemporary work on life narratives and storytelling, which has underpinned oral history methodology for the last 50 years.[44] Indigenous feminist standpoint theory has forged its place within standard methodological practice, though only Indigenous academics (female and male) and a very few non-Indigenous scholars have legitimized it, despite the fact that Indigenous narrators have consistently challenged the life history template from the beginning.

Western concepts of linear time have also largely dictated the interview format: we begin with a person's birth and lead them through to the present. However, Indigenous notions of circular or cyclical time do not align with a chronological approach and important events, whether in Dreaming, or in one's physical life, are more likely to be the starting point for an Indigenous life story. While working in the Yukon, Cruikshank learned early on to allow her narrators to guide her, giving them the much-needed space required to structure their interviews and decide what form the content would take.[45] Jaimee Hamilton understood going into her PhD research (when she interviewed her intellectual Elders) that she had to allow *Dadirri* to flow to ensure the yarn was meaningful. One of her narrators, an Indigenous academic, explained that both Jaimee and she were engaged in a very deep and spiritual connection where trust, respect, and reciprocity had to be allowed to develop or the yarn would be deemed useless. Our oral history work with Indigenous Australians has taken a similar course since stories are at the root of life and culture. In her PhD research, Barker also learned to listen to her narrators' cues, particularly her mum and dad, who reintroduced her to potential narrators, reminded her of family/community obligations and responsibilities, advised on suitable members for group interviews (both male and female), and, in some instances, directed discussions to ensure social and cultural protocols were adhered to. Barker applied the cultural convention and research methodology of "hangin' out and yarnin'" with members of her family and community by participating in different cultural and social activities, stating:

> In order to engage a participant I had to first hang out, have a yarn, partake in a meal, or various activities: playing cards, having a flutter on the pokies [poker/slot/gaming machines] or socializing at the local pub or club, some days and sometimes, even weeks before an interview took place.[46]

Anderson was an interviewer for the National Library of Australia's "Bringing Them Home Oral History" project, which served as the first recommendation of the Report of the National Inquiry into the Separation of Aboriginal and Torres Strait Islander Children from their Families.[47] When conducting her first interview with Ngarrindjeri Elder, Dr. Doreen Kartinyeri, Anderson was nervous about using very expensive recording equipment for the first time. Kartinyeri noted, "You look nervous, Sue." Anderson responded that she was, so Kartinyeri put her at ease by saying, "It will be all right as long as you don't interrupt me too much." While this is an amusing anecdote, and Kartinyeri and Anderson have a good relationship that later flourished and led to a significant collaboration, it demonstrates Kartinyeri's need to direct the interview process.[48] For real meaning to be made of an individual's life, they must have control of the narrative so they can present it in a way that is culturally appropriate and relevant. Thus, by challenging the life history model, we may finally be coming full circle, back to where orality all started, with yarning.

Conclusion

For us, the growing interest in oral history recording, which has been a predominant feature of the field over the last 50 years, has its roots in traditional Indigenous yarning practices, where the transmission of cultural and practical knowledge has been valued for tens of thousands of years. In an increasingly globalized world, these strong traditions have been largely lost to Westerners and they have been devalued under patriarchy. Hence the urge to capture, for the record, knowledge that can otherwise be fleeting, but that has real meaning for everyday lives.

For Indigenous cultures, the oral tradition is a powerful mechanism for cultural cohesion and wellbeing and has implications for oral history recording, particularly in the collective sense. Furthermore, women are not only instrumental in the education of children, and serve as prolific oral historians and contributors to the discourse, but they have introduced important challenges to the field and continue to do so. Let us listen more to women's words.

Postscript

Following the 2015 Oral History Australia Conference, Indigenous presenters Lorina Barker, Elfie Shiosaki, and Brenda Gifford, together with Sue Anderson, decided to establish an Indigenous oral history research group. The response was enthusiastic, and Shiosaki immediately secured funding from her university for a symposium on Indigenous approaches to oral history that took place at Curtin University in May 2016. The aim was to encourage more Indigenous participation in the field and to examine the contributions that Indigenous practitioners can and do make to it. With the support of prominent Māori oral historian Dr Nēpia Mahuika from the University of Waikato in Aotearoa/New Zealand, who was the symposium's keynote speaker, the Indigenous oral history research group hopes to broaden international networks, and draw on the works of other Indigenous oral historians and their methods and approaches of recording stories in their own way. Plans are underway for another symposium in 2018, with consecutive symposiums to be held thereafter at each of the founding members' universities, providing a culturally safe space to explore Indigenous research methodologies, and to decolonize oneself and the oral history discipline from within.

Notes

1   We use the term "Indigenous" in the Australian context to describe both Aboriginal and Torres Strait Islander peoples. While the term is debated within Australia, it is the only inclusive term we have at present. We also use the term to refer to Indigenous peoples globally.

2   "Meaning of 'Oral History,'" accessed 20 October 2015, http://dictionary. cambridge.org/dictionary/english/oral-history; "Oral History Defined: Oral History Association," accessed 20 October 2015, www.oralhistory.org/about/ do-oral-history/; "Definition of Oral History," accessed 20 October 2015, www.oxforddictionaries.com/definition/english/oral-history.

3   Dawn Bessarab and Bridget Ng'andu, "Yarning About Yarning as a Legitimate Method in Indigenous Research," *International Journal of Critical Indigenous Studies* 3, no. 1 (2010): 37; M. Terszack, *Orphaned by the Colour of my Skin: A Stolen Generation Story* (Maleny, Qld: Verdant House, 2008), 90; Melissa Walker et al., "'Yarning' as a Method for Community-Based Health Research with Indigenous Women: The Indigenous Women's Wellness Research Program," *Health Care for Women International* 35, no. 10 (2014): 1216.

4   In her comparative analysis of the Australian penchant for "telling yarns" and the storytelling practices of the Pitjantjatjara and Yankunytjatjara peoples of the Western Desert, Daniele Klapproth concludes that there are three significant differences between the two: in Western Desert culture, orality carries high prestige in comparison with recordings or written work, while the opposite is true in Western culture; Western Desert stories are sacred, while Western stories are secular; Western Desert stories represent "a body of socially distributed cultural knowledge" and hence are collective, as opposed to individualistic Western stories (which, in psychological terms, involve personal interest). See her *Narrative as Social Practice: Anglo-Western and Australian Aboriginal Oral Traditions* (Berlin: Walter de Gruyter, 2004), 380.

5   Greg Dening, *Mr. Bligh's Bad Language: Passion, Power and Theatre on the Bounty* (Cambridge, New York: Cambridge University Press, 1993).

6   Karen L. Martin, "Ways of Knowing, Being and Doing: A Theoretical Framework and Methods for Indigenous and Indigenist Re-search," *Journal of Australian Studies* 27, no. 76 (2003): 203–214.

7   Aileen Moreton-Robinson, "Towards an Australian Indigenous Woman's Standpoint Theory," *Australian Feminist Studies* 28, no. 78 (2013): 331.

8   Moreton-Robinson, 331; Maggie Walter, "The Nature of Social Science Research," in *Social Research Methods*, ed. Maggie Walter (Melbourne, Vic: Oxford University Press, 2010), 13.

9   Traditionally, when boys reach the age of initiation, men take over their education and pass on secret/sacred knowledge when it is suitable. Note that this relationship

is more fluid in urban environments. See Ronald Berndt, Catherine Berndt, and John Stanton, *A World that Was: The Yaraldi of the Murray River and the Lakes, South Australia* (Carlton, Victoria: Melbourne University Press at the Miegunyah Press, 1993). For a connected discussion, see Couchie and Miguel in this volume (Chapter 16).

10 Australian Aboriginal people use the Aboriginal-English term "Country" to describe the area of land their ancestors and relatives came from or are still living on. It is used when describing and locating the area of land where an Aboriginal person was born and/or grew up and the area from which they locate their identity as an Aboriginal person. It is the place or places where they have kin affiliations and connections with the Dreaming and Law that is associated with this land. Anthropologists use the term when referring to Aboriginal peoples' definitions of their cultural landscape.

11 Stuart Rintoul, *The Wailing: A National Black Oral History* (Port Melbourne: William Heinemann Australia, 1993), 240.

12 Mona Ngitji Ngitji Tur, interviewed by Sue Anderson, "Bringing Them Home Oral History" project, Croydon, SA, Australia, 9 March 2001, Oral TRC 2000/253, National Library of Australia.

13 See, for example, R. Struthers and C. Peden-McAlpine, "Phenomenological Research Among Canadian and United States Indigenous Populations: Oral Tradition and Quintessence of Time," *Quality Health Research* 15, no. 9 (November 2005): 1264–1276.

14 Bob Randall, *Kanyini*, directed by Melanie Hogan (Hopscotch Films, 2006).

15 Terri Janke, "The Application of Copyright and other Intellectual Property Laws to Aboriginal and Torres Strait Islander Cultural and Intellectual Property," *Art, Antiquity and Law* 2, no. 1 (1997): 13–26.

16 Larissa Behrendt, "Aboriginal Women and the White Lies of the Feminist Movement: Implications for Aboriginal Women in Rights Discourse," *The Australian Feminist Law Journal* 1 (1993): 28; Graham Jenkin, *Conquest of the Ngarrindjeri* (Point McLeay, South Australia: Raukkan Publishers, 1995), 19.

17 Klapproth, 381.

18 Julie Cruikshank and Tatiana Argounova-Low, "'On' and 'Off' the Record in Shifting Times and Circumstances," in *Oral History Off the Record: Toward an Ethnography of Practice*, eds. Anna Sheftel and Stacey Zembrzycki (New York: Palgrave Macmillan 2013), 45, 49.

19 Klapproth, 14; Linda Tuhiwai Smith, *Decolonizing Methodologies: Research and Indigenous Peoples* (Dunedin, NZ: Zed Books and University of Otago Press, 1999).

20 Richard Broome, *Aboriginal Australians: A History since 1788* (Crows Nest, NSW: Allen and Unwin, 2010), 14.

21 Moreton-Robinson, 340.

22 bell hooks, "Ain't I a Woman: Black Women and Feminism," in *Philosophy of Gender, Race and Sexuality* (Pluto Press, 1982); J.J. Pettman and P. Jan, *Living in the Margins: Racism, Sexism and Feminism in Australia* (Crows Nest, NSW: Allen and Unwin, 1992); Razia Aziz, "Feminism and the Challenge of Racism: Deviance or Difference?" in *Identity and Diversity: Gender and the Experience of Education*, eds. Maud Blair and Janet Holland with Sue Sheldon (Adelaide: Multilingual Matters Ltd, 1995), 161–172; Nancy Caraway, *Segregated Sisterhood: Racism and the Politics of American Feminism* (Knoxville: The University of Tennessee Press, 1998).

23 Lynore K. Geia, Barbara Hayes, and Kim Usher, "Yarning/Aboriginal Storytelling: Towards an Understanding of an Indigenous Perspective and its Implications for Research Practice," *Contemporary Nursing* 46, no. 1 (2013): 13.

24 Gladys Idjirrimooya Milroy and Jill Milroy, "Different Ways of Knowing: Trees Are Family Too," in *Heartsick for Country: Stories of Love, Spirit and Creation*, eds. Sally Morgan, Tjalaminu Mia, and Blaze Kwaymullina (Fremantle, WA: Fremantle Press, 2008), 162.

25 Bronwyn Fredericks et al., "Engaging the Practice of Indigenous Yarning in Action Research," *ALAR Journal* 17, no. 2 (October, 2011): 13.

26 Greg Lehman, "Telling us True," in *Whitewash: On Keith Windschuttle's Fabrication of Aboriginal History*, ed. Robert Manne (Melbourne, Vic: Black Inc Agenda 2003), 175.

27 "Miriam Rose Ungunmerr-Baumann," accessed 21 April 2016, http://nextwave. org.au/wp-content/uploads/Dadirri-Inner-Deep-Listening-M-R-Ungunmerr-Bauman-Refl.pdf.

28 Andrea O'Reilly, *Toni Morrison and Motherhood: A Politics of the Heart* (Albany: State University of New York Press, 2004), 23.

29 Tuhiwai Smith, 12.

30 See Bessarab and Ng'andu, 37–50; Walker et al., 1219; Geia, Hayes, and Usher, 13–17; Fredericks et al., 13–24; Lorina Barker, "'Hangin' out' and 'Yarnin': Reflecting on the Experience of Collecting Oral Histories," in *History Australia* 5, no. 1 (2008): 09.1–09.9.

31 Jimmie Barker (as told to Janet Mathews), *The Two Worlds of Jimmie Barker: The Life of an Australian Aboriginal, 1900–1972* (Canberra: Australian Institute of Aboriginal Studies, 1980). Janet Mathews recorded Barker just once, and he made another 109 recordings of himself. See Heather Goodall, "Barker, James (Jimmie) (1900–1972)," *Australian Dictionary of Biography*, accessed 20 April 2016, http://adb.anu.edu.au/biography/barker-james-jimmie-9433.

32 Lorina Barker's PhD dissertation includes a video of this journey and she has since created a short documentary about it.

33 All three women presented their projects at the Oral History Australia Conference, September 2015, Perth, Western Australia.

34 bell hooks, *Feminist Theory from Margin to Center* (Boston: South End Press, 1984); Toni Morrison, *The Bluest Eye* (London: Picador, Chatto and Windus, 1994); Gwendolyn Etter-Lewis, "Black Women's Life Stories: Reclaiming Self in Narrative Texts," in *Women's Words: The Feminist Practice of Oral History*, eds. Sherna Berger Gluck and Daphne Patai (New York: Routledge, 1991), 44.

35 With a simple Google search using the words "Indigenous" and "feminism," one can access Indigenous feminist publications by authors from around the globe, accessed 22 October 2015, https://scholar.google.com.au/scholar?q=indigenous+feminism&btnG=&hl=en&as_sdt=0%2C5.

36 Behrendt, 34.

37 Bronwyn Fredericks, "Reempowering Ourselves: Australian Aboriginal Women," *Signs* 35, no. 3 (Spring 2010): 546.

38 Lester-Irabinna Rigney, "Internationalization of an Indigenous Anticolonial Cultural Critique of Research Methodologies: A Guide to Indigenist Research Methodology and Its Principles," *Wicazo Sa Review* 14, no. 2 (Autumn 1999): 115, 116–117.

39 Sherna Berger Gluck, "Reflecting on the Quantum Leap: Promises and Perils of Oral History on the Web," *Oral History Review* 41, no. 2 (2014): 248.

40 In *Women's Words*, see, for example, Sherna Berger Gluck and Daphne Patai, "Introduction," 3; Kristina Minister, "A Feminist Frame for the Oral History Interview," 36; Judith Stacey, "Can There be a Feminist Ethnography?" 112; Tess Cosslett, Celia Lury, and Penny Summerfield, *Feminism and Autobiography: Texts, Theories, Methods* (New York: Routledge, 2000), 16; Michael Frisch, *A Shared Authority: Essays on the Craft and Meaning of Oral and Public History* (Albany:

State University of New York Press, 1990). Also see the editors' Introduction to this volume.

41 Koni Benson and Richa Nagar, "Collaboration as Resistance? Reconsidering the Processes, Products, and Possibilities of Feminist Oral History and Ethnography," *Gender, Place and Culture* 13, no. 5 (October 2006): 583.

42 "National Library of Australia, de Berg Collection," accessed 21 October 2015, www.nla.gov.au/selected-library-collections/de-berg-collection.

43 It is worth noting that de Berg's daughter, Diana Ritch, is also a dedicated oral historian.

44 See, for example, Cruikshank and Argounova-Low, 48–49; Sherna Berger Gluck, "From California to Kufr Nameh and Back: Reflections on 40 Years of Feminist Oral History," in *Oral History Off the Record*, 25–42.

45 Cruikshank and Argounova-Low, 49.

46 Barker, 0.94.

47 Human Rights and Equal Opportunities Commission (Commonwealth of Australia, 1997).

48 Their collaboration led to Doreen Kartinyeri and Sue Anderson, *Doreen Kartinyeri: My Ngarrindjeri Calling* (Canberra, ACT: Aboriginal Studies Press, 2008).

13 "This thing we are doing here"

Listening and writing in the "Montréal Life Stories" project

Stéphane Martelly

It was "as if" the voices carrying stories and memory were also becoming a place. During the interviews conducted for the "Montréal Life Stories" project, the voices of the speakers used to bounce against the bare walls of our small interview room, risking to come back to us, indecisively attributed and violently unassigned. Given its objective of collecting stories, oral history is a discipline and practice of displacing and relocating voices. Collected voices are carefully organized in archives, travelling through place and time because of violence, exile, or a wish to preserve; voices secretly drawing out a space that might finally contain or echo them; looking, in that imagined place, for the right vehicle to carry them home. It was "as if," with the absence of the physical location of origin, voice became an impossible place, but a place nevertheless where stories or words were laid, where they rearranged themselves, in the hopes of understanding, resisting, listening, or resonating.[1] The interview itself is a fleeting place of strangeness and belonging, of permeable subjectivities, where a difficult negotiation is nevertheless possible.

Starting with voice, and its amplitude and effects, is a good place to begin a conversation about margins, what moves in and beyond them, what is troubled by them, and also what sometimes becomes possible in a long-term oral history project. One of the strengths of the "Montréal Life Stories" project was how it worked to resolve the question of the "Other."[2] The project defined all interview subjects as Montréalers—whether they were from Haïti, Rwanda, Eastern Europe, or Cambodia; whether they defined themselves as "rescapés," Shoah survivors, refugees or exiles, or as first or second-generation immigrants or displaced peoples. This important decision served as a per-formative act that placed everyone involved (interviewers and narrators, academics and "communities") in the same frame, in the same space, and, tentatively, with the same legitimacy—a principle articulated in the notion of "shared authority."[3] Montréal thus served as a "third space," a composite space already redesigned and transformed by the stories we were hearing, a place that allowed the displacement not only of the voices, but also of the margins, that were in that sense *moved*.[4]

In this chapter, I reflect on those margins, on what is created by and for them within the stories of violence and displacement, and on how they were approached, addressed, and negotiated in the context of oral history interviews with Haitians in Montréal. Drawing on literary analysis, empirical oral history methodology, and arts-based research, I aim to (re)present the interviews carried out with the women of *Les femmes endeuillées de La Maison d'Haïti*, a post-earthquake (2010) grieving group, as the best actualizations of these questions about margins, space, and voice.[5] A multidisciplinary approach provides me with the methodological framework to consider critical issues related to marginality and center women's deep voices. It is a form of reciprocity to let women's voices permeate my writing, to never completely transcribe them but *preserve* them in memory as living traces that never rest in certainty or completion, but as resounding echoes of the powerful yet incomplete experience of interviewing.[6]

Etymologically, margins are a complex concept.[7] They signal secondary location: something considered to be at the center while another is considered to be "outside" of that center or relatively less important than the center. They evoke an object destined to be identified as other, destined to be differentiated, opposed to, confronted by, and produced in a distinct "supply" of meaning.[8] Therefore, there are a few rhetorical operations involved with the delimitation of margins: a center has to be identified or asserted from a form of outsideness to be delimited and differentiated; a negotiation must also take place that both separates the margins from the center and keeps them connected. For example, by decisively recognizing all narrators as Montréalers rather than (for example) "native Quebecers," "immigrants," or "exiles," the "Montréal Life Stories" project attempted to level the playing field, to put them in the same category and therefore, redefine what could be considered the content and nature of the center.

But is such a performative act, with clear political implications, sufficient to smooth out all tensions and disparities? The initial difficulty of obtaining interviews with Haitians, of gathering their stories indicated otherwise. This was not only because the power dynamics between an inquiring center, mainly situated in academia, and a dissonant "displaced" person (even if not necessarily underprivileged in some ways) could always find multiple ways to persist.[9] It was also because within the stories themselves, in their inevitable brokenness between past and present, here and there, and because of the violence that initiated the dislocations and movements, there was tension and already shifting centers and margins as well as a necessary negotiation between spaces and identities. This implicit negotiation existed, in fact, within the subjects themselves, within their fractured experience and their ability to convey it to us, the researchers, for the always elusive purpose of memory and archive. If, as a Shoah survivor tellingly stated, "the life that I was supposed to live was gone," then who is this new "I" that tells?[10] If, as one of the narrators of the Haitian working group told us, it is not just the person who is displaced, but that there is also movement situated within, we must take into account that it is not simply the story that speaks of the narrator's displacement, but indeed the narration itself that is dis-located, re-situated; the narrator him/herself that is travelled and reinvented; the narrative itself that has to conjure up other ways to exist and organize itself in a different way.[11]

However, first and foremost we had to find people who were willing to share their stories with us. For the Haitian working group, at the beginning, the interviews were simply not taking place. We had to fully appreciate some of the cultural forms of resistance associated with Haitian culture (where a conception of the self as separated from the community is less prevalent) and the specific context of dictatorship and organized violence many experienced, and which created a culture of silence and of resistance in regards to institutions of all kinds. In relation to the project's methodology, which drew on Michael Frisch's concept of "shared authority," we also had to expect, and accept, that the narrators' stories might not fit tidily into the broad narratives of militant or academic discourses on contemporary Haitian history, that there would be dissonant voices among the narrators, and dissonance even within a single interview or a single story.[12]

The Haitian working group began by soliciting testimonies from victims/survivors of the (father and son) Duvaliers' bloody dictatorship (1957–1986) and the military regimes considered to have been a continuation of it (1986–1994). But, ultimately, we decided to listen to witnesses of the subsequent regimes, including the Lavalas movement, mainly led by Jean-Bertrand Aristide (1986–2004). This was a decisive step, because, while it generated much discussion and controversy, it offered a way to include and listen to everyone who would speak to us.[13] There was an understanding that the interviewing process should be entirely independent from a more traditional academic approach and that we should let the narrators define themselves, whether as militants or citizens, victims or survivors. It was up to them to name themselves and identify the "perpetrator(s)" of the violence they experienced (as often there were multiple ones). This approach validated personal stories, even when they apparently "didn't fit," or seemed "beside the point," or even felt "inconvenient."

It became evident almost immediately that women narrators, from a range of classes, professions, and educational backgrounds, were most willing to denounce and dis-locate the broad narratives of Haitian contemporary history, choosing instead to offer highly personal accounts of the events of their lives. Perhaps this was because they were never really part of the broad narrative to begin with, or their gendered presence and participation in historical narratives was always complex and multifaceted. Later on, we discovered just how much the women's words disrupted the life story narrative, not only in terms of content, but also through the processes of remembrance and storytelling.

In the midst of the project, and quite suddenly, the 12 January 2010 earthquake happened, as did the return to Haïti of Jean-Claude Duvalier, Jean-Bertrand Aristide, and many of their successors. While these events added uncertainty and urgency to our process, they also made our work all the more necessary. All of the destruction, both material and symbolic, as well as the unexpected resurgence of the past, compromised the examination and remembrance of past scars for all those involved, but also made this collaborative work all the more relevant.

As soon as we shifted the power to our narrators, interviews slowly started to take place. In less than two years, we conducted 30 interviews, ranging from 4 to 10 hours in length, with a diverse range of narrators in terms of gender, age, profession, and status with first- and even second-generation Montréalers of Haitian descent, and with recent or past immigrants. Together, the narrators composed a very complex and nuanced portrait of Haitian contemporary history, including (but not limited to) the persistent and violent imprint of the Duvalier and subsequent regimes. The situation called for a broader reflection on structural and organized violence in the Haitian context, its ability to persist and permeate all aspects of culture and society, but also the capacity of individuals as well as Haitian society to find multiple modes of resistance, inventive capabilities of self-empowerment, and the persistence of subjective identities in line with the spirit of the 1804 revolution.[14]

Interviewing itself became, more than ever, an unexpected shared experience: I was interviewing of course what could be considered my own community, while also being considered somewhat of an outsider. Our group of inter-viewers was also a mix of sameness and otherness—some were of Haitian descent, others were not—but our varied origins did not necessarily pre-determine proximity to our interlocutors. These varied positionalities between proximity and distance actually created an open space for listening, a space that we might also consider a third space, not yet saturated by already completed and legitimized narratives. Further, this space allowed new stories to emerge. To me, following a "shared authority" ethos was simply about recognizing the narrators as the sole *authority* of their narrative, the *authors* of their stories. "I am the master of my word," as one of our narrators proudly proclaimed.

Within the interviews themselves, however, the form of the narrative was always shifting. Whether it was the classic narrative of A.B. the painter, the matriarchal re-construction of lineage by Monique Dauphin, the analytic perspectives of writer Raymond Chassagne that both replaced, revealed, and obscured the more personal memories of traumatic events, the silences and artistic elaborations of D.B. the musician, the amazing anecdotes of Ghislaine Charlier, the infernal circular, traumatic, and repetitive words (and sounds) of A. Larochelle, survivor of Fort-Dimanche, or the stories of the grieving women of *La Maison d'Haïti*, all the narrators reinvented the interview's form to fit their voices, spaces, and stories. It was "as if," during the course of the interview, the margins moved to accommodate many centers and many disarticulations, many displacements. It was "as if" these different "I"s belonging to different spaces and times were not always the same, not always equal to themselves, but subtly and continuously travelled into themselves to find other ways of existing and telling and being heard. It was "as if" there was a knowledge of violence breaking apart stories, lives, and selves. But there was also a knowledge of creativity, which allowed narrators to envision the lives "they were supposed to live" but had been taken away from them, and to imagine other selves, perhaps repaired selves or new selves in spaces where all was lost, but also where everything was not fixed and already written, where everything had to be reinvented anyway.

I then chose to explore the possibility of reinventing the margins encountered during the interviews by freeing narrators from the limited constraints of life-course interviews and autobiographical discourse. I suggested a creative writing class where both narrators and interviewers explored what emerged from a creative process in the margins of oral history. I wanted to see what would happen in these silences, particularly when there were profound and haunting scars of organized violence. I hoped that the silences and opacity not acknow-ledged by autobiographical narrative could be more fully understood through storytelling. How could one tell a story, a personal story, when an all-consuming narrative takes charge and eradicates personal journeys, both in bodies and in words? How does one negotiate such an overwhelming narrative? What remains of the self when trauma complicates identity and memory?

I worked with other groups in the "Montréal Life Stories" project to devise a creative writing class to explore these questions. In freely writing their own texts, the participants, I hoped, would find an unhindered space within which to approach the parts of their stories that history had killed and that autobiography does not always permit to exist. The results were remarkable. Many selves emerged, including selves that were *allowed* to be angry or violent, that were *allowed* to be silent, that were *allowed* to evoke unacceptable emotions. The result was often a longing for silence and for better words to insert meaning where meaning was abolished, which also served as a sharp and poignant criticism of the power dynamics that were not eradicated even within a project as ethically aware as ours.

Out of the silence, individual voices emerged that started to aggregate, autobiographically or creatively, diversifying perspectives as well as modes of expression. There emerged a chorus of voices, a body of memory concerning both Haïti and Montréal. It was "as if" this chorus was separately, but instant-aneously, building a community of experience and story.

This chorus of stories came full circle in an interview with women from the *Maison d'Haïti*, when they unexpectedly chose to speak as a group, anonymously combining their voices into a powerful and shared experience of the past. The echo of their mingled voices reflected the chorus of the many interviews we had done before, while also propelling them to the most radical form of their possibilities, into the unchartered territories where the subject, the destination, and the very form of the narrative, were profoundly trans-formed. Their intent was more complex, as they sought not only to leave a memorial trace—like all the other narrators did—but also to consciously and deliberately empower and heal themselves; to hold each other up and recreate a community. Thus, the form of the narrative itself became both a poignant metaphor and a complete break from all of the interviews that came before: it evoked them in many ways, while also completely shattering the form and content of those narratives. The interviewers were not interviewing anymore, as the women were asking most of the questions to us and each other. The subject was not defined and singular anymore, as it was diffracted in indistinguishable ways and plural in voice. The narration itself ceased to be linear, as it was characterized by the fragmentation and overlapping of voices. The sentence was no longer the favored rhythm of speech, as repetition and "call backs" punctuated all the intertwined self-narratives, within this single, audio interview. The women also refused to be filmed or identified, choosing instead the relative anonymity of the audio interview. Interpretation itself was not the interviewers' or speakers' prerogative, as everybody chimed in to finish each other's sentences; to offer strength and care through yet another narrative, emerging from the previous one, consolidating it or breaking it apart, and, in a way, anticipating the next one and legitimizing it. Indeed, the women told their stories in a way that did not erase their individual paths, but enhanced them through dialogue, resonance, contradiction, and dissonance. It was "as if," all of a sudden, a knowledge of uncertainty, a knowledge of resonance instead of reason and meaning, began to appear as a distinct possibility.[15]

In a grave moment for all of us, J., one of the ten women involved, warned us about what was to come. She started to weave an incredible tale that other women in the group continued—with stories of memory and self—built from one another's voices:

> It is something very grave, this thing we are doing here. I recognize that it is grave. I won't tell it all, but I'll explain some of it. The conscious that you were living, we have to [finally] decipher it.[16]

And so we did. Reflections were not just isolated academic interpretations; they also became a continuous story where selves and voices interwoven, permeable, were never standing still. And another history, one that was never

Figure 13.1 Mafalda Nicolas Mondestin, *Chita pale* (Sit Down and Talk), mixed technique on paper, 2016, 61 x 47.5cm.[17]

190   *Stéphane Martelly*

definitive, suddenly became possible, allowing us to think in an opaque and broken way about opaque and broken things.

In this amazing reinvention of selves, the selves themselves were moving and porous, as margins should be. Magnificent and unpredictable narration, finally becoming, in the face of violence, the infinite, necessary, providential possibility of "another side." In the face of all-consuming and destructive centers, resisting and unyielding, the unbearable hopefulness of margins offered possibilities of moving beyond for all of us.

Notes

1 Marie Chauvet, "Folie," in *Amour, Colère et Folie* (Paris: Gallimard, 1968), 333. On Chauvet's usage of "as if" (*"comme si"*) in her writing, I suggest that she uses the expression to mark the shared subjective space occupied by the writer and reader, a mediated and composite perspective that evokes both a narrative and its effects on the reader/listener. For more, see my interpretation of *Amour, Colère et Folie* in Stéphane Martelly, *Les Jeux du dissemblable. Folie, marge et féminin en littérature haïtienne contemporaine* (Montréal: Nota Bene, 2016), 31–35.
2 The "Montréal Life Stories" project was a five-year (2007–2012) oral history project that explored "Montréalers' experiences and memories of mass violence and displacement." The team of 160 university- and community-based researchers and practitioners conducted and recorded interviews with over 500 Montréal residents. With seven working groups focused on the Holocaust, Great Lakes [Rwanda], Haïti, Cambodia, education, performance, and youth refugees, the project aimed to "create cultural and historical materials for Montréal's diverse communities and foster collaboration and partnership between them." It also "[developed] interdis-ciplinary pedagogical tools and [made] a significant, original contribution to the preservation of historical memory in Canada, by raising questions about the long-term repercussions of crimes against humanity." A project that was rooted in collaborative work between researchers, and also blurred the lines between researchers and participants at every stage, it employed Michael Frisch's concept of sharing authority: "an effort of collaboration, in all directions, and at all levels." Rather than "being considered research objects," the participating communities had "a role as associates and real partners in the dialogue." Centre for Oral History and Digital Storytelling (COHDS) (collective), *General Training, Part 1: Introduction to the Life Stories Project*, PowerPoint document, September 2011, slides 1–3.
3 Michael Frisch, *A Shared Authority: Essays on the Craft and Meaning of Oral History* (Albany: State University of New York, 1990).
4 I purposefully use that word in two ways: in the sense of emotion and of dis-placement, i.e. personal involvement and varied identification(s) within the space of the oral history interview. Margins are also about delimitations: in my approach, I ponder the ways that we allow ourselves to move with and beyond them to more uncertain, but also more fluid definitions, questioning hierarchies while transforming spaces and distinctions. Note that I am also paraphrasing the title from Toni Morrison's famous Nobel Prize acceptance speech: "What moves at the margin." See Toni Morrison, *What Moves at the Margin* (Jackson, MS: University Press of Mississippi, 2008).
5 On 12 January 2010, Haïti was struck with a massive earthquake that left more than 250,000 people dead and most buildings and institutions completely destroyed. Many of the women in the grieving group were recent refugees who settled in Montréal with the help of *La Maison d'Haïti*.

6 This relates to my own work regarding the opacity of the text/narrative in which not every aspect has to be revealed or made transparent in interpretation: Stéphane Martelly, *Le Sujet opaque. Une lecture de l'oeuvre poétique de Magloire-Saint-Aude* (Paris: L'Harmattan, 2001). On the uses of the archive, where some aspects are preserved (meaning is kept in memory and in secret) while others are deliberately not made public, see Grace Sanders Johnson, "Archival Cadences: History, Sound and Collective Memory," paper presented in the *Modalités du récit de vie* round-table series (Concordia University, Montréal, Quebec, 29 February 2016).

7 Of the Latin *margo* (ledge), the root *mark* (sign, mark) of Germanic *marka* (step, border), the word was used in the 18th century to designate available quantities, reserves (like in the expression *une marge de manœuvre*). In the 19th century, the idea of deviancy or eccentricity was introduced. The idea of separation came in the 20th century, when margins were used to describe deviant and separate elements of society. See Christine Noille-Clauzade, "Rhétoriques de la mise en marge," in *Théorie des marges littéraires*, eds. Philippe Forest and Michelle Szkilnik (Université de Nantes, s.l: Éditions Cécile Defaut, 2005), 39. I complete these definitions by referencing Alain Rey, *Le Petit Robert, Dictionnaire culturel de langue française* (Tome III, Paris: Dictionnaire Le Robert, 2005), 367.

8 Noille-Clauzade, 39.

9 Over time, the academic/public divide became more porous because of the community members who were involved as researchers in the project.

10 Henry Greenspan, "Re-inventing Testimony," Keynote address at the "Remembering War, Genocide, and Other Human Rights Violations. Oral History, New Media and the Arts Conference", Concordia University, Montréal, Quebec, 5 November 2009. Also see Greenspan, "Voices, Places and Spaces," in *Remembering Violence. Oral History, New Media, Performance*, eds. Steven High, Edward Little, and Thi Ry Duong (Toronto: University of Toronto Press, 2014), 35–48.

11 Raymond Chassagne, "I travelled into myself," interview by Stéphane Martelly, Montréal, 18 June 2010.

12 I borrow this concept, of "Grands récits," from Marc Angenot, *Les Grands Récits militants des XIXe et XXe siècle: religions de l'humanité et sciences de l'histoire* (Paris: L'Harmattan, 2000).

13 Since organized violence takes many forms, to some members of the group talking to all victims put us at risk of false equivalencies between the specific violence of totalitarian regimes, sporadic state-sponsored violence, violence perpetrated by various armed groups, or collateral violence from social unrest. Also, the Lavalas movement, with its liberatory and autocratic moments, is still quite polarizing in recent Haitian history. See Jana Evans Braziel's "Introduction" in *Duvalier's Ghosts. Race, Diaspora and U.S. Imperialism in Haitian Literatures* (Gainesville, University Press of Florida, 2010) and, for a thorough analysis, see the special issue of the Haitian-Caribbean journal *Chemins Critiques* entitled "La tentation de la tyrannie," 5, no. 1 (2001).

14 Martha C. Nussbaum, *Creating Capabilities. The Human Development Approach* (Cambridge, MA: Belknap Press of Harvard University Press, 2011), 17–49.

15 Shoshana Felman, *La Folie et la chose littéraire* (Paris: Seuil, 1978), 15–16.

16 Anonymous, interview with the women of *La Maison d'Haïti*, Montréal, 2011. My translation of the original *Kreyòl*.

17 Contemporary Haitian artist Mafalda Nicolas Mondestin created this piece of art for this chapter. When I sent her my first draft to find out if she had available images, she was inspired instead to create this new piece of artwork. I am very grateful for her generosity and talent. With this painting, she adds another voice from Haïti to mine, as well as to the intermingled voices of our elders.

14 Intersubjective experiences and a depiction beyond written words

Doing ethnography with wartime children in northern Uganda

Grace Akello

In 2004, when I visited the war-torn district of northern Uganda as an ethnographer and doctoral student interested in researching the impact of violence on children, the region had been engulfed by war for more than two decades. In that period, tens of thousands of people, including children, were displaced, and many of the children witnessed or experienced violence in various forms. My theoretical approach involved treating children as social actors in their own right. What I did not originally understand, however, was the degree to which my research would ultimately be influenced by the experiences I shared with the children who were my research subjects. This chapter is about that revelation. In reflecting on my positionality, and how it shaped my project, it contributes to the growing scholarship on intersubjectivity and "the autobiographic" in anthropological fieldwork. However, in contrast to much of the literature on self-reflexivity, which is dominated by white, Western scholars, including global North feminists who conduct research in African and other non-Western contexts, I highlight my positionality as a non-Western researcher who shares a history with the children I studied. While my discussion of "empathetic enmeshment" and writing "autobiographic" ethnography draws mainly on the medical anthropological scholarship in which I am situated—and I thank the collection's editors for not imposing one literature on all authors—I also acknowledge that feminist oral historians have contributed much to the study of intersubjectivity and the embrace of reflexive writing.

When I began my doctoral research, northern Uganda was a war zone, the result of prolonged fighting between the Lord's Resistance Army (LRA) and the Uganda People's Defence Forces (UPDF). Headed by the rebel leader Joseph Kony, the LRA's militaristic ways, which received assistance from the Sudanese government, exposed many civilians in the northern Uganda districts of Kitgum, Gulu, and Pader to years of war, violence, displacement, abductions, and death. Following mediated negotiations between the Government of Uganda and the LRA, relative peace was restored in January 2007. Since then, the Ugandan government has failed to eliminate the LRA, which, based in the Democratic Republic of Congo forests, continues to initiate occasional civilian attacks in the Central African Republic.

During the armed conflict, many of the people affected by the war settled in displaced persons' camps, also called protected villages. These villages were unsafe, however, because the UPDF imbedded themselves in these locations, a military strategy that frequently exposed civilians to dangerous gunfire exchanges between the two warring parties.[1] Furthermore, the LRA tactics, involving the abduction and forceful enlistment of children in its armed group, instilled fear and distrust in children living in this war zone. Many had either witnessed or heard about the LRA's tactics of using children to unleash various forms of violence, including sibling abduction, killings, and maiming civilians. These were also typically children who had lost parents and caretakers to armed conflict as well as girls and child mothers who had experienced or witnessed acts of sexual and gender-based violence. In addition, people had to cope with social, health, security, and economic challenges daily. The children, who were mostly dependent on food hand-outs from emergency aid agencies, attended schools for displaced children in the daytime, but spent their nights in night commuter shelters where they constantly negotiated dangerous and risky contexts. These "wartime children" were the main focus of my doctoral study, which employed qualitative techniques of data collection between 2004 and 2005.[2]

I recruited the respondents for my doctoral work, which was later published as a monograph, through schools for displaced children, non-governmental organizations (NGOs) that targeted children for assistance, such as World Vision and Noah's Ark, and from night commuter shelters.[3] Located mainly in the comparatively safer municipality of Gulu, the night commuter shelters existed in many forms. At St Mary's Hospital Lacor and Gulu Regional Referral hospitals, tents were erected at specific points within the hospital each night for children and adults. At Kaunda grounds, children and adults gathered every evening to spend the night in a relatively safe place where partially locked classrooms and tents served as shelters. In some night commuter shelters, various NGOs offered counselling services, which included medical advice and opportunities for the children to play. A common therapy was to have the children tell their stories and then either perform the traditional songs and dances of the Acholi tribe to which many of them belonged, or sing church music.[4]

Conceptualizing children as social actors

To conceptualize children as social actors in their own right, and with their own points of view, is to understand them not as passive recipients of support (and culture) but active individuals who play an important role in their own development, relationships, and protection.[5] This theoretical orientation, which informed my study, represents a paradigm shift of sorts. The notion that children have little autonomy from adults, and that their experiences are quite removed from the adult world, originates from Western concepts of childhood. However, in non-Western societies children often have considerable everyday responsibilities related to household tasks, sibling care, income generation, and healthcare. In their work with children in Western Kenya, for instance, Ruth Prince et al. found that Luo children had a strong knowledge of medicines as treatments for common illnesses. Similar results have been reported for other African countries, and, indeed, also for developed nations where children play active roles in their healthcare.[6]

Elsewhere I have indicated that, consciously or unconsciously, my work with wartime children could be interpreted as an exploration of, and also confrontation with, my childhood experiences.[7] It was what Marian Tankink and Marianne Vysma describe as a round-about-way of assessing oneself by assessing the "Other's" experience.[8] While I reflected upon wartime children's experiences as well as my own, the boundaries between the two became blurred, thereby making my study an exploration, analysis, confrontation, examination, and writing of "our" experiences. I will return to this point below through a discussion of intersubjectivity, stressing the need for researchers to be aware of the past and present experiences they may share with their respondents.[9]

Dilemmas in the field

My ethnographic study focused primarily on northern Uganda's Gulu District. As many of the displaced people moved to Gulu town, they settled in different, congested suburbs that offered cheap and affordable huts for rent. Outside Gulu town, displaced people lived in gazetted (government-designated) areas that were also called protected villages or displaced persons' camps. Although I underwent a rigorous ethics review that was designed by the National Council of Science and Technology and sought additional permission from Gulu district administrators—including the then Directorate of District Health Services, the District Education Office, the Chief Administrative Office, and the Resident District Commissioner—I only became aware of how ill prepared I was once I entered the field, especially given my inability to objectively assess the experiences of others.[10] For example, I arrived with four pre-set criteria meant to enable me to select a few children for my ethnographic study: they had to be displaced from their livelihood; be caretakers of kin suffering from HIV/AIDs; be living in abject poverty; and be orphans living in child-headed households (a child who had assumed the main responsibility of caring for the sick and dying members of their household, whether adults, such as a parent, or other children, either kin or not). These criteria were, however, of little help in limiting my study given that many children met all of them.

During my first three months in the field, more than 400 children participated in my study in various ways. Some depicted their experiences pictorially (120) or wrote compositions (100) about their recent illnesses, noting which medicines they had taken. Others responded to semi-structured questions

(165) suitable for their ages, and still others participated in focus group discussions (87). Out of all of these children, I then selected 24 for extensive follow up, even though many more were eligible and agreed to continue to participate in my study. Until now, I have been unable to explain how I came to select only those particular 24 children. What I know is that we had many shared experiences between us, which transcended gender and age boundaries. Also, like many other oral history practitioners, I made an emotional connection with them.

Encountering intersubjectivity

As I typed up my field notes, I reflected on my findings' implications. How had my presence in the field consciously or unconsciously influenced my observations and investigations? How did it impact how I responded to the children's stories of their experiences?[11] As I sorted my data into themes, I often found it very painful to type or write up my field notes, and so I decided to discuss this issue with a then senior psychiatrist and expert on the experiences of child survivors of war. He evoked transference and counter-transference to help me understand my feelings, an understanding that well fits with the analytical framework of intersubjectivity—the importance of the relationship between the interviewer and her subject—and which, in my case, involved shared biographical experiences.[12] My personal involvement with the children influenced, consciously or unconsciously, my research process, my selection of informants, and my data analysis and reporting. So much so that I now recognize my study represents the outcome of the particular interactions that occurred between the researcher and the researched within an intersubjective space that transcended racial, class, and socio-economic boundaries.[13]

To return to the psychiatrist's terms of "transference" and "counter-transference," I found helpful, for example, the notion that the informant's recollection of their current experiences of violence can trigger, in the researcher's sub-conscious, a re-enactment and reminder of a similar experience. The psychiatrist made me aware that my constant worrying about the children's circumstances—whether they could care for their mothers suffering from tuberculosis without themselves getting sick or make it through the night without getting beaten or raped—and also the significant attention that I paid to a child who had been taken advantage of by his paternal aunt, could be my own way of dealing with a similar childhood experience. It was not, however, a conscious choice at the time of the study, which was meant to study suffering, and to recruit, listen to, and examine children's experiences that were similar to mine. In fact, by the time I started my fieldwork, I had even managed to repress some of my painful childhood experiences to the point of forgetting them. And yet, I kept feeling a tremendous sense of guilt. In retrospect, what guided the organization of my field notes and their analysis was both the children's narratives and my own experiences. In part, my embodied knowledge was reflected in the different themes on which I reported, and my interpretations of the children's narratives. And, as Judith Okely puts it, "My data interpretation came also from the whole person, body, mind, emotion, through memory and re-enactment."[14] Therefore, in contrast to the many traditional anthropological works that have been carried out in Africa, and which read like a representation of bounded, homogenous, and static cultures, my findings emerge out of a multi-site study, which evolved over time and involved an ethnographic interaction with a heterogeneous culture.[15]

In retrospect, I attribute much of what happened in my study to shared experiences. I think the questions I asked and analyzed, the ways children openly discussed their points of view with me, and my selection of respondents all underpinned my need to document "our" shared experiences. If ethnography is in its concise sense "writing about people," then how do I classify a study where the researcher and the respondents compose a narrative depicting a weaving together of their joint past and present experiences in an intersubjective space?[16] Is it engaged medical anthropology? Is it (auto)ethnography and (auto)biography? And, when is it possible to move beyond doing ethnography?

Shared experiences and the research process

In describing my fieldwork experiences elsewhere, I suggested that my own embodied fears and past childhood experiences led me to try to avoid and leave unexplored my own childhood.[17] Now, I am more convinced than ever that this is what happened. Just like the wartime children I interviewed, who lived in tents and open spaces, went to sleep hungry, and carried many burdens on their shoulders, I had a range of traumatic childhood experiences, including living in abject poverty and misery, and lacking basic needs such as food and clean water. In addition, I spent three years living in a house with broken doors and windows where I constantly feared that I would be attacked. I found that assessing wartime children's experiences and writing about them was like writing about my own experiences. Still committed to a model of the detached researcher, I nevertheless worked hard to avoid confronting what I had actively suppressed for such a long time. I attempted again and again to repress the constant and painful thoughts about why I wanted to assess what the children identified as "their" common health complaints and quests for therapy. At this point, I told myself that I was only interested in what "others" had experienced, and I wanted to write about "them." Nonetheless, I now realize that my embodied experiences influenced my entire research process, extending even to my treatment of the literature I consulted and reviewed in connection with my work. For example, I read many ethnographies that not only presented African experiences as exotic, and Africans as possessing only folk and subjective beliefs, but also argued that these "primitive" folkways affected how people managed illness, whether they requested help, and to whom they turned for therapy. In short, they were singularly unhelpful.[18] Without being conscious of my choices, I actively ignored these works because they did not reflect either the daily realities of my life or the everyday experiences of wartime children in northern Uganda.[19] At the same time, I was pulled toward those authors who wrote about doing anthropology at home, or autoethnography, especially those pondering how "native anthropologists" deal with subjective feelings that arise in the context of carrying out their research, particularly with vulnerable subjects (usually women). Their depictions were closer to how I wanted to share my findings in light of my own reality. To some extent, it was confusing to me to find ethnographies that dealt with other contexts—those outside Africa, and sometimes not even directly focused on children—were more relevant to my work than many African ethnographies.[20] I did not connect with depictions of what I can now call insider ethnography, done by Africans researching Africans, probably because of differences in theoretical stance or, to a greater extent, the absence of any acknowledgement of the importance of intersubjectivity.[21] In terms of the questions I asked in the field, I focused on everyday experiences without looking for the strange, the exotic, and what makes wartime children "different."[22] I also interpreted the children's narratives within the framework of my embodied experience and, to a lesser extent, within the context of what contemporary anthropologists had done in their ethnographic studies in Africa or in work written about Africans. Moreover, I also did not want to engage in endless critiques of the anthropological "classics" and how they represent white imperialist renditions of "other" cultures and societies because, by that point in time, I wanted to communicate the shared experiences of wartime children, including my own, and write autoethnography.

This meant writing a different kind of anthropology, a process that turned out to be more emotionally draining and painful than a "detached" assessment would have been. Anthropologists, like Alan Bryman, describe qualitative research as seeing through the eyes of people you are studying, while Jennie Popay explores the meanings people attach to their experiences (i.e. emic views) and describes the processes that shape these meanings.[23] Increasingly, I found that these insights resonated with me as I worked in the field. As I examined the children's experiences, as well as their ways of coping and their viewpoints—for example, the children wanted to earn money to help their families rather than play and they did not always follow the medical advice to not eat the leftovers of sick family members because they had so few resources—I simultaneously reflected upon and examined my own childhood and present experiences. What I experienced is consistent with Okely's claim that the anthropologist does not arrive in the field as an innocent observer, but instead brings the flotsam of prior representations and alternative knowledge with them, which affects their initial experiential understandings. She adds that the engaged anthropologist, rather than the necessarily anonymous psychoanalyst, stimulates revealing dialogue through mutual trust and shared participation even when done vicariously.[24] In their critique of social science research that neglects embodied knowledge, Edmund Husserl and Edith Stein argue that the researcher embraces personal thoughts, feelings, stories, and observations to understand the social context they are studying.[25] I now recognize that I engaged in certain procedures that were mediated by my embodied knowledge and shared experiences with wartime children. For example, I would sometimes volunteer to take care of some of my narrators' sick kin, who had been admitted to hospital because of HIV and AIDs, actions that went beyond what was required of me in these contexts, but that can also be largely explained by my own more recent experience of caring for a relative with HIV.

The stories children told about themselves and how they dealt with their wartime distress were very much their experiences, but listening to them gave me the impression that I was studying myself "in a round-about way through the other's experiences."[26] While the outcomes of such studies show greater understanding on the part of the researcher, Marian Tankink and Marianne Vysma have also demonstrated how, when engaged with such a dynamic, it is often easy for the researcher to lose sight of boundaries and become a helper instead.[27] John Wilson and Jacob Lindy report that emotional involvement and empathic enmeshment implies that a researcher/therapist's interaction with the researched/client can border on over-identification and personalization, hence they advise researchers to limit such involvement as much as possible during their fieldwork. Otherwise, they argue, emotional enmeshment will adversely affect their work. However, my position is closer to the one advocated by Nelson Coelho and Luis Figueiredo, who assert that we can only understand another person in terms of ourselves and ourselves in terms of the other.[28]

Indeed, I suggest that by losing my "boundary" as a researcher, and sometimes becoming a helper, I authentically examined these children's experiences. Certainly, at times, my actions caused me even more pain. When, for example, my decision to give money to some of my child narrators led them to become the target of slander at the hands of other children, and the landlord of one child to raise the child's rent, I felt both guilt and outrage. Distancing myself from the children's experiences likely would have led to different outcomes, but at the cost of leaving much out. There is plenty of debate over the role of the researcher and their subjects in scholarship. Within social science research, there is presently agreement that, as Johannes Fabian explains,

> If an anthropologist does not want to use intersubjectivity—that is to actively gain insight into his(her) own fully conscious intersection with his(her) subjects—s/he runs the risk of producing mere categories of social artefacts with doubtful historical and intellectual significance.[29]

Upon further scrutiny, however, I suggest that many insider anthropologists, including Indigenous anthropologists who were born and raised in the same locale and speak the same language as those they research, sometimes come up with unexpected outcomes that hardly reflect the respondents' realities. This is partly because they either assume certain theoretical standpoints that lead them to certain kinds of conclusions, or adopt a positioning as detached researchers that blinds them to the role their own personal history plays in shaping their results. In my view, acknowledging the intersubjective space that one inhabits along with one's research subjects offers a far more useful approach than the previously espoused model of seeking to access the respondents' (insider) point of view. This applies even to anthropologists doing research among members of their own racial, ethnic, or gender group. Similarly, Donna Gabaccia and Franca Iacovetta's recent analysis of Luisa Passerini's scholarship underscores the fact that Passerini long ago "insisted that oral history material be treated primarily as cultural, rather than literal or wholly individual, narratives and that scholars understand that memory incorporates dimensions of ideology and subconscious desires as well as an informant's contemporary positioning."[30] Acknowledging and embracing such shared experiences enables the researcher to transcend racial and ethnic boundaries precisely because the starting point in data collection signifies the realities or everyday experiences of both the researched and researcher. They unify rather than divide both sides, leading to a mutually agreed upon narrative. Acknowledging and scrutinizing such shared experiences further enables the researcher to avoid the pitfalls created by researchers who have their own preconceived ideas and prejudices about the people they are observing/interpreting and the issues at stake. Engaging in this practice allowed me to make the following conclusions. The key health complaints children identified were malaria, diarrhoea, and diseases of an infectious nature. They used pharmaceuticals, which they accessed from state-aided hospitals or they bought cheap and affordable medicines from pharmacies. Although the children did not readily discuss their stressors, they addressed them through appropriate ways of coping, engaging, for instance, in income-generating activities and seeking help from well-wishers. Others mentioned that they used the local plant *atika* (Labiate species) to ward off *cen* (evil spirits), or when they had frequent episodes of nightmares. I thereby argued that children prioritized infectious disease management over psychosocial complaints, even though wartime interventions largely focused on "offering psychosocial support" to vulnerable people.

Conclusion

In "doing anthropology at home" as autoethnography, the researcher's self-reflection and writing depicts personal experiences that are enmeshed within broader political, social, and cultural meanings, and which respondents also attribute to their experiences.[31] Autoethnography reflects a shared subjective experience between the researcher and the researched, rather than a presentation by the "expert" of past and present experiences, and the beliefs and practices of "others."[32] Unlike empiricist-oriented research, such approaches embrace and foreground the researchers' subjectivity rather than attempting to limit it. In essence, autoethnographers are themselves the primary participant/subject of the research, and, in the process, they write personal stories and narratives. Laura Ellingson and Carolyn Ellis describe autoethnography as a "social constructionist project that rejects the deep-rooted binary oppositions between the researcher and the researched, objectivity and subjectivity, process and product, self and others, art and science, and the personal and the political." Introspective research and autoethnography based on the principle of inter-subjectivity are also modes of analysis in which many feminist oral historians from different disciplines engage. These ethnographers have helped to bring about a profound paradigmatic shift in our understanding of knowledge-production by rejecting the concept of research as objective and the notion that neutral knowledge is produced though scientific methods applied by a researcher who is detached from the researched. To this list, I could also add feminist anthropologists such as Ruth Behar, a strong advocate of empathetic listening and of embracing the subjective in field research, and feminist oral history scholars such as Passerini and Sherna Berger Gluck.[33] All of these scholars, and others, have demonstrated that introspective research can facilitate the collection of valid and valuable "data"—that is, stories which evoke in readers a feeling that the experience described is life-like, believable, possible, and could be true.[34] Also, Amadeo Giorgi suggests that validity, in a phenomenological sense, can be achieved "if the essential description of a phenomenon truly captures the intuited essence.[35] The ability to draw comparisons between the experiences of the researcher and researched with-out striving to highlight difference, which usually implies the researcher's superior position and thus inequality, or by "othering," can produce more egalitarian scholarship even if, as Judith Stacey observed in the original *Women's Words*, we cannot eliminate every inequality.[36] When, in relation to our research subjects, we position ourselves as co-researchers and co-narrators of phenomenon, the power relations between researcher and respondent are minimized significantly. As Immy Halloway states, recognizing the researcher as the research instrument, and the plan of inquiry as a process that evolves as it will, also means that qualitative researchers cannot rely on standardized procedures to deal with concerns like bias and reproductivity.[37] Admittedly, studying one's own culture means one understands many or most of the issues involved, but such closeness might also mean neglecting certain aspects of that culture, thereby producing data that is not generalizable. Nevertheless, the strength of knowledge produced from qualitative studies rooted in inter-subjectivity and autoethnography shows that the researcher can develop a deeper understanding of the issues at stake.

Notes

1   For more details on the war, see Grace Akello, *Wartime Children's Suffering and Quests for Therapy in Northern Uganda* (Leiden: African Studies Centre, 2010).
2   In 2004, UNICEF estimated that the LRA abducted and recruited up to 20,000 children between ages 7 and 17 years as fighters and sex slaves. On the efforts of UNICEF and national and international NGOs to rehabilitate and reintegrate the children who escaped from the LRA or were rescued, see Grace Akello, Annemiek Richters, and Ria Reis, "Silencing Distressed Children in the Context of War: An

Analysis of Its Causes and Health Consequences," *Social Science & Medicine* 71, no. 2 (2010): 213–220; Akello, "The Impact of the Paris Principles on the Reintegration Processes of Former Child Soldiers in Northern Uganda," *Annals of Psychiatry and Mental Health* 3, no. 5 (2015): 1038–1047.
3 My dissertation was published as Akello, *Wartime Children's Suffering.*
4 Akello, *Wartime Children's Suffering.*
5 Alan Prout and Allison James, "A New Paradigm for the Sociology of Childhood? Providence, Promise and Problems," in *Constructing and Reconstructing Childhood. Contemporary Issues in the Sociological Study of Childhood,* eds. Allison James and Alan Prout (London: Falmer Press, 1990), 7–34; Alan Prout and H. Pia Christensen, "Hierarchies, Boundaries, and Symbols: Medicine Use and Cultural Performance of Childhood Sickness," in *Children, Medicines and Culture,* eds. Patricia. J. Bush et al. (New York: The Haworth Press, 1996), 31–50; Pia Christensen and Allison James, *Research with Children: Perspectives and Practices* (London and New York: Falmer Press, 2000), 77–99; Allison James and Alan Prout, "Hierarchy, Boundary and Agency," *Sociological Studies in Children* 7 (1995): 77–99.
6 Ruth Prince et al., "Knowledge of Herbal and Pharmaceutical Medicines Among Luo Children in Western Kenya," *Anthropology & Medicine* 8, no. 2/3 (2001): 213–235; Prout and Christensen, 31–50; A. Engelbert, "Worlds of Children: Differentiated but Different. Implications for Social Policy," in *Childhood Matters: Social Theory, Practice and Politics,* eds. J. Qvortrup et al. (Aldershot: Avebury Press, 1994); Prince et al., 213–235; David Lancy, *Playing on the Motherground* (New York: Guilford Press, 1996); Akello et al., "Silencing Distressed Children"; James and Prout, 77–99.
7 Grace Akello, "Understanding Wartime Children's Suffering, Uganda: Inter-subjectivity at the Centre," *Medische Antropologie Journal* 19, no. 1 (2007): 39–58; Akello, "The Importance of the Autobiographic Self during Research among Wartime Children in Northern Uganda," *Medische Antropologie* 24, no. 2 (2012): 289–300.
8 Marian Tankink and Marianne Vysma, "The Intersubjective as Analytic Tool in Medical Anthropology," *Medische Antropologie* 18, no. 11 (2006): 249–265.
9 Tankink and Vysma, 249–265; James and Prout, 77–99; Prince et al., 213–235; Akello, "Understanding Wartime Children," 39–58; Akello, "The Importance of the Autobiographic Self," 289–300.
10 Akello, "Understanding Wartime Children," 39–58.
11 Akello, "Understanding Wartime Children," 39–58.
12 John P. Wilson and Jacob D. Lindy, *Counter Transference in the Treatment of PTSD* (New York: Guilford Press, 1994); Danieli Yeal, "Psychotherapists' Participation in the Conspiracy of Silence about the Holocaust," *Psychoanalytic Psychology* 38, no. 1 (1984): 23–42.
13 Akello, "The Importance of the Autobiographic Self," 289–300; James and Prout, 77–99; Prince et al., 213–235.
14 Judith Okely, "Fieldwork Embodied," in *Embodying Sociology: Retrospect, Progress, Prospects,* ed. Chris Shilling (Oxford: Blackwell, 2007), 66–79.
15 See Judith Stacey, "Can There Be a Feminist Ethnography?" in *Women's Words: The Feminist Practice of Oral History,* eds. Sherna Berger Gluck and Daphne Patai (New York: Routledge, 1991), 111–120.
16 Alan Bernard, *History and Theory in Anthropology* (Cambridge: Cambridge University Press, 2000), 141.
17 Akello, "Understanding Wartime Children."
18 For example, African anthropologist Christine Mbabazi Mpyangu claimed that engaging the children in cleansing rituals and other Acholi religious practices, such as stepping on an egg, would be "unquestioningly significant in the process of

reintegration." These ideas were not reflected in young people's point of view. See Mpyangu, "The Acholi Worldview: Why Rituals are Important for the Reintegration of Formerly Recruited Girls in Northern Uganda," in *Culture, Religion, and the Reintegration of Female Child Soldiers in Northern Uganda*, ed. Bard Maeland (Peter Lang: New York, 2011), 101–104, 108.

19 George M. Foster, "Disease Etiologies in Non-Western Medical Systems," in *The Art of Medical Anthropology*, eds. S. Van der Geest and A. Rienks (Amsterdam: Het SpinHuis, 1998), 141–150; Robert Pool, *Dialogue and the Interpretation of Illness* (Amsterdam: Aksant Academic Publishers, 2003); Dennis M. Warren, "The Techman-Bono Ethnomedical System," in *African Health and Healing Systems: Proceedings of a Symposium*, ed. P.S. Yoder (Los Angeles: Crossroads Press, 1982), 120–124.

20 Johannes Fabian, *Time and the Other of Anthropology: Critical Essays, 1971–1991* (Chur: Harwood Academic Publishers, 1996); Johannes Fabian, *Time and the Other: How Anthropology Makes its Object* (New York: Columbia University Press, 2002), 5–164; Athena Mclean and Annette Leibing, "Ethnography and Self-Exploration," *Medische Antropologie* 23, no. 1 (2011): 183–201.

21 Harriet Ngubane, *Body and Mind in Zulu Medicine* (London: Academic Press, 1976).

22 Yeal, 23–42.

23 Alan Bryman, *Mixed Methods: A Four-Volume Set* (London: Sage, 2006); Jennie Popay, "'My Health Is Alright But I Am Just Tired All the Time': Women's Experiences of Ill Health," in *Women's Health Matters*, ed. Hellen Roberts (London: Routledge, 1992), 99–120. See also Patricia J. Bush, *Children, Medicines and Cultures* (New York: Pharmaceutical Products Press, 1996).

24 Judith Okely, "Fieldwork as Free Association and Free Passage," in *Ethnographic Practice in the Present*, eds. Marit Melhuus, Jon P. Mitchell, and Helena Wulff (New York: Berghahn Books, 2010), 28–41; Okely, "Vicarious and Sensory Knowledge of Chronology and Change: Aging in Rural Frame," in *Social Experience and Anthropological Knowledge*, eds. Kirsten Hastrup and Peter Hervik (London: Routledge, 1994), 45–64.

25 Edmund Husserl, *Ideas Pertaining to a Pure Phenomenology and to a Phenomenological Philosophy: General Introduction to a Pure Phenomenology* (Boston: Kluwer Academic Publishers, 1982), 5–8; Edith Stein, *A Biography* (New York: Harper & Row, 1985).

26 Akello, "Understanding Wartime Children," 39–58.

27 Tankink and Vysma, 249–265.

28 Wilson and Lindy; Nelson E. Coelho Jr. and Luis C. Figueiredo, "Patterns of Intersubjectivity in the Constitution of Subjectivity: Dimension of Otherness," *Culture & Psychology* 9, no. 3 (2003): 193–208.

29 Fabian, *Time and the Other*, 9.

30 Donna R. Gabaccia and Franca Iacovetta, "Borders, Conflict Zones, and Memory: Scholarly Engagements with Luisa Passerini," *Women's History Review* 25, no. 3 (May 2016), 345–364.

31 Edward Bruner, "Introduction: The Ethnographic Self and the Personal Self," in *Anthropology and Literature*, ed. Paul Benson (Urbana: University of Illinois Press, 1993), 1–26.

32 Daniel Stern, *The Present Moment in Psychotherapy and Everyday Life* (Norton Books: 2004); Akello, "Understanding Wartime Children," 39–58; Tankink and Vysma, 249–265.

33 Laura Ellingson and Carolyn Ellis, "Autoethnography as Constructionist Project," in *Handbook of Constructionist Research*, eds. James A. Holstein and Jaber F. Gubrium (Guilford Press, New York, 2008), 445–466. Ruth Behar, *The Vulnerable*

Observer: Anthropology that Breaks Your Heart (Beacon Press, Boston 1996); on Passerini, see, for example, Gabaccia and Iacovetta, "Borders, Conflict Zones, and Memory." Besides her many publications, which are cited throughout this volume, Sherna Berger Gluck was honored by an international and intergenerational panel at the Oral History Association's recent 50th anniversary meeting, Long Beach, CA., October 2016.

34 Norman K. Denzin, *The Interpretative Heritage: Symbolic Interactionism and Cultural Studies* (Oxford: Blackwell, 1992); Carolyn Ellis, Tony C. Adams, and Arthur P. Bochner, "Autoethnography: An Overview," *Forum: Qualitative Social Science Research* 12, no. 10, 282. (2011); Dan Zahavi, *Self-Awareness and Alterity: A Phenomenological Investigation* (Evanston: North Western University Press, 1999); Fabian, *Time and the Other*, 5–164.

35 Amadeo Giorgi, "Validity and Reliability from a Phenomenological Perspective," in *Recent Trends in Theoretical Psychology*, eds. W. Baker, L. Mos, H. Rappard, and H Stam (New York: Springer-Verlag, 1988), 167–176.

36 Stacey, 111–120.

37 Immy Halloway, *Qualitative Research in Healthcare* (Open University Press: New York, 2005).

15 Putting the archive in movement

Testimonies, feminism, and female torture survivors in Chile

Hillary Hiner

In regards to oral history and the creation of oral history archives, Latin America occupies a unique position because of the region's many countries that were shaken by Cold War-era dictatorships at roughly the same time, from the 1960s to the late 1980s. As torture, exile, death squads, and forced disappearances became the norm under these dictatorships, strong human rights movements, many led by female family members of the victims, arose in response.[1] Many of the first oral histories emerged during the continuing repression, usually in the form of *denuncia* (denouncement) testimonies issued by those affected, several of whom were in exile.[2] In post-dictatorship settings and transitional democracies, a *nunca más* (never again) discourse commonly came to the fore, as did truth commissions and trials, typifying what has come to be known as memory politics. While particular national contexts differ, Latin American human rights groups have generally sought to protect patrimonial memory sites, such as ex-torture centers or political prisons, to install victim-related memorials, and establish oral and written archives, many of them related to memory sites.[3] Oral history methodology has produced an intense and critical scholarship focused on Latin American Recent History and Memory Studies.[4] Since the 1990s, oral history and oral archives in Latin America have been closely associated with truth, justice, and memory projects linked both to repudiating authoritarian pasts and to shoring up democratic presents and futures. In the 21st century, greater attention has begun to be paid to the gendered and sexualized nature of political violence.

This chapter addresses women's memories of trauma through a comparison of an oral history archive in Chile—the Villa Grimaldi Oral Archive in Santiago—and my personal archive of 162 interviews conducted with women in Chile. Elsewhere, I have analyzed women's testimonies to evaluate the multiple and complex dimensions of gendered and sexualized violence, and the role of feminist theory in unpacking these socio-historical constructions.[5] Here, I draw on my experience as a dual American-Chilean citizen working as an academic and feminist activist in Chile to consider the practical and theoretical issues related to using oral archives of "terror" and undertaking oral history with female survivors of torture. My reflections can be read alongside Rina Benmayor's chapter on the use of *testimonios* in the classroom

(Chapter 5) and Theresa de Langis' chapter on the Cambodian Women's Oral History Project (CWOHP; Chapter 11).[6]

Archiving terror: The Villa Grimaldi memory site and oral archive

Villa Grimaldi, also called *Cuartel Terranova* by the military, was a notorious torture center and political prison located in an outlying area of the Peñalolén neighborhood of Santiago. It housed more than 4,500 political prisoners, 239 of whom were killed or forcibly "disappeared" between 1974 and 1978.[7] This former country house and restaurant was transformed into a concentration camp under the control of the DINA (National Intelligence Agency, headed by Colonel Manuel Contreras between 1973 and 1978), with designated torture areas, including the infamous "Tower," and cramped, unhygienic living quarters for male and female prisoners. Many leading members of the Communist (PC) and Socialist Parties (PS), and the MIR (guevarist-inspired Revolutionary Left Movement) passed through Villa Grimaldi, but perhaps the best-known ex-political prisoners are current president Michelle Bachelet (PS) and her mother Angela Jeria, who were detained there in 1975.[8] Due to international outrage over the 1976 killing of Orlando Letelier and Ronni Moffitt, important opponents of the regime, by DINA operatives in Washington, D.C., and internal power struggles in Chile, the DINA was officially shut down and replaced with the CNI in 1977.[9] The following year, when the Pinochet dictatorship sought greater legitimacy through the 1978 Amnesty Law and repressive methods became more focused, Villa Grimaldi was closed. While torture continued under the newly formed CNI (National Information Agency), which replaced the DINA, Villa Grimaldi was increasingly viewed as a political liability during the 1980s. Its original infrastructure no longer remains, as its buildings were demolished between 1988 and 1990, but its symbolic presence is enormous. Thus, much like Cambodia's Tuol Sleng Genocide Museum discussed by Theresa de Langis, which is housed on the former premises of the infamous S-21 prison and interrogation center, the mobilization of a human rights movement in Chile led to the preservation of the physical space on which Villa Grimaldi is located. In 1994, a memory site was opened there, and in 1997, a Parque de la Paz (Peace Park) was created. In 2004, the National Monument Council declared Villa Grimaldi a Historical Monument. Today, it is one of the best-known memory sites in Chile, visited annually by an average of 18,000 Chilean and foreign visitors, a third of which are students on guided tours.[10]

Currently, Villa Grimaldi (hereafter VG) houses a number of historical monuments and plaques dedicated to the executed and disappeared, and re-constructed areas that are shown during memory site tours, usually with K-12 and university students, but also foreign tourists. The site's strong cultural and educational aspects are evident from the small library, medium-sized outdoor amphitheater, and area reserved for the Oral Archive. With the consulting assistance of international and regional leaders in historical memory sites, such as those involved in the Argentinean memory site *Memoria Abierta*, and the technical and practical supervision of the University of Chile's Communication and Image Institute, the Villa Grimaldi Oral History Archive (VGOA) was founded in 2005 and began operations in 2006.[11] The archive is composed of 168 life histories, 99 of them done with men (59 per cent) and 69 with women (41 per cent).[12] The majority of these interviews, each of which lasts approximately three hours, were conducted with VG ex-political prisoners, though some family members of the executed and disappeared were also interviewed. Of the 69 female interviews, I reviewed the 26 that most dealt with the topic of gendered and sexualized violence and involved female survivors. These life histories are available for public viewing on DVDs that must be watched in situ (no copies or loans are allowed), using one of the VGOA's four computers equipped with headphones. Scholars may take notes and transcribe the interviews, but no official transcripts exist. Each video includes a brief narrator biography and strict guidelines are in place for researchers who wish to cite interviews.[13] VG prefers anonymity for its interview subjects but permits the use of last names or initials.[14] With the help of the archive's coordinators, scholars may search the Oral Archive's database—it contains references to topics such as sexual violence, for example—but locating specific testimonies can be difficult as the database is missing information and/or more recent oral testimonies are not necessarily catalogued. Also, the life history format used means interviews may include many hours of testimony not focused on the subject's detention in VG. Depending on one's project, one may find the historical detail either deeply enriching or frustrating given the time needed to manually advance to the most pertinent sections.

As an oral historian who belongs to the Oral History and Oral Archives Network, of which VG forms a part, I have come to better understand how the testimonies have been incorporated into the VGOA through conversations with its staff.[15] For example, although the script of oral interviews has largely remained unchanged over time, structured around a life history format with a political orientation, the particular interests of each interviewer have meant that certain recorded testimonies have a more pronounced gender perspective.[16] While gender-sensitive questions were common in earlier interviews, due largely to the flexible nature of the interview process and interviewers' familiarity with gender theory, later teams did not necessarily pay equal or consistent attention to this issue. Individual interviewers also have different interviewing techniques; some are more prone to follow the narrator's lead, improvising questions and leaving "space" for reflection, while others stick to their script and/or nervously fill in the lulls with additional rapid-fire questions. Gender may also influence interview style and whether a rapport is established with narrators. Before filming an interview, survivors underwent a pre-interview process during which they were shown the questions and given the opportunity to identify any topics as "off-limits." They signed a written consent form, in which they ceded all property rights pertaining to their recorded testimony in exchange for the

VGOA's promise of appropriate archival care. There is a standing "no-edit" policy for the interviews, but staff try to accommodate narrators' needs by allowing them "last cut" privileges in the video editing process, though very few requests have been made to date.[17]

The VG archive has been an invaluable resource for my research project, which focuses on the lived experiences of female survivors of the gendered and sexualized violence of state terrorism. In the interviews, women narrate, sometimes in great detail, the myriad ways this type of violence affected them in VG, both during the torture sessions and in "everyday" spaces, such as bathrooms and hallways. Women in particular were subjected to a constant barrage of gendered and sexualized violence from the moment of their detention, and it was often naturalized and internalized by the survivors themselves as shameful. Here, the power of filmed testimonies is clear; as they recall the violence, images say more than words, pauses become longer and more frequent, and emotions well up. These testimonies also shed light on limited spaces of resistance and solidarity among prisoners: women's stories tell of sharing foodstuffs and clothing, comforting one another after torture sessions, and devising activities to boost morale and combat boredom during long periods of forced collective sitting or standing, often in small cells while subject to extreme heat or cold. Individual details of experiences vary, but, generally, the women note their extreme dissatisfaction with the "*nunca más*" process. In Chile, the process has taken several forms, including two truth commissions: the 1990–1991 Rettig Commission for detained disappearances and executions; and the 2003–2004 Valech Commission for political prison and torture.[18] There have also been a number of trials, especially after Augusto Pinochet's 1998 detention in London, and a series of reparative measures that include pensions, scholarships, and lump-sum payouts, as well as the ongoing public health PRAIS program, which provides physical and mental health services for victims of human rights abuses and their families. As the survivors themselves note, few of the reparation measures, however, have specifically targeted female survivors of sexual political violence and, to date, none of the sexual violence or sexual torture trials have provided favorable rulings for women. They feel that their own experiences have not been fully recognized and that true "reparation," symbolic or material, is non-existent or extremely insufficient. In the testimonies of survivors who became feminists, and thus reflect on the past through that theoretical lens, clear linkages are drawn between the sexual and political violence experienced and the role of patriarchy as an oppressive force. In these interviews, present-day reflections on past trauma also become much more related to the anti-violence demands of the current feminist movement.

Seeking new voices: Survivors in Chile's different regions

Funded by a Chilean state Fondecyt project grant on gender violence, my project on state-initiated gender violence in Chile is called *Una historia inconclusa: violencia de género y políticas públicas en Chile, 1990–2010*

("Unfinished History: Gender Violence and Public Policy in Chile, 1990–2010"). I completed 162 interviews, all in Spanish, 25 of which were done with women from different Chilean regions who identified specifically as survivors of state terrorism, and approximately 15 with women who, when interviewed, disclosed past experiences of political violence during the dictatorship years (1973–1990). The semi-structured nature of the interviews and a relatively wide interpretation of what constitutes "gender violence" meant that, in many cases, women who were chosen to speak about their work with gender violence in the present also spoke about their experiences as survivors of past state terrorism. Instead of a life history format, I conducted semi-structured interviews (a few key questions and some follow-up questions) that focused on experiences of gender violence and interactions with, and opinions of, state and non-state (i.e. activist) efforts to eradicate, sanction, and repair gender violence. Interviews were also done with women who were "family members" of human rights victims, but who, for this project, are also considered survivors because they too lived through extreme episodes of psychological violence while searching for disappeared or executed loved ones. Some of these women experienced gender violence in their homes, police stations, or political prisons because of their connection to a detainee or their own political activities as party militants and/or human rights crusaders.

The primary research assistant during the project's fieldwork phase was Catalina Flores. As the grand-daughter of the coordinator of a local chapter of *Agrupación de Familiares de Detenidos Desaparecidos* (AFDD), the Organization of Family Members of Disappeared Detained Persons, in the south of Chile, she used family and political connections to approach contacts and build trust with women survivors. This "trust factor" was paramount. As many still consider sexual political violence a taboo subject, survivors are understandably reluctant to speak with an outsider. Considerable trust is thus required before a narrator will disclose what happened to her. That we could find women who wanted to speak about it may also reflect the fact that, 40 years after the military coup, we are seeing the increasing denouncement of sexual political violence. Interestingly, we found that women survivors from the regions, as opposed to the city of Santiago, were more willing to share their stories, perhaps because the former know their stories are nationally unknown. With many of Chile's major universities located in Santiago, students and researchers have been conducting interviews with women survivors there for some time, leading some of them to experience interview "burnout." The VGOA also proved helpful to us because it reduced the need for additional interviews, many of which would have duplicated the contents of that archive.

Conducted between July 2014 and December 2015, the interviews generally lasted between one and three hours. They were audio recorded and later transcribed. Given the time constraints—our interview trips to the different sites in the regions outside Santiago each lasted ten days or less—we did not conduct pre-interviews, although we usually sent a summary of the project to narrators ahead of time and engaged in a follow-up phone or email conversation afterwards. Although in the majority of cases we had only recently met our participants, the interviews were always intense and frequently marked by expressions of deep emotion. Some women were more accustomed than others to telling their stories and "bearing" witness to the horrors of the dictatorship, while others had not spoken frequently and publicly about their past experiences of trauma. Some of the latter had not told close family and friends. In these instances, my own training while working in a battered woman's shelter as well as previous experience conducting interviews on sensitive human rights and feminist issues proved salient.[19]

We were pleasantly surprised to find a high level of interest in the project and in being interviewed, a process that involved informed consent procedures that allowed women to participate as anonymous or named subjects. That the great majority of narrators let us use their given names reflects a widely shared sentiment among survivors of the need to "bear witness," speak out, and promote "*nunca más.*" Women's desire to "break the silence" more than 40 years after the violent military coup d'état that took place on 11 September 1973 came through strongly in the interviews. A post-interview process allowed them to review and modify the texts produced. I have been pleased with the positive feedback the project's related publications have received from narrators, especially given the time restrictions on reviewing the transcripts and, as the authors of *Women's Words* demonstrated, the likelihood that narrator and researcher might diverge in their interpretation of recorded memories.[20] Our collaborative and feminist approach has strengthened the project's insights.

These interviews were set up through various contacts, including local and national Chilean human rights groups such as the already mentioned AFDD and *Agrupación de Familiares de Ejecutados Políticos* (AFEP, Organization of Family Members of the Politically Executed), which have local chapters throughout Chile, and groups involved with local memory sites, local human rights activism, or with issues related to female survivors.[21] As we hoped, doing oral histories in the regions allowed a more complex and varied experience of state terrorism to emerge, as class, ethnicity, and race informed the experiences of women in the northern and southern regions in ways that were different from those in Santiago.

The narratives in these interviews differ from those in the VGOA in several ways. First, as previously noted, whereas the VGOA deals primarily with political violence that occurred in designated torture centers and political prisons, some of the regionally based women also survived episodes of state terrorism in their own homes (especially during *allanamientos*, or search and seizure procedures by the military or police), in police stations and police vehicles, and in public spaces related to detentions and/or protests. Additionally, the Mapuche women interviewed in the highly militarized Araucanía region see little if any difference between past and present state violence as their communities in the denominated "conflict zones" are frequently subject to dictatorial *allanamientos* (raids) carried out by militarized police forces. During such raids, violations of human rights are common, even against the elderly and small children, who have been shot at and otherwise treated with great violence during police operations.[22] Second, while the VGOA tends to circumscribe the perpetrators of violence to a small number of state agents who worked at specific torture centers during a limited time frame, the testimonies that we compiled speak of both state agents and civilians who took part in state repression over many years, including years *after* the end of the dictatorship. Police targeted many of the trans women who worked as sex workers during the dictatorship for infringing laws on morality (*buenas costumbres*) and sodomy, and the lack of rule of law and high levels of impunity within the police favored many transphobic acts, such as cutting hair, removing make-up, changing of clothes, or forced sex. Many of these women agree that mistreatment under the dictatorship was "worse," but they still face widespread transphobic violence at the hands of the police. Finally, the women of the VGOA tend to see and position themselves as primarily political subjects, as ex- or current militants of certain political parties or groups (usually the PS, PC or MIR), and as former political prisoners. Perhaps because we tended to recruit survivors of political violence through the different routes described above, our narrators exhibit a plethora of identities and group adhesions. Some no longer see themselves as being primarily linked to a particular political party, for example, or see their party militancy as secondary to their feminist activism. The large number of feminist activists we interviewed also meant that the feminist lens through which sexual political violence could be interpreted was even more present, and more sharply focused, in the project's interviews.

Oral history as a *gringa chilena*

Working with the VGOA interviews and the ones I conducted has greatly enriched my understanding of the gendered and sexualized torture and political imprisonment suffered by women who participated in leftist groups and parties. It has enhanced my understanding of how feminism informs these survivors' memories and current political activism, their perceptions of truth, justice and reparations, and how memory politics and party politics sometimes intersect, and sometimes are at odds, in post-dictatorial Chile. In my Spanish publications, I have argued that former female political prisoners are both survivors of acute and gendered human rights abuses and women whose narrations exhibit a great deal of resilience, capturing as they do instances of resistance, negotiation, solidarity, and feminism.[23] A study of the different types of women who became female militants in the 1970s and 1980s suggested that there was some correlation between, on the one hand, a narrator's willingness to disclose in-formation and the type of prison memories conveyed, and, on the other, her political trajectory, relationship to feminism, self-identity, and geographical location. Most recently, in an English publication, I have assessed the interviews of former female political prisoners in Chile in light of the critical theoretical insights of oral historian Luisa Passerini, including that "memory speaks from today," and, more specifically, her interpretations and self-analysis of the memory of Italy's 1968.[24] The latter particularly allowed me to think more transnationally about female militants in the left-wing groups of 1960s and 1970s in Italy and Chile, and their subsequent turn towards feminism. And about the transmission of intergenerational memory between older and younger feminists in Chile and the nature of current intergenerational activism that has drawn links between gender violence and sexual political violence: this activism may well represent a form of socio-political "reparation" on the part of female survivors.

Utilizing interviews in the two archives has made possible the construction of new gendered and feminist histories previously silenced and marginalized from mainstream Chilean History, including even Recent History, which has focused almost exclusively on men, whether workers, politicians, or even political prisoners or detained-disappeared. That 41 per cent of VGOA comprises women's testimonies means that, for generations to come, feminist researchers will be able to access women's life stories that address the gendered nature of state terrorism.[25] Indeed, given its importance and open access, the VG archive is *underused*, as many researchers do not know about it or have yet to visit the site, which is located some distance from downtown Santiago. Or they prefer to conduct their own interviews, a reflection of the cachet currently surrounding the practice of creating our own archives. In particular, young undergraduate students could learn an enormous amount from using the VGOA's invaluable testimonies, whose quality would be hard to replicate, as could non-Chilean students interested in women's experiences of state violence.

While these testimonies also proved important to my own research, my interest in capturing a diversity of stories meant interviewing women in the regions outside Santiago: self-identified "survivors of state terrorism" who also identified as lesbian and trans women, as Mapuche and Aymara women, and as Afro-Chilean women. This opened up a whole area of experience and historical interpretation that went beyond the circle of women whose torture occurred in a political prison like VG, whose archive is defined geographically (Santiago) and by such structural factors as the political parties whose members were most likely to have spent time there, and the types of political action most likely to result in detention during the years that VG was in operation.

My own positionality is also noteworthy here. When seeking out interview subjects, Catalina Flores and I generally used the snowball method, but generating the first "snowflakes" depended on securing contacts with human rights or feminist individuals and organizations. Catalina was a great resource for the project as she had many personal and activist connections to the world we were researching. Her "familiar face" allowed us to downplay one aspect of the project, which is that, although I have spent most of my adult life in Chile, I was born and trained as an undergraduate and master's student in the United States, making me (as some of my friends call me) a *gringa chilena*: a non-Chilean who has lived long-term in Chile, is a dual citizen, and who teaches and writes primarily in Spanish. Being a *gringa chilena* historian who works on Chilean History in Chile has not always been easy—a product, I think, of the Cold War history of US intervention in Chile. US involvement in the overthrow of Allende, CIA training of state agents responsible for torture and state terrorism, and the propping up of the Pinochet dictatorship and its neoliberal model, among other actions, has fomented a deep-seated mistrust and, at times, direct dislike of US-based researchers, especially, and understandably, among those directly affected by these nefarious policies, such as survivors of state terrorism.

Because I am frequently, if not always, perceived as "non-Chilean" also for reasons of appearance and/or accent, Catalina's role as a research assistant was critical to my project. Other US-born academics seeking to do oral histories in places where they are unknown may also use other strategies, such as the anthropological method of living with a family or immersing oneself in a place for an extended period of time, or working in a local human rights or feminist NGO. But I found that having a highly informed and deeply connected research assistant solved many problems. Also key was my fluent Spanish, my long-time residence in Chile (over ten years), and my being a feminist activist and academic in Chile. Being able to reference my own dense network of activist contacts also shifted somewhat the relations between interviewer and narrators, so that participants were less suspicious of me as a potentially untrustworthy "outsider," or at least tolerated me enough to let me in the door for a first encounter. Meeting many of these women through Catalina, or already knowing "friends of friends" through my feminist activism, also meant, in many cases, that interviewing and socializing went together. In many cities, we could turn to a few main feminist activist contacts who believed that helping us with the project also served a greater feminist good. Since completing the interviews, I have kept in contact with many of my narrators through email and Facebook. Sending them publications to review is not just about getting approval, but also about "checking in" to see how they are. Additionally, we share information about feminist activism in the regions and in Santiago. Hence, my title's meaning: conceiving of an archive "in movement" or academic work accompanied and nurtured by activism, and vice versa.

Women's Words and feminist oral history

In *Women's Words*, Kathryn Anderson and Dana Jack as well as Judith Stacey address debates raised in this chapter. Anderson and Jack identify a sort of baseline "feminist oral history" approach outlining the issues common to feminist researchers in the field: being aware of our own role as researchers in the oral history process, and listening carefully and respectfully when our narrators talk about "feelings as well as activities." There is also the still widely shared conviction that doing oral history with women is an appropriate methodology that can "pull back the curtain" on previously hidden "her-stories" that help us understand women's struggles in a predominantly patriarchal culture.[26] However, Stacey calls into question many of Anderson and Jack's presuppositions and prompts us to question the supposedly "objective" or naively "innocent" altruistic interactions between feminist ethnographer and her subject, and to explore the tensions surrounding the practice of feminist oral history. Given the inherently unequal power relation between ethnographer and subject, she argues, there cannot be a fully "feminist" ethnography, but

> there also can and should be feminist research that is rigorously self-aware and therefore humble about the partiality of its ethnographic vision and its capacity to represent self and other. Following the loss of my ethnographic innocence, I agree that the potential benefits of "partially" feminist ethnography are worth the serious moral costs involved.[27]

As an academic and activist oral historian keen to redress underrepresented histories, I stress the particular importance of interviews being done with women from LGBTQ+, Indigenous, black, and migrant communities in Chile, as these groups remain marginalized from mainstream Chilean History. Given the structural constraints of various oral archives in Santiago, including the VGOA, doing oral history is a necessary methodology for doing feminist Recent History work in Chile. As Stacey also noted, the process of recovering and using women's narratives—whether to mount exhibits as part of a large archival project or to write history using smaller collections—raises important ethical issues. There are other omissions as well. I suspect that the unevenness with respect to gender-related questions in the VGOA indicates that it has been only tangentially informed by feminist theory: while a few initial researchers were clearly informed by feminist theory, there is little evidence of a continuing dialogue with the current feminist movement in Chile. Consequently, not all women affected by the military regime are represented in the collection. In using my own oral histories, I have been particularly mindful of Stacey's admonition for feminists to be "rigorously self-aware" while also realizing, as she notes, that self-awareness alone cannot eliminate all inequities: we still have the final say in how we edit and tell our subjects' stories. Significantly, my project incorporated two requirements which I believe contributed towards feminist efforts to redress the unequal dynamics of oral history work: first, an informed consent process that requires devolution of all texts for participant review prior to publication—many written in Spanish, but if not, then with portions translated to Spanish or explanations in Spanish so narrators can understand the text and how they were quoted; and, second, particularly when interviewing feminist and human rights activists, recruitment of researchers who are themselves active feminists. This last principle is perhaps downplayed in some academic circles, but it applied to all the researchers in my project, creating a "virtuous" cycle between the feminist community, feminist oral history, and a feminist Recent History research project.

Finally, the principle of engagement in a larger activist community beyond the geographical restraints of one's project is also particularly important for feminists who research in regions outside of where they live. Clearly, not all researchers who work on Latin America can live or work full-time in the country where they do research, and the debate as to whether "outsiders" should work on the histories of "others" will continue. But if we wish to broaden our thinking about the use of oral history and transnational feminist history, I propose that our starting point be a continued and constant engagement with local feminist social movements. In that sense, and with the express interest of generating dialogue on this matter, I believe that what matters most is perhaps not *who* conducted the interview or consulted the oral archives—though, of course, this is vitally important for understanding the analyses offered in published works—but rather *how* they chose to dialogue with the local feminist movement and its activists while doing their research, and whether they put the "movement" back into their personal and professional archives.

Notes

1 For just a few examples, see Da Silva Catela Ludmila, *No habrá flores en la tumba del pasado. La experiencia de reconstrucción del mundo de los familiares de desaparecidos* (La Plata: Ediciones Al Margen, 2009); Feijoó María del Carmen and Mónica Gogna, "Women in the Transition to Democracy," in *Women and Social Change*, ed. Elizabeth Jelin (New York: Zed Books, 1990), 79–114; Elizabeth Jelin, *Los trabajos de la memoria* (Buenos Aires: Siglo XXI, 2001); Vidal Hernán, *Dar la vida por la vida: Agrupación Chilena de Familiares de Detenidos Desaparecidos* (Santiago: Ediciones Mosquito, 1996).

2 Bunster-Burotto Ximena, "Surviving Beyond Fear: Women and Torture in Latin America," in *Women and Change in Latin America*, eds. Nash June and Helen Safa (South Hadley: Bergin and Garvey, 1985), 297–327; Elizabeth Burgos, *Me llamo Rigoberta Menchú y así me nació la conciencia* (México: Siglo XXI, 1998 [1983]); Alicia Partnoy, *The Little School: Tales of Disappearance and Survival* (Berkeley: Cleis Press, 1998 [1986]).

3 In Latin America, Argentina leads the way in transforming former torture centers and political prisons into museums and archival projects, which include Archivo Provincial de la Memoria/Ex D2 in Córdoba (www.apm.gov.ar/apm/portada) and the Espacio Memoria y Derechos Humanos/Ex ESMA in Buenos Aires (www.espaciomemoria.ar/).

4 A few examples include Isabella Cosse, *Pareja, sexualidad y familia en los años sesenta* (Buenos Aires: Siglo XXI, 2010); Daniel James, *Doña María's Story: Life History, Memory, and Political Identity* (Durham: Duke University Press, 2000); Victoria Langland, *Speaking of Flowers: Student Movements and the Making and Remembering of 1968 in Military Brazil* (Durham: Duke University Press, 2013); Florenica Mallon, *Courage Tastes of Blood* (Durham: Duke University Press, 2005); Heidi Tinsman, *Partners in Conflict: The Politics of Gender, Sexuality, and Labor In the Chilean Agrarian Reform, 1950–1973* (Durham: Duke University Press, 2002).

5 See the citations below.

6 See their respective chapters (Chapter 5 and 11) in this volume.

7 On the Villa Grimaldi website there are 236 officially recognized victims: "Historia," Villa Grimaldi Corporación Parque de la Paz, accessed 4 August 2016, http://villagrimaldi.cl/historia/. Sagredo provided the new 239 number and also said it includes 18 people who were executed and 221 who disappeared. Email message to author from Omar Sagredo, 12 December 2016.

8 According to ex-prisoner and Villa Grimaldi activist Pedro Matta, the largest number of political prisoners in VG came from the MIR (455), followed by the Socialist Party (145) and Communist Party (139). Gabriel Salazar, *Villa Grimaldi (Cuartel Terranova)*. *Volume 1* of *Historia, testimonio, reflexión* (Santiago: LOM, 2013), 200.
9 For more on the Letelier/Moffitt Case and related human rights activism, see John Dinges, *The Condor Years* (New York: The New Press, 2004); Steve Stern, *Reckoning with Pinochet* (Durham: Duke University Press, 2010), 136–142.
10 Email message from Sagredo.
11 "Transitions. From Dictatorship to Democracy in Latin America Gallery," Memoria Abierta, accessed 4 August 2016, www.memoriaabierta.org.ar/eng/. According to two relatively young scholars who worked at the VGOA in its formative stages, the first ten recorded VG testimonies were undertaken in 2006 with the technical and monetary support of Memoria Abierta. In 2007, six more were recorded with the help of the NGO Kolat and the following year, 2008, the VGOA won a Ford Foundation grant that allowed it to operate in a more stable fashion. See Elisabet Prudant and Raúl Rodríguez, "Archivo y testimonio: Reflexiones para una historia de las memorias" (unpublished paper provided by authors).
12 Details from the website "La colección," Villa Grimaldi Corporación Parque de la Paz, accessed 4 August 2016, http://villagrimaldi.cl/archivo-oral/la-coleccion/; email message to author from Omar Sagredo, 9 August 2016. He also said another 30 interviews will soon be added to the archive.
13 All work using archive material must also include a footnote that thanks the Corporación Parque por la Paz Villa Grimaldi for access to the Villa Grimaldi Oral Archive and states: "All results of this study are my responsibility and in no way reflect the said Corporación."
14 The use of sensitive material related particularly to sexual political violence remains controversial. The archive's protocol for citing testimonies does not specify how people should be identified but is decided on a case-by-case basis. In my case, the archive coordinators and I decided on the use of last names only to preserve some confidentiality. This issue will likely be resolved given current controversies surrounding published works, or proposed published works, that have not followed VGOA citation protocols.
15 Conversations with former coordinator, Anahí Moya, and current coordinator, Sagredo. Both are very knowledgeable about the archive and the wider Chilean human rights movement context in which it was conceived.
16 I thank Raúl Rodríguez for clarifying this point about the scripts.
17 Follow-up telephone conversation between author and Anahí Moya, 13 December 2016. She was adamant that for most interviews what appears on the tape is the entirety of the interview, but also recognized that, in a few special cases, narrators have sought to re-record portions (which were later edited into previous tapes) or the entirety of their video testimonies—done, in many cases, because of the fragility of memory itself and the narrators' desire to "set the record straight" by providing detailed testimonies.
18 On this subject, see my "Voces soterradas, violencias ignoradas: discurso, violencia política y género en los Informes Rettig y Valech," *Latin American Research Review* 44, no. 3 (2009): 50–74.
19 Both my undergraduate and doctoral theses were based on oral history methodology and involved conducting numerous interviews with women in Spanish, in the former case, primarily with women from the AFDD, and, in the latter, with women from a shantytown women's group dedicated to dealing with violence against women. In 2003–2004, I trained as a peer counselor and worked in the Women's Crisis Support/Defensa de Mujeres (now called Monarch Services) in Santa Cruz and Watsonville, California, and surrounding areas.

20 See the discussion and citations below.
21 Such as *Corporación Ex Presos Políticos de Pisagua* in the north, and Temuco-based *Centro de Investigación y Promoción de los Derechos Humanos* in the south.
22 UDP Human Rights Center, *Annual 2013 UDP Human Rights Report* (Santiago: UDP, 2013), 243.
23 Hillary Hiner, "'Fue bonita la solidaridad entre mujeres': género, resistencia, y prisión política en Chile durante la dictadura," *Estudos Feministas* 23, no. 3 (2015): 406, 867–892; Hiner, "'Somos memoria y sangre de mujeres combatientes': ex presas políticas feministas, represión autoritaria y memoria colectiva en Chile," in *Memoria, historiografía y testimonio,* eds. Pablo Aravena and Walter Roblero (Universidad de Valparaíso/Museo de la Memoria y los Derechos Humanos: Red de Historia Oral y Archivos Orales, 2015), 43–49; Hiner, "Mujeres resistentes, memorias disidentes: ex presas políticas, militancia e Historia Reciente en Chile," *Conversaciones del Cono Sur* 2, no. 2 (2016): https://conosurconversaciones. wordpress.com/.
24 Hillary Hiner, "'Memory Speaks from Today': Analyzing Oral Histories of Female Members of the MIR in Chile Through the Work of Luisa Passerini," *Women's History Review* 25, no. 3 (2016): 382–407.
25 The durability of the VGOA is critical given the limitations of my own archive. Under the terms of the Chilean National Research Council, I may keep my interview materials for up to ten years after the project's completion (2027), after which time they must be destroyed. This requirement reflects the domination of the biomedical ethics "experts" in the Chilean informed consent process, whose understanding of research with human subjects differs enormously from humanities- and social-science-based oral history practitioners. It might also represent overzealous compensation, as ten years ago virtually no informed consent protocols or institutional oversight for oral history projects existed at state research councils or in individual universities.
26 Kathryn Anderson and Dana C. Jack, "Learning to Listen," in *Women's Words: The Feminist Practice of Oral History,* eds. Sherna Berger Gluck and Daphne Patai (New York: Routledge, 1991), 15.
27 Judith Stacey, "Can There Be a Feminist Ethnography?" in *Women's Words,* 117.

Section 4

Feminists in the field: Performance, political activism, and community engagement

Introduction to Section 4

Feminists in the field: Performance, political activism, and community engagement

Paul Ortiz

This is an indispensable group of chapters that speak to the collective labor of memory work, collaborative storytelling, and how feminist oral historians create new and more democratic relationships between interviewers and narrators, performers, audiences, and territories, as well as museum professionals and surrounding communities. Oral historians work today in a time of global crisis. Our narrators demand more than ever that we use digital technologies to engage in the fight to combat oppression in all forms.[1] The authors in this section demonstrate how feminist oral history positions itself in opposition to global capitalism's destruction of the commons, and how narrative storytelling can challenge the frightening intensification of misogyny, racism, and economic inequality that plagues the world. In their piece, Shahrzad Arshadi, Hourig Attarian, Khadija Baker, and Kumru Bilici point toward the vital role that oral history and performance play in these struggles by noting that the wounds they talk about and retell have "deep historical roots." Their performance "enabled us to explore a history that comes out of a specific place, of lands lost, to imagine and reclaim them."[2]

These powerful essays build on the brilliant base created by *Women's Words*, while forging ahead to address the most serious problems of our time including endless war, displacement of people into refugee camps and prisons, and the relentless pursuit of profits, which has led to atrocities such as the mass poisonings in Bhopal, India recounted in Suroopa Mukherjee's chapter. Union Carbide's industrial malfeasance is a harbinger of the environmental injustices of the 21st century where the poorest of the poor are forced to pay the highest price for catastrophic global climate change. Three decades of neglect transformed the Bhopal gas tragedy into a medical, legal, scientific, and political disaster: "Only the state and the corporation had the resources required to care for those affected by the disaster, but the promise of long-term rehabilitation was false propaganda. Compensation was barely mentioned. Nobody spoke about justice."[3] Mukherjee shows how the process of interviewing survivors and amplifying their voices enabled dissident stories and demands for justice to pierce the fraudulent state tale of recovery that covered up the realities of birth defects, chronic illness, and displacement in Bhopal.

Feminist oral historians situate their work at sites where people strive to achieve self-respect and wholeness whether that is through a washtub, a union hall, an interactive theater performance, or other locations. While each of these places contains historically-imposed silences, and contested interpretations of the past, Sady Sullivan points toward commonalities of feminist praxis: "Oral history is collaborative work . . . Oral historians regularly talk about care for the narrator—building trust, establishing rapport, honoring reciprocity, and protecting privacy."[4] Sullivan's evocative description of the practice of radical storytelling illustrates the convergence between feminist oral history and incipient movement building. The creation of relationships of trust is the beginning of every meaningful revolt.

These remarkable essays, grounded as they are in acts of insurgency and the search for belonging and liberation, reveal the closeness between feminist oral history and social movement building. Oral history becomes a way to affirm the dignity of the oppressed, beginning with Penny Couchie and Muriel Miguel's Indigenous methodology of "storyweaving," and Sarah K. Loose's and Amy Starecheski's conceptualization of oral history as "aid[ing] in the process of humanization—of challenging stereotypes, and facilitating identification with individuals who were once perceived as 'other' but who can now be recognized in their full humanity."[5] Storyweaving explicitly challenges elitist dichotomies of active performers/speakers and passive listener/audiences: "In storyweaving a piece is sometimes created from the tiniest grain of sand. Everyone in the room is engaged in the discovery of the story, whether it's an epic or tiny story."[6] Similarly, Loose and Starecheski vividly portray how oral history's participatory narrative format has the ability to support the efforts of movements trying to transform consciousness in the present.

Furthermore, each author honestly discusses the challenges that confront feminist oral history methodology. Arshadi writes of her imperfect efforts to connect with refugees in Iraqi Kurdistan: "I intended to write about [my memories of community and laundry], but talking to refugees brought pain to my heart. They complained about their lost sense of community, of trust." Camp residents told her about how the lack of very basic facilities created much distance between them.[7] For her part, Sullivan cites the initial hurdles in the Brooklyn Historical Society's "Crossing Borders, Bridging Generations" project's effort to bring together narrators and interviewers through a predominantly white institution in an area of New York where the majority are people of color. In spite of these difficulties, however, the authors are unified in recognizing the potential of oral history to enhance intergenerational understandings of the past. As Loose and Starecheski note:

> While feminist oral historians have shown us that the interview itself is political, fraught with complex power dynamics and rich with liberatory and oppressive potential, there has been less scholarly work on the intentional use of oral history to make change in the world in the context of social movements, activism, and advocacy.[8]

These essays offer great lessons on how professionals who work in academia, museums, non-profits, and state institutions can forge connections to individuals, groups, and neighborhoods grappling with displacement, inequality, and sexism. At the same time, however, the authors remind us that institutionally based oral historians will need to adjust their methods and become more flexible in the pursuit of unsanctioned truths that often challenge the official myths of their respective societies. While academics insist on "objectivity," chronology, and impartiality, oral historians in the field must become students of subjectivity, and thrive in what Couchie and Miguel call the "non-linear time" of Indigenous cultures. For their part, Loose and Starecheski are refreshingly blunt about the need to shatter the artificial divide between scholarship and social justice: "Here we are thinking about oral history primarily as activism, often without a home or allegiance in the academy."[9] Each of the writers—all of whom work in collective team settings—strives to share, acknowledge, and affirm interconnections between people. This is a welcome contrast to traditional university-based practices that often sequester, individualize, and even control and patent knowledge for the sake of profit.

These essays confirm the power of community-based oral history fieldwork and the necessity of consciousness-raising discussions, performances, and collaborative research to create mutual understanding and social change. In recent years, oral historians have rightly focused on technological innovations that have provided our narrators with broader and more accessible platforms. The authors in this section remind us, however, that we must use these technologies to serve communities, and that we must continue teaching and listening for the sounds of solidarity, empathy, and righteous outrage, which underpin the best radical oral history work. In this vein, we have much to learn from Couchie's and Miguel's joint production, *Material Witness*, which teaches audiences the incredibly nuanced power of Indigenous knowledge in the dialogic format of participatory theater.

As we revisit and build upon the wisdom of *Women's Words*, we would do well to circle back to another important breakthrough in oral history, which was equally grounded in the crises, struggles, and anti-colonial insurgencies of its time: the activist journal *Southern Exposure*, which first appeared in 1973. Many of *Southern Exposure*'s contributors were inspired by an earlier generation of women movement organizers, especially iconic civil rights activists Virginia Foster Durr and Anne Braden. Braden told Sue Thrasher, "You think you are the first generation who's ever done this; you ought to go out and learn some things"[10]—which is exactly why Thrasher and her colleagues began using oral history to uncover forgotten histories of anti-black massacres, the interracial Southern Tenant Farmers Union, and a women's movement in the South that had direct ties to 1930s anti-lynching struggles.[11] *Women's Words*, *Southern Exposure*, and *Beyond Women's Words* demonstrate that the best oral history scholarship is grounded in popular struggles, social movements, and efforts to break down barriers between academics and the communities that sustain them.

Notes

1 Paul Ortiz, "Oral History in a Time of Crisis," for "Oral History, Now (and Tomorrow)," plenary session, Oral History Association Annual Meeting, Long Beach, California, 13 October 2016. On global crisis, see Jordan T. Camp and Christina Heatherton, eds., *Policing the Planet: Why the Policing Crisis Led to Black Lives Matter* (London: Verso, 2016); Michelle Alexander, *The New Jim Crow: Incarceration in the Age of Colorblindness* (New Press, 2012); Ruth Wilson Gilmore, *Golden Gulag: Prisons, Surplus, Crisis, and Opposition in Globalizing California* (University of California Press, 2007); John Brown Childs, *Hurricane Katrina: Response and Responsibilities* (North Atlantic Books, 2008).
2 Shahrzad Arshadi, Hourig Attarian, Khadija Baker, and Kumru Bilici, Chapter 20 of this volume, 264.
3 Suroopa Mukherjee, Chapter 18 of this volume, 246.
4 Sady Sullivan, Chapter 19 of this volume, 252.
5 Sarah K. Loose, with Amy Starecheski, Chapter 17 of this volume, 237–238.
6 Penny Couchie and Muriel Miguel, Chapter 16 of this volume, 230.
7 Shahrzad Arshadi, Chapter 20 of this volume, 265.
8 Sarah K. Loose, with Amy Starecheski, Chapter 17 of this volume, 236.
9 Sarah K. Loose, with Amy Starecheski, Chapter 17 of this volume, 236.
10 Sarah Thuesen, Bob Hall, Jacquelyn Dowd Hall, M. Sue Thrasher, "Learning from the Long Civil Rights Movement's First Generation: Virginia Foster Durr," *Southern Cultures* 16, no. 2 (Summer 2010): 72–89.
11 *Southern Exposure*'s 1974 special issue featured pieces on Zora Neale Hurston, the Elaine Massacre, and the 1930s "Federal Writers'" project on ex-slave narratives. See Sue Thrasher and Leah Wise, "The Southern Tenant Farmers' Union," *Southern Exposure* 1, nos. 3–4 (Winter 1974): 5–8; Paul Ortiz, "Tearing Up the Master's Narrative: Stetson Kennedy and Oral History," *Oral History Review* 41, no. 2 (Summer/Fall 2014): 279–289.

16 Storyweaving, Indigenous knowledge, and process in *Material Witness*

Penny Couchie and Muriel Miguel

Preface

When I was asked to write about my work, I immediately wanted to collaborate with Muriel Miguel, my long-time mentor, colleague, and friend, and reflect on the technique of storyweaving developed by the company she and her sisters founded, Spiderwoman Theater.[1] There is much to be learned from writing on Indigenous process, particularly when dialogue emerges from practitioners within. For so long, understanding has come from outside our communities and efforts to listen, from inside, move us beyond histories of colonialism in important ways. In this light, I center my story and reflect on my relationship to Spiderwoman's methodology through conversations with Muriel Miguel about our co-production, *Material Witness*, and various aspects of our twenty-year working relationship.[2]

Within the research, development, and rehearsal phases of creating a production such as *Material Witness* we look at stories from many directions. We acknowledge the finite circles of relationality that create it and rather than attempt to direct how an audience receives a story, we open as many doorways to understanding as possible. For instance, education, a multitude of training modalities, and the Indigenous knowledge that I carry, shape my artistic practice. With deep respect, I acknowledge all of the other artists who have brought and continue to bring their practice and Indigenous knowledge to the storyweaving process. On stage, within *Material Witness*, we illuminate one another's stories: echoing, underscoring, casting both light and shadow, contradicting, re-enforcing, and affirming. These elements are familiar to me. I have witnessed them in Anishinaabe ceremony; I have heard them in Indigenous storytelling, songs, and dance; and, I have seen them in Indigenous clowning.[3] From an Anishinaabe worldview, there is nothing contradictory about learning through these relationships, using, for instance, any genre of dance, song, or theater technique, even that which we might identify as Western—a tap dance number and grass dance can exist within the same story. These are the relationships between stories that help us facilitate our way through the story we want to share.

Creation stories, non-linear time and space, and intergenerational storytelling

In the beginning, DuTuKapsisis, both ancient and present day, calls the witness and ancestors, preparing the space for us to tell our stories. She helps to make it safe. Throughout the play she is our grandmothers, our aunties, our mothers, our sisters, our daughters. She has her own stories of violence and facilitates a collective scream. She reminds us to use our voice to express the anger and rage as well as the joy and hope. She is what initiates the crack in the fabric/sky/earth that leads us towards voice and those initial steps towards health and wellness. She is the voice we never heard or the voice we can't stop hearing. At the end of the play she closes the doorways by taking down the guardians. She acknowledges the good work that's been done. She leads us towards hope by connecting us to our past, present, and future.[4]

PENNY: One of the things that I've been thinking a lot about storyweaving is when you say "A long, long, long, long time ago . . ." And this idea that one way of talking about the present is by locating ourselves within our lineage, and within our creation stories.

MURIEL: Once I said in a performance, "A long, long, long, long, long, long time ago when animals could talk . . ." and a little kid in the audience said "Those were the days!" I never thought about creation stories in terms of them being creation stories. I always thought of them as being very long stories.

I think it's when I started to talk about, the Kuna, you know, daughters from the stars, that I realized that, "Oh! That's what creation stories are. They're long, long stories." Because they're from a long, long time ago and if you're going to make a creation story you have to make it. And if you make it, it's like making the mountains and the moon and the stars. You know. You have to make it, so you have to start someplace that's a very long time ago. Then I realized that with creation stories, I could create a creation story. That was really fascinating, the idea that I could make a creation story and that it is just as valid as other ones.

You come to a long, long, long time ago, and those were the times like that little person said, "Those were the days." These are the stories we carry with us. Sometimes they break down, and sometimes they're mended, but they're still carried on to the present. When I say I can make my own creation story, I'm just adding on. I'm just adding on to the creation story that was made already. It's like a very long train.

The women come tumbling, charging, running out of the doorway. They ask one another, "What is your name and where did you come from?" Our names and origins are connected to our roles and responsibilities in this world. We remember where we come from and sometimes we lose connection and have to find our way back. In *Material Witness*, the line, "she was plucked . . .," refers to the magnitude of the loss when Indigenous women are murdered or go missing. In Anishinaabe welcoming ceremonies for newborns they say, "So nice to see you. We've been waiting for you. We've already known about you for generations. We've listened to the name you already carry." That name carries great importance and weight. When we lose our names or they are taken away through genocide, extinguishment, or assimilation, we lose connection with who we are. We lose connection with the gifts and bundles we carry, leaving us and our communities with bits and pieces scattered.

PENNY: In our Full Moon Ceremonies, one of the ways I've heard Anishinaabe women introduce themselves, is to say, "My name is . . . (their spirit name) I come from the waters of (her mother's name), and she came from the waters of (her grandmother's name)." They trace their matrilineal line back as far as they can. Some of our teachings talk about knowing our ancestors seven generations back. Within our teachings and stories in the Anishinaabe worldview this would eventually connect us to our grand-mother moon. It's a way of locating ourselves within our creation stories. It's like when I go to Bear Island, my mother's territory, and someone says, "Oh! You're Tendacii's granddaughter," and they tell me stories about my grandmother or my great-grandmother and what she was like. They say, "Oh! You have the same eyes." Or, "You walk just like her." Or "The way you smile reminds me of her." Through this I realized that my grandmothers' stories are within me. I can begin to trace my history all the way back to my creation stories. I came from the stars. Those are the stories that are from my community and within my family.

In storyweaving, I'm experiencing the weaving of stories that I'm both conscious and unconscious of. I'm experiencing those stories that I'm carrying within my breath and body. Those stories are the ones that are directly linked to my creation stories, both personal and communal and tied to the land that is in my body.

In the beginning of *Material Witness*, DuTuKapsis is heaving, bubbling, building pressure until she begins to erupt. A crack forms and she seeps out. She reminds us that the stories are present in the air, land, rocks, and water. Our stories are connected and already woven together; between each other, woven into stories of the land, woven with our stories and those of our ancestors, our future generations, our families, our communities, the spirits around us. We are part of the web of all creation. In this sense, we are not so much storyweaving but are listening and acknowledging what is already woven.

MURIEL: With storyweaving a lot of times it's the present, the future, and the past; and you can feel it. It's like the web, you know, one piece goes ahead, one piece stays, one piece is something that you took from there and brought to here. Sometimes you don't even recognize it anymore;

it shatters into five or ten pieces and goes out again. And that to me is really the idea of storyweaving. It goes in and out and in and out, and then something comes and pushes them down to the next weave.

PENNY: About 20 years ago, I participated in a workshop funded through reconciliation monies.[5] The facilitator said sometimes it's like we're standing in a stream and the water's flowing by us. We throw our past upstream and when it comes downstream, we say "Ah! I knew it was going to turn out this way." But it's us, throwing it upstream. He had us write about big stories in our lives, the tough ones we carry around. He asked us to look at these stories and showed us how many of the stories were similar." He asked things like, "What is the one question that you were asking the universe in this story? Am I wanted? Am I loved? Am I worthy?" These are the big questions that he wanted to look at in these stories. I have thought a lot about that since. This idea that the stories we tell, whether they seem small, funny, or sad, tend to tell the same thing. We carry these stories and sometimes we share them without realizing it. In storyweaving, this process is at play.

MURIEL: For a long time, I've been thinking that these stories all come from the sky. The woman who fell to the earth, sky woman falling, and all the stories of daughters from the stars, your Anishinaabe stories about coming from the stars, and our version of the star family; I think they are the same thing. These stories of stars and people falling; falling through the hole, looking at the root, falling through the hole past the root—they're all the same story.

I was also thinking that the hole doesn't necessarily have to be something that you took a spade and dug into the earth. There are all kinds of holes and webs, including a web being made in a hole or a hole being made into a web. That hole could be a space in the sky or next to your bed. Now I see all these holes that I connect with past and present and future. It is a recognition of being through our relationships.

PENNY: My aunt, Carol Guppy, was talking to someone who thought the Full Moon Ceremony was about worshipping the moon. She explained that we actually have a relationship with the moon, that there is a difference between worshipping the moon and talking to the moon. The moon is our grandmother and we remember her as our grandmother. It goes as far back as time immemorial. That's why we have those creation stories. We locate ourselves within time and space: "A long, long, long, long, time ago" is how we continue talking about our relationship to all of creation. In 2000, when I worked on your piece, *Throw Away Kids*, for the first time in Banff, I struggled to understand the complex layers of meaning within the text.[6] Ten years later, with a deeper level of understanding about Anishinaabe creation stories, I understood that as with the character, Cosmos, I can't talk about my daughter without talking about the event of her birth, connecting us to all of creation and locating us within our own history.

Piles, heaps, bundles, and mounds

The backdrops begin to stitch together what has been torn apart or fragmented, piecing together the parts of our lives that have been torn apart, acknowledging the many layers of our stories. When one character speaks about the loss of her daughter, saying, "Her body was plucked from the river, she was plucked from me." She tells us that her daughter was plucked from the present and the future. She was part of a constellation.

In *Material Witness*, we wear our trauma and survival within our costumes, stitched and glued together. What is often unseen is highly visible. We can't, or won't, let it go because we are not done with it. We are not done, "picking, scratching and pinching at it until we find an end to pull." We need to understand the impact these stories have had on us. At the end of the play, we remove a bra, an apron, a grenade, and a feather tutu. We add it to the piles, heaps, and bundles, and then throw it up to see where it all lands.

MURIEL: A long time ago, I sang an honor song at an opening for a woman's festival in North or South Carolina. I can't remember where. But there were mounds there. When I sang I could hear the song coming back. It really shook me because I felt those mounds saying "Hello!" to me. Every time I say it, I fill up with emotion, because it shook me. I almost couldn't get through the song. At the same time, I heard these people—these mounds—say, "I haven't heard you in a long time. How nice to see you." They were talking to me. When I got off the microphone, I was really shaken. I told my friend Louis Mofsie, "I sang, and the mounds talked to me." And he said, "Yeah. Isn't that something?" He knew it too. I was thinking, "I wonder how many people know that?" I think this happens. This really happens and it happens to all of us. Maybe the wonderful thing about it is that each one of us thinks we're special because it happens like that.

PENNY: We're not just talking about creation stories. We're talking about death stories too and the passing of loved ones. My husband, Sid Bobb, wrote a play about a man who saw a clear-cut cedar forest for the first time. The man was devastated, knowing that he had broken his contract with the cedars to always protect them. The cedars were his family. People talk about the hills or mountains being family as well. We recognize the land, like you recognized those mounds and we know that they recognize us, too. When we return to the land, or the dirt, sky, or water, we go back to family.

MURIEL: It's funny to hear people say, "Well, you know, this is where they put their garbage. That's why there are big mounds." And they're not realizing that garbage is life. We're going to leave mounds, too. When mankind is gone, the next one, if there is a next one, is going to see mounds too. This world doesn't think that way, so it's always strange for people to hear us talk about them. Even though I come from the city, and I live in a house on a concrete street, there is a way of seeing the world in an Indigenous way that is with me all the time. And I think there are many of us that are that way. It isn't anything special. It's allowing yourself to see that.

PENNY: Throughout *Material Witness*, there are heaps, piles, and mounds. They are sacred and irreverent, beautiful and ugly, profound and mundane. It's all piled one on top of the other, our storied lives, and very long histories. It's all woven together.

MURIEL: When any of us talk about bundles, we may not know *exactly* what is in the bundle, but we know some of what is in our bundles. I think somehow that piles—that's where we store a lot of these stories that we don't want to tell. We store them neatly, layer upon layer, upon layer. When we start to look at them, we throw them into heaps. These heaps are things that are trash to other people.

PENNY: What we're wearing is one layer. But the piles and the heaps are the many, many layers of our lives and our histories. In *Material Witness* we're looking at the heaps. The surface of the person you see in front of you is just one story, the one they're most willing to tell. The heaps and the piles are all the other ones.

Continuously shifting emotional experience

Interwoven in our sad, tragic, horrific stories is absurdity and humor. It's the tricksters reminding us not to take ourselves so seriously. We can land anywhere in a story if we throw it up in the air. We acknowledge the power of our stories, but they don't have absolute power over us or any other stories we carry. Whether we shot down from the stars, rose up from the earth, or erupted from a volcano, we have landed in this place together. DuTuKapsis holds the space for us to tell our stories. We listen, feel, experience, shout out, deny, echo, minimize, and fully acknowledge the gravity and weight of each story. We accept that in this place, the "holding cell," we are safe to tell our stories. We witness one another's stories so that we can begin the process of putting down what makes it difficult for us to move forward. We listen in the most exaggerated form of humanity, sometimes compassionate, sometimes as clowns. We are compassionate and loving, shaming and vindictive, jealous and oppositional, kind and honest. We allow the rascals their biggest voices, as in ceremony, we speak the unspeakable because we know we must, for our survival, health, and wellbeing.[7]

PENNY: I was sitting in the theater during a performance of your daughter, Murielle Borst's play *Don't Feed The Indians*. The man next to me saw me writing notes and asked, "Are you a theater critic?" I said, "No, I'm the Assistant Director." He said, "Oh. Okay." After the play, he said, "That was great. With other plays, sometimes it's as though I know how I'm supposed to feel right away. In this play, there's a constant shifting of emotional states; I never could get my footing. Sometimes I was laughing, sometimes I was crying, but I was always unsteady. I never knew what was coming next."

That is something I've heard you say a lot, in the storyweaving process, that you throw something up in the air. Certainly, for me, I often feel an impulse to stay with an emotional state much longer. But you'll do a quick switch of directions and I think "Oh, that was too fast." When I look at it again, however, I feel that same unsteadiness in my body. Whether I'm watching it from the outside as a choreographer, or I'm in it as a performer, I know that unsteadiness is a part of Indigenous storytelling. In *Material Witness*, we're in tragedy and then immediately we're laughing, and then we're back into something serious, and then it's very mundane. The fast shifting of emotional states is what life is like. It's the nature of the world in which we live.

MURIEL: Well I always go back to that point when I was growing up in feminist theater. I would get so impatient because it would go on about how we were suffering, how we were beaten, woe, woe, woe. That really drove me crazy. I started to think, "If I'm going crazy with this way of telling stories, other people must be feeling the same way." I thought, "How do we grab attention, make our point, make the audience think, and then take them someplace else? When we take them someplace else, and make it funny, and then we realize or the audience realizes, it's both not funny and funny, that, to me, is the kernel.

A lot of times I'm looking for places in the story like that. A friend of mine just reminded me that I told her story a long time ago. She wrote it in a book. It's an old Native story about this person fighting a bear. He's fighting the bear, and he's fighting the bear, and finally he opens the bear's mouth and sticks his hand all the way down the bear's throat. He grabs the bear by the tail and pulls the tail out, so the bear is inside out and he tickles himself to death. I tell that story all the time because of the absurdity, the absurdity of doing this to a bear without losing your whole body.

That desire to use stories to change things through the absurdity is what I was interested in; the absurdity of another person stopping an abused woman from walking out; the absurdity of killing someone because they don't want to live with you; the absurdity of sending a child to live as a prostitute at 13. It boggles the mind and it's absurd. It's absurd that people are not investigating it. That twitches in my brain. It's just like sticking your hand down that bear's throat and pulling it inside out by his tail. How do you make that transition from being someplace and staying there? I think life is like that. You hold on to something too long and "Good God!" you really do sink into the earth. I think about alcoholics, drug addicts, and people who are really mean, like that. If you hold onto something for so long it changes you.

When I was dramaturging for *When Will You Rage?*, I said, "The dancer upstage has to do something." You said, "She's not supposed to be there."[8] And I replied, "But she's there." And then we started to talk about it. I said, "Well, she is there. No one told her to leave." We started to work from that position. We're there and it's a surprise. The question is what do you do with that surprise?

PENNY: For me, a big revelation occurred in the development of *When Will You Rage?*. I was desperately trying to hang on to one moment, and I thought if I sped it up, or if I had the dancers drop it and then walk around and start again I would lose the moment. You asked me to change the tempo and I thought, "If I speed it up, it's all going to unravel." However, I was able to see the nature of it much more when I just allowed it to be. I was hanging on too tightly and trying to control what the audience would see, hear, or feel. I was struggling with it being very flat. I didn't know how to get out of that flatness, but I'm starting to learn how to identify when I'm standing in my own way. As an improviser, I don't have to be so careful about every single moment. I can throw this up in the air and then trust that it's going to come back down.

MURIEL: That's very true. I do that a lot. I throw it up in the air a lot. If it doesn't fall in the right place, there's nothing wrong with picking it up and putting it in the right place. I don't write from the beginning and go to the end. I end up with all these little monologues and thoughts and I know that it's going to be messy.

PENNY: People who are trained in ensemble, and trained a certain way, find a way through the mess by exploring the sound and movement in a story. You can't think your way through it. That is the way that you train people.

MURIEL: Yeah. That's the trickiness of it. But it's also the adventure and delight of it. It's what I see in the young students when they get it, it's more than that light bulb. But you have to be ready. You have to know why you told the story. Now if you can't figure it out, because you're not past certain events in the story, that is what the story is. A lot of times, that's what's interesting where people are at when they're telling their stories. Some of them will never get past a certain place.

PENNY: There are mainstream ideas in commercially driven art about what belongs on the stage. Here the arts become a place only for those who sing, dance, act, and tell stories within a very narrow value system. It is a system that determines who is worthy to tell a story or who makes it on that stage and it pushes out and silences exciting, diverse, innovative, and excellent art.

Yet, within your process, there's a place for people to come in who are not trained in mainstream performance techniques. The stories are sometimes seemingly mundane, they're not fantastical, although some are, and sometimes they're only two sentences long. In storyweaving, a piece is sometimes created from the tiniest grain of sand. Everyone in the room is engaged in the discovery of the story, whether it's an epic or tiny story.

There is a process of tuning in to the stories in the room. We are asking someone to tell his or her story and the way it gets brought up or coaxed out; it's all part of the process. People come at it in different ways.

MURIEL: When we're talking about our stories, or how our stories face the world, we all have a common ground. Most of us know where that rope is that we're all hanging onto, and when we present the work Native people get it almost right away. They sit there and watch it, the chaos, they watch everything exploding or the absurdity and they laugh because everyone makes a connection to that rope. Where I have a hard time is when people try to analyze my work or how I teach or how I like to work in teams. I have a hard time explaining where it came from. I have no idea, but most of us come from storytellers. We come from a culture of storytelling. I think a lot of times it is opening up channels that are already there. A lot of times, we don't trust that, so working in teams makes it easier to explore a taboo place for someone without sending them into another world or scaring the shit out of them. It's just trying to explore a little bit.

I think that there are a lot of people who can teach. I don't feel really special. I'm with other teachers sometimes and I think, "Oh yeah, I do that too." You realize that you combine a lot of things to get that point across. This comes from working with you and others; the work of taking an exercise and putting another facet on it. Like when we're working together and I build on something you've started and we continue layering it. I realized that it was the beginning of me understanding that you have to go in with all your fingers out, like combing through hair. What happens a lot of times is students don't connect one thing to another. They don't know they have to take this and integrate it in their next class. How do you teach them to carry all their embroidery, sewing and layering with them, as they're going to other places with you? I don't know why people are on stage. I teach people who are asking, "How do you do this?" Some of us are doing this for very different reasons, not to win an Oscar.

PENNY: Some of us are doing it for community, for family, or for a greater understanding of how to move forward in a good way.

MURIEL: There are many different paths.

PENNY: With regards to who has a right to take the stage and which stories have a right to be on stage, I don't think we have a right to decide that. We have no idea. We're here to pass on what we've learned and the ways we have learned to do it. As teachers, we help with one step, which helps to facilitate someone on their path. It's within our culture that everyone is an Elder to someone younger than themselves. We have a responsibility to teach others.

Legacy

DuTuKapsis says, "These are my hands, a little wrinkled and arthritic, but beautiful." Within the play, for the first time, we look at ourselves; we look into our palms, the people we've touched, the people we've loved, and our actions. We consider what we want to make and leave behind when we're gone.

MURIEL: I see it in the younger ones, teaching each other without any bullying. I see it in a 6-year-old, her teaching. Anybody can teach someone else. As you get older, it's the younger ones I talk to, because they are the ones who are listening.

In the *Pulling Threads* fabric workshop, which is connected to *Material Witness*, the last layer that we investigate within the cloth squares that we create is legacy. It's one of the things I always remember. It's the thing now, after everything I've done, that I really have to look at. I look and look. What do I want to leave behind and what do I want to pull out? I truly believe we should be sharing and not trying to eat each other up. What's happening in New York City within the Indigenous theater community, it can't happen anymore. We have to talk to each other. We have to stop fighting each other.

PENNY: That's been happening for years and years in our communities. We've been so busy fighting each other, that there are all kinds of crazy things going on around us. Non-native companies are telling our stories without us. They misrepresent us, appropriate our culture, perpetuate stereotypes, devalue our knowledge, and undermine the work we've done to be heard. And they get away with it because we're not mobilizing to the degree that we need to. When I went to Australia, for Yirama Yangga-na,[9] it opened my eyes. This is about more than Canadian Indigenous or North American Indigenous issues. These are global issues. Sometimes I feel pulled in all directions, but I do have a sense that all those directions are part of the same path. Perhaps it's just that I'm not seeing the links yet. The idea of being part of reconnecting or revitalizing our relationships to one another is really exciting to me. The idea of visiting one another's territories to affirm our commitments to good relationships is integral to the health and wellbeing of our planet. I think the affirmation of good intention is critical in times of crisis. If we don't come together, share our knowledge, revitalize, and rebuild, or see ourselves as part of a global community, we can't possibly fight. It's just too hard to fight a good fight on your own.

With regards to legacy, I think because the way of storytelling is different, the training is different. I recently gave a keynote address for a dance educators' conference. I talked about the spring fasting my family and I have been doing for the past 20 years and how much I regard that as some of my biggest teachings in dance. When I am fasting, I am engaged in a process of shedding and being reborn. I sit with myself and all of Creation, really deeply. As a dance artist, my ultimate goal is to dance as closely connected as possible to my spiritual, physical, mental, and emotional self, in relationship to the rest of Creation.

Coming out

In the end, we emerge and break through the wall that separates the storytellers from the audience, from our community, larger world. We push, bump, beat, and punch our way through, to see ourselves as part of a larger whole.

MURIEL: If I did not have my sisters and their encouragement in saying, "The sky's the limit!" I would not have gone out there. I mean, I went out there pretty raw. When Louis Mofsie was talking at Liz's memorial he said, "If it was not for Liz, then none of us would have gone out. She was the first one out; she came back and told us." A lot of us went out there and got banged on the head. I didn't know that I was getting banged on the head. Others got banged on the head, noticed it, and just retreated. This was called racism, and it made me feel bad. Within the family itself, Liz was saying, "Get out there!" and Gloria was saying, "It's because you don't have a degree. That's why they didn't pick you. So, you need a degree. It's because you never took ballet that they did not pick you. You need to take ballet."

I think that this is still happening. I think that's probably why I wanted to teach at the Centre for Indigenous Theatre (CIT) so badly. At CIT, it was really important for me to try to figure out how to get the students to understand that what we're giving to them is much more important. The other stuff they can learn, but to go in to class with a sense of self is really important.

PENNY: It's important that our body of knowledge is respected. It's important that we can be part of mainstream schools without being devalued, humiliated, and degraded.

MURIEL: That's why it's important for us to create our own vocabulary.

PENNY: Our vocabulary, methodology, creative process, pedagogy, and curriculum arises out of our worldview and Indigenous knowledge. When I hear you talk about your sisters and how they paved that way for you, how our Elders pave the way for all of us, I think of all the *Coming Out* ceremonies that we have as Indigenous Peoples. Beginning from the first moment we arrive on this earth, we have a *Coming Out* ceremony. Here in the Nipissing area, we hold the baby up to the guardians, helpers, to the ancestors, family, and community. We introduce the baby, exclaiming their name loudly, joyously. We acknowledge them, that we've been waiting for them and that we're so happy that they are here. When a young woman has her first Moon Time that is another *Coming Out* ceremony. When we complete our regalia, our dance, and the *Give Away* that follows, this is another *Coming Out* ceremony. When you come from a culture that has those values, and that worldview, and you try to engage with another society and culture with an opposing worldview, that's where the problems start.

MURIEL: When I talk to some of the actors and acting teachers that I know, I hear them talk about how, in these schools, they break you down to build you up again. I could not understand that. A teacher tried to do that to me very young. I was maybe 18 years old, in a dance class. His philosophy was, "If you don't do it this way, it's not right." My clown or my trickster came out. I started to really taunt him. He got very angry with me.

PENNY: That whole ideology behind knocking someone down to build them up again, is so counter to the idea of helping someone to connect their mind, body, spirit, and emotions to all of creation. It's so counter to the belief that we are here to help each other discover what our gifts are, what is in our bundles, and celebrate that.

MURIEL: That was why I had such a reaction to him trying to break me down, because I knew what he was trying to do. That way of teaching is coming from a different direction. One time, I was sitting on a dune. The waves were coming in and out. I looked up at all the stars, trillions of stars. I remember feeling very small and getting scared. Then I realized, "I am a part of this." I started to feel the joy of being a part of something. In some schools of thought, they think if they break you down, you will see that you are part of something bigger. But if they break you down, you're just in pieces, instead of recognizing all these pieces as a part of you and you as a part of the whole.

Notes

1 Founded in 1976, Spiderwoman Theater is North America's longest running Native Feminist theater company.
2 Storyweaving is a theatrical creation and performance process developed by Muriel Miguel and Spiderwoman Theater. Within *Material Witness* there was a collaborative process, which often began with a discussion about a topic or goals and then led performers to bring forth their individual stories. The director, in collaboration with the performers and or/choreographer, guided a development process of unveiling the story and performance style through investigating motifs, phrases, songs, and dances that layered, connected, and juxtaposed the stories.
3 Clowning has a long history and an important spiritual function in a wide variety of Indigenous cultures.
4 *Material Witness*, a co-production of Spiderwoman Theater and Aanmitaagzi, comprises a full-length theater production and a community-engaged textile installation. The performance reinvestigates Spiderwoman's 1976 inaugural production *Women and Violence*, carrying forward some of the original scenes. DuTuKapsis, played by Spiderwoman co-founder Gloria Miguel, carries Miguel's writings from *One Voice* and *Women and Violence* as the initiating and closing figure within *Material Witness*. All quotes in this chapter are drawn from *Material Witness*.
5 Over the last 20 years, the Canadian federal government has offered grant money in support of reconciliation for and with Indigenous Peoples. Recently, the Truth and Reconciliation Commission generated more substantial funding for healing, reconciliation, and relationship building: www.trc.ca/websites/trcinstitution/index.php?p=3.

6 For more on Muriel Miguel's productions see: www.spiderwomantheater.org/
   CreativeMMiguel.htm.
7 Within Anishinaabe thought, the "rascals," inferiority, envy, resentment, not caring,
   and envy, are juxtaposed with the seven grandfather teachings. See Herb Nabigon,
   The Hollow Tree: Fighting Addiction with Traditional Native Healing (Montreal &
   Kingston: McGill-Queen's University Press, 2006).
8 For more on *When Will You Rage?*, see: http://aanmitaagzi.net/events-projects/
   when-will-you-rage/.
9 For more on the Yirima Yangga-na (meaning "spirit singing") gathering see https://
   www.britishcouncil.org.au/yirama-yangga-na, last accessed 7 March 2018.

17 Oral history for building social movements, then and now

Sarah K. Loose, with Amy Starecheski

In the Afterword to their edited collection *Women's Words: The Feminist Practice of Oral History*, Sherna Berger Gluck and Daphne Patai remind us that:

> [W]e must not be lulled into the belief that the mere doing of this kind of work [oral history] is likely to bring about social transformation, but even less should we give in to the scholar's doubts by demeaning the powerful contribution that oral history can make to the process of change.[1]

While feminist oral historians have shown us that the interview itself is political, fraught with complex power dynamics and rich with liberatory and oppressive potential, there has been less scholarly work on the intentional use of oral history to make change in the world in the context of social movements, activism, and advocacy. Building on the work of academic-activists writing in and since the publication of *Women's Words* and drawing from many recent conversations between oral historians, activists, and artists working for social justice, this chapter highlights the potential limits and possibilities of oral history for movement building.[2] For the most part, the authors of *Women's Words* framed oral history as research, positioning themselves as scholars trying to balance political and intellectual commitments. Here we are thinking about oral history as activism, often without a home or allegiance in the academy. As feminist scholarship has helped to show, all knowledge is produced through relations of power and from a particular standpoint. How is oral history different when led by people directly affected by oppression who are trying to use oral history to change their lives?

While we will focus on the possibilities, we begin by noting that, in addition to the ethical, political, and logistical challenges that arise when doing any kind of research or social justice work, there are real limitations to oral history's use for social change inherent to the form of the craft.[3] For example:

- **Oral history takes time.** The time-sensitive demands of certain types of organizing can conflict with oral history's more measured pace and longer-term vision.

- **Oral history is a relatively private encounter.** It is not always obvious how to use the one-on-one experience of an oral history interview for broader collective impact.
- **Oral history is a generative process.** It is good at raising questions, creating and recording powerful narrative accounts, and fostering relationships, but translating story into action requires more than oral history alone.
- **Oral history produces specific knowledge.** The "data" of oral history is not easily generalizable or quantifiable.

Such limitations notwithstanding, certain characteristics of oral history make it uniquely suited to movement building. Understanding these characteristics can help organizers, archivists, scholars, and artists draw on the full potential that oral history offers to movement work. The text that follows is a brief exploration of three attributes that contribute to oral history's effectiveness as a method or tool that can be used in the process of social change.[4] None of these is wholly unique to oral history (other forms of storytelling, interviewing, and documentation share some of these same characteristics), but they come together in a single form with distinctive possibilities for the work required to create a more just world.

Narrative form

As a form of communication and mode of discourse, oral history is fundamentally a narrative act. Oral histories are made up of stories—stories shared and interpreted by their narrators in a sometimes creative, other times didactic fashion. Humans have always used story as a primary mode of persuasion and communication. Recent scholarship in the field of oral history reflects on the distinct emergence of a neo-liberal-influenced storytelling phenomenon since the 1970s.[5] However, an accompanying rise in the study and use of narrative in social movements by social movement theorists and organizers alike, who recognize the power of story to shape opinions, impart lessons, and mobilize in the service of justice movements, has not received the same critical attention.[6]

Oral history narratives are often complex, rich in the contradictions and ambiguities that characterize human beings and our interactions and decisions. They differ from other forms of autobiography and storytelling, in part because of the active role an interviewer plays in shaping the narrative. A well-prepared interviewer's precise or probing questions can lead a narrator to think of a new idea or develop a creative, deeper reformulation of a familiar account. Oral history's dialogical nature, together with its longer format, can allow for more nuanced accounts of a person or a community's experience.

Oral history, in which an individual is offered the narrative space to convey a more holistic portrayal of their self and their story, can also aid in the process of humanization—of challenging stereotypes, and facilitating identification with individuals who were once perceived as "other" but who can now be recognized in their full humanity. In contrast to the simplified storylines of individuals reduced to a single identity or experience (for instance "the undocumented immigrant" or "the victim of intimate partner violence"), the flexible and expansive form of an interview allows a narrator, in their own words with their own frameworks, to contextualize their experiences within a broader socio-political and historical milieu, and in the process more fully represent the many dimensions of their identity.[7] In response to the insights and critiques of black feminists, contributors to *Women's Words* were actively navigating the shift from an essentialized and universal view of woman-hood to an intersectional and dynamic understanding of identity, gender, and oppression. Given its complexity and life history focus, oral history offers, as they came to understand, great opportunity for a listener to find points of common concern and difference, and to recognize that our identities are not singular.[8] In other words, we learn not only that an Arab American was unjustly detained and tortured, but also that he is a poet who writes words of resistance from his cell, cannot stand lima beans and answering machines, and takes indescribable pleasure in the easy laugh of his only daughter. Kathleen Blee's chapter in this volume (Chapter 4), which examines "awkward" research in interviews with racist women, provides further examples of the lasting importance of this approach.

Moreover, oral history narratives reveal how forms of oppression overlap and coexist in individuals' lives and can point towards effective and inclusive strategies for confronting oppression and injustice. In this way, oral history may be a resource for today's social movements, many of which are moving from single-issue campaign models to values-based approaches rooted in a recognition of intersectionality. Contemporary oral history projects, such as Texas After Violence, the "Trans Oral History" project, and the "Anti-Eviction Mapping" project's Narratives of Displacement and Resistance, point to this power; each are recording and sharing interviews with individuals with particular experiences or identities (i.e. persons directly affected by murder and the death penalty, transgender and gender non-conforming people, and individuals experiencing displacement and eviction) but whose narratives reflect compli-cated stories about place, belonging, intimacy, violence, and corporeality. This adds texture and nuance to related social movement-oriented research and organizing efforts.[9]

Francesca Polletta's important research on storytelling in social movements suggests that it is precisely this complexity and moral ambiguity that char-acterizes the narratives most likely to influence listeners and thus serve as a political resource to disadvantaged groups. According to Polletta, a narrative's power comes from its collaborative nature and "openness to interpretation." She delineates three types of narrative ambiguity—polysemy, perspectival ambiguity, and semantic dissonance—each of which offer distinct possibilities to groups who share stories in the service of social change. Polysemy (the use of words or phrases that can have multiple meanings) in stories engages listeners in the act of interpretation in ways that create opportunities for "groups to forge agreement across diverse interests." Perspectival ambiguity (where the perspective from which a story is being told is unclear or shifts within the narrative itself) creates "new foundations for political authority," while semantic dissonance (stories with seemingly contradictory elements) can foster empathy across difference.[10] In one case study, Polletta examines students' narratives of the 1960 lunch counter sit-ins to explore why they proved so effective in expanding the movement. In the end, it was stories of the protests as "spontaneous," which engaged other students as co-authors, denied "individual intention" in organization and, in this "ambiguity" supported widespread "collective action."[11] It is impossible to predict or control what a narrator will say, but social movements can employ stories produced in interviews to communicate the nature and moral legitimacy of their struggle and mobilize allies.

Affective engagement

Oral history's personal nature can foster relationships, and the collective identity and emotional connections that facilitate and sustain collective action.[12] Through rich sensory descriptions and first-person narration (usually including both "I" and "we") narrators invite their listeners to join an imaginative space, and be active participants in the story. This can be transformative for both interviewers and narrators and lead to social change by building identification between listeners and movements. Activist oral history, and oral history more generally, have roots in feminist consciousness-raising practices and popular education methods, which sought to develop collective political analyses through personal narrative and group listening.[13]

Moreover, the affective content of an oral history interview can evoke outrage, compassion, and empathy in a listener and, in the process, compel action. The aurality of a recorded interview is especially evocative in this regard, as hearing a person share their narrative brings the listener into closer relationship with the person and their story, amplifying its emotional impact. Tone, volume, and velocity convey emotion, while the visual information of a videotaped interview can add another layer of affective content. Affective power can be harnessed, strategically and intentionally, towards movement ends by creating opportunities for listeners to channel their emotion into action. In 2015, the Groundswell: Oral History for Social Change network in Oregon collaborated with the Portland Immigrant Rights Coalition (PIRC) to record oral history interviews with immigrant families affected by detention and deportation. They edited them into a series of emotionally resonant audio slideshows and shared them via social media and in community forums to mobilize community support for immigrant families and challenge the collaboration that occurs between police and Immigration and Customs officials more broadly.[14]

Described as a "dialogical encounter," a "conversational narrative," and a "multivocal art," oral history is clearly an *exchange between individuals*.[15]

The distinction in roles between the listener and teller makes for a particular kind of interpersonal experience that creates space for hearing and speaking with a depth, care, and intention largely absent from most daily interactions. In this sense, narration in interviews is fundamentally different from other forms of storytelling, which imbues it with another characteristic relevant to social change. Oral history holds a special capacity for relationship building that is "intergenerational," enduring, and powerful for movement building. Two powerful examples include: VivesQ, where Emmanuel Garcia's interviews with LGBTQ+ elders established an intentional, intergenerational movement-building experience; and No One Is Illegal, an anti-colonial migrant justice group on Coast Salish territory that inspired the "Inheriting Resistance" project, as a way to honor and learn from their movement elders.[16] In movement building, relationships sustain activity, increase commitment, and form the basis of trust and action that underlie the willingness of individuals to risk their personal security and safety for the sake of the wider group or collective cause.[17] Formal and intentional use of interviewing can augment or accelerate the process of relationship building that occurs within social movements to build trust within an affinity group, solidarity among participants of sister movements, and understanding between allies and those directly affected by injustice.[18]

Historical content

In defining the genre of oral history, Alessandro Portelli argues that what distinguishes oral history from other forms of storytelling, fieldwork, and interviewing is "the combination of the prevalence of the narrative form on the one hand, and the search for a connection between biography and history, between individual experience and the transformations of society, on the other."[19] Just as the highly personal, individual character of oral history is of value for building movements, historical parts of an interview are assets for social change too.

Understanding the history of communities or issues deepens our understanding of the causes of contemporary problems. How and why did current struggles emerge? A historical understanding can reduce individual guilt and isolation, inspire pride in the struggles and successes of elders, and compel allies to support the cause by highlighting broader structural or ideological problems beyond the control of individuals. At the Marian Cheek Jackson Center for Making and Saving History, organizers recorded oral histories to document the civil rights history of a community facing gentrification. The process and resultant stories energized elder activists, inspired a new generation to join the cause, and convinced the university and local nonprofits to support community control of development.[20] Further to this, oral history is often the only format in which the histories of marginalized communities and social movements can be documented and made accessible, particularly in cases where people and communities cannot, do not, or simply will not interact with written texts.

Oral histories can also demystify the process of organizing. What worked and did not work in the past? Why? Through the "Rural Organizing Voices Oral History" project, rural Oregon's grassroots progressive leaders critically examined the organizing experiences of those who fought white supremacists and far right groups in their communities in the early 1990s, which strengthened their present-day organizing work.[21] Given the centrality of consciousness-raising and cultural transformation to many social movements, an oral history approach can provide insight into individual worldviews, value systems, and historical consciousness, as well as wider processes and moments of transformation that can further movement building and support organizers by providing access to how individuals make sense of their history and the world.

Conclusion

As we settle into the 21st century, the activist oral history visions put forth by both the editors and contributors to *Women's Words*, as well as those in this volume, continue to inspire new generations of organizers, scholars, and artists. Our collective knowledge has begun to point the way to a future in which more organizers have access to and understanding of the unique and powerful tools of oral history, and more oral historians see the radical potential of their work to document and create social change.

Notes

1 Sherna Berger Gluck and Daphne Patai, "Afterword," in *Women's Words: The Feminist Practice of Oral History*, eds. Sherna Berger Gluck and Daphne Patai (New York: Routledge, 1991), 221.
2 See Sherna Berger Gluck, "Advocacy Oral History: Palestinian Women in Resistance," in *Women's Words*, 201–219. This chapter is adapted from Sarah K. Loose, "Groundswell: Oral History for Social Change: A Synthesis" (Master's thesis, Columbia University, 2011), last accessed 6 October 2017, www.oralhistoryfor socialchange.org/blog/gs2011synthesis.
3 The *Oral History Review* 30, no. 1 (January 2003) special issue on "shared authority" identified many of these issues.
4 For more see Mary Marshall Clark, "Oral History Art and Praxis," in *Community, Culture and Globalization*, eds. Don Adams and Arlene Goldbard (New York City: The Rockefeller Foundation, 2002), 87–106.
5 Alexander Freund, "Under Storytelling's Spell? Oral History in a Neoliberal Age," *Oral History Review* 42, no. 1 (Winter/Spring 2015): 96–132.
6 Anthologies such as Rickie Solinger, Madeline Fox, and Kayhan Irani, eds., *Telling Stories to Change the World: Global Voices on the Power of Narrative to Build Community and Make Social Justice Claims* (New York: Routledge, 2008), Joseph E. Davis, ed., *Stories of Change: Narrative and Social Movements* (Albany: State University of New York Press, 2002), and the research of academics such as Francesca Polletta, *It Was Like a Fever: Storytelling in Protest and Politics* (Chicago and London: University of Chicago Press, 2006) are advancing conversations around the role of story in social movements. From an organizing perspective, the advent

of digital storytelling as a tool to raise awareness about critical justice issues has led to an explosion of documentation projects. The Center for Story-Based Strategy, a training and strategy development organization, harnesses "the power of narrative for social change" (www.storybasedstrategy.org). The Transgender Law Center recently released a storytelling campaign and toolkit for transgender and gender non-conforming youth, families, and allies (http://transgenderlawcenter.org/archives/11847). Furthermore, scores of new community organizers are trained each year in Marshall Ganz's story-based model (https://dash.harvard.edu/handle/1/30760283). See this training from 350.org: http://workshops.350.org/toolkit/story/.

7 As early as 1979, Luisa Passerini cautioned against an uncritical approach to this notion of oral history as capturing narrators' experiences "in their own words": "Work Ideology and Consensus under Italian Fascism," *History Workshop* 8 (October 1979): 82–108. The point is critical for practitioners seeking to employ oral history as a method for radical social change, as it underscores the need for a multi-layered approach to our practice, whereby critical consciousness becomes a central aim.

8 Sherna Berger Gluck and Daphne Patai, "Introduction," in *Women's Words*, 2.

9 See: http://texasafterviolence.org; https://www.nyctransoralhistory.org/; and www.antievictionmappingproject.net/narratives.html.

10 Polletta (*It Was Like a Fever*, 174) makes an important point, however, that the capacity of narrative to achieve these ends is largely contextual; the normative conventions of storytelling in a particular setting or institution influence how stories are heard and received.

11 Polletta, *It Was Like a Fever*, 28.

12 On collective identity in movement building, see Francesca Polletta and James M. Jasper, "Collective Identity and Social Movements," *Annual Review of Sociology* 27 (August 2001): 283–305, and Chapter 4 in Donatella della Porta and Mario Diani, *Social Movements: An Introduction*, 2nd edition (Malden, MA: Blackwell, 2006). Goubin Yang presents a survey of (mostly sociological) research on the connections between emotion, collective action, and social movements in "Emotions and Movements," in *Blackwell Encyclopedia of Sociology, Volume 3*, ed. George Ritzer (Oxford: Blackwell Publishing, 2007), 1389–1392.

13 Daniel Kerr, "Allan Nevins Is Not My Grandfather: The Roots of Radical Oral History Practice in the United States," *Oral History Review* 43, no. 2 (Summer/Fall 2016): 367–391; Anne Valk, " 'Recalling Our Bitter Experiences': Consciousness Raising, Feminism, and the Roots of Radical Oral History," unpublished conference paper, Oral History Association Annual Meeting, 14 October 2016.

14 For examples, see: www.forcedtrajectory.com.

15 Ronald J. Grele, *Envelopes of Sound: The Art of Oral History*, 2nd edition (New York: Praeger Paperback, 1991), 135; Clark, "Oral History Art and Praxis," 94; Alessandro Portelli, *Battle of Valle Giulia: Oral History and the Art of Dialogue* (Madison: University of Wisconsin Press, 1997), 24–25.

16 VivesQ, accessed 13 December 2016, www.facebook.com/vivesq/ and http://vives-q.tumblr.com/; "No One Is Illegal," https://noii-van.resist.ca/about/community-history-project/, last accessed 14 December 2017, Inheriting Resistance: A Community History Project.

17 Many researchers have studied the significance of personal relationships and networks in mobilization processes and social movements. See Suzanne Staggenborg, *Social Movements*, 2nd edition (New York: Oxford University Press, 2015), 31–38; Mario Diani and Doug McAdam, *Social Movements and Networks: Relational Approaches to Collective Action* (New York: Oxford University Press, 2003).

18 Amy Starecheski discusses this in *Oral History Review* 41, no. 2 (Summer/Fall 2014): 213–214.

19 Portelli, *Battle of Valle Giulia*, 6.
20 Marian Cheek Jackson Center, accessed 13 December 2016, www.jacksoncenter. info/.
21 Rural Organizing Voices, accessed 13 December 2016, http://ruralorganizing voices.org/.

18 Women power and feminine solidarity

Oral history, life stories, and trauma in the context of an industrial disaster

Suroopa Mukherjee

In my first serious foray into oral history, I focused on the women survivors of an industrial disaster that took the world by storm. On the night of 3 December 1984, as 40 tons of Methyl Iso Cyanate (MIC) leaked from inside the premises of Union Carbide India Limited (UCIL), the Indian Subsidiary of the American-owned Union Carbide Corporation (UCC), the streets of Old Bhopal, capital of Madhya Pradesh in India, turned into a gas chamber. Anyone in the path of the gas was killed or maimed for life. More than three decades later, the site of this human-made environmental disaster continues to be one of the world's most dangerous "toxic hotspots."[1] Thousands of women, who suffered from gas-related illnesses like lung cancer and liver disease, and children, suffering from various birth defects as a result of genetic mutations in their parents' reproductive systems, are among the 550,000 people ravaged by the disaster's fallout.

To better understand this disaster's social, political, and cultural ramifications, I carried out an ethnographic study on the people affected. Like Theresa de Langis and Hillary Hiner in this collection, I wanted to explore people's memories of trauma, and the role women played in assisting local leaders to set up survivor organizations. Initially, my academic training compelled me to focus on feminist oral history and its impact on the study of disasters. I was particularly interested in the social justice movement in Bhopal, which had its genesis in the death-ridden streets of Old Bhopal at the threshold of the killer factory. Its aim was twofold: to keep Bhopal and its issues "alive" as "breaking news"; and to create a database of stories to fight misinformation. In disaster contexts, government data is often responsible for misrepresenting facts and falsifying research, creating narratives that contradict those told by survivors. After the government's short-lived relief measures and the volunteers carrying out specific agendas disappeared, the social movement began to intensify its actions and "volunteering" took on a more political character as "intervention" by people committed to a sustained battle against the state and the corporation.[2] Women played highly public and critical roles in the social movement that emerged.

Doing fieldwork

When I entered the field, I carried my own baggage, drawn from my literature background, which included teaching Renaissance drama and ethnographic novels such as Joseph Conrad's *Heart of Darkness*. A three-year stint as Fellow at Nehru Memorial Museum and Library gave me the opportunity to explore oral history. I soon became involved in a research project that was undertaken by Queen Margaret University, Edinburgh, on the ethnography of Bhopal's social justice movement. Eurig Scandrett, the Principal Investigator, formed the Bhopal Movement Study Group (BMSG). I acted as the Indian Researcher, and we also hired two Bhopal-based research assistants. The study group conducted 40 interviews, which employed a feminist approach and were recorded on digital video and audiotapes. This proved to be an important training ground for me. The testimonials used in this chapter combine my earlier pen-and-paper ethnographic accounts with these later interviews. Gathering information "in the field" through interviews drew my attention to the "experiential" nature of sharing narratives of pain and trauma, as many of the recordings occurred at protest sites in both Bhopal and Delhi, where I became immersed in a colorful mélange of banners, T-shirts, street plays, die-ins, and other forms of collective action that embodied the resistance movement.[3]

The majority of those protesting were from marginal communities and they found strength in numbers as they invaded and disrupted public sites. My presence here, iPad in hand, was quaintly anachronistic, but the streets were my classroom, as I participated in this theater of resistance. Initially, I gained entry into memories of trauma through the "contentious performances" I witnessed.[4] The protestors took over parts of the city never occupied by gas survivors, their bodies visually enacting the fight for justice and challenging the establishment through slogans printed on T-shirts and armbands. The short YouTube videos of these protests created for the www.bhopal.net website offered opportunities to expand action plans.

In ethnographic terms, I was the "outsider" far removed from my academic space. Like many others who came to the protest site, I thought the disaster was a one-time event without ongoing consequences.[5] This false sense of security enjoyed by the privileged classes is precisely what ethnographic research can challenge. At protest sites, activist groups created photo-exhibitions-on-wheels with images of Bhopal's congenitally defective children that served to "embody" and deny claims to progress. The strategy drew attention to those "living" in this lifelong nightmare. It explained why rehabilitation—or, rather, the state's refusal to provide meaningful rehabilitation—became the grounds for claiming denials of justice. Having entered the field as a novice, I came to see that the only way of working towards the task of saving Bhopal was to join the movement as an activist. I collected stories-in-the-making to intentionally replace hegemonic narratives that downplayed the disaster's horrific effects and kept the middle class at a safe distance from the carnage.

Feminism and feminine solidarity

From the beginning, women workers were at the forefront of street actions. The more visible they became, the more their responsibilities increased. They acquired a new identity as the "voices" and "faces" of the movement, and played a major role in recruiting people like me to join them. In interviews, I listened carefully to women's narratives of acute trauma and became increasingly aware that I was collecting "evidence" of gross neglect by various state institutions. The amount of paperwork needed to file claims and achieve justice was well beyond the victims' paying capacity. Moreover, the invisibility of women in the official documents—legal, medical, bureaucratic, and those used in compensation courts—meant that they did not trust the "written word."[6]

The women understood their responsibilities for surviving the industrial disaster in material terms, and they built solidarity with one another by sharing personal narratives of trauma. The BMSG intentionally created space for the participants to "share memories" and, if desired, "relive" the experience of trauma in individual interview sessions. Group discussions provided opportunities to share memories of pain and loss and face feelings of anger and despair together. Recorded memories also expanded evidence of the disaster's catastrophic impact, furthering movement leaders' political agendas. The fact that the women were illiterate and deeply disadvantaged, and had very little prospect of changing the material conditions of their lives, made their testimonials even more important in the fight for justice.

Opposition narratives emerged to challenge the women. Some questioned their veracity and dismissed their medical conditions as "fake." Still others, who were more powerful, denounced the women as "parasites" in a forward-looking and fast-developing country. But the women fought back. When the government told the world it was giving survivors support, the survivor groups, most notably the Bhopal Group for Information and Action, responded. They stressed that the short-term measures passed at the time of the accident—for example, the government set up workshops, which lasted three months, soon after the gas leak to teach the women how to sew clothes and make stationery— did not begin to address the real need for continuing rehabilitation. When I visited one of these stationery sheds, its outdated machines were dormant; there were a few bundles of stationery papers and women were cutting, pasting, numbering, and putting them into piles. Only the state and the corporation had the resources required to care for those affected by the disaster, but the promise of long-term rehabilitation was false propaganda. Compensation was barely mentioned. Nobody spoke about justice. In truth, the workshops were designed to curb activism; anyone who dared engage in protest was fired.[7]

As the Bhopal tragedy attracted international attention, the women as well as gender-related issues received considerable attention as part of a worldwide battle against corporate power. When women activists from different countries arrived in Bhopal, they brought Western understandings of feminism that did not resonate with the movement's women. For them, feminism was an alien discourse that did not speak to the material reality of their lives. The Bhopal women's activism also compelled them to grapple with unfamiliar ideas. When they took to the streets, women had to discard their purdah (the black head and face covering worn by some Muslim women), join protest marches, and become wage-earning members of their families. Bhopal's revival in the national memory also renewed the "visibility" of women. In the streets of Bhopal and New Delhi, the women and their dancing bodies became a testament to their resilience in the fight for justice and the disaster's ravages.[8]

Women's narratives

Although the interviews required the women to "relive" the trauma of the disaster, most were keen to participate. Their narratives highlighted the different ways they entered the public domain, taking part in processions, hunger strikes, and padyatra—a protest marathon that covered the distance from Bhopal to New Delhi. Most of the women were illiterate so did not relate to words or text, but they used photographs, and their stories of trauma, to flood social platforms with a "live" display of their toxin-filled, ravaged bodies.[9] The more the movement grew, the harder the government worked to suppress information.

Although the women did not explicitly adopt Western feminism, they offered a strong image of female solidarity. "We are flames not flowers" became the women's signature song and "We are not asking for dole" their ideological point of view. "We want justice" united them with the worldwide demands of marginalized people. Bhopal women also called for rehabilitation and compensation from the government they had voted into power. Arguably, it was a "feminist" battle cry launched by empowered marginalized women, which helped shape the narrative of the social movement. As the story of Bhopal reached other marginalized communities, it inspired others to have courage in the face of corporate power. "No more Bhopal" became the clarion call of activism and "listening" to the "voices" that narrate stories of acute trauma became of paramount importance to making change.

The voices of female gas survivors speak powerfully to the human cost of this industrial calamity and how it politicized them. As Hazra Bi said:

> I feel strong enough to fight the government and I will fight till I get whatever is rightfully ours. We will not just take our rights but snatch them by force from the government, because we are not begging. We are taking what is rightfully ours. In the campaign, most of the participation is by the women; there are less men. I was a woman before the gas disaster and I am a woman today but in between I was someone's daughter, someone's wife, someone's mother. A woman needs to think, analyze the situation, and then make a decision to participate. Many men do not allow their daughters and wives to participate. Especially in the Muslim community you will see a lot of such things. I am a Muslim too.[10]

Hamida Bi's recollection of how involvement in the movement changed her speaks to the lifetime of struggle these women faced too:

> My perspective changed slowly. I felt very awkward for some time. I do not need to wear a Burkha to show that I am a dignified woman. In our meetings, we raised all sorts of women's rights issues like dowry, cheating, and abusing women. A lot of women also changed after they came to meetings and after they saw their leaders without the Burkha. They also gave it up. My family has never opposed my involvement because I have managed to fulfill all my responsibilities. My daughter was not a bride even for one night and her life was destroyed over the issue of dowry. They demanded money from the first compensation and a car, when I could not even buy a cycle. After marriage, they abandoned my daughter. I sued them and fought the case for three years and made them return the dowry that I had already given them. I am a fighter. When life was most chaotic, my husband left me. I could not educate my other children. How was I to send them to school? Where would I get books and uniforms for them? This is the story of my life.[11]

In her interview Rabiya expressed her deep resentment towards the "politicians" who want votes, "[talking] big" but serving only to "fill their pockets." She added:

> I don't even feel like talking to you about the corruption that is taking place today. Today, India is an independent country but who helped her win it. It was yours and my ancestors who struggled and fought with honesty. They did not think about saving their homes but their country, their city, their *mohalla* [local residence]. They struggled for all this and not for themselves. Whereas the leaders today want to come to power for their own benefit. People of Bhopal have become objects of pity. For me pity is an abusive word. Our government and Anderson made us pitiable.[12]

The women's stories underscored the enormous importance of accountability and how their disappointment with the government workshops politicized them. Rashida Bi highlighted the inadequacy of "the stationery and sewing centers" by discussing the workshop in which she, one of 50 Hindu and 50 Muslim women, had participated:

> We would get to the work shed at ten in the morning and come back after five in the evening. We got 5 rupees for a day. By the end of the month we were paid and asked to go home, and work from home and sell the finished products.[13]

Interestingly, Bi's narrative revolved around notions of self-development, a growing political consciousness, and the severe limitations she faced as an illiterate woman born and raised in a patriarchal family. Following this, she spoke about how the fight for justice moved out of the work shed and into the streets:

> It was decided that we would gather at Valabh Bhavan (Secretariat) and protest for our demand. [The] Gas Secretary said that this demand cannot be met, and that we should continue to work the way we were working, or else we would lose the job as well. We did not take any notice. . . . After about six to seven days of dharna we decided to go on a hunger strike . . .[14]

Bi's story became a carefully drafted narrative that shapes a larger story and vision of people's resistance:

> The air is polluted in most parts of the world. Developed countries are equally affected by the growing industrialization and the spread of corporations. Hence the fight today in Bhopal is not limited to the rich or poor but is the fight of the world for the environment. If the environment is not clean then humanity itself cannot survive.[15]

Conclusions: Contentious performances, political constraints

By the time Bhopal's social movement acquired an international presence in 2004, it had entered its second decade and the political scenario had changed considerably. The venues for protest had changed too. The Dow-Carbide offices in Mumbai and Noida were sites of protest, while weekly meetings were held in Bhopal, in Neelam Park and the Aloo factory.[16] The internet and social networking expanded support, enabling petitions to circulate on websites and list-serves, and technology made it possible to fax protest messages directly to the Prime Minister's and President's offices. These methods proved to be as evocative as street actions.

Always eclectic in nature, the Bhopal movement combined disruptive actions with those that were peaceful and commemorative in nature. Highlighting Bhopal's relevance in the face of middle-class apathy remained a primary concern. However, rifts also developed between movement intellectuals and rank and file workers, some of which occurred over evidence of political opportunism. Many felt that familiar faces got aired on talk shows and primetime debates in ways that diluted serious issues. The political immunity that the infamous Supreme Court-directed settlement of 1989 granted to government and corporations gave them cover. Nonetheless, as long as women remained visible as stakeholders in the public domain, their narratives had political consequences. The Bhopal gas tragedy offers a classic case study in how systemic failure, accompanied by the lack of political will, results in the travesty of justice. The pressing issues, like environmental cleanup and medical treatment for the second generation, continue to be contentious issues because there has been limited compensation.

As a "participant observer" who became politically involved through my experiences in the field, I learned that memory can take us anywhere, but there are limits when it comes to replicating "our" experience. Bhopal is perennially "outside" our consciousness.[17] Yet, to forget Bhopal is to engage in the politics of "disengagement," which gets replicated in discourses on marginality. After all, who wants to live with other people's "monstrous" memories? The more women I interviewed, the closer I came to a political understanding of why these survivors have become "outsiders" to the aspirations of modern India. That said, a politics of disengagement was impossible for me. I remain inspired by the women of Bhopal and, for me, engaged ethnography and feminist oral history continue to act as effective tools for activism and protest.

Notes

1 Amnesty International, *Clouds of Injustice. Bhopal Disaster 20 Years On* (London: Amnesty International, 2004).
2 Bridget Hanna, Ward Morehouse, and Satinath Sarangi, eds., *The Bhopal Reader* (Goa, The Other India Press, 2005). This collection offers comprehensive coverage of the tragedy and includes materials gathered by survivor organizations like the Bhopal Group for Information and Action.
3 On stereotyping and defining trauma victims in Bhopal, see Tara Jones, *Corporate Killing: Bhopals Will Happen* (London: Free Association Press, 1988).
4 In Charles Tilly, *Contentious Performances* (Cambridge University Press, 2008), he argues that participants in contentious gatherings draw their claims-making performances from familiar repertoires, applying available scripts to local circumstances.
5 See Andre Beteille and T.N. Madan, eds., *Encounters and Experience: Personal Accounts of Fieldwork* (Delhi: Vikas Publishing House, 1975); and Vinay Kumar Shrivastava, *Methodology and Fieldwork* (New Delhi: Oxford University Press, 2004) on the challenges of fieldwork in India. Though I disagreed with many of its basic premises, also useful is Kim Fortun, *Advocacy after Bhopal: Environmentalism, Disasters and New Global Orders* (Chicago: Chicago University Press, 2001); Meenakshi Thapan, *Anthropological Journeys: Reflections on Fieldwork* (New Delhi, Orient Blackswan, 1998).
6 Jones, *Corporate Killing*; Vandana Shiva, *Staying Alive: Women, Ecology and Survival in India* (New Delhi: Kali for Women, 1988); Meena Menon, "Bhopal: Poisoned Lives," in *Bhopal Revisited*, The Hindu Survey of the Environment, 2003.
7 Suroopa Mukherjee, *Surviving Bhopal: Dancing Bodies, Written Texts, and Oral Testimonials of Women in the Wake of an Industrial Disaster* (New York: Palgrave Macmillan, 2010), 117.
8 Mukherjee, 118, 157–163.
9 See the photographs on the Bhopal Disaster by Raghu Rai, Pablo Bartholomew, and Maud Dorr, "International Campaign for Justice in Bhopal," accessed 31 January 2017, www.bhopal.net/resources/photographs/.
10 Hazra Bi, interviewed by author and the Bhopal Movement Study Group (BMSG).
11 Hamida Bi, interviewed by BMSG.
12 Rabiya Bi, interviewed by BMSG. Warren Martin Anderson was Chairman and CEO of the Union Carbide Corporation at the time of the Bhopal disaster.
13 Rashida Bi, interviewed by author.

14 Rashida Bi, interviewed by author.
15 Rashida Bi, interviewed by BMSG.
16 Stephen Zavestokshi, "The Struggle for Justice in Bhopal. A New/Old Breed of Transnational Social Movement," *Global Social Policy* 9, no. 3 (2009): 383–407.
17 James Clifford, *The Predicament of Culture: Twentieth-Century Ethnography, Literature, and Art* (Boston: Harvard University Press, 1988), 34; Clifford Geertz, *The Interpretation of Cultures: Selected Essays* (Waukegen, Illinois: Fontana Press, 1993); Evans Pritchard, *Social Anthropology* (London, England: Cohen and West, 1951); Claude Lévi-Strauss, *Structural Anthropology*, trans. Claire Jacobson and Brooke Grundfest Schoepf (New York: Basic Books, 1963).

19 Public homeplaces

Collaboration and care in oral history project design

Sady Sullivan

Oral history is collaborative work. But while oral historians regularly talk about care for the narrator—building trust, establishing rapport, honoring reciprocity, and protecting privacy—much less is said about the care required to maintain a spirit of open collaboration as projects develop. This chapter explores the ethics of care that deeply informed a collaborative oral history and public humanities project I directed at Brooklyn Historical Society (BHS) between 2011 and 2015: "Crossing Borders, Bridging Generations" (CBBG). In doing so, I address how feminist relational-cultural theory informed the project and how an ethics of care can usefully link oral history praxis and feminist research methodology.

The project's design was inspired by feminist relational-cultural theory, a revolutionary psychological theory that, as Christina Robb writes, provided a way by which "the women's movement and other human rights movements of the 1960s moved into psychology."[1] Within relational-cultural theory, the term "connected," as in "connected knower" and "connected teacher," conveys the premise that caring for relationships can not only be intertwined with intellectual pursuits but actually enhance inquiry.[2] Very much a "connected" pursuit, the CBBG project explored the history and experiences of mixed-heritage people and families in Brooklyn, New York, and concepts of cultural hybridity, race, ethnicity, and identity.[3] An award-winning project praised for its "open-ended, collaborative, community-based approach to exploring mixed-heritage populations," its final results included three years of public programming, a digital humanities website (with online and indexed access to many of the oral histories), and free curriculum material for middle- and high-school students.[4]

Brooklyn Historical Society is a historically white institution located in a borough of New York City where people of color are currently the majority. Therefore, greater inclusivity in programming and diversifying its collections are among BHS's priorities. The CBBG project met this mandate by building on existing community ties and creating spaces for people to have conversations about race, ethnicity, identity, and privilege.[5] Enacting an ethics of care, our working community engaged a national team of 20 scholars, a local team of 25 oral history interviewers, and over 100 narrators. In addition, nearly 1,800 people participated in our public events. Including a multiplicity of voices in its planning and implementation was essential to the project's success. An overlap in groups—narrators and audience members joined the interviewing team, and some interviewers were also interviewed as narrators—unsettled any perceived hierarchy of authority. We prioritized communication with all those involved to ensure we mobilized principles of care. Following Paolo Freire's radical precepts, everyone acted as "co-investigators" in the sense of partners in a democratic partnership of learning, and we engaged in concentric circles of dialogue that require love, humility, faith, and hope.[6]

As CBBG co-director, I focused on what was needed to ensure everyone felt valued and heard. For CBBG advisors, the public programs and digital humanities site created opportunities for public scholarship and amplified their work beyond BHS' walls. We honored advisors' contributions by paying them for their involvement in meetings, although this hardly compensated them for their countless hours of advice and inspiration. Regular meetings with members of the interview team provided opportunities for new learning, skill sharing, and networking. Interviewers also gained experience by presenting at public programs, teaching workshops, and publishing contextual essays on the digital humanities site. They were paid for interviews they conducted and other contributions, but not for attending meetings. To foster an atmosphere of open communication and collaboration, I was intentionally transparent about decision-making and finances. Moreover, we responded and were adaptive to feedback along the way, dealing with issues that arose by changing language, programming content, event structure, and the online oral history archive.[7] Such strategies were critical given that institutions like BHS are not accessible to everyone as repositories for family papers, photographs, or oral histories. Many people have seen their histories misrepresented or erased by schools, museums, and other public institutions, and that sits heavily in community memory. To help build trust, we decentered BHS as an authority, making clear that the CBBG was a project by and for Brooklyn's varied communities.

CBBG explored the politics of interpersonal relationships. In the United States, interracial married couples who happened to cross into one of the sixteen states that legally prohibited interracial marriage until 1967 faced prosecution, jail time, and violence. While not legally proscribed, interfaith and interclass marriages also met with opposition from family and community. And yet, in less than two generations since the removal of the last anti-miscegenation laws, multiracial and multiethnic children are one of the country's fastest-growing demographic groups.[8] Our project used care to document this trend and the political power of love that made it happen through oral history. As Black, intersectional, and postcolonial feminists note, forming loving partnerships in a racist, sexist, homophobic, and transphobic world can be a radical act.[9] This ethics of care includes decolonizing the self, looking inward for personal and community healing, and rejecting the individualistic values of a hierarchical culture. Social justice movements such as Black Lives Matter include self-love, empathy, and loving engagement among its guiding principles.[10] Arguing that "decolonial love" is a goal for racial justice activists, Dominican-American writer Junot Díaz adds: "We're never going to get anywhere as long as our economies of attraction continue to resemble, more or less, the economies of attraction of white supremacy."[11]

The project created opportunities for people to listen to one another with empathy and care. Community-based learning involves encouraging participants to historicize their understandings of mixed heritage, identity, and culture, and engage in racial justice dialogues. CBBG invited white people to take an active part in interrupting racism. Through the sharing of personal stories, we hoped to uncover the complexities of culture and identity, including how laws and social mores affect our private lives, and inspire reflection on the roles we play in building a more equitable world. "Telling about experiences invites listening," writes feminist and anti-racist activist Peggy McIntosh, while "opinions invite argumentation."[12] CBBG events were places to practice the careful listening necessary to address white supremacy, undo racism, and heal.

What are you? I'm a story

I began my work by reaching out to people already organizing around concepts of mixed-heritage, and multiethnic and multiracial identity.[13] We agreed that public dialogue would be a good way to complicate cultural representations of mixed-heritage people. The tropes invoked have shifted from that of the

Figure 19.1 Audience break-out group at the second annual "What Are You? A Discussion About Mixed Heritage," Brooklyn Historical Society, 2012. Credit: Willie Davis, Brooklyn Historical Society

"Tragic Mulatto" to contemporary notions that mixed kids are a panacea for racism. We called our first event, which became an annual one, "What Are You?" because it is an invasive and dehumanizing question that mixed-heritage people are often asked.

All CBBG events, whether film screenings, visionary fiction workshops, or panel discussions, encouraged audience participation. To help ensure that all public programs felt welcoming, we provided food and drink, and elicited audience involvement through break-out groups, pair sharing, and question-and-answer sessions. This also blurred the boundaries between the presenters and the audience. Audience members' generous and brave contributions never ceased to amaze me. Nearly 1,800 people attended 32 events between 2011 and 2014; of the presenters, 75 per cent were people of color, more than half of them women.[14]

Many narrators learned about the CBBG oral history project through these public events. We left the definition of "mixed heritage" open so narrators could self-identify for interviews.[15] In the United States, people tend to think about race first and foremost when discussing mixed identity. By resisting this impulse, we maintained the project's acknowledgement of intersectionality and the social constructions of race. Self-identification provided a unique window into what Brooklynites thought about cultural heritage. Manissa McCleave Maharawal, a member of the interviewing team as well as a narrator, wrote: "Oral history allows for multiplicity: for the varied, nuanced, and complicated

Figure 19.2 Audience break-out group at "Science Fiction and Multiraciality: From Octavia Butler to Harry Potter," Brooklyn Historical Society, 2013. Credit: Willie Davis, Brooklyn Historical Society

stories of identity to be told—not flattened to static racial categories."[16] We heard from interracial and interethnic families, interfaith and international families, Third Culture Kids (children raised in a culture other than their parents' culture), and people who identified as mixed because they grew up in neighborhoods that were predominantly of a race/ethnicity that was different from their culture at home. CBBG mobilized care by honoring and valuing complex stories and experiences of identity.

Prioritizing what was best for those involved, the project devoted energy and resources to spaces for public dialogue and community engagement—such as Listening Meetings where narrators and interviewers collaboratively analyzed interviews, workshops, a digital humanities site, and free curriculum—rather than scholarly output. However, the CBBG oral history collection is now open to researchers at Brooklyn Historical Society. Critical race scholars, such as historian Renee Romano, stressed just how "incredibly useful" this collection will be because it captures the stories of people of mixed heritage invited to speak for themselves, while most of the (limited) historical sources "used to document racial border crossing, have been mediated by others, and usually, colored by stigma."[17]

The project's success was due to the readiness of our oral history narrators, interviewers, advisors, public programming presenters, and audiences, as well as BHS staff, especially CBBG project staff, to attend, connect on a personal level, and learn along with the project.[18] Sherna Berger Gluck, Margaretta Jolly, and others have written about the limits of life history interviews in documenting collaborative movements like feminisms.[19] I feel a similar limitation in writing about a community-engaged project, my alternating between "I" and "we" reflecting the difficulty of writing about collaborative work in a way that credits the team without erasing my own ideas and labor. As the labor of care is still undervalued, we need to make more visible the achievements of caring and empathetic and connected leadership.[20]

Relational-cultural theory helps to do that. Beginning in the 1970s, and inspired by feminist and anti-racist activism, psychologists challenged models of mental health based on (white, straight, cisgender) men that value individual achievement over interconnectedness.[21] This led to the development of relational-cultural theory, which values connection for individual psychological health and challenges patriarchy and white supremacy.[22] Early writings were in some ways essentialist but there is much that still resonates, including Carol Gilligan's research on morality, which inspired the concept of radical (or politicized) empathy.[23] Relational-cultural practitioners continue to work for social justice by "promot[ing] healing, empathy and mutual respect to sustain positive connection and create powerful change."[24] Further, this methodology has much in common with oral history, especially its focus on interview-based research, active listening, collaborative authorship, grappling with power dynamics, and finding voice.[25]

Relational-cultural theorists' notion of "public homeplaces" is also relevant to CBBG. Developed in the 1990s, public homeplaces refers to the community-based, personal-is-political movement-building common to the 1960s–70s civil rights and women's movements whose leaders were "intensely interested in the development of each individual, of the group as a whole, and of a more democratic society."[26] For instance, the inimitable Dr. Bernice Johnson Reagon, leader of the Student Nonviolent Coordinating Committee (SNCC) Freedom Singers, and Sweet Honey in the Rock, called a public homeplace "a nurturing space where you sift out what people are saying about you and decide who you really are."[27] CBBG sought to provide this sort of nurturing and inclusive space. Through Listening Meetings with narrators, the idea of *belonging* shifted CBBG's focus from personal identity—"What are you?"—toward community: "Where is home?" Explaining why she joined the project, narrator Elizabeth Velazquez said: "I feel like stories have a way of making connections with people. Our society now is not really nurturing that connection. It's really cold and fast-paced. And policy makers are disconnected . . ."[28] As oral historians, we carefully consider the ethics of asking narrators to share their personal histories with the public. By prioritizing collaboration, CBBG extended a feminist ethic of care to participants and tried to pave one path toward a more just future.

Over the past decade, I have shied away from words like "care" and "connection" when discussing my work. While I have long been politically and morally committed to acting with empathy and love, I started my career during the feminist backlash and neoliberalism of the late 1990s. As a woman working

Figure 19.3 Workshop participants: "Racial Realities: Writing about Race in the First Person," Brooklyn Historical Society, 2013. Credit: Willie Davis, Brooklyn Historical Society

mostly outside academia (and without a PhD), I realized that speaking about nurturing relationships—despite its importance to oral history and public humanities projects—lessened my authority. I have also witnessed the workplace racism, sexism, and other offensive actions dismissed as "personality" conflicts to be handled privately, or not at all. As relational-cultural theorists argue, this disconnection between our public and private selves is not healthy for individuals or communities. For many women, people of color, and LGBTQ+ people, this disconnection manifests itself as imposter syndrome. When colleagues and institutions fail to acknowledge racism, sexism, homophobia, and transphobia, we experience a further disconnection between our personal and professional selves. In my experience, the devaluing of emotional labor—such as nurturing community and mentoring the next generation—contributes to self-doubt. Oral history interviews allow narrators to (re)connect with their personal experiences and transform private reflections into public sources of knowledge— a process that is both validating and healing. To this end, CBBG participants were thankful to have public spaces in which to discuss race, ethnicity, and their experiences of cultural heritage, self, and relationship.

Notes

1 Christina Robb, *This Changes Everything: The Relational Revolution in Psychology* (New York: Picador, 2007), ix.
2 Mary Field Belenky et al., *Women's Ways of Knowing: The Development of Self, Voice, and Mind*, 10th anniversary edition (New York: Basic Books, 1998).
3 *Crossing Borders, Bridging Generations*, accessed 14 August 2016, http://cbbg. brooklynhistory.org.
4 CBBG won the US Oral History Association's 2015 Elizabeth B. Mason Project Award and the 2016 American Association for State and Local History's Leadership in History Award. To learn more about the project, go to: "Crossing Borders, Bridging Generations": *Listen*, accessed 7 January 2017, http://cbbg.brooklyn history.org/listen.
5 BHS has conducted socially engaged oral history work since the 1970s: Karen Olson and Linda Shopes, "Crossing Boundaries, Building Bridges: Doing Oral History among Working Class Women and Men," in *Women's Words: The Feminist Practice of Oral History*, eds. Sherna Berger Gluck and Daphne Patai (New York: Routledge, 1991), 199.
6 Paolo Freire, *Pedagogy of the Oppressed*, 13th anniversary edition (New York: Bloomsbury Academic, 2000), 87–124.
7 For example, we used settings for search engines to limit access to the archive and add an extra level of privacy: "CBBG and Google Find-ability," accessed 18 February 2017, www2.archivists.org/groups/oral-history-section/spotlight-privacy-academic-freedom-and-the-law-0.
8 "2010 Census Shows Multiple-Race Population Grew Faster Than Single-Race Population," United States Census Bureau, accessed 14 August 2016, www.census. gov/newsroom/releases/archives/race/cb12-182.html.
9 Cherríe Moraga and Gloria Anzaldúa, eds., *This Bridge Called My Back: Writings by Radical Women of Color* (Watertown: Persephone Press, 1981); bell hooks, *Ain't I a Woman? Black Women and Feminism* (Boston: South End Press, 1981); Audre Lorde, *Sister Outsider: Essays & Speeches by Audre Lorde* (Trumansburg: Crossing

Press, 1984); Patricia Hill Collins, *Black Feminist Thought: Knowledge, Consciousness, and the Politics of Empowerment* (Boston: Unwin Hyman, 1990); Chandra Talpade Mohanty, Ann Russo, and Lourdes Torres, eds., *Third World Women and the Politics of Feminism* (Bloomington: Indiana University Press, 1991); Adrienne Rich, "Compulsory Heterosexuality and Lesbian Existence," *Signs: Journal of Women in Culture and Society* 5, no. 4 (Summer 1980): 631–660.
10 "Black Lives Matter Guiding Principles," accessed 22 December 2015, http://blacklivesmatter.com/guiding-principles.
11 "Junot Díaz's Keynote Speech at Facing Race 2012," accessed 6 February 2017, www.youtube.com/watch?v=F3ZoiFxeiEs.
12 Peggy McIntosh, "White Privilege: Unpacking the Invisible Knapsack" and "Some Notes for Facilitators", accessed 5 November 2016, http://nationalseedproject.org/white-privilege-unpacking-the-invisible-knapsack.
13 Jen Chau-Fontán of Swirl, Inc., a national multi ethnic organization; Ken Tanabe of Loving Day, a global network of annual celebrations honoring the *Loving versus Virginia* decision; and several members of MAVIN Foundation, an organization of mixed race people and heritages, were generous with their time and ideas.
14 For event summaries and photographs, see http://cbbg.brooklynhistory.org/news/events.
15 Initially, we asked interview team members to write one-page "personal/professional" biographies for the archive so that narrators could make informed decisions when it came to choosing an interviewer, but the narrators tended to reply: "Whomever you think is best!"
16 *Crossing Borders, Bridging Generations*, "Making Space to Talk about Race," accessed 22 December 2015, http://cbbg.brooklynhistory.org/learn/making-space-talk-about-race?page=3#slides.
17 "Hidden No More," BHS newsletter, accessed 14 August 2016, http://cbbg.brooklynhistory.org/blog/hidden-no-more.
18 Endless gratitude to Margaret Fraser, Nayantara Sen, Julia Lipkins Stein, Abigail Ettelman, Emily Potter-Ndiaye, Heather Miller, Judy Pryor-Ramirez, and Walis Johnson.
19 Sherna Berger Gluck, "Advocacy Oral History: Palestinian Women in Resistance," in *Women's Words*, 205–219; "From California to Kufr and Back: Reflections on 40 Years of Feminist Oral History," in *Oral History Off the Record: Toward an Ethnography of Practice*, eds. Anna Sheftel and Stacey Zembrzycki (New York: Palgrave MacMillan, 2013), 25–42; "Has Feminist Oral History Lost Its Radical Edge?" *Oral History* (Autumn 2011): 63–72; Margaretta Jolly, Polly Russell, and Rachel Cohen, "Sisterhood and After: Individualism, Ethics and an Oral History of the Women's Liberation Movement," *Social Movement Studies* 11, no. 2 (2012): 211–226.
20 Two projects that work towards this are the "Montréal Life Stories" (www.lifestoriesmontreal.ca); and "nindibaajimomin: A Digital Storytelling Project for Children of Residential School Survivors (http://nindibaajimomin.com/).
21 Kathryn Anderson and Dana Jack cite Carol Gilligan's work on moral frameworks in "Learning to Listen: Interview Techniques and Analyses," in *Women's Words*, 20.
22 Jean Baker Miller Training Institute, "The Development of Relational-Cultural Theory," accessed 22 December 2015, www.jbmti.org/Our-Work/the-development-of-relational-cultural-theory.
23 Michelle Caswell and Marika Cifor, "From Human Rights to Feminist Ethics: Radical Empathy in the Archives," *Archivaria* 81 (Spring 2016): 23–43, accessed 6 February 2017, http://escholarship.org/uc/item/0mb9568h.
24 Jean Baker Miller Training Institute (JBTI), accessed 6 February 2017, www.jbmti.org/.

25 JBTI, "The Development of Relational-Cultural Theory," accessed 22 December 2015, www.jbmti.org/Our-Work/the-development-of-relational-cultural-theory. Also see Jean Baker Miller, *Toward a New Psychology of Women* (Boston: Beacon Press, 1976); Carol Gilligan, *In a Different Voice: Psychological Theory and Women's Development* (Cambridge, MA: Harvard University Press, 1982); Lyn Mikel Brown and Carol Gilligan, *Meeting at the Crossroads: Women's Psychology and Girls' Development* (Cambridge, MA: Harvard University Press, 1992); Judith V. Jordan et al., *Women's Growth in Connection: Writings from the Stone Center* (New York: The Guilford Press, 1991); Judith V. Jordan, ed., *Women's Growth in Diversity: More Writings from the Stone Center* (New York: The Guilford Press, 1997); Mary Belenky et al., *Women's Ways of Knowing*; Robb, *This Changes Everything*; Daniel Kerr, "'We Know What the Problem Is': Using Video and Radio Oral History to Develop Collaborative Analysis of Homelessness," in *The Oral History Reader*, 2nd edition, eds. Robert Perks and Alistair Thomson (New York: Routledge, 1998), 485–494; Amy Starecheski, "Squatting History: The Power of Oral History as a History-Making Practice," *Oral History Review* 41, no. 2 (Summer-Fall 2014): 187–216.

26 Mary Field Belenky et al., *A Tradition that Has No Name: Nurturing the Development of People, Families, and Communities* (New York: Basic Books, 1997.), 14.

27 As quoted by Belenky et al., *A Tradition that Has No Name*, 163.

28 "A Look at Looking Different: 'Crossing Borders' at Brooklyn Historical Society," accessed 6 February 2017, www.nytimes.com/2014/12/03/arts/design/crossing-borders-at-the-brooklyn-historical-society.html?_r=0.

20 Come wash with us

Seeking home in story

Shahrzad Arshadi, Hourig Attarian,
Khadija Baker, and Kumru Bilici

The contours of our story

The members of our collective originally come from the Middle East. Hourig is Armenian, but born in Lebanon; Khadija is Kurdish from Syria; Shahrzad is Iranian; and Kumru is Kurdish hailing from Turkey.[1] Having lived in volatile regions before calling Canada home, all four of us have inherited memories of atrocities from our families, just as we have all lived through civil wars, military coups, bloody revolutions, and political repressions. It is these inherited and difficult lived memories that compose the fabric of our individual interdisciplinary work and the broader canvas of our collective work together.

Our idea to create a process-based performance—*Come wash with us*—was born coincidentally on a bright sunny day in late May 2014. We came together to eat and discuss our current projects; our conversations centered on joyful memories of our grandmothers doing laundry and the laundry blue they used. We were quickly immersed in childhood memories, talking passionately about how they evoke story through the symbolism of women's work and metaphors of water, washing, and clotheslines, together with our sense of the embedded aesthetics of these moments.

Over time, the threads in these stories became a performance piece, which highlighted the commonalities in our experiences and gave us the opportunity to look critically at the deeper folds of memory. We envisioned sitting together to wash clothes in *tashts* (traditional metal washtubs), transforming the performance area into a laundry space as we remembered it from "back home."[2] As we washed, we intended the space to be open, interactive, and dialogic among ourselves and with audience members. The "process of washing" uniting us, three women from different communities—Armenian, Iranian, and Kurdish —and audience members, as we explored laundry stories.

Since we come from different disciplines, we wanted to create a (methodological) language that would allow us to talk about difficult memories through performance.[3] We located this language at the interlocking axes of feminist oral history, dialogue, and narrative inquiry, which manifested through the collaborative aspects of our work. Our starting point was our personal stories and family memories of doing laundry, which, woven together with shared

Figure 20.1 Our washtubs. Credit: Shahrzad Arshadi

history from our home countries, became the springboard for creating community as we sat around the *tashts* to explore individual and collective stories of loss, dispossession, war, genocide, and exile. For us, the act of washing and doing laundry evoked memory and created space for dialogue. Critical questions emerged that centered on concepts of "homecoming" as well as homeland lost, imagined, and experienced through memories. We yearned to understand: Where is home? Can we find home in the story? Or within the process of the performance we create? Can home exist through the imaginary and mythical concepts we have of a place?

Following what seemed like unending conversations over more than a year, together around tables overflowing with food and apart through email and Skype, we had our first performance in October 2015, at Concordia University's Centre for Oral History and Digital Storytelling (COHDS) in Montréal, Canada.[4] We recounted the stories of mothers, daughters, and granddaughters through our "laundry performance" and, in the process, struggled to come to terms with our memories of war and genocide, to face the pain of loss and dispossession strewn across the life paths of our families, and to heal. We also regard the process of our performance as a conduit, bringing the "mundane" from our grandmothers' and mothers' lives into our practice in the present. We highlighted the simple act of doing laundry, of women's work, to evoke shared childhood memories as a form of resistance to the violence engulfing the regions from which we come.

Our invitation to people to bring "dirty linen" and wash with us was deliberately multilayered and meant to signify both the literal and metaphorical

Figure 20.2 Washing. Credit: Shahrzad Arshadi

gradations of interpretation, from actual clothes to conflicts seeking resolution through dialogue. By carrying the conversations into the space of "doing laundry" together we hoped to break down barriers between "audience" and "artist," and create an alternative methodological language in which *the process becomes the performance* and generates further conversations. This chapter is structured around such dialogue.[5] What we share here through multiple voices may feel disjointed and even point to a dissonance between performance and text. Writing in this case is not a mirror, but rather, like the water flowing during the washing in our performance, it is fluid and ever changing, refracting and shifting our voices to reveal our continuing conversations, about the first iteration of our project—its process, impact, and the many new questions and stories it engendered.

Conversations around the kitchen table

HOURIG: Laundry memories have preoccupied me for some time. Writing elsewhere about the ways clotheslines speak to our lives, I have divulged how recounting the childhood memory of doing laundry with my mother and grandmothers became a benign memory that provided refuge.[6] Through it I could escape the heavy residue left by the retelling of other family narratives—those of my grandparents who were genocide survivors and of my adolescence scarred by the Lebanese civil war.[7] However, writing soon led me to discover that what I regarded as gentle and even joyous memories often triggered stories of loss and trauma. One of the recurring images of clotheslines from the war years that remains etched in my mind is an excerpt from Palestinian poet Mahmoud Darwish's powerful poem "Birds Die in Galilee"—"My homeland is clotheslines / For the handkerchiefs of blood / Shed every minute." I have recited those lines countless times, over those years, seeking a balm in words that I could not find elsewhere.

Working with Khadija, Shahrzad, and Kumru on our performance offered a new opportunity to ponder the different and complex layers of laundry stories and memories. From our first discussions, I envisioned a collective performance featuring my paternal grandmother's hometown Dikranagerd, now called Diyarbakir, in Southeastern Turkey. There would be a huge *tasht* in a courtyard somewhere in *gyavur mahalesi*, as the Armenian quarter was known.[8] I have fantasized about that place all of my life, imagining where my grandmother must have grown up and where my father was born. I imagine the four of us sitting and wringing the laundry, then stomping in the *tasht* to clean it some more, rinsing it in cold water, adding *leghak-chivit-nil* (laundry blue), and finally hanging the clothes.[9] What better homecoming from *ghurbet*, as Kumru called it, than a "return" to a mythical place that has taken hold of my imagination ever since I was a child; the city where part of my beginnings are scattered, the city that remains an open wound.[10]

The personal narratives and family histories we delve into inevitably create a link to collective histories and memories: these wounds have deep historical roots. The performance enabled us to explore a history that comes out of a specific place, of lands lost, to imagine and reclaim them. Sifting through our memories together, in communion, also helped us find a connection between the personal and *our* collective, the community we created sitting together around the washtubs. Doing the laundry in this space of dialogue, evoking story, became a metaphor for attempting to wash away an unwashable pain deeply embedded under our skins.

SHAHRZAD: In November 2015, I was walking around and inside "Barika," a refugee camp 30 minutes outside Sulaymaniyah, in Iraqi Kurdistan. It was a beautiful, sunny day, colorful laundry hanging all around, on top of the United Nations High Commissioner for Refugees (UNHCR) tents and on the half-built cement walls. Mesmerized by the scene, I felt overwhelmed by the sadness of the refugees' living situations. I had returned to Kurdistan after a long absence to present my latest documentary film, *Dancing For Change*, at a film festival, and to conduct research for a new project about Kurdish/Iranian women *Peshmarga* (freedom fighters).[11] The situation I observed was worse than what I had witnessed ten years prior. A rapid rise in religious fundamentalism was undeniable, and poverty soared along with the number of refugees—Kurds and Arabs from Syria as well as those fleeing the horrors of ISIS in other parts of Iraq. At every traffic light, boys and girls asked people to buy gum, napkins, or water. It was so hard for me to look into their eyes! Early on I wanted

Figure 20.3 Barika refugee camp, near Sulaymaniyah in Iraqi Kurdistan (Northern
      Iraq), November 2015. Credit: Shahrzad Arshadi

to talk to these children's families. Where are they? What are they doing?
I wondered.

For a long while, I just walked with my camera in my hand without
taking a single photograph. A beautiful little girl with a lovely smile
approached and, pointing at my camera, said, "*Rasme-kam le begra* [take
my picture]!" Her contagious smile woke me up. I returned her smile and
started taking pictures, to capture her stories, and my stories, in that
moment. Little did I know that the laundry hanging everywhere along the
dusty roads of "Barika" camp would become a critical line in our collective
stories.

Here I want to write about our laundry project and about my distant
memories of childhood—the act of doing laundry with close family and
neighbors in our garden—but other images rush to mind. Washing clothes
for me always meant community, friendship, and joy, particularly when I
was a child. In "Barika" camp, though, I suddenly felt like those memories,
which I had tended so carefully from my years of living at home in
Northern Iran, had been erased from my mind! It was as if the broken
walls, ripped UNHCR tents, and children with empty stomachs in cold
tents were defying my happy childhood, telling me to stop remembering.
I intended to write about these memories but talking to the refugees
brought pain to my heart. They complained about their lost sense of
community, of trust, of the distance created by the absence of basic
facilities. Instead of the spotless white laundry of our performance, as I
write this I see invisible red spots all over it.

KHADIJA: When I was a child, I never thought that one day I would find beauty in washing clothes. I cannot remember how old I was when I started helping my mother, perhaps six, but I know I was too tiny to squeeze the laundry perfectly. My mother had to redo all of my work, and I would ask myself, why am I doing this? I never said this aloud, however, because I felt responsible for helping my hard-working mother. On cold winter days, the water saved for washing froze and its glassy surface only melted from the boiled water of cotton whites. The cold water made my tiny hands bleed. They would hurt for days and then heal. Remembering these details, I feel the love and engagement of my family in my memories of daily work.

Thinking about my parents' jobs, I always thought that women's work was the hardest.[12] Pride was tied to perfect housework for women, even encouraging competition between them. But my mother never told us how to be perfect. I learned that being a woman meant being independent and doing what we had to do—unavoidable issues when we speak of washing, women, labor, and perfection. It brings the home as a gendered cultural space into view. Laundry was about the place of women in the home and men tended not to get involved. Once my grandmother was so angry and ashamed that my young uncle had hung clothes for his wife that she criticized my aunt for not being a good woman and wife.

KUMRU: There are few household chores that connect me to my mother as strongly as washing, drying, folding, and putting away laundry. Growing up I saw my father and three older brothers doing most of the other

Figure 20.4 Piled up laundry during the performance, October 2015.
Credit: Shahrzad Arshadi

chores at home, but never the laundry. Where did this attachment— woman to laundry or laundry to woman—come from? I vividly remember the day, early in my marriage, when I realized that I was going to do the laundry willingly, without questioning it. My husband and I share other chores, but not this. I do laundry every week: separate the darks from the whites, and then wash, dry, and fold them without any complaints, hesitations, or regrets. It is therapeutic, soothing, to clean the dirt away and make the clothes and fabrics in our life smell fresh. I do not think my mother liked washing laundry this much, until maybe she got her first automatic washing machine. But she did it. She had to. Every week she sorted the dirty clothes, washed them by hand, wrung them, hung them to dry, and folded them without complaining. Her clean laundry was her badge of honor, the symbol of her skills as a homemaker; her shield against the outer world.

KHADIJA: In the "home" I came from in a Kurdish town in Northern Syria on the Turkish–Iraqi borders, washing was a way for women to get rid of the dirt. It happened weekly and required much preparation. We collected water for days. Since we only had tap water at night, we woke up early, around four in the morning, or stayed up very late past midnight; more often my father would do that part. We collected rainwater whenever it rained. The "home" was also where women showed off and competed with other women through their neatness. We used to call the bad behavior of people "dirty" and it was the women's job to get rid of that dirt, whatever that entailed. Connecting these two issues, I can see how much women are engaged in family and community-building, education, and even morality.

The acts of remembering and storytelling are central to our laundry project. It is about memory and nostalgia, a starting point for sharing stories of today and seeing ourselves, in the process of retelling and learning through the past, recreated through our words and thinking. It is about four women who desire change and look for hope together.

SHAHRZAD: Feminism for me is a philosophy that has shaped and affected my lifestyle, my everyday life, and, most importantly, my work as an artist. I come from a tradition of learning the history of my country through individual stories, especially my grandmother's and my friend's grand- mother's memories about their difficult everyday lives during World War II. Most importantly, though, my father's stories of his generation, those who experienced the aftermath of World War II in Iran with the dictatorship and the ensuing 1953 American-orchestrated coup d'état, helped shape my ideas and beliefs.

I think all four of us come from similar storytelling traditions. Growing up in environments of tyranny, you understand that most history books are written from the perspectives of those who wield power. Such story- telling defies that locus of power. For me, our project is an act of resistance storytelling. It is an act of sharing, of creating new community through washing and cleansing. I think that in all of our cultures, water brings light and clarity. Through our performance, we are trying to use our history to spread light into our personal stories and out into the world.

KHADIJA: In talking about Palestinian artist Mona Hatoum's installations, Edward Said described our times aptly: "In the age of migrants, curfews, identity cards, refugees, exiles, massacres, camps and fleeing civilians," Hatoum's works of art are created with "the uncooptable mundane instruments of a defiant memory facing itself." They are "precious fragments placed before us to recall our mortality and the precarious humanity we share with each other."[13] Through performance we face our memories and respond to what is happening in the Middle East, back "home." We re-witness, resist silence, and share knowledge of ongoing violence.

In Middle Eastern (including Kurdish) culture, we regard forgetting as a mercy or a blessing; yet, we also celebrate remembrance. When someone dies we often keep their clothing as one of our most precious things. We keep our babies' clothing to remember the moment they were given to us. For our performance, we collect white clothing and wash it in a public space where we exchange stories. There are three elements in our work—water, clothes, and sound (which includes the sound of the water and our voices)—that come together with indirect tales of the ongoing conflict we witness today in terms of displacement, violence, and injustice.

Figure 20.5 Kawergosk Syrian refugee camp in the Kurdish region of Northern Iraq, near Erbil City, 2012. Credit: Khadija Baker

HOURIG: The first "live" experience of our performance was very different for each of us. We talked about it endlessly for over a year, imagining various possibilities. We told and listened to each other's childhood recollections of laundry—washing, soaking, boiling linens, rinsing, water, lots of flowing water, laundry blue, wringing, squeezing, hanging, matching colors and sizes, early teachings in the aesthetics of perfect clotheslines—with much joy and laughter. We also reflected on the nostalgia and sadness linked to a deeper layer of loss in these memories. Not all of our laundry memories were joyful, not all of the stories benign. Displacement, dispossession, trauma, survival, and resilience were reoccurring themes in our narratives.

It took time and debate to decide how to "conduct" the first iteration of our performance—would we only be in conversation with each other? Or would we interact with the audience too? Would we each concentrate on our own personal memories or take cues from one other? How much did it matter that Khadija and Shahrzad are experienced multidisciplinary artists with a background in performance, while Kumru and I were embarking on our first public performance? In the end, we decided to dwell on memories that surfaced on the spot as we each went into our personal spaces, while still connected to one another, as we did the wash. We allowed the act of washing to lead to spontaneous memories "poured out" at that moment in performance.

I remember feeling dazed in the days following the performance. I oscillated between the contradictory feelings of "walking on air" and a new heaviness weighing heavily inside. We discussed the reaction of the audience-participants who so generously shared some of their own stories, the impact the memories that surfaced during the performance had on us and others, and also their unexpected fallout. Unavoidably, questions about our own discomfort, vulnerability, and fragility emerged. Some of the spontaneous memories had led down unexpected paths during the performance, divulging "family secrets." The questions we asked ourselves in retrospect circled around the right to tell our family stories while being mindful of intrusions and a feeling that our inner selves lay naked in public. How do we story without either sensationalizing or deepening an existing wound, when the act of remembering and retelling resembles more of an excavation than a storytelling session?

KHADIJA: I have answered this question about sharing personal and family stories for myself. I do not want it to stop me from reaching my goal and realizing our greater intention unless it puts someone's life in danger. I view breaking the rule of keeping the family's life private and exposing it in public through art as the artist's statement. The other rule-breaking here is putting the Middle Eastern female body doing housework and laboring for this very private act of washing clothes in public view. This action is not a critique of the position of women as much as it is an act of remembrance meant to provoke public memory and resist ongoing violence.

SHAHRZAD: I agree deeply with Khadija that it is an artist's privilege to be able to break rules, rules that have been created by family or society. In that sense, I find our performance's intention of sharing memory, performing oral history, and telling story as well as our history resonates with performance studies specialist Della Pollock's argument that

> history can not be held privately. No one person "owns" a story. Any one story is embedded in layers of remembering and storying. Remembering is necessarily a public act, whose politics are bound up with the refusal to be isolated, insulated, inoculated against both complicity with and contest over claims of ownership.[14]

Our performance taught us the importance of understanding and familiarizing ourselves with the actual space of the performance and the need to deeply connect with it. We first performed at COHDS—a place about which Khadija, Hourig, and I were very familiar, while Kumru was new to the space, coming from Ottawa to Montréal to wash with us. This was brave of her; in retrospect I think our shared moments made it possible for her to be fully in the moment.

To prepare for the performance we set up a simple choreography: who started the washing, did the second wash, and rinsed and hung the clothes. We decided how to create a "live soundtrack" that mixed the sound of water with our stories and our silences. The atmosphere encouraged spontaneous memories from the near and distant past, and created a space for audience members to participate.

During that first performance, I remembered our two-floor house in Rasht, a city in Northern Iran near the beautiful Caspian Sea. It had a lovely garden with walnut, sour pomegranate, and wild pear trees. There were geraniums everywhere. I remembered washing days with my mother and her best friend. I remembered my friend's grandmother with her *narghile* (water pipe) sitting on top of the porch telling us stories. How I wished I would become just like her when I grew up!

KHADIJA: For us, washing during our performance was an invitation to wash away hatred and attempt to heal—revealing injustice, sharing the burden of the history we carry, and affecting change. Doing the performance, at least for me, was a way to learn to express the truth and move beyond stereotypes and the painful repetition of stories about suffering. In the performance, the act of sharing stories was the main component, as the same story and the memories it evokes can change with every retelling. In one instance it may evoke tears and in another sweet bitterness. In the performance we wanted our most immediate memories to surface through the process of washing itself, without any prior rehearsal or preparation. Our intention was to initiate "the pouring out" of memory. We imagined that washing would wash our hearts from the daily pain of the stories we carry. A major issue we encountered was how much and what to reveal through our stories. Was it about generating empathy without making ourselves victims? For me, it was about being able to talk about the recurring injustice in the region without being regarded as a victimized Middle Eastern woman.

During the performance, I touched the water, colored the white with another white, heard the sound of the past through the sound of the other women, of the audience, and shared it or kept it private—these are all parts of the work. The stories we shared did not have to be heavy ones. They did not have definitions or roles. We shared them to highlight problems, seek change, and renew hope.

SHAHRZAD: Here I am after four months of traveling in the Eastern part of the world. It is six in the morning. I am sitting in my kitchen in Montréal wondering where I belong. I am very happy to come home to my family and to this familiar city, yet also feel part of my heart is far away. For many years I told myself home is where I feel happy, where I feel safe, where my heart is, where people I love live. Yet, none of these definitions satisfy me any more.

During my travels, I often asked myself, "What is home? Will I ever find it? Do I carry home with me everywhere I go?" One evening, after a long day of photographing Kurds and Syrians in a refugee neighborhood in Istanbul, the question of "home" hit me particularly hard. Is the answer encapsulated in the moment I stepped outside of Iran and joined the great multitude of people with different cultures, backgrounds, and races destined to be homesick for the rest of time? Is "homesickness" my/our new nationality, our new understanding of home?

Maybe if we survive the challenge of leaving home and being uprooted, we allow ourselves to look for connections in the creation of a community much larger and much more diverse than we can imagine. Perhaps this is a strong community that allows us to spread our hands far enough to reach others. Because, maybe, as Gil Scott-Heron sang in one of his songs, "Home is where hatred is / Home is filled with pain and it / might not be such a bad idea if I never went home again." It is a painful thought but sometimes I cannot stop thinking about it!

HOURIG: I regard myself as an in-betweener, constantly living between "here" and "there," forever torn between shifting locations. When I am in Armenia my soul soars, I feel alive in a different way. I realized this during a four-month trip in Spring 2015. I had forgotten about that feeling of "here," that I have in Montréal. For years I have contemplated home, where and what it is, theorizing that it is among friends and like-minded thinkers, or what I create. But, ask me where I belong and the boundaries shift, they blur.

Maybe Shahrzad's question about home needs no answer. Maybe the answer is to ask more questions. In our ongoing conversations about uprootedness and displacement, we have so often asked whether we can find home in story and create it through performance. Apart from what we have left behind in lands overseas, there are the inherited, imaginary, and mythical concepts of a lost home. Maybe the only answer I have these days is seeking home in the telling and receiving of stories.

KHADIJA: Home and identity are the first things that change when we cross borders. How we relate to place and people, how we reflect on our memories, all we remember, forget, and relate through stories; all of our new ideas, connections, and even the mundane in our daily lives, are home.

KUMRU: In thinking about home, I remember my mom's stories of her past sufferings, saying, "I raised four children without any help. Nobody even washed their one snotty handkerchief." Each time she repeats "snotty handkerchief" I imagine with a giggle this "unimaginable" scenario of my father washing the handkerchiefs in the basin with his shirtsleeves rolled up. This is an image that is tantamount to defying the laws of physics. Laundry, my father thinks, is "strictly the chore of women."

But if my father and brothers never helped my mother, I did. Since I was the only other woman in the house, I suppose this collaboration was understood to be natural. I usually sat next to her on a small stool in the bathroom. In different cities of Anatolia, different bathrooms of houses, some bigger and brighter than others, we washed laundry side by side

Figure 20.6 Historical Armenian fountains, Hebap/Ekinözu village (Havav in Armenian) Kovancılar district of Elazığ province, Turkey, October, 2016. Kumru's mother remembers doing laundry with her mother at these fountains as a child. Credit: Kumru Bilici

every Sunday. I helped with the small items like socks, mittens and, yes, handkerchiefs, too. I watched her body move around the washtubs, rubbing the clothes, dumping them in the water again and again. She always looked bigger, stronger, and more majestic when she was washing the laundry. I felt smaller and fragile next to her. I used all of my strength to prove to her that I could do it too, wringing the clothes as tight as she could with my little hands, waiting for her to tell me "*afferim* (good job)" after each attempt. I still do in fact . . .

During laundry days, I was instinctively more careful about what I would say or do to not upset my mother. On those days she was exhausted and more rigid, but also sadder. Part of me respected and tried to share this immense labor, the other part wished I could disappear to avoid her deep sadness. I always imagined she was washing the laundry and rubbing away her frustrations, squeezing her old pains, rinsing her regrets, and refreshing her self-esteem. Or, maybe, she only washed the clothes. Either way, I wanted to give her mundane, unpaid, unappreciated labor some meaning. It had and has meaning to me.

While we did the laundry together, my mother always shared memories of her youth and the community she used to have when the women washed together. In those days, she talked as if the laundry was an easier job, the clothes less dirty, and the soaps more effective. For her they were. She spoke of going to the village fountain together with her sister and sisters-in-law, of how much fun they had washing together. In these cold, lonely bathrooms being by herself, maybe washing underlined her

Figure 20.7 Barika refugee camp, near Sulaymaniyah in Iraqi Kurdistan (Northern Iraq), November 2015. Credit: Shahrzad Arshadi

displacement, reminded her of separation from family more than anything else. She missed those days; the ones when she felt she belonged to a family, village, and community. Being aware of this unending longing made me uncomfortable as a little girl. I wanted her to be happy that she had us and that we lived in a safe place. I was naïve and did not know that homesickness creates a big hole in your chest.

SHAHRZAD: Let me recount a dream for you. Towards the end of my 2016 trip to the lands we used to call home, I woke up in tears. We were all washing impeccably clean and well-hung white dresses. As we draped and fastened the bluish-white dresses on the clotheslines, red stains appeared on our beautiful dresses out of nowhere. We started taking them down one by one and washing them over again. As soon as we hung them up, the red stains reappeared! Eventually our *tashts* were filled with reddish water instead of the clear laundry blue.

HOURIG: Let me recount the story of Lusya's *tas*.[15] The antique bath bowl or *tas* we used in our performance belonged to my great grandmother, Lusya Mamlakatian. It is inscribed with her name and the date 1900. From Dikranagerd, Lusya brought the *tas* to her husband's home as part of her dowry. She did not survive the Armenian Genocide, but her bath bowl did. For me, Lusya's family name Mamlakatian, signifying hometown and country in Turkish, encapsulates a portrait of loss and historical irony.[16] My grandmother Zohra kept her mother's bath bowl as a precious memento, hidden in the recesses of her wardrobe for years. I found out about its existence only when my mother moved to Montréal and brought it with her. In my possession, it has become a revered "museum piece" on my bookshelf, a symbol of loss.

Figure 20.8 Khadija pouring water over Hourig's hands with Hourig's great grandmother Lusya's bowl during the performance. Credit: Shahrzad Arshadi (still photo from video)

Since the bowl had not been used since 1915, our performance restored it to its original usage. The same *tas* that poured water over Lusya's body was used to pour water on my hands as I washed laundry. The water breathed life into the bath bowl and into Lusya's memory. The *tas* became the medium to connect, across time and space through washing, her with me, as well as to the other members of our collective.

Notes

1 Hourig, born in Lebanon, lived through the Lebanese Civil War of 1975–1990. Khadija grew up in a Kurdish town in Northern Syria, close to the Turkish border. She witnessed her first bomb—planted on the border to stop Kurdish fighters from joining Kurdish militants in Turkey—explode at the age of 5. It killed her uncle. Shahrzad is Iranian and lived through the horrors of the 1979 Islamic Revolution in Iran and the subsequent Iran–Iraq war. Kumru grew up in Turkey witnessing successive military coups and the suppression of Kurdish and other minority rights on a daily basis.

2 *Tasht* is washtub in Armenian and Farsi. In Kurdish it is pronounced *tesht*.

3 See the authors' biographies listed in the collection (pages xiii–xix).

4 Our first performance took place in an enclosed space, in front of an audience of oral history scholars and practitioners, community activists, and artists.

5 Since writing this text, we performed in the garden of the Grey Nuns Residence, in Montréal, as part of a COHDS-SOHC Summer Institute in 2016. Plans for other performances are in progress.

6 See Hourig Attarian, "Stories Fluttering in the Wind: How Clotheslines Write Our Lives," in *Was It Something I Wore? Dress, Identity, Materiality*, eds. Relebohile Molestane, Claudia Mitchell, and Ann Smith (Cape Town: HSRC Press, 2012), 41–56; Hourig Attarian, "Lifelines: Matrilineal Narratives, Memory and Identity" (PhD diss., McGill University, 2009).

7 Hourig's four grandparents survived the 1915 Armenian genocide perpetrated by the Ottoman Turkish Empire.

8 *Gyavur mahallesi* means "neighborhood of the infidels" in Turkish, marking it as the quarter where most of Diyarbakir's Armenians, Greeks, Assyrians, and Jews lived. Much of it lies in ruins after heavy fighting between the Turkish military and the PKK (Kurdistan Workers' Party) in 2015–2016. While state propaganda proclaims that the city will be restored, many cultural heritage sites belonging to minorities, including Armenian churches, have suffered severe destruction and been confiscated by Turkish authorities.

9 *Leghak* is laundry blue in Armenian, *chivit* in Turkish, *nil* in Farsi.

10 Signifying emigration in Turkish, *ghurbet* or *gurbet* also denotes deeper meanings of yearning, longing, homesickness, and even exile. *Ghorbat* in Farsi and *kharibi* in Kurdish carry the same meaning.

11 *Dancing for Change*, which focuses on six Kurdish Iranian women from three different generations, is a story about secular and socialist women in the Islamic world, and their ideals, activism, and visions for a better world.

12 As women who cared for children and did the housework, we were also responsible for preparing food all year; this was intense labor, especially in the summer.

13 Joseph Massad, "Affiliating with Edward Said," in *Edward Said: A Legacy of Emancipation and Representation*, eds. Adel Iskandar and Hakem Rustom (Berkeley: University of California Press, 2010), 38–39. Mona Hatoum's works reveal a sense of displacement and estrangement. Like other Palestinian refugees, Hatoum is a stranger in exile who has never felt at home.

14 Della Pollock, "Introduction: Remembering," in *Remembering: Oral History Performance*, ed. Della Pollock (New York: Palgrave Macmillan, 2005), 5.
15 In Armenian and Turkish, *tas* is "bowl".
16 Originating etymologically from Arabic, *mamlakat*, meaning kingdom, is pronounced *memleket* in Turkish and means country and hometown. Connections to a concept of home and belonging would easily be detected in a figurative sense of the word.

Listening to and learning from stories in the digital world

Introduction to Section 5

Listening to and learning from stories in the digital world

Anna Sheftel

Feminists have long talked about the perils and promise of technology. From discussions of standpoints and situated knowledges as ways of exposing patriarchal domination and creating space for feminist epistemology in the history of science, to conceptions of "cyborg" feminism as a way of imagining emancipatory futures that reject essentialism and move beyond rigid categories, feminist approaches to technology and the digital world have always been equal parts critical and constructive.[1] From the beginning of these creative and boundary-pushing discussions, the newness and speed of technology has compelled feminist scholars to ask two seemingly opposing questions: How can we seize the possibilities of this brave new world for our theories, ethics, and practices? And, in what ways does this brave new world mimic, replicate, and transform the practices of domination that continue to marginalize, ignore, and exclude women and LGBTQ+ peoples.

The authors of the chapters in this section play with the push and pull of these concerns within the context of their own oral history practices, experimenting with the ways that new technologies give them opportunities to push their feminist methodologies further, while also musing about how the kinds of feminist concerns that *Women's Words* raised play into the dilemmas posed by the digital world. Alistair Thompson famously warned us to take seriously how the digital turn in oral history would transform our practice and impact the ways we understand memory and life stories. Feminist scholars, due to their sensitivity to questions about power, narrative, subjectivities, and audience, are uniquely well positioned to ponder these issues, as we see in the following chapters.[2] Not only do they deftly use a feminist oral history lens to grapple with the digital turn, but they also demonstrate how debates around it cast classic questions about feminist oral history in a new light.

The digital has made the world bigger—giving us access to unprecedented amounts of information and resources—and smaller—making it easier to connect with people and their stories—and for better or for worse, it forces us to balance questions of transparency and privacy. In her chapter, Mary A. Larson uses the classic feminist adage that "the personal is political" to examine how the digitization of oral history practice has created opportunities for the amplification of that idea and reversed it, by making the personal more visible in the political, bringing an intimacy to more abstract debates. Putting women's oral histories online allows us to see more specificity in women's lived experiences, recentering those experiences in powerful ways. Margo Shea, however, unpacks what "personal" meant during the second wave feminist movement and what it now signifies in social media contexts, wondering if the two are reconcilable. Certainly, the online world as it exists today places a high value on personal narratives, but she points out that this does not necessarily translate into oral history, nor does it necessarily facilitate a collaborative, emancipatory, and ethical feminist vision of personal narratives.[3] Larson argues that the notion of "public" is manifestly different—bigger and less easily delimited—when dealing with the online sphere, while Shea grapples with how that sphere values and contextualizes the personal narratives that are everywhere online. These narratives are autobiographical, fleeting, curated, confessional, and commodifiable, forcing us to consider what this means for the slow, deliberate practice of documenting people's whole lives. She concludes that, "the telling matters."[4] Both authors see the promise in a medium that allows for the amplification of and complexity inherent in women's and subaltern voices, and which quite literally allows those actual voices to be shared more easily. But, they also argue that this does not happen by default; we must craft oral history's relationship to the digital to make it an inclusive and thoughtful feminist method.[5]

Along with complicating the relationship between the personal and the political, the digital turn forces us to reassess our conceptions of intimacy and distance in the oral history process. Oral historians have long debated the balance between these two poles and technology forces us to reconsider what either can really mean in a fluid, expansive, and rapidly changing context.[6] In terms of the digital world, intimacy is not just about the relationship between interviewer and narrator; it is also about how digital tools allow us to actually hear the voices of the people we interview rather than relying on transcription, a point highlighted by Larson as well as Ruth Percy and Heather Howard. In particular, Percy argues that the temporal, political, and physical distance that comes from accessing archived interviews and working with narratives that one has not collected oneself can allow for new insights that help us better understand the subjectivities and co-construction of the interview. That distance, while illuminating, can also complicate matters, as one must negotiate how language has transformed over time and trace the "discursive origins" of the narratives with which one is engaging. In a digital context, this call for complexity is important; the seeming permanence of digitized material can too easily divorce online interviews from their contexts, their histories, and their idiosyncrasies. As Percy puts it, "historians using archived oral histories thus require an astute ear and a comprehensive and flexible lexicon to piece together histories of resistance."[7] In a similar vein, Howard reflects on the challenges of working within a medium like app development when trying to properly contextualize and represent Indigenous women's voices for multiple audiences, especially given that colonized voices have so often been misrepresented and exploited in the past. Larson similarly takes on this question of context, citing both the ways that digital tools can help to situate excerpts of life stories, while also critiquing how such practices can decontextualize those narratives. How do you bring people closer when they may be a world away? While Howard describes the ways that First Story Toronto impressively ensured that the app it created justly represented the voices of its narrators to multiple audiences, she also acknowledges the limitations of the form and cites the power of "shutting the tape off."[8] Oral historians have long acknowledged that no matter how intimate an interview is, not everything can be said within that space, and the context of digitization compels us to acknowledge silence as a deliberate and sometimes necessary choice given the breadth and limitations of the medium.[9]

Finally, all of the authors engage with questions of ethics—namely, how to represent and do justice to their narrators' stories, and how to ethically engage with the sometimes exploitative and misogynist medium that is the Internet. Elise Chenier, in explaining her project, "The Archives of Lesbian Oral Testimony" (ALOT), gets down to the brass tacks of digitization, explaining how complicated it is to gain permission from people who were interviewed before the digital turn to put oral histories online, and how this differs from traditional archiving. She argues that the process of getting consent regarding the dissemination of women's stories is separate from the process of gaining consent to be interviewed. She also points out the various logistical barriers to overcome in this kind of work, and emphasizes the importance and benefits of partnering with museums, archives, and libraries at the start of a research project. In her work, we can see an extension of the feminist ethic of collaboration, here applied to the post-interview digitization process, and not just to the recording of a life story. When it comes to feminist ethics of justice and inclusivity, Larson points out, first, how feminists have critiqued the replication of patriarchal structures in a space that is purported as being inclusive and democratic like the Internet. She also highlights what she calls "the 800-pound gorilla in the room, the digital divide. There is a feminist impulse toward democracy and inclusion, but there are large numbers of women internationally who are not online."[10] This brings us back to Shea's interest in the kinds of personal stories that are shared online, and what, if anything they have to do with oral history. There are millions of voices on the Internet, and yet not everyone is represented, or listened to, or willing to put themselves out there. A feminist ethic of digital oral history needs to make space for that: to see the boundaries, as much as the abundance, and as Howard points out, it must include the possibility of refusal.

What the following chapters demonstrate is that the same debates—around ethics, intimacy, collaboration, and interpretation—with which *Women's Words'* authors engaged manifest themselves in new and yet familiar ways in the context of digitization and technology. As a result, feminist oral historians are uniquely positioned to grapple with these issues and to add complexity to the field's discussion of innovation, moving us beyond merely fetishizing technology to critically engaging with it. Like feminist scholars working in the History of Science and the Digital Humanities, feminist oral historians critique and create at the same time.

Notes

1 Donna Haraway, "A Cyborg Manifesto: Science, Technology, and Socialist Feminism in the Late Twentieth Century," in *Simians, Cyborgs and Women: The Reinvention of Nature* (New York: Routledge, 1991), 149–181; Donna Haraway, "Situated Knowledges: The Science Question in Feminism and the Privilege of Partial Perspective," *Feminist Studies* 14, no. 3 (Fall 1988): 575–599; Sandra Harding, "Rethinking Standpoint Epistemology: What Is 'Strong Objectivity?'" in *The Feminist Standpoint Theory Reader: Intellectual and Political Controversies*, ed. S. Harding (New York: Routledge, 2004), 127–140.
2 Alistair Thomson, "Four Paradigm Transformations in Oral History," *Oral History Review* 34, no. 1 (Winter–Spring 2007): 50.
3 Alexander Freund has also been critical of the conflation of autobiographical storytelling and new media projects that use oral history: "Under Storytelling's Spell: Oral History in a Neoliberal Age," *Oral History Review* 42, no. 1 (Winter–Spring 2015): 96–132.
4 Margo Shea, Chapter 21 of this volume, 295.
5 See also Anna Sheftel and Stacey Zembrzycki, "Slowing Down to Listen in the Digital Age: How New Technology Is Changing Oral History Practice," *Oral History Review* 44, no. 1 (Winter/Spring 2017): 94–112.
6 See Valerie Yow, "'Do I Like Them Too Much?': Effects of the Oral History Interview on the Interviewer and Vice Versa," *Oral History Review* 24, no. 1 (Summer 1997): 55–79; Alan Wong, "Listen and Learn: Familiarity and Feeling in the Oral History Interview," in *Oral History Off the Record: Toward an Ethnography of Practice*, eds. Anna Sheftel and Stacey Zembrzycki (New York: Palgrave Macmillan, 2013), 97–111; Stacey Zembrzycki, *According to Baba: A Collaborative Oral History of Sudbury's Ukrainian Community* (Vancouver: UBC Press, 2014); Katherine Borland, "'That's Not What I Said': Interpretive Conflict in Oral Narrative Research," in *Women's Words: The Feminist Practice of Oral History*, eds. Sherna Berger Gluck and Daphne Patai (New York: Routledge, 1991), 63–75; Franca Iacovetta, "Post-Modern Ethnography, Historical Materialism, and Decentring the (Male) Authorial Voice: A Feminist Conversation," *Histoire sociale/Social History* 32, no. 64 (November 1999): 275–293.
7 Ruth Percy, Chapter 24 of this volume, 315.
8 Heather A. Howard, Chapter 25 of this volume, 331.
9 See also Anna Sheftel, "'I Don't Fancy History Very Much': Reflections on Interview Recruitment and Refusal in Bosnia-Herzegovina," in *Oral History Off the Record*, 255–272.
10 Mary A. Larson, Chapter 22 of this volume, 301.

21 Feminist oral history practice in an era of digital self-representation

Margo Shea

This chapter has its origins in a Facebook thread prompted by *Oral History Off the Record*. While reading the anthology, I considered the students I had introduced to oral history since 2010. We had delved into shared inquiry and authority, and the power of the co-constructed narratives we fashion with diverse people out of performances of talking, listening, interpreting, and reflecting. Yet, the students seemed unenthused by the power of oral history. For them, the prospect of co-creating narratives and making space for "ordinary people's" experiences and reflections was passé, even boring. While the power of "I" in eyewitness accounts, oral histories, and feminist scholarship continued to captivate me, the old shibboleths of oral history critique—accuracy, veracity, and, of course, "truth"—preoccupied my students.

In *Oral History Off the Record*, Sheftel and Zembrzycki's insistence on the importance of valuing people instead of studying them seemed relevant.[1] As I reflected on the difference between valuing people and extracting memories from them in the transactional mode feminist oral historians have long castigated, I could not escape the dual meaning of "value." It led me to make the following observation in a Facebook post: "Perhaps the plethora of subjective interpretations of experience available on the internet has made the very idea of charting ordinary people's experiences not only less unique, but less interesting, less evocative of something larger."[2] Millions of people now narrate and share their thoughts and experiences to ever-broader groups of people via social media. No longer is the unremarkable life unremarked upon. In ways Carl Becker could never have imagined, everyone really is their own historian.[3]

I wondered, had we spent too much time thinking about the promises of digital media and not enough considering the implications of digital culture? Perhaps oral historians might need to work differently to bring people's experiences and memories to bear to facilitate their own meaning-making and contribute to public spaces of dialogue about how and why the past matters now and for the future.

A former student and avowed feminist, Caroline Correia, responded by defending oral history. She suggested that while most online first-person narratives are self-censored to curate and display the best versions of ourselves, oral historians privileged, performed, and ultimately brought into being fuller representations of individual experience. Correia raised critical issues of time, perspective, and the shifting and settling of experience into coherent narrative forms, querying:

> I wonder what it means to reflect immediately on an experience—as in the case of social media—versus being asked to bring forward past memories in an interview. What happens to them in that "downtime?" Is the knee-jerk telling more authentic than a retelling of an older memory?[4]

Even as she admitted that the choreographies of talking and listening made oral history performance very different from self-representation and self-disclosure via social media, Correia insisted that oral history's significance transcended the individual: "Oral histories and the process of shared authority have to be so much more than the capturing of subjective experiences, no?"[5] This chapter argues that the message cannot be disentangled from its medium. Oral history, self-representation, and feminism are all in the process of significant paradigm transformations, each influenced by digital culture in their own right and all implicated in broader processes of cultural change. After a discussion of transformations in oral history and their connections to the history and current state of feminist practice, this chapter highlights how digital culture has altered both the concepts and the practices of self-representation. Computer-mediated communication, specifically user-generated content shared through social media, and the cultures that shape, mediate, and respond to them, are altering our understandings of both oral history practice and feminist engagements with heritage formation and history.

Through a discussion of oral histories collected in Derry City, Northern Ireland in 2014, I argue that the new obligations of feminist oral history for practitioners are three-fold: to continue the tradition of shared meaning-making with narrators; to animate the notion that oral history's purpose and unique contribution to broader political discourse is to disturb and reveal ambivalence; and, finally, to create, share, and leverage digital products in ways that provide the most opportunity for diverse personal and political voices to, in the words of Deborah Withers, "create and reinvent intangible cultural heritage" to contribute to an array of important conversations.[6]

Alistair Thomson, Linda Shopes, Michael Frisch, Steven High, and Stacey Zembrzycki have illuminated critical shifts in the theory and practice of oral history, particularly in North America. Thomson states that transformations in oral history have always reflected "broader and wider historiographical and methodological shifts" as well as broader social change.[7] While he charts the history of the movement/field to the "digital revolution," Frisch, High, and Zembrzycki's work reflects how rapidly oral history has changed with the advent of digital technologies and the cultural, ontological, and epistemological transformations that have accompanied them. Linda Shopes cautions against linear and progressive historical understandings of oral history practice and argues for a move away from merely "collecting" and towards more intentional "curating."[8]

The postwar period saw emergent enthusiasm for oral sources and efforts to argue for their legitimacy for both archival and evidentiary purposes. Oral historians established methodological guidelines in the hope of capturing and amplifying the voices of elite citizens who played important roles in public, political, and economic life and "ordinary" people whose experiences were often overlooked in historical narratives of the era and thus disenfranchised and dislocated from the historical record.[9] Oral history was understood to mean specifically material that became part of that record—recorded, transcribed, and archived.

The rise of social change movements and developments in women's history, social history, subaltern studies, and public history in the 1970s and 1980s saw the next major transformation in oral history. Proponents reacted against empiricists critical of the methodology and derisive of subjective first-person accounts. Two things happened as a result. First, oral history struck out on its own as an explicitly multidisciplinary methodology, drawing tools and frameworks for assessment from anthropology, sociology, and social psychology. Like public history during this period, oral history ceased to be a subfield of history and became a field in its own right. Second, oral historians asserted the unique and valuable contributions of their field, arguing that memory was a strength to be celebrated instead of a weakness to be expunged from historicity. Indeed, they argued that memory's caprices were in many ways its strengths, "that the subjectivity of memory provided clues not only about the meanings of historical experience, but also about the relationships between past and present, between memory and personal identity, and between individual and collective memory."[10]

Alessandro Portelli's work on memory and oral history exemplifies the advances and contributions during this period, though his is not the only work to make the arguments that characterized paradigm transformation.[11] Portelli argued that acts, expressions, and performances of memory needed to be understood in their own right in relation to historical meaning-making and insisted that it was unproductive to continue to cast memory as history's delusional twin. He posited that memory served symbolic, psychological, and formal functions, thus illustrating the ways in which even memories deemed inaccurate or counter factual were actually rich in meaning and valuable in their own right:

> The discrepancy between fact and memory . . . is not caused by faulty recollections, but actively and creatively generated by memory and imagination in an effort to make sense of crucial events and of history in general . . . beyond the event as such, the real and significant historical fact which these narratives highlight is the memory itself.[12]

The third paradigm shift in oral history involved an intentional and direct engagement with politics as well as international and global partnerships and information sharing among oral historians. The explicitly political nature of much oral history practice during the 1980s and 1990s behooved interviewers to grapple with their own subjectivities and to include these machinations within their scholarly products and other oral history collections. Debates and discussions over the relationship between oral history and advocacy were shaped by the fact that "the center of gravity for oral history [was] moving away from Europe and America" to the "majority world," low and lower-middle income countries that comprise 75 per cent of the globe and have historically been negatively impacted by colonialism.[13]

The fourth paradigm transforming oral history to date has received much attention from oral historians. It is important to recognize that the "digital revolution" itself has undergone rapid change and oral historians' commentaries on the implications for our work have also changed. Less than a decade ago, Michael Frisch observed that one of the most significant implications of the digital revolution was of a systematic nature. The digital mode resulted in a collapse of categories of information because digitally "there is simply no difference between text, photographs, drawings and models, music and speech, and visual information; [they] can all be expressed as digital information that can be organized, searched, extracted and integrated with equal facility."[14] For Frisch, the other major shift was one of availability. Information was no longer accessed in a linear way—data ceased to correlate to a fixed point with clearly delimited avenues of access.[15] Technological change meant a changed technical working environment for oral historians, creating opportunities for the use of audio and video materials after the interview itself. Accessibility of the materials meant that researchers could "mark, assess, analyze, select and export" clips and passages for a variety of uses.[16] With the digital revolution, oral history was liberated from the transcript.

However, Thomson saw the technical shifts having significant cultural and scholarly corollaries, predicting deeper implications:

> [T]he medium is part of the message, and digital technologies are trans-
> forming so many aspects of our work as oral historians—and indeed the
> ways in which people remember and narrate their lives—that they will,
> over time, also change the way we think about memory and personal
> narrative, about telling and collecting life stories, about sharing memory
> and making histories.[17]

Steven High has outlined the cross-disciplinary possibilities of digital oral history and life story practice, arguing that new media can bring partners, colleagues, and participants into closer collaborative contact with one another to co-create meaning after the interview itself is over.[18] The digital revolution, he argued, does not simply change the product; it allows for a more intentional commitment to participatory and democratic processes even as it shifts focus away from the interview itself. Zembrzycki expanded on these ideas and implemented democratic participation in her community-based research on the Ukrainian communities of Sudbury, Canada; she created a website with the express goal of reaching out to those whom she had interviewed. This process allowed her "to create a virtual and evolving outlet where the sharing of stories (could) continue to take place."[19] For Zembrzycki, this marked the beginning of thinking about the possibilities digital technology and new media bring to our ethical responsibility to "make informed decisions that consider and ultimately respect the humanism that is at the heart of oral history."[20]

Key periods within feminist movements, long referred to as "waves," have found broad correlation in oral history's first three paradigm transformations, though periodization does not match neatly. As many have argued, reference to "waves" to discuss feminism's history may be unproductive for a variety of reasons. The waves metaphor makes gender *the* primary category of analysis, privileging a white, middle-class, Western movement and thus limiting and obscuring what Benita Roth calls "[f]eminisms that were plural and characterized by racial/ethnic organizational distinctiveness."[21] Other problems exist, beyond collapsing significant disharmonies between feminism and struggles organized and implemented by women against colonialism, racism, and their legacies. Historians such as Glenda Gilmore, Premilla Nadasen, and Eileen Boris have invited students of feminism to rethink the chronology itself as overly simplistic and exclusive of activities that may indeed be construed as part of a feminist project. Finally, the waves metaphor conceals the fluid, organic, and uneven work of feminism: "In these time-specific and narrowly focused accounts, the multidimensional aspects of feminism too often are excluded."[22] In the context of this study, however, the waves metaphor remains productive if problematic. The focus here returns again and again to key movement goals and projects as they relate to and otherwise parallel oral history and testimony; the problematic nature of the term "wave" itself is built into the arguments herein.

Dating to the 1848 Seneca Falls Convention, with origins in abolitionism and other reform movements, early feminism focused on making space for women in the public sphere, primarily through securing the right to vote. Just as oral history had served a largely additive function during its first major period, so feminism's first major period focused on broadcasting the contributions of women and arguing for their rightful roles as full citizens. If "mainstream" oral history during its first phase focused on collecting interviews of elites (often white men) but had a more radical element interested in broader stories, early feminism's mainstream platform was generally white and wealthy or middle class with a radical vanguard whose protests, hunger strikes, and other tactics were pivotal to the movement.

"Second-wave" feminism, also known as radical feminism or the women's liberation movement, dated from the 1960s to the 1990s and coalesced with the second and third major phases in oral history practice in important ways. As Charlotte Kroløkke and Anne Scott Sørensen recount, activist politics were central to this wave, which sought legislation granting women autonomy over their bodies and created women-centered spaces focused on empowerment.

Second-wave feminists produced slogans like, "'Sisterhood is powerful,' 'consciousness raising,' 'The personal is political,' 'the politics of housework,' the 'pro-woman line,' etc."[23]

Second-wave feminist oral historians embraced the idea that in speaking "for themselves," women could change the historical record because, quite simply, their everyday experiences *were* history.[24] While in retrospect, veteran Sherna Berger Gluck reported that she was "terribly embarrassed by the naïve assumptions of gender solidarity" that shaped the earliest thinking about the purpose of feminist oral history, the fact remains that additive work was necessary, that women's voices required inclusion, and that history itself was recast as a result. Claire Bond Potter reflected that "women and other marginalized groups had been overlooked or deliberately ignored by empirical practitioners in an earlier generation" and viewed social history, inspired by feminism, as a "grand corrective to dominant historical narratives skewed by such exclusions." She continued, "Feminism, we believed, *was* our ethical commitment to our subjects."[25] If early feminist oral history was unsuccessful at challenging race and class hierarchies, as veterans of the movement have suggested, it challenged both patriarchy and normative structures of knowledge production.[26]

Undoubtedly influenced by the work of their feminist colleagues, many oral historians explicitly rejected "objective" research on political as well as epistemological grounds. Second-wave feminists, especially feminist oral historians, shaped an entire generation of scholars who began to question the assumptions on which empiricism was built, though the debate seems to be a chicken/egg one. Some activist scholars argued that second-wave feminism itself emerged as a reaction against the idea that value-free and "objective" knowledge was anything other than "andocentric."[27] As politics became more deeply implicated in scholarship, feminist scholars extolled, instead of merely justifying, methodologies that embraced the subjective. As Stanley and Wise put it:

> We reject the idea that scientists, or feminists, can become experts in other peoples' lives. And we reject the belief that there is one true reality to become experts about. We feel that feminism's present renaissance has come about precisely because many women have rejected other people's (men's) interpretations of our lives.[28]

Even as the third wave of feminism emerged in the 1990s, Gluck insisted that the work of feminist oral history had to continue its efforts to "recover, recover, recover."[29] She and other feminist oral historians, in keeping with the paradigm transformations in oral history more broadly, began to work globally and to see international oral history and international feminist activism as deeply intertwined.

In the meantime, third wavers focused on querying essentialist notions of both the feminine and feminism, moved towards feminism as a commitment to intersectionality, and insisted on boisterousness and playfulness as a rejection of the pieties of the second-wavers who had earned them the right to assert themselves on their own terms.[30] According to Kroløkke and Sørensen, "third-wave feminists are motivated by the need to develop a feminist theory and politics that honor contradictory experiences and deconstruct categorical thinking."[31] Third-wave feminism's contributions to oral history might be best summed up by Tamar Carroll, who noted, "Feminist oral history shares with feminist activism more broadly the disruptive potential to upset oppressive dichotomies such as public/private and good girl/bad girl."[32]

The effects of these tendencies can be seen in the theoretical sophistication that marked reflections in feminist oral history during the same period. As Gluck and Armitage reflected on the state of the field in 1998, the complexities of oral history performance were of central concern. Explicitly rejecting the notion of an unmediated interview, Gluck declared the notion that informants should "speak for themselves" to be a disingenuous position:

> If we believe that the narrative is a partial story, is a representation and is governed by a host of complicated determinants, then I think we have an obligation to contextualize and historicize.[33]

These questions about situatedness, the incompleteness of the oral history performance, and the ethical responsibilities to both narrators and to the historical record in an era, point to new paradigm transformations in oral history and feminism, which cannot be untangled from digital culture. The "digital revolution" that marked a major shift in oral history practice has also reshaped feminism, symbolizing a fifth paradigm transformation in oral history practice and, arguably, a fourth wave in feminism.

As Nancy Thumin has argued, digital culture is marked by porous "analytic boundaries between production, text and reception."[34] In ways that would have been unthinkable even a decade ago, people have the power to create, share, and evaluate an exhaustive array of digital subjective/first-person expressions on a variety of platforms. From comment sections to video blogs to Twitter feeds to Facebook profiles to the StoryCorps app to anonymous crowd-sourcing of everything from secrets to text messages, our capacity to produce, consume, and rebroadcast ordinary and extraordinary accounts from across the street to around the globe has exploded. Just as significantly, the speed with which information is disseminated and then replaced by new stories confounds efforts to consume and process them.

The self-produced narratives that have marked digital culture are simultaneously ubiquitous and disposable, intimate and public, remarkable in their departure from earlier forms of self-representation and yet utterly forgettable, centered around claims to authenticity and, paradoxically, rarely verifiable. As communications and digital media scholars have noted, genres of self-representation are premised on expectations of authenticity and are read through the lens of implicit understandings that productions are inherently socially (not politically or commercially) motivated.[35] At the same time, journalist Jeremy Garner reminds us that these representations and productions exist within a field of cultural production wherein social positions are constantly evaluated and negotiated according to cultural and social norms that condition how we respond.[36] He states:

> Now, for the first time, one's sense of belonging is externally documented, expressed and graded on an ongoing basis in the form of tweets, posts, pins, comments and other shares . . . these digital expressions are immediately sorted and categorized. Some are popular, celebrated and accepted . . . (they) can also be rejected, dismissed or called into question by a suspicious, distrustful audience. Or they can be condemned to remain pedestrian, unremarkable and average . . .[37]

As digital communication technologies change, communications scholar Adi Kuntsman urges us to consider the effects of "reverberation—not only the movement of emotions and feelings in and out of cyberspace through bodies, texts, psyches and machines," but also the "multiplicity of effects of this movement might entail."[38] The new wave of feminism might best be understood as a series of engagements with reverberation in digital culture. Feminist self-representations, political activism, social media campaigns, feminist performance art, and hashtag activism illustrate how digital culture has reconceived the movement as something fragmented and diffuse, framed by and through digital culture. As Deborah Withers points out, feminism itself operates generationally according to modes of transmission of its own inheritances; an already scattered process of transmission grows ever more complex.[39]

Oral historian Linda Shopes pointed to some of the issues confronting oral history in this era of self-representation when she recommended that we plan for and frame oral history projects intentionally "to curate instead of to collect."[40] Shopes was talking specifically about the hundreds of thousands of oral histories already collected, but she could have been referring to the broader culture of subjective self-representation when she asserted:

> While an oral history interview is indeed individual and deeply personal, history as lived and written isn't. It's relational, it's social; and part of our job, I submit, is to make clear the connections between the "I" of the interview and the "we" of the rest of the world.[41]

For feminist oral historians, the politics of transmission have changed radically. It might be tempting to suggest that the work has run its course, that feminism itself as it is currently constituted is dedicated to the kinds of representations, inclusions, and complications that once were the purview of feminist oral historians. Indeed, oral history's longstanding purpose of "giving people a voice" has lost meaning in the chorus of individual voices telling their own stories. Self-representation is now central to the ways we narrate, create, and negotiate meaning and identity and to the ways we seek, understand, and evaluate authenticity.

Yet, our work is not done, especially if we maintain that "the stories, the narratives of individual lives, in the end . . . are the source of oral history's particular power, neither as document nor text for scholarly assessment, but as a medium for public engagement with the past."[42] As Sheftel and Zembrzycki point out, the ethical, scholarly, political, and community expectations of and demands for oral history are in constant flux, pulling oral historians in multiple directions at the same time.[43] Our work must commit to tracing and querying the fault lines between public and private, to testing the façade of authenticity, always insisting that narratives have consequences, even, perhaps especially, unintended ones. In a world fuelled by discourse, feminist oral history must continue the tradition of shared meaning-making with narrators. It must animate, and indeed complicate, the notion that oral history's purpose and unique contribution to broader political discourse is its power to disturb, to reveal ambivalence, and to highlight memory as a search for meaning without according innocence to that process.[44] Finally, we need to create, share, and leverage digital products in ways that provide the most opportunity for diverse personal and political voices to contribute to important conversations.

In 2014, I conducted oral history interviews in Derry City, Northern Ireland, with women over 65 in an effort to glimpse their mothers' worlds. Irish historiography, especially Northern Irish historiography, is still fairly quiet on the subject of women's cultural and social history, and little research has been done on women in the 1920s and 1930s—the period when the mothers of the women I was interviewing were young. I research the construction of historical consciousness from the turn of the 20th century until 1969 and I have struggled with the gendered nature of memory work, found few women's voices in my non-oral sources and also sought insight into the ways those who came of age at the beginning of the Troubles—the 35-year period of civil conflict beginning in 1969—received or inherited a sense of history.

My narrators were more than sources. We each brought very different senses of history to our conversations. My sense of history was an acquired one, the result of a decade of research as an outsider; it was also in many ways a public sense of history because of the nature of my access and the scholarly questions I brought to my work. Theirs, on the other hand, was a reflexive history—one they carried and lived through, but did not necessarily reflect critically on. It was also an intimate history, private, contained, and rarely shared. The twinned processes of co-creation and co-curation of meaning, through questions posed and questions answered, offered insights about history and memory in Northern Ireland that otherwise would have remained unconsidered.

A telling example is the transmission of values and memory through Catholic religious practices. Many Catholic women in Derry remember their mother's being "churched"—that is, barred from going to mass or receiving sacraments after giving birth on the grounds that they were seen as impure in the eyes of God until a service of purification took place. Another compelling issue is the history of single motherhood in Ireland and the ways the Catholic Church shamed unmarried pregnant women and separated children from their mothers. At the same time, my research suggested that the Catholic Church was a critical site of memory and a crucible for building and sustaining identity for Northern Catholics after Partition, the division of Ireland in 1921. These issues were opaque and positions could hardly be considered clear.

My interviews revealed something fascinating. If the textbooks present an unbending and often inhumane Catholicism, women themselves remember their mothers having a much more instrumental relationship with their faith and with Church authority figures. Maeve McCuigan described the evening ritual of gathering around after her prayers as her mother read from *The Book of Saints*:

> Well, I thought she would read from it. But it would be, "St. Teresa was born and she was this lovely little girl. And she was very good to her mammy and all of this." So, she just told us stories and I thought they were in this book. When my mother died, I got this book, *The Lives of the Saints*. Teresa, born, such and such a date. Died. Venerated at Lisieux. I mean. So. She just told us stories and I thought they were all in this book. And I was dying to get this book.[45]

Church doctrine might have dictated some of the rituals that formed the architecture of family life, but it did not penetrate as deeply as one might assume. Improvisation was an integral part of Catholic cultural life. It is important to note that for Maeve, storytelling was just as much a part of her inheritance and her identity. In explaining her mother's penchant for making up her own "stories of the saints," Maeve took us back to Donegal, to the family homestead where she spent summers as a child. Specifically, she talked about gatherings of neighbors:

> It was known as a "ceili" house. "Ceili" means together. So people would come and tell stories and yarns and all that. We of course were sent off to bed. But, my great aunt always left a mattress on the floor and that kept the door open. So we would lie down and listen to these stories. So, I mean, becoming, late in life, a storyteller, it was just natural. I could see where my mother got that from.[46]

Pamela Kelly looked back and considered the intrusiveness of the Church:

> The nuns had the funniest way of getting news out of the young ones. They'd always ask them at school to stand up on the Monday and tell what was happening at home, and that was how they'd find out everything.[47]

At the same time, Kelly explained that there were issues around which the resolve of the Church came up against an equally potent determination in the community. The most sensitive issue may have been unplanned pregnancies by unmarried young women. While in much of Ireland, young women were sent away to convents and worked through their pregnancy, gave birth, and allowed their children to be adopted out through programs run by the convents, Derry seemed to be an anomaly. There was only one such convent in the northwest. When I asked Pamela Kelly to confirm that Derry families were not willing to let their daughters go, her response was adamant, "Not at all. Absolutely not. They kept them within the family."[48] She joked that as a child she thought there was the "biggest epidemic of appendicitis in Derry," because girls seemed to be forever coming down with that particular ailment, not to be seen for several months:

> I remember one particular girl. I was probably 15, she might have been just a little older. I'd never seen her standing up for months. They had a working table and there was a chair behind that. And she sat there. She just sat there. That was her form of, you know what I mean?[49]

Pamela Kelly's reflections on children born to Catholic women outside of marriage suggest shame, some kind of "punishment," and a desire to shield family members from the physical and emotional trauma many Irish women experienced in homes for pregnant women and their children. A comparison with Facebook comments on a page dedicated to the history of the Good Shepherd Mother and Baby Home in Tuam, County Galway, is instructive. Local historian Catherine Corless engaged in a long, tedious process of determining how many babies and children died there between 1925 and 1961. The project began in an attempt to erect a plaque for an unmarked gravesite on the grounds of the former home run by the Bon Secours order. Looking to name the children, Corless expected to find a few. The county registrar came back with 796 death certificates. The historian cross-referenced the list of dead children with many area cemeteries. None of the names appeared, raising the question of where the bodies were buried. Further investigation revealed that the gravesite was not the only burial ground at the home; in the 1970s, bones had been discovered onsite, the story silenced. Corless developed a public Facebook page associated with her research.[50]

Comments there reveal the raw and unresolved nature of memories surrounding the Tuam site and others like it. Margaret Baxter O'Reilly wrote in response to a post by her sister, who was born at Tuam:

> You tell them how it really was, sis, of the horrendous abuse and torture in that hell hole. It was that bad our mother took the secrets of you and her to her grave And suffered more. Than most. (sic) Hope those animals who ran that place rot in HELL.[51]

Rosie Rodgers wrote:

> It looks just like a prison which it was, my sister was there up until she
> was seven and by the looks of things she may well have been among the
> last of the children there as it closed in 1961 . . . my adopted mother said
> she was starved and scared with very little hair, she became quite hardy
> from plenty of fresh cow's milk, and turned into a lovely woman.[52]

It is difficult to find and make meaning from the self-representations presented
in these extracts. They are deeply personal and emotive, and they tell the story
of two women "in their own words." At the same time, it is almost impossible
to determine what influenced their telling. Was it the reverberations of stories,
images, and news articles about the Tuam scandal? The film *Philomena*, which
told a very similar story and had been in theaters just a few months earlier?
How are we to represent Rosie's and Margaret's experiences outside of any
context, bereft of any relationship?

   Another issue that seemed impossible to examine through traditional sources
had to do with the day-to-day issues of male unemployment and family poverty.
While oral histories conducted in the 1980s provided ample evidence of both
of these issues, there were few interviews that talked specifically about women's
responses. I was curious, though, because ample ghost stories seemed to
address this. While I have argued elsewhere that many Derry ghost stories
originating in the 1920s and 1930s held within them an array of preoccupations,
concerns, and lessons, I was curious if stories held in memory were similar. For
example, in the tale of the "haunting on Wellington Street," a family with
many children saw the unexpected death of their mother. The family's eldest
daughter, Mary, had to take responsibility for caring for the younger children;
her father was little help as he had begun to drink heavily and was rarely home.
The ghost of the mother appeared regularly, and continued to have a presence
compelling enough to convince Mary's father to go to his priest, who suggested
that the wife could not rest in peace since she worried that her children were
not being looked after properly. So, the father took the pledge, swearing not
to drink again. The mother's ghost never returned.[53]

   When Maeve told the story of her family's arrival in Derry City from their
home in Donegal, themes of poverty, alcoholism, and family blended with a
kind of memorial solidarity. She told of her grandfather's pub on the Lecky
Road in Derry's Catholic neighborhood, just a few blocks from the Wellington
Street described in the ghost story:

> Actually, he bought a pub here, in the Lecky Road and it was open and
> they lived above it and it was very busy one night. And they asked my
> grandmother to come down. And a docker came in and he put his wages
> on the counter and he said, "Throw me out when that's finished."
> And my grandmother said, "Go home to your wife. I'll keep the money."

She took the money and she brought it to his wife. And then she came home and she said to my grandfather, "We're not, I'm not going to be in a business that deprives a woman of the money to feed her children." So they left, then.[54]

As a cultural historian seeking to understand the ways memory operates over time in a community which for so long had little recourse to official, legitimized forms of history-making and therefore relied on memory to produce and nurture historical consciousness, the parallels between the oral history account of alcoholism, its effects on family life, and the ways women acted as moral authority are fascinating.

For the purposes outlined in this chapter, they are equally compelling. These stories do not simply write women "back into" Northern Irish history, although they certainly do that. Nor do they provide an easy antidote to the self-curated, often self-centered representations of lives and experiences produced and consumed as a part of digital culture—although, once more, they are far more detailed, thoughtful, and evocative than most Twitter confessions. Instead, they reveal the ways we construct meaning and identity both through what we remember and through how we speak about it. The telling matters. In this way, they bridge the distance between public and private, creating a co-curated history with the feminist oral historian that allows for broader *and* deeper public engagements with the past and the ways it continues to shape us.

In this sense, my student Caroline Correia's reflections make a compelling case for contemporary feminist oral history as something separate from—though interwoven with—both feminism and oral history. Moving forward, feminist oral history must be understood as a practice as much as a stance, and *as a way through* as opposed to simply an opening into silenced, marginalized, contested, depoliticized, and otherwise disempowered narratives. By utilizing an array of digital spaces and embracing the democratic possibilities of social media while maintaining focus on *how* we tell stories and construct meaning together, feminist oral historians stand poised to amplify their own work while inserting an important counterpoint to the shape and tenor of the curated narrative self-representations that proliferate in social media and other digital platforms.

Notes

1 Anna Sheftel and Stacey Zembrzycki, eds., *Oral History Off the Record: Toward an Ethnography of Practice* (New York: Palgrave Macmillan, 2013).
2 Margo Shea, "Margo Shea's Facebook Page," accessed 25 January 2014, https://www.facebook.com/margo.shea.3/posts/10151884032831444.
3 Carl Becker, "Everyman His Own Historian," *American Historical Review* 37, no. 2 (January 1932): 221–236.
4 Caroline Correia, "Margo Shea's Facebook Page," accessed 25 January 2014, www.facebook.com/emmclaughlin2/posts/10204959895257369.
5 Correia, www.facebook.com/emmclaughlin2/posts/10204959895257369.

6 Deborah Withers, "Deborah Withers," International Network for the Theory of History, accessed 30 October 2015, www.inth.ugent.be/directory-of-researchers/deborah-withers/.

7 Alistair Thomson, "Four Paradigm Transformations in Oral History," *Oral History Review* 34, no. 1 (Winter–Spring 2007): 50.

8 Linda Shopes, "Insights and Oversights": Reflections on the Documentary Tradition and the Theoretical Turn in Oral History," *Oral History Review* 41, no. 2 (Summer/Fall 2014): 257–268.

9 Thomson, 7.

10 Thomson, 54.

11 As Linda Shopes reminds us, archivist William Moss certainly pre-dated Alessandro Portelli in his own observations that memory was as much about selection, emphasis, and, indeed, forgetting. See William Moss, "Oral History: An Appreciation," in *Oral History: An Interdisciplinary Anthology*, eds. David K. Dunaway and Willa K. Baum (Nashville: American Association for State and Local History, 1984), 91, 93, 97, as cited in Shopes, 259.

12 Alessandro Portelli, *The Death of Luigi Trastulli and Other Stories: Form and Meaning in Oral History* (Albany: SUNY Press, 1991), 26.

13 Thomson, 66–67.

14 Michael Frisch, "Oral History and the Digital Revolution," in *The Oral History Reader*, eds. Robert Perks and Alistair Thomson (New York: Routledge 2006), 103.

15 Frisch, 103.

16 Frisch, 103–104.

17 Thomson, 70.

18 Steven High, "Telling Stories: A Reflection on Oral History and New Media," *Oral History* 38, no. 1 (Spring 2010): 102.

19 Stacey Zembrzycki, "Bringing Stories to Life: Using New Media to Disseminate and Critically Engage with Oral History Interviews," *Oral History* 41, no. 1 (Spring 2013): 103.

20 Zembrzycki, 106.

21 Kathleen A. Laughlin et al., "Is It Time to Jump Ship? Historians Rethink the Waves Metaphor," *Feminist Formations* 22, no. 1 (Spring 2010): 78.

22 Laughlin et al., 82.

23 Charlotte Krølokke and Anne Scott Sørensen, "Three Waves of Feminism: From Suffragettes to Grrls," in *Gender Communication Theories & Analyses: From Silence to Performance*, eds. Charlotte Krølokke and Anne Scott Sørensen (Thousand Oaks: Sage Publications 2006), 9.

24 Sherna Gluck, "What's So Special About Women? Women's Oral History," *Frontiers: A Journal of Women Studies* 2, no. 2 (1977): 3.

25 Claire Bond Potter and Renee C. Romano, "When Radical Feminism Talks Back: Taking an Ethnographic Turn in the Living Past," in *Doing Recent History: On Privacy, Copyright, Video Games, Institutional Review Boards, Activist Scholarship, and History*, eds. Claire Bond Potter and Renee C. Romano (Athens: University of Georgia Press, 2012), 156.

26 Sherna Berger Gluck, "Has Feminist Oral History Lost Its Radical/Subversive Edge?" *Oral History* 39, no. 2 (2011): 65.

27 Susan Geiger, "Women's Life Histories: Method and Content," *Signs* 11 (1986): 338, as cited in Valerie Yow, "Do I Like Them Too Much? Effects of the Oral History Interview on the Interviewer and Vice Versa," in *The Oral History Reader*, 61.

28 Liz Stanley and Sue Wise, "Back into the Personal or Our Attempt to Construct Feminist Research," in *Theories of Women's Studies*, eds. Gloria Bowles and Renate Duelli Kein (London: Routledge, 1983), 193–194.

29 Susan Armitage and Sherna Berger Gluck, "Reflecting on Women's Oral History: An Exchange," in *Women's Oral History: The Frontiers Reader*, eds. Susan Hodge Armitage, Patricia Hart, and Karen Weathermon (Lincoln: University of Nebraska Press, 2002), 79.
30 Kr6løkke and Sørensen, 15.
31 Krøløkke and Sørensen, 16.
32 Tamar Carroll, email correspondence with Sherna Berger Gluck, 21 January 2010, cited in Gluck, "Has Feminist Oral History Lost Its Radical/Subversive Edge?," 70.
33 Armitage and Gluck, 80.
34 Nancy Thumin, *Self-Representation and Digital Culture* (New York: Palgrave Macmillan, 2012), 15.
35 See Amy Shields Dobson, *Postfeminist Digital Cultures: Femininity, Social Media and Self-Representation* (New York: Palgrave Macmillan, 2015).
36 In *The Field of Cultural Production* (New York: Columbia, 1993), Pierre Bourdieu developed the idea of the field to bridge ideas of agency and structure.
37 Jeremy Garner, "How Our Digital Lives Are Impacting Our Shifting Sense of Belonging," last modified 2 June 2014, www.12ahead.com/how-our-digital-lives-are-impacting-our-shifting-sense-belonging.
38 Athina Karatzogianni and Adi Kuntsman, eds., *Digital Cultures and the Politics of Emotion: Feelings, Affect and Technological Change* (New York: Palgrave Macmillan 2012), 1–2.
39 Deborah Withers, *Feminism, Digital Culture and the Politics of Transmission: Theory, Practice and Cultural Heritage* (London: Rowman and Littlefield, 2015), 11.
40 Andrew Shaffer and Linda Shopes, "Reflections on the Urge to Collect," Oxford University Press Blog, last modified 6 March 2015, http://blog.oup.com/2015/03/linda-shopes-oral-history-curation/.
41 Shaffer and Shopes.
42 Shaffer and Shopes.
43 Anna Sheftel and Stacey Zembrzycki, "Who's Afraid of Oral History? Fifty Years of Debates and Anxiety About Ethics," *Oral History Review* 43, no. 2 (Summer/Fall 2017): 338–366.
44 Some of these ideas emerged in a lecture by Alessandro Portelli, "Riley Fellowship Lecture: On the Uses of Memory," last modified 15 October 2015, www.youtube.com/watch?v=X0PJsPGqU8I.
45 "Maeve McCuigan" (real name changed to a pseudonym), interview with author, Derry, Northern Ireland, 20 June 2014.
46 McCuigan, interview.
47 Pamela Kelly (real name used with permission), interview with author, Derry, Northern Ireland, 26 June 2014.
48 Kelly, interview.
49 Kelly, interview.
50 "Mother Baby Home Research," accessed 20 November 2015, www.facebook.com/MotherBaby-Home-Research-1381096678815670/.
51 Margaret Baxter O'Reilly, Facebook comment, 26 July 2014, accessed 20 November 2015, www.facebook.com/MotherBaby-Home-Research-1381096678815670/.
52 Rosie Rodgers, Facebook comment, 25 May 2014, accessed 20 November 2015, www.facebook.com/MotherBaby-Home-Research-1381096678815670/.
53 Jenni Doherty, *Yarns and Stories* (Derry: Guildhall Press, 1994).
54 McCuigan, interview.

22 The medium is political and the message is personal

Feminist oral histories online

Mary A. Larson

When *Women's Words* was published over 25 years ago, personal computers were fairly new and the World Wide Web was less than a year old. The terrain for oral history research and dissemination has shifted significantly since then, making it incumbent on us to revisit questions central to feminist oral history practices through this particular frame. Since multimedia, online presentations became possible in the mid-1990s, there have been ongoing discussions within the oral history community about the ethics of placing interviews online and disseminating them in ways that chroniclers could not have envisioned at the time of their interviews. These conversations are even more important when discussing feminist oral histories, given the way that women's words have previously been silenced/ignored, interpreted/misinterpreted, appropriated/misappropriated, and otherwise mediated.

An active subset of oral historians has tried to use evolving digital technologies to address a number of issues that were originally raised in the chapters of *Women's Words*, including but not limited to the mediation of women's voices; concerns about inadequate representation of the oral history performance; and the inability to make meaning from uncontextualized interviews. Some of these efforts have been successful, while others are still largely unrealized. There also remain serious, unasked questions about the changing nature of media and mediation and how those concepts interface with activism in politicized online platforms. This chapter discusses both the attempts made to solve problems identified by feminist oral historians and those unraised questions that need to be brought to the forefront.

An early feminist (and more generally activist) slogan, "the personal is political", frames this chapter.[1] While we learned in the late 1960s and early 1970s that the personal was, in fact, political, this chapter discusses how the political is also personal when it comes to feminist oral histories and their online dissemination. Although women's words can be politicized when they are placed online, they also represent personal stories as they are pushed out into that very public sphere. These words may embody the problems of the collective, certainly, but they also belong to specific women and their individual contexts, and as feminist oral historians it is important not to lose sight of those personal considerations in our larger efforts to ensure that women's voices and their particular words are heard.[2]

We must start with an understanding of how putting feminist histories online is a political act, even if their content is not overtly activist. In her essay in *Women's Words*, Kristina Minister posed the question, "Why is it that many North American and British women are not used to speaking in public? Feminist research points to the cause: postagrarian culture has assigned women to the private sphere."[3] With that consideration in mind, feminist oral histories themselves represented a political act, as women broke into the public arena to tell their stories. I would argue, though, that another layer of politicization is added when these voices are amplified online, due in part to the nature and origins of the Internet itself.

At the beginning of the 1990s, cyberfeminists were among the first to critically assess the potential of networked cyberspace. While they were optimistic about the liberating possibilities that online communities could offer, the Internet in its early years was not as welcoming to women as they might have hoped.[4] Explanations have pointed to the sociocultural scaffolding on which the Internet was built. As Virginia Barratt observed, "The techno-logical landscape was . . . uncritical and overwhelmingly male-dominated. It was a masculinist space, coded as such, and the gatekeepers of the code (cultural and logos) maintained control of the productions of technology."[5]

Given that the Internet was largely designed by men and many of the assumptions we may make about its platforms and appropriate uses are informed by that original infrastructure, what, then, could be more political than to use it as a means of dissemination for feminist oral histories? Women's voices are being highlighted not just in a public sphere, but in perhaps *the most* public sphere, using as amplification a tool that was not designed with them in mind. Using the medium of the Internet, in this case, is almost certainly political by its very nature.[6] There is also the consideration that feminist oral history privileges the voices of an under-documented/marginalized group, in terms of historical narrative particularly, which makes online speech additionally subversive.

Another political issue that concerned some of the authors of *Women's Words* was the mediation of women's voices, particularly in the form of transcripts, which inadequately represent the fullness of actual interviews.[7] After all, women's words had been misconstrued, mistranslated, and misrepresented for years, and written transcripts had the potential to do this yet again, either through sins of overt commission or covert omission. Text versions left out nuances, pauses, and other audio (and video) signifiers that could help someone better understand what a woman was trying to express. Kathryn Anderson and Dana Jack called attention to this specifically when they noted: "Those aspects of live interviews unavailable in a written text—the pauses, the laughter—all invite us to explore their meaning for the narrator."[8] Gwendolyn Etter-Lewis noted the importance of speech patterns and how they can "reveal status, interpersonal relationships, and perceptions of language, self, and the world."[9] It is unlikely that anyone would be able to read any of those cues from a standard written transcript. Evolving digital technology, however, has made it increasingly easy to put full audio online (and video as well, if one has the bandwidth and storage). This capacity to present original recordings rather than just transcripts gives listeners and viewers the opportunity to better understand these oral histories, as the sarcasm or uncertainty in a speaker's voice, for instance, can change how we make meaning from an interview. This shift is something that new technologies have enabled. We are not just seeing textual representations of women's words, we are able to hear them in the voices of the women themselves. This is a significant change in the level of mediation inherent in the presentation of oral histories.

Digital formats have also allowed us to address another concern, both political and personal, that was raised in *Women's Words*—the potentially negative effects of uncontextualized (or under-contextualized) interviews.[10] Just as a transcript only represents one aspect of an interview, so, too, does any oral history recording, regardless of medium. While audio and video provide additional layers of information relative to a written version, there are those who would argue that the interview is still incompletely represented. Two aspects of an oral history remain undocumented in many instances: the specific context of the oral history event itself, which I would argue falls more in the personal than political realm; and the larger cultural context, which tends more to the political. David Dunaway was an early advocate for understanding an oral history as an event or performance, carried out at a precise time for a particular audience in a specific venue.[11] The issue of audience is complex, since a chronicler likely chose their words in response to at least two audiences—the interviewer as well as a wider perceived audience, which might have included people physically in attendance or the "ghostly audience" of future listeners/viewers.[12]

While the smaller-scale, personal context of an oral history event is important for our understanding of an interview, the larger cultural and political context is equally crucial. Knowing what community a woman came from and understanding that community's culture, acknowledging her class and educational background, and recognizing the political circumstances of the time enable us to grasp an interview in a fuller context. Indeed, Alexander Freund argues that this rich situatedness may be one of the things that distinguishes oral history from the recent enthusiasm for storytelling, noting the problematic nature of apolitical, non-contextualized stories (such as those broadcast weekly by StoryCorps), as opposed to the more heavily documented oral histories that we hope to produce.[13]

The question is, how do we address the lack of information—both for the specific, performance-related context and the larger, more encompassing cultural and political context? While some of these details could have been addressed earlier in transcript notes, more often than not they remained undocumented. The presentation of material online, though, allows linked documents, images, and other information to be unobtrusively appended to complete recordings, transcripts, or other representations of an interview. "Project Jukebox", which began in the early 1990s at the University of Alaska Fairbanks and was one of the first digital oral history undertakings, worked closely with communities to provide context statements with its oral histories, along with slideshows, linked maps, and scanned historical materials that helped to build a robust framework for understanding the oral histories and cultural settings presented.[14] More recent projects such as Anne Valk's and Holly Ewald's collaborative community documentation of Rhode Island's "Mashapaug Pond", which has a methodology grounded in feminist sensibilities, have developed context in other ways, disseminating oral histories in a researcher-friendly database while also enhancing and interpreting interviews through a number of different public manifestations, including online exhibits, audio tours, and on-site installations.[15]

Something that *Women's Words* did not address because it was not a consideration at the time was the question of whether oral histories should be put online. Now part of a much larger conversation in oral history, many of the more general aspects of that issue have been addressed, although not necessarily resolved, elsewhere.[16] For feminist oral histories, however, that decision necessarily involves balancing the personal and political. As oral historians, we tend to develop trusting relationships with chroniclers, and our impulse is to act in what we believe to be their best personal interests. This sense of responsibility is reflected in the many conference-based conversations over what to do when a chronicler wants their interview disseminated online but an oral historian feels it might be damaging to that person.[17] While we are used to thinking about this from the standpoint of an interviewee's personal concerns, we have to understand that someone's reasons for wanting their oral history placed online may be political rather than (or as well as) personal. If they are willing to get past their own discomfort in order to make a political point, the principle needs to be respected by the oral historian curating the material, either online or in an archive. Conversely, we may think that certain interviews need to be placed online to provide viewers with a fuller political context, but when a chronicler is reluctant to do so for personal reasons we need to allow them to privilege those reasons. In either case, it requires oral historians to recognize that their chroniclers may be operating from both political and personal considerations.[18]

Finally, we need to mention the 800-pound gorilla in the room—the digital divide. There is a feminist impulse toward democracy and inclusion, but there are large numbers of women internationally who are not online. That may be by choice, since not everyone sees the utility of engaging with technology in this way, but in many cases, it is due to a lack of access. Before we congratulate ourselves too heartily on the global span that our online oral histories have (or potentially will have), we need to recognize that the audiences we are reaching are more limited than we like to think, and probably more privileged. Recent figures indicate that only about 30 per cent of the world's population has the capacity to merge onto the information superhighway, and considering that women around the world tend to be politically and economically disadvantaged, it is fair to assume that those who do have access (or are creating content) are disproportionately male.[19] While it is very important to do the work that feminist oral historians do—negotiating with communities, collaborating with chroniclers, and amplifying voices online—we have to recognize that our reach, however good our intentions, is limited. Because of that, though, it may be even more crucial that we get it right and work with women to make sure that their voices are amplified, honored, and appropriately presented.

Digital technology has provided new ways of reaching many of the goals that feminist oral history has set for itself. It is now easier to collaborate, hold researchers accountable for the work they do with communities, and offer more holistic oral histories through contextualization. On the other hand, that same technology has opened the door to online bullying, gendertrolling, and real-life threats against women. Like the cyberfeminists of the early 1990s, we have to be critical in our assessment of these tools, ever vigilant for the downside while celebrating those aspects of cybercommunication that will allow us to better document and disseminate women's words for the next 25 years.

Notes

1 The title of a Carol Hanisch essay first widely published in 1970, the phrase became shorthand for the understanding that the personal struggles of individual women were really the political struggles of women as a collective: "The Personal Is Political," in *Notes from the Second Year: Women's Liberation*, ed. Shulamith Firestone (New York: New York Radical Women, 1970), 76–77.

2 For a discussion of collective versus individual emphases in oral histories with feminists, see Margaretta Jolly, Polly Russell, and Rachel Cohen, "Sisterhood and After: Individualism, Ethics and an Oral History of the Women's Liberation Movement," *Social Movement Studies: Journal of Social, Cultural and Political Protest* 11, no. 2 (2012): 211–226.

3 Kristina Minister, "A Feminist Frame for the Oral History Interview," in *Women's Words: The Feminist Practice of Oral History*, eds. Sherna Berger Gluck and Daphne Patai (New York: Routledge, 1991), 29.

4 It is arguable that not much has changed, as the anonymity that cyberfeminists initially hoped would empower them has also empowered the misogynistic perspectives evident in Gamergate and gendertrolling more generally. See Jessica Megarry, "Online Incivility or Sexual Harrassment? Conceptualising Women's Experiences in the Digital Age," *Women's Studies International Forum* 47, no. A (November–December 2014): 46–55; Karla Mantilla, "Gendertrolling Misogyny Adapts to New Media," *Feminist Studies* 39, no. 2 (2013): 563–573.

5 Claire L. Evans, "An Oral History of the First Cyberfeminists," *Motherboard* (blog), last modified 11 December 2014, http://motherboard.vice.com/read/an-oral-history-of-the-first-cyberfeminists-vns-matrix. Also see Rachel Wexelbaum, "Introduction," in *Queers Online: LGBT Digital Practices in Libraries, Archives, and Museums*, ed. Rachel Wexelbaum (Sacramento: Litwin Books, 2015), 7.

6 Curiously, there is little written on this topic. While there is an emphasis in scholarship on issues like networked feminism, cyberactivism on organizational levels, and the politicization of social media, discussion about the political impli-

cations of the individualized act of having one's voice posted online as opposed to the collective voice, which is very much a part of Hansich's original essay, does not exist. For more on collective versus individual identity in activist contexts see Stacey Sowards and Valerie Renegar, "Reconceptualizing Rhetorical Activism in Contemporary Feminist Contexts," *The Howard Journal of Communications* 17 (2006): 57–74.

7   On format mediation, see Mary Larson, "'The Medium is the Message': Oral History, Media, and Mediation," *Oral History Review* 43, no. 2 (Summer/Fall 2016): 318–337.
8   Kathryn Anderson and Dana C. Jack, "Learning to Listen: Interview Techniques and Analyses," in *Women's Words*, 23.
9   Gwendolyn Etter-Lewis, "Black Women's Life Stories: Reclaiming Self in Narrative Texts," in *Women's Words*, 44.
10 Sherna Berger Gluck and Daphne Patai, "Introduction to Language and Communication," in *Women's Words*, 9; Gluck and Patai, "Introduction to Authority and Interpretation," in *Women's Words*, 61–62; Etter-Lewis, 44.
11 David Dunaway, "Transcription: Shadow or Reality?" *Oral History Review* 12 (1984): 113–117.
12 Minister, 29. For another discussion on the complexities of audience and contextualization, see Heather Howard's chapter in this volume (Chapter 25).
13 Alexander Freund, "Under Storytelling's Spell? Oral History in a Neoliberal Age," *Oral History Review* 42, no. 1 (Winter/Spring 2015): 96–132.
14 "Project Jukebox Projects," University of Alaska Fairbanks, accessed 1 December 2015, http://jukebox.uaf.edu/site7/all-projects.
15 "Mashapaug Pond," Brown University, accessed 3 December 2015, www.brown.edu/academics/public-humanities/initiatives/mashapaug-pond. Not all scholars agree, however, on the relationship between oral history contextualization and digital technology. See Anna Sheftel and Stacey Zembrzycki, "Slowing Down to Listen in the Digital Age: How New Technology is Changing Oral History Practice," *Oral History Review* 44, no. 1 (Winter/Spring 2017): 94–112.
16 For a recent overview, see Mary Larson, "Steering Clear of the Rocks: Ethics and Oral History," *Oral History Review* 40, no. 1 (Winter/Spring 2013): 36–49. Most oral historians are aware of the ethical care required when putting interviews online. Current conversations tend to revolve around *which* oral histories could be made publicly available online (and for whom) rather than *whether* oral histories belong there in the first place. These discussions, which emerged out of Indigenous and feminist communities of practice, hark back to more general issues of access to sensitive oral histories—whether they are online or in a public archive. See, for example, "Mukurtu Software Preserves Indigenous Digital Heritage through Technologies of Today," Institute for Museum and Library Services, accessed 14 August 2016, https://goo.gl/UDDKNZ; Sherna Berger Gluck, "From California to Kafr Nameh and Back," in *Oral History Off the Record: Toward an Ethnography of Practice*, eds. Anna Sheftel and Stacey Zembrzycki (New York: Palgrave Macmillan, 2013), 38–40.
17 If it might be damaging to someone else, then that is a separate ethical issue that should be addressed separately.
18 See Elise Chenier's chapter in this volume (Chapter 23).
19 T.V. Reed, *Digitized Lives: Culture, Power and Social Change in the Internet Era* (New York: Routledge, 2014), 180.

23 Oral history's afterlife

Elise Chenier

Not too long ago, original recordings of oral history interviews ended up in an attic or a basement. At a project's completion, only the most organized and dedicated oral historians sorted out their tapes, transcripts, and, at the end of the 20th century when institutions began to require them, consent forms, and donated them to a community or institutional archive for preservation. If anyone ever consulted one of these archived oral interview collections, it was usually to view the transcripts; hardly anyone listened to the actual recordings. The voice of the past was just that: past.

Such is no longer the case. Digital technologies and the Internet have created new possibilities for oral history's afterlife. In many parts of the world low-cost digital recorders and cameras, easy-to-use editing software like Audacity and iMovie, content managers like YouTube, and massive distribution networks like Facebook have made short film and radio documentary production a ubiquitous part of everyday life. Consequently, for hearing audiences at least, transcripts have taken a back seat and the aural has been put back into oral history.[1] Fulfilling oral history's commitment to democratizing knowledge and helping to empower marginalized and oppressed peoples by gathering and sharing oral testimonies is easier than ever.

In 2010, I founded the Archives of Lesbian Oral Testimony (ALOT), www.alotarchives.org, with all of this in mind. I knew that numerous collections of interviews conducted with lesbians had never been archived, yet had tremendous value for future researchers. However, archiving collections produced more than a decade ago raised a host of ethical issues. Detailed information about individual narrators is not often available. People like me who undertook interviews in the 1990s, well before online archives existed, could not have prepared for the opportunities to share these rich stories with such broad audiences, but today we can.

Taking advantage of opportunities afforded by digital technologies and the Internet requires foresight, a working knowledge of copyright issues, and a deep engagement with ethical questions regarding dissemination and copyright ownership. The opportunity to engage, challenge, and empower new and much broader audiences with women's and feminist issues makes this more than worth the effort.[2] This chapter addresses three essential issues that practitioners undertaking oral history interviews must now consider: planning a project's afterlife during its earliest phase; collaborating with an archive, museum, or library, and, when creating one's own online exhibit, with design and technical specialists; and curating materials for public consumption. Making the most of the extraordinary opportunities to engage and involve other scholars, students, and various publics hinges on integrating these steps into our project plans. At the end of the chapter, I will discuss how some projects are implementing an online archiving and dissemination strategy as part of the research process.

The opportunities digital technology and the Internet afford are available to every oral historian, of course, but considering how underrepresented women—including transwomen—remain, these opportunities are particularly valuable for feminists.[3] Inequalities that our oral history projects strive to challenge remain entrenched: according to the United Nations Statistics Division's report "The World's Women 2015, Trends and Statistics," nearly two-thirds of the world's illiterate population over age 15 are women (the vast majority residing in Northern Africa, sub-Saharan Africa, and Southern Asia). Globally, women do two-to-three times more domestic and unpaid work than men, earn between 10 and 40 per cent less than men (depending on sector, region, and race), and receive much less formal education than their male counterparts. Moreover, women are underrepresented among researchers: they constitute 44 per cent of researchers in the humanities, but when all fields are combined, including the social sciences where most oral historians are situated, for the last ten years women have yet to surpass the 30 per cent mark. Outside the academy, stories about women's lives are filtered through male-dominated news media: from 2008 to 2010 women represented an estimated 35 per cent of the news workforce, including the world of documentary film.[4] Digital technologies offer a more democratic way to overcome these obstacles, and to share our stories with each other.

Women's lives, experiences, and viewpoints are still marginalized in official records, and many women lack the literacy skills needed to create a lasting record in the first place. In such situations, the oral interview remains the best method available to capture women's lived experiences. This is particularly true for Indigenous women, women of color, disabled, and economically marginalized women, gender non-conforming women, and lesbian and queer women, as well as women in the majority world.[5] Moreover, putting interviews online makes it easier for our narrators to use their stories for their own purposes. However, because women's oral testimonies are more likely to deal with matters of a personal and intimate nature, such as intra-familial relations and sex and sexuality, including emotional, physical, and sexual violence and abuse, preparing interviews for donation to an archive requires time and skill on the part of the interviewer. For example, these interviews will likely require more intensive editing than might normally be the case. Talking about the post-fieldwork tasks that online archives and exhibits demand allows us to implement more fully the principles that initially informed feminist oral methodologies: to produce work/knowledge about women rooted in grass-roots, non-hierarchical, and collaborative cultural and intellectual exchange production.

For the first-time project leader, archiving one's interviews is likely the furthest thing from one's mind, but every interview-based research project, no matter how modest the endeavor, should develop a preservation plan even before the first interview is undertaken. Ironically, it is the very people whose experiences are most marginalized that are the least likely to recognize the value of their material beyond their own research project. Indeed, their research may be devalued within the institutional or social context in which they undertake their work. Doubly and sometimes trebly marginalized, feminist and other historians must continue to insist on oral history's legitimacy. Archiving and curating our interviews is an important step in this direction.

Permission to archive and post online is critical. Without it an archive will not likely accept interviews for donation, nor should interviewers post an interview online without the permission of the narrator. Acquiring permission at the end of a project is a time-consuming undertaking even the most dedicated person will struggle to complete, and if narrators have died, one faces the more onerous task of locating next of kin to acquire permission to share or archive interviews. Discussing a long-term preservation strategy upfront with narrators, as well as outlining different types of uses for the interview, ensures that, where the narrator is agreeable, others can access oral histories.

The interviews I undertook for my own Master's research were completed in the mid-1990s. Most of the first collections ALOT received were from the same decade, and none of the donors used consent forms, since they were not standard practice at the time. Most of my narrators have since died, and others I cannot locate. In instances like this, ALOT allows researchers to access the material by applying for a password and agreeing to comply with requirements regarding the preservation of narrators' confidentiality. In this way, we are able to adhere to archives' traditional custodial responsibilities and protect the interests of both interviewer and narrator. Conversely, when in the 2010s I undertook interviews for a research project on intimate relationships between white women and men of Asian heritage in Toronto in the 1910s through to the 1950s, I obtained permission to post the interviews online at the time of the interview. When I began the project I had no plans other than to publish my research in the conventional manner and donate the interviews to the Multicultural History Society of Ontario (MHSO). As the research project unfolded, however, I developed the idea for www.interracialintimacies.org, an open access archive and research-learning tool. Because I had obtained permission to share the material online, I was able to proceed. More recently produced collections in the ALOT archive such as Nadine Boulay's oral history of lesbians in British Columbia offer rich details about the project participants, and because permission to post them online was obtained at the time of the interview, they require no password protection and are more readily accessible.

There is no standardized preservation procedure to follow, but there are plenty of resources (some of which are listed at the end of this chapter) to help interviewers decide the best approach for their project. Each project is unique, and a preservation plan should be considered in light of the subject, the researcher's goals, and the narrators' desires. In my own practice, if a narrator agrees to allow the interview to be archived, I suggest an archive I have in mind for the project. I will already have confirmed that the archive is interested in and able to accept the donation. Not all of them will be. I also volunteer to make available a copy of their interview to an archive of their choosing, and of course to provide them with their own copy. Narrators may choose to restrict the use of the interview to me alone and request that they be anonymized. Most of the women I interviewed in the 1990s for my research on butch and femme bar culture in the 1950s and 60s chose anonymity. Conversely, only two of the people I interviewed two decades later about Toronto's Chinatown requested anonymity. In the first project—also *my* first project—I had not given a moment's thought to preservation; in the second project I worked with each participant to develop a preservation plan.

In the digital age, it is vital to establish a relationship with an archive, museum, or library at the earliest possible opportunity, ideally before one conducts their first interview. Why? To accept a donation an institution requires oral historians to provide them with all kinds of information, including, most likely, permission from the narrator to donate their interview, as well as metadata, which comprises details about the interview such as the narrator's name, the place and date of the interview, and the topics discussed. Knowing the metadata categories in advance means one can collect the right information at the time of the interview, which will make the donation process simpler and smoother.

Reviewing an agreement to donate an interview is best done at the interview's conclusion when the narrator knows what they said, and therefore what they are agreeing to share with others. It may be a good idea to briefly mention preservation options before the interview begins. Waiting until the end of an interview to broach the subject may cause anxiety for some people who imagined they were having a conversation with you alone. Leaving it to the end may cause a person to feel deceived and could compromise the trust so necessary for a positive interview experience. Raising the option of archiving an interview before one turns on any recording equipment prepares the narrator for the discussion that will follow at the interview's end, which can be done following the process of reviewing consent forms.

A consent form is distinct from a donation form. It explains the purpose of the research project to the narrator, and what the interviewer intends to do with the information gathered in the interview. It also lays out the narrator's rights. One should not combine the consent form and the donation agreement in a single document (although the archive to which one may donate the interview will require both forms; publishers also require consent forms, therefore always keep originals.) Keeping the donation form separate from the consent form signals to the narrator that consenting to an interview and permitting their interview to be archived are distinct issues, and that donation to an archive is not required or even expected.

In addition to donating interviews to brick-and-mortar institutions, researchers must address the possibility of interviews being put online. Even if one has no plans to do so, the archive to which one donates may at some future time pursue an online strategy. Stories people took the trouble to share will not likely be among those made available online unless a narrator gave explicit consent or signed a Creative Commons license (see page 311 in this chapter) that permits such usage. Furthermore, researchers who consult the collections created by others may want to use clips to create a documentary or short film, but without explicit permission that permits this usage, they will not be able to do so. By pursuing a preservation plan with narrators at the conclusion of an interview, researchers ensure that the fullest range of future uses of the material is possible, so far as a narrator permits.

At ALOT, where permission to post online has been acquired from both interviewer and narrator, interviews can be viewed by anyone. The rest of the collection can only be accessed by formal request, and by agreeing to the terms of use. Other collections, such as "The Voices of Feminism Oral History" project, provide online access to transcripts only. Video recordings can only be viewed on a university campus computer.[6] Similar restrictions apply to the "Mormon Women's" and the "Latin American Women's Oral History" projects.[7] The downside of such precautions is that by limiting access, the collection will not be as widely used as it could. Determining if and what parts of a collection should be put online need to be addressed by individual collectors of oral histories and must be considered in light of the nature and content of the interviews themselves, in addition to protecting narrators' interests.

If a narrator allows their interview to be shared online, they must also determine how and for what purpose the interview can be used. For example, they may want to prohibit reproduction of their voice or image. They may want to restrict access to bona fide researchers, or prohibit commercial uses. Researchers need to know and be prepared to explain the range of options available to a narrator, and the potential advantages and disadvantages of each. For this, Creative Commons licensing is quite simple and straightforward. It provides several options: Attribution only; Attribution-ShareAlike; Attribution-No Derivatives; Attribution-Non-Commercial; Attribution-Non-Commercial-ShareAlike; and Attribution-Non-Commercial-No Derivatives— the most restrictive of the licenses and the one ALOT uses when narrators are deceased or cannot be located.[8]

Carefully reviewing licensing options with narrators is tremendously important. Most people choose a non-commercial license, but would they if they understood that this prohibits documentary filmmakers from using their stories? While only a few documentarians profit substantially from sales of their films, most operate on a for-profit basis, thus they would be prohibited from using material with a non-commercial license. What about posting our interviews on YouTube or Facebook? Facebook retains legal ownership of any data uploaded to its site, thus both interviewer and narrator relinquish their rights to their recording. It is essential that interviewers fully understand the legal and privacy implications of each platform they might want to use to disseminate an interview, and be able to explain the issues at stake to narrators.

Community-based researchers, faculty, and graduate students are taking advantage of open source software that enables people with patience and perseverance but not necessarily technical skills to produce sophisticated online exhibits and archives.[9] Interviews can be uploaded to commercial servers such as YouTube or Vimeo, and shared on blogs and web pages. Theresa de Langis, an independent consultant on women, peace, and security issues based in Cambodia, used the web page platform squarespace to share the experiences of women survivors of sexual and gender-based violence during the Khmer Rouge regime (1975–1979).[10] An innovative site, which incorporates oral history clips to tell the story of civil rights activist Ann Braden, used Weebly.[11] More complex projects require professional design and technical services, the costs for which should be included in a budget proposal. Both ALOT and www.interracialintimacies.org required such expertise since, in the first case the content, and in the second case the layout and design, demanded a complex structure that required advanced coding and design skills.

That said, more and more tools are being built that allow almost anyone to compile engaging online oral history exhibits and archives. The gold star among them is Omeka, an open-source web-publishing platform well suited to projects with diverse data types, including oral interviews.[12] Designed with non-IT specialists in mind, building an online exhibit with Omeka is comparable to creating a WordPress page. No programming skills are required, allowing users to focus on content and interpretation.[13] "From Farms to Freeways: Women's Memories of Western Sydney [Australia]" is but one example of a feminist scholar taking an oral history project, applying a Creative Commons license, and using Omeka to share her data in a public exhibit.[14] These new opportunities are also transforming teaching. Using Omeka and other programs, students are producing comprehensive archival collections and exhibits as part of their undergraduate and graduate training.[15]

Omeka allows creators to do one of the most valuable things one can do in online archives: curate their oral and other historical research. Preparing materials for public consumption means providing interpretive and contextual information to guide and inform audiences about the purpose for which an interview was collected. An excellent example of effective oral history curation is the British Library's "Sisterhood and After" project, which features interviews with Women's Liberation Movement activists to tell the story of modern feminism.[16] Preparing oral interviews for online dissemination in a similar manner should be accounted for in research training, workflows, funding, and academic recognition. Such curatorial projects are not typically recognized as publication of research results, but those working in the digital humanities are pushing for such changes. In the meantime, scholars concerned about publication recognition might approach their chair to request that external reviewers include a review of online oral history projects for this purpose.

Another innovative use of Omeka is Washington University's "Documenting Ferguson" project, which seeks to "preserve and make accessible the digital media captured and created by community members following the shooting death of Michael Brown in Ferguson, Missouri, on August 9, 2014" with the "ultimate goal of providing diverse perspectives on the events in Ferguson and the resulting social dialogue."[17] Created not long after Brown's death, it is an example of how the Internet enables a rapid response to public events, and facilitates broader community engagement in creating archives. To this end, "Documenting Ferguson" uses "Contribute," a plug-in (a piece of software code that enables an application or program to do something it could not do by itself) developed for Omeka. "Contribute" allows users to upload their own data, including interviews, to the site. "The Kentucky Women in the Civil Rights Era" project, whose site is hosted by MATRIX, employs a similar approach.[18] By enabling Internet users to capture and search stored data, and to upload documents, images, and other data to the site, "Contribute" and similar plug-ins allow oral historians to use the Internet for much more than simple dissemination. These sites double as an outreach tool that builds community and increases data collection capacity. They can also facilitate greater collaboration, an advantage creators of the University of Washington-based "Women Who Rock" project are currently exploiting. Their site "brings together scholars, musicians, media-makers, performers, artists, and activists to explore the role of women and popular music in the creation of cultural scenes and social justice movements in the Americas and beyond." Like "Documenting Ferguson," it mobilizes collective methods of research, teaching, and community and scholarly collaboration.[19]

When in the 1970s Sherna Berger Gluck interviewed women involved in the American suffrage movement, neither she nor her narrators could have anticipated the Internet. Gluck had the foresight to archive her interviews, but the main means through which we would first learn about those stories was through her 1976 book *From Parlor to Prison*.[20] Today, thanks to forward thinking on Gluck's part, students can listen to those extraordinary interviews, and are much more likely to do this than they are to read her book.[21]

As a method, oral history has always placed additional requirements on researchers. The authors in *Women's Words* raised in forceful ways a number of those responsibilities. Today, we must take on yet another responsibility: that we take the necessary steps to plan for the afterlife of our oral interviews.

Resources

The Winter/Spring 2013 issue of *Oral History Review* is a special edition on oral history in the digital age. See especially Mary Larson, "Steering Clear of the Rocks: Ethics and Oral History," *Oral History Review* 40, no. 1 (Winter/Spring 2013): 36–49.

Douglas A. Boyd and Mary A. Larson, eds., *Oral History and Digital Humanities: Voice, Access, and Engagement* (New York, NY: Palgrave Macmillan, 2014).

Creative Commons Licenses: http://creativecommons.org/licenses/.
Lauren Kata, "Not Another Schema: Describing Oral Histories," http://ohda.matrix.
msu.edu/2015/10/the-oha-metadata-task-force-the-force-behind-our-task/.
Nancy MacKay, *Curating Oral Histories*, 2nd edition (Walnut Creek: Left Coast Press,
2015).
"Oral History in the Digital Age," http://ohda.matrix.msu.edu/.
"Best Practices," http://wiki.ohda.matrix.msu.edu/index.php/Best_Practices.

Notes

1 Michael Frisch, "Oral History and the Digital Revolution: Toward a Post-
Documentary Sensibility," in *The Oral History Reader*, 2nd edition, eds. Robert
B. Perks and Alistair Thomson (London: Routledge, 2006), 102–114.
2 Developing expertise in the digital humanities is also advantageous from a career
development standpoint.
3 See Elspeth Brown, "Trans/Feminist Oral History," *Transgender Studies Quarterly*
2, no. 4 (November 2015): 666–672.
4 United Nations Statistics Division, "The World's Women 2015: Trends and
Statistics," 2015.
5 Marc Silver proposes "majority world," a classification based on data, replace "the
developing world" and "third world" classifications based on the viewpoint of the
globe from the perspective of the wealthiest of nations: Silver, "If You Shouldn't
Call It The Third World, What Should You Call It?" *Goats and Soda: Stories of Life
in a Changing World*, National Public Radio, 24 January 2015, accessed 22 July
2016, www.npr.org/sections/goatsandsoda/2015/01/04/372684438/if-you-
shouldnt-call-it-the-third-world-what-should-you-call-it.
6 "Voices of Women Oral History" project, accessed 22 July 2016, https://library.
osu.edu/find/collections/the-ohio-state-university-archives/digitalcontent/voices-
of-women-oral-history-project/.
7 "Mormon Women's Oral History Project at Claremont Graduate University,"
accessed 22 July 2016, www.mormonwomenohp.org/; "'Immigration and Identity'
Latin American Women's Oral History Project Collection," accessed 22 July 2016,
www.memorybc.ca/immigration-and-identity-latin-american-womens-oral-history-
project-collection.
8 For more on the value of Creative Commons licensing, see J. Dougherty and
C. Simpson, "Who Owns Oral History? A Creative Commons Solution," in *Oral
History in the Digital Age*, eds. Doug Boyd et al. (Washington, DC: Institute of
Museum and Library Services, 2012), accessed 10 July 2013, http://ohda.
matrix.msu.edu/2012/06/a-creative-commons-solution/.
9 Oral historians may also want to consider using a content management system such
as "Stories Matter," accessed 22 July 2016, http://storytelling.concordia.ca/
storiesmatter/ to manage recordings. See also Dean Rehberger, "Getting Oral
History Online: Collections Management Applications," *Oral History Review* 40,
no. 1 (Winter/Spring 2013): 83–94; Sara Price, "Collection Management Systems:
Tools for Managing Oral History Collections," in *Oral History in the Digital
Age*, accessed 22 July 2016, http://ohda.matrix.msu.edu/2012/06/collection-
management-systems/.
10 "Cambodian Women Oral History" project, accessed 12 October 2017, http://
cambodianwomenoralhistory.squarespace.com/. For more on this project, also see
Chapter 11 by de Langis in this volume.
11 "Anne Braden: Advocate, Radical, and Revolutionary," accessed 12 October 2015,
http://50473743.nhd.weebly.com/index.html.

12 See "Omeka Feature List," accessed 22 July 2016, http://omeka.org/files/docs/Featurelist.pdf. For a list of sites currently using Omeka, go to: "See What You Can Do with Omeka," accessed 22 July 2016, http://omeka.org/codex/Sites_Using_Omeka.
13 "Omeka: Serious Web Publishing," accessed 22 July 2016, http://omeka.org/about/.
14 "From Farms to Freeways: Women's Memories of Western Sydney," accessed 22 July 2016, http://omeka.uws.edu.au/farmstofreeways/.
15 See "Goin' North," accessed 22 July 2016, https://goinnorth.org/about; "Activist Women's Voices," accessed 22 July 2016, http://activistwomen.commons.gc.cuny.edu/activists/. Also see Aishwarya A. Gautam, Janet H. Morford, Sarah Joy Yockey, "On the Air: The Pedagogy of Student-Produced Radio Documentaries," *Oral History Review* 42, no. 2 (Summer/Fall 2015): 311–351.
16 "Sisterhood and After," accessed 22 July 2016, www.bl.uk/sisterhood.
17 "Documenting Ferguson," accessed 22 July 2016, http://digital.wustl.edu/ferguson/.
18 Another option can be found at Michigan State University's MATRIX: The Center for Humane Arts, Letters and Social Sciences Online, creator of MediaMatrix and Project Builder applications: www2.matrix.msu.edu. The African Studies faculty at the university has created a number of online exhibits including "African Oral Narratives (AON)," accessed 22 July 2016, http://africanactivist.msu.edu/; "South Africa: Overcoming Apartheid Building Democracy," accessed 22 July 2016, http://overcomingapartheid.msu.edu. MATRIX also hosts "Oral History and the Digital Age," a valuable resource: http://www.matrix.msu.edu/oral-history-in-the-digital-age/.
19 The interviews are archived in the University of Washington Library, http://content.lib.washington.edu/wwrweb/, and the project maintains a WordPress site at "Women Who Rock: Making Scenes, Building Communities," accessed 22 July 2016, http://womenwhorockcommunity.org/who-we-are/.
20 Sherna Berger Gluck, *From Parlor to Prison: Five American Suffragists Talk About Their Lives* (New York: Vintage Books, 1976).
21 Gluck was one of the first to move oral histories online, by creating The Virtual Oral/Aural History Archive: http://symposia.library.csulb.edu/iii/cpro/CommunityViewPage.external?lang=eng&sp=1000026&suite=def. See Sherna Berger Gluck, "Why Do We Call It Oral History? Refocusing on Orality/Aurality in the Digital Age," in *Oral History and the Digital Humanities: Voice, Access, and Engagement*, eds. Douglas A. Boyd and Mary Larson (New York: Palgrave Macmillan, 2014), 35–52.

24 Women's words from the archives

Ruth Percy

When asked in the 1970s about their feminism, two trade unionists active in the 1910s and 1920s gave strikingly different answers. While one boldly stated "I was probably a born feminist," the other distanced herself on the grounds that "We weren't interested in sex. We weren't interested in brassieres."[1] These contrasting responses illustrate feminism's complex history and the potential archived oral sources hold for writing that history.[2] They open up new lines of enquiry around contested language and evolving meanings within women's struggles for equality, emotional responses to feminist language, generational shifts, and an interviewer's or a project's own positionality and biases.

This chapter considers how archived oral histories can contribute to our understanding of the shifting and contested meanings of gender equality and women's rights over the course of the 20th century by shedding light on how former trade unionists engaged with the term and concept of "feminism." I also consider the methodological problems for historians who use archived collections, in particular changes in activist language and the different ways collections have been archived. I argue that by focusing on language and contextualization and supplementing with close readings of other sources we can overcome these challenges.

To this end, I discuss two different collections that originated in the 1970s, employed a life history approach, and focused on the narrators' activism in the opening decades of the 20th century. "The Feminist History Research Project," a Los Angeles-based community project co-founded by Sherna Berger Gluck and Ann Forfreedom, began recording oral histories of women's struggles in 1972.[3] Founded explicitly as a feminist, community-based research project removed from the academy, it initially focused on women who had been active in the labor and suffrage movements.[4] In contrast, the "Twentieth Century Trade Union Woman" had a more institutional parentage. Inspired by the bourgeoning interest in women's history, the leaders of the University of Michigan and Wayne State University's Institute of Labor and Industrial Relations' Program on Women and Work realized that labor historians had, up to that point (1975), ignored blue-collar women workers and trade unionists, and they set about trying to rectify this absence.[5] Both collections thus had a feminist positionality and aimed to collect the life histories of women active within the labor movement.

Before discussing the collections in more detail it is worth considering their form, as Elise Chernier does in her chapter in this collection. "The Feminist History Research Project" has been fully digitized and audio files are accessible through an online platform. While transcripts are not provided, in order to help with what Michael Frisch has identified as the "shoebox" problem of having an overwhelming amount of audio information entered into a site, written summaries and biographical information accompany each file.[6] In contrast, the "Twentieth Century Trade Union Woman" has no digital presence at all, other than in library catalogue records.[7] Although the original tapes are archived at the University of Michigan, these are not available to researchers because of their delicate state. Instead, I accessed the material via microfilmed and microfiched transcripts. As many historians have discussed, the transcript is limited to representing the "segmentary traits" of an interview, missing the meanings conveyed in the pace, volume, and rhythm of speech.[8]

As with all oral history, memory is central. In both collections, the women's recollections of their activism in the era of first-wave feminism were filtered through their contemporary experiences of second-wave feminism. If memory only gets associated with language through recounting, a key question arises: in which language is it constructed, the language used at the time of the memory, or the language used at the time the memory is recounted?[9] In other words, how does an individual's later relationship with feminism affect how they speak about their earlier activism? Are narrators' attitudes constructed independently of the interview and interviewer? Does feminism mean now what it meant at an earlier time?

Focusing on the differences in language over this extended timeframe offers unique insight into the evolution of the word and concept of "feminism." What "feminism" means has been a subject of fierce debate since it first entered the English language from the French in the late 19th century. It was the 1910s before it was commonly used—mostly in the context of the suffrage movement—and even then its meaning was fluid; it was not until 1933 that its political meaning appeared in the *Oxford English Dictionary*.[10] The focus on labor in these collections adds a further complication. Unlike "feminist" oral histories, such as those Lynn Abrams considers in this collection, these women's activism was located within the labor movement, and they thus lacked the feminist framework that Abrams discusses in her piece. Consequently, they were highly unlikely to have used or related the term to their own activism in the early 20th century. Indeed, in each interview discussed in this chapter, the interviewer introduced the term "feminism." As Gluck reminds us, when using oral history to study feminism we must remember that actions are rarely as distinct or coherent as ideologies and thus the language used to recall them is less precise or defined.[11] Since all of these women were interviewed because of the role they played in the labor movement, their choice of language sheds light on the complex relationship between gender- and class-based politics, the relationship between interviewer and narrator, and the passage of time.

Given that I approached these interviews for evidence of working women's engagement with ideas of women's rights and equality, I was excited to find women using the words "feminism" or "feminist" in both collections. However, written primary sources suggested that it was highly unlikely that they would have used this language in the periods that they recalled. Moreover, the words had a particular association at the time of the interviews; the press regularly reported on "feminist" actions, such as the 1970 Women's Strike for Equality, the 1972 launch of *Ms.* magazine, and the 1973 *Roe v. Wade* Supreme Court decision that established a woman's right to an abortion. Ascertaining how the developments of the intervening decades had provoked a reconceptualization of their earlier activism thus had the potential to add a new perspective to the fundamental question I was asking, about the fluid, shifting, and contested nature of "feminism." The interviews thereby provide narratives of the past as well as a window into processes of self-construction in a particular discursive context. Following Penny Summerfield's advice, I needed to "understand not only the narrative offered, but also the meanings invested in it and their discursive origins."[12]

As I thought more deeply about these interview collections, I wondered why some women embraced the term "feminism" while others rejected it. Did this tell us something about their activism, the nature of the questioning, or the context of the interviews? While these are issues the original interviewers could well have considered as they analyzed the material, my greater historical distance facilitated a deeper identification and understanding of the fluid nature of politicized language, as well as the interviewers' own feminist biases. The particular uses (or absences) of "feminism" could shed light on the individual's self-presentation and her relationship to the interviewer and the contemporary feminist movement.

Interviewed about women trade unionists' struggles for women's rights and equality, Pauline Newman connected the activism of the Women's Trade Union League, a cross-class organization that mobilized and represented working women, to a broader history of feminist activism. However, "feminism" was not in her lexicon. The women of the League, she argued, "were probably advocating equality long before the equal rights people came on board."[13] Newman's interview is fairly typical of the interviews in the two collections in that it skirts around the issue of equality without actually using the term "feminist." The absence of the term suggests that feminist ideas can be expressed without necessarily embracing the word. Removed from the interview process, historians using archived oral histories thus require an astute ear and a comprehensive and flexible lexicon to piece together histories of resistance.

In recounting her experiences as a trade union organizer, Rebecca Holland not only avoided using the term "feminism," but actively rejected any association between her own activism and second-wave feminism. When asked if she was a feminist, Holland, who is quoted at the outset of this chapter, argued that her time was:

> entirely different . . . because we fought for something . . . Our girls were not the type of girls that you see now. We weren't interested in sex. We weren't interested in brassieres. We weren't interested in all these things . . . We were at that time interested in equality of respect, work, wages, and organization.[14]

Holland's unwillingness to connect her own struggles for equality to those of 1970s feminists reveals a significant generation gap. This disjuncture also highlights the value of archived oral histories to our understanding of the intersection of class- and gender-based politics. Although Holland fought for workplace improvements and spoke at length about the struggles she faced as a *woman*, it was only through dialogue with the interviewer that a feminist framework was considered and essentially rejected.

The labor movement also framed trade unionist Sara Fredgant's engagement with struggles for women's equality. When the interviewer asked her if the Bryn Mawr School for Working Women was feminist, her reply—"Feminist?"— suggests surprise or even confusion at the use of the term in this context. Here the limitations of the transcript became all too evident; it is impossible to identify her tone and we thus have to be more speculative. The course of the conversation indicates some disjuncture between the interviewer's understanding of the word and her own. The interviewer explained that she meant "talking about women's issues and encouraging women to be more active politically and more active professionally and so forth," to which Fredgant replied, "That was the purpose of the school!" The exclamation mark again suggests a tone of surprise. Although Fredgant had a more empathetic under-standing of the 1970s women's movement than Holland and thus could relate the term to her own activism, she also felt that it was too limited in its reach: "You're working now in a field where feminism is the important aspect of every part of a woman's life who is interested. I had so many concerns . . . You cannot work in a trade union and just be concerned about one thing."[15] As a consequence she was unsure about her identification with feminism:

> I don't know whether I could have carried a feminist banner . . . I was concerned about women. That's true. I wanted women in a position of leadership . . . I wanted them to assume more leadership. But I also worked in a field where there were other important parts which I wanted them to be active in and to participate in and to make their contribution as *human beings* and as *workers*, and not only as women.[16]

These interviews highlight fissures among women activists and remind scholars that even active participants in political movements have a variety of motives and understandings behind their actions. Identifying them with a single word thereby belies their complexity.

Only two of the women (out of the admittedly small sample of twenty-one interviews I accessed) actively embraced the language of feminism. Sarah Rozner, a Chicago trade union organizer, explained that her "feminism" came simply from her experiences of "injustice"; "How can I be anything else but a feminist?" she replied rhetorically. However, as she continued, her identification with feminism became more ambivalent: "It doesn't make any difference if it's a man or a woman. It's the injustice that bothered me most . . . the majority of workers . . . in the clothing factories were women, that's why I had to be a feminist." Again, Rozner did not independently choose the word "feminist" to explain her activism, although she was comfortable applying that language to her experiences. However, ultimately she distanced herself from the term, saying: "I call myself a unionist, that's what I call myself."[17] Having struggled to find a voice within the labor movement, but then spending decades working for her union, her identity as a feminist was anchored in a clear sense of class solidarity.

The woman who most assertively self-identified as a feminist was Rebecca Beck August, who is also quoted at the start of this chapter. Even so, she used the term only after being asked whether she would call her 1910s self a feminist; she confidently answered "Oh yes" and later on stated "I was probably a born feminist."[18] Unlike Rozner, August had no problem filtering her union experiences through the language of feminism. For her, being a feminist was common-sense: "Women should have the same rights as men . . . that's what I fought for because I thought, women, we are *human beings*."[19] In her explanation of why she was a feminist, she used the same language that Fredgant employed when explaining why she was *not* a feminist.

We can turn to Luisa Passerini's analysis of subjectivity to explain the varying associations with feminism in these interviews.[20] Narrators' self-presentation often conformed to culturally specific schema that framed and lent meaning to their recollections.[21] Perhaps it was August's and Rozner's self-presentation as "rebels" that led them to more easily claim a feminist identity. However, Holland also professed to be a rebel and yet rejected an association with 1970s feminism. Holland presented herself as the rebellious *worker* and thus slotted her memories into a labor history schema instead of a feminist history one. In contrast, when offered a feminist framework, August and Rozner more readily filtered their experiences through 1970s gender politics. When using such archived collections, then, we must consider the forces shaping the schema that influence how memories are recalled. Only by taking such factors into account can we understand these women's varied relationships to "feminism" and thus also begin to explain why many women within the trade union movement have rejected feminist language over the years.

Although all of the narrators talked about their struggles to advance women's status within the labor movement or workplace, not all of the interviews contain words we might expect. Significantly, the women who used the terms "feminism" or "feminist" did so only when prompted to do so by their interviewers. Distance from the interview process allows us to appreciate the intersecting subjectivities that are central to the interviews' construction. While the narrator understands her own activism through a particular framework, the interviewer is situated differently and might draw connections across time and place. A close reading of the interviews' construction, including the language, tone, and pace—far more challenging with only transcripts available—can thus shed light on how narrators and interviewers may have engaged, unwittingly or knowingly, with feminist discourses. From there, scholars can begin to construct a genealogy of feminism that transcends the rather restrictive first-wave/second-wave dichotomy.

These interviews, which I first approached as examples of early 20th century women's engagement with feminist ideas, and tend to be labeled as first-wave, are in fact mediated through the decades that have passed since the women's activist period, through the lens of so-called second-wave feminism, and through the process of self-presentation. The feminist language of the 1970s offered earlier activists a vehicle through which to reconsider their own experiences. In the end, only a few of them whole-heartedly adopted the "feminist" label and even then only when interviewers offered them the term. Nevertheless, these interviews reveal the ease with which women of the first-wave relate to those of the second, even if they rejected the exact language, suggesting that the wave dichotomy is little more than a linguistic construction. These competing interpretations of their early activism reveal oral history's unique value and highlight the importance of locating narrator, interviewer, and interview within their particular historical contexts. What is different about using *archived* collections in a project such as this is the distance afforded to the listener or reader. In effect, we can use them to write the history of two different periods, the one being asked about and the one in which the interviews were conducted, with the benefit of hindsight and greater awareness of bias that distance can bring. Furthermore, the potential for such dual readings highlights the value to historians of digitization projects, for only in the original audio files can we get the inflection, pauses, and tone that can give added meaning to words that might appear less complex in a transcript. By digitizing the original recordings, the "problems" identified by oral history critics become the key to making such collections so rich.

Notes

1   Rebecca Beck August, interviewed by Sherna Berger Gluck, Los Angeles, California, 19 March 1973. The Virtual Oral/Aural History Archive, California State University, Long Beach (hereafter VOAHA II), audio file 3, accessed 11 August 2016, http://symposia.library.csulb.edu/iii/cpro/DigitalItemViewPage.external?lang=&s p=1001920&sp=T&sp=1&suite=def; Rebecca Holland, interviewed by Patti Prickett, Los Angeles, California, 12 November 1974, VOAHA II, audio file 2, accessed 11 August 2016, http://symposia.library.csulb.edu/iii/cpro/DigitalItem ViewPage.external?lang=&sp=1001923&sp=T&sp=1&suite=def.

2 For reflections on working with oral histories conducted by other practitioners, and the issue of authority therein, see Sheyfali Saujani, "Empathy and Authority in Oral Testimony: Feminist Debates, Multicultural Mandates, and Reassessing the Interviewer and her 'Disagreeable Subjects,'" *Histoire sociale/Social History* 45, no. 90 (November 2012): 361–391.

3 "Living History," *Off Our Backs* 3, no. 6 (February–March 1973): 24.

4 Sherna Berger Gluck, interview by Dara Robinson, Los Angeles, California, 2 December 1988, VOAHA II, audio file 2, accessed 12 January 2016, http://symposia.library.csulb.edu/iii/cpro/DigitalItemViewPage.external;jsessionid=5E0F2 4D69E9203CB8F3A95F5984F2C46?lang=&sp=1001667&sp=T&sp=1&suite=def.

5 Daryl Hafter, "The Twentieth Century Trade Union Woman: Vehicle for Social Change," *International Labor and Working-Class History* 9 (May 1976): 11–12.

6 Michael Frisch, "Oral History in the Digital Age," *Australian Historical Studies* 47 (January 2016): 97.

7 Digitization has not been ruled out, and when I approached the Bentley Historical Library about accessing the collection while editing this article the archivist explained that if researchers plan to use materials deemed fragile they will endeavor to digitize them, a process which takes six to eight weeks.

8 See Alessandro Portelli, "The Peculiarities of Oral History," *History Workshop* 12 (Autumn 1981): 98; Luisa Passerini, "Attitudes of Oral Narrators to Their Memories: Generations, Genders, Cultures," *The Oral History Association of Australia Journal* (1990): 15–16.

9 Walter Benjamin, "The Image of Proust," in *Illuminations*, trans. Harry Zohn, ed. Hannah Arendt (London: Pimlico, 1999 [1970]), 209; Donald Spence, *Narrative Truth and Historical Truth: Meaning and Interpretation in Psychoanalysis* (New York: W.W. Norton, 1982), 56–57.

10 *The Oxford English Dictionary* (Oxford: Clarendon Press, 1933); *The Oxford English Dictionary: Supplement* (Oxford: Clarendon Press, 1933); Jane Rendall, *The Origins of Modern Feminism: Women in Britain, France, and the United States, 1780–1860* (Chicago: Lyceum, 1985), 1; June Hannam, *Feminism* (Harlow: Pearson Longman, 2007), 3–5.

11 Sherna Berger Gluck, "Whose Feminism, Whose History?" in *Community Activism and Feminist Politics*, ed. Nancy A. Naples (London: Routledge, 1998), 31–56.

12 Penny Summerfield, "Culture and Composure: Creating Narratives of the Gendered Self in Oral History Interviews," *Cultural and Social History* 1, no. 1 (2004): 67.

13 Pauline Newman, interviewed by Barbara Wertheimer, 1976 "The Twentieth Century Trade Union Woman: Vehicle for Social Change" (hereafter TCTUW) (Sandford: Microfilming Corps., 1979), 77.

14 Holland, interview.

15 Sara Fredgant, interviewed by Alice Hoffman, 1976, TCTUW, 98.

16 Fredgant, interview, 98–99. Emphasis in the original.

17 Sarah Rozner, interviewed by Sherna Berger Gluck, Los Angeles, California, 9 October 1973, VOAHA II, audio file 3, accessed 12 August 2016, http://symposia.library.csulb.edu/iii/cpro/DigitalItemViewPage.external;jsessionid=7F61FEE543C 74C2EC8EC844BBEF3F0F8?lang=&sp=1001929&sp=T&sp=1&suite=def.

18 August, interview.

19 August, interview. Emphasis added.

20 Luisa Passerini, *Fascism in Popular Memory: The Cultural Experience of the Turin Working Class*, trans. Robert Lumley and Jude Bloomfield (Cambridge: Cambridge University Press, 1987), 59–60; Passerini, "Women's Personal Narratives: Myths, Experiences, and Emotions," in *Interpreting Women's Lives: Feminist Theory and Personal Narratives*, eds. Personal Narratives Group (Bloomington: Indiana University Press, 1989), 192.

21 See Jeffrey Prager, *Presenting the Past: Psychoanalysis and the Sociology of Misremembering* (Cambridge, MA: Harvard University Press, 1998); Carolyn Steedman, "Enforced Narratives: Stories of Another Self," in *Feminism and Autobiography: Texts, Theories, Methods*, eds. Lucy Cosslett and Penny Summerfield (London: Routledge, 2000), 25–39.

25 "Shut the tape off and I'll tell you a story"

Women's knowledges in urban Indigenous community representations

Heather A. Howard

In the 1990s, when I started working on my dissertation examining the production of Indigenous community in the urban context of Toronto, one of my goals was to critically consider both feminist and Indigenist approaches to research. I was intrigued by the primacy of orality and oral history in the current scholarship on the production of women's and Indigenous knowledge, particularly as these shaped community organizing and resistance to the structural forms of violence sustaining the triumvirate of patriarchy, colonialism, and capitalism.[1] Many of the contributors to *Women's Words* spoke about the need for feminist oral historians to balance the responsibility of illustrating these "larger cultural formations" and women's experiences within them, while grappling with the potential to misrepresent.[2] Calling for innovative community-based approaches to conducting oral history projects, they examined oral history as processual and engaged intersectional analyses and dynamics that might prove transformative for individuals, communities, and social justice work.[3]

My position as a researcher within the Indigenous community was and remains informed by a commitment to feminist oral history practice, which reciprocates the benefits of research and empowers local community development, and by critiques of social science studies of Indigenous peoples, especially anthropological ones, which implore researchers to co-direct research with communities, situate our work within the critical decolonizing frameworks emerging from the Indigenous communities in which we conduct research, and apply our work to improving quality of life.[4] I was challenged to design relevant methodologies, produce interpretations that continue to be valued, and engage with community-based theorizing about the complexities of Indigenous women's orality.[5] The organizing work involved in co-founding the Native Canadian Centre of Toronto community-based history program, "First Story Toronto," in 1995, provided a structure for attending to these responsibilities in the production of knowledge with, by, and for Indigenous peoples in the city.

Recently, "First Story Toronto" developed a mobile phone app as part of its mandate to carry out community-engaged popular education programs and generate tools to promote accurate representations of urban Indigenous people. In this chapter, I consider transformations in representations of urban Indigenous women's knowledge and orality, as collected and disseminated by "First Story Toronto" within the specific context of urban Indigenous community practice. My analysis takes account of broader debates arising from the digitization of oral traditions, and is in conversation with contemporary critical Indigenist feminist work. I focus on the "First Story Toronto" mobile phone app to explore how women's leadership in community organizing is featured, and highlight the ways in which Indigenous community-created and disseminated oral histories have the potential to transform human relations of co-existence in urban contexts.

Urban Indigenous/digitizing oral history

Although there has been a "second wave" of scholarly analysis of Indigenous peoples' experiences in urban areas since the 1990s, only a fraction of this literature critically considers oral history and even less urban Indigenous women's orality.[6] As I describe in the text that follows in this chapter, the community-directed structuring of "First Story Toronto" research centered oral history as the choice methodology. In the 1990s, oral histories were collected through video-recorded "living history circles," wherein several narrators sat together to reminisce and tell stories that interwove personal biographical, cultural, and general historical content.[7]

In 1998, I presented this research in a panel called "Issues in the Oral History of Indigenous Peoples," at the annual meeting of the US Oral History Association, wherein all of the panelists' projects focused on urban Indigenous communities. As discussant for the panel, Indigenous Studies scholar Winona Wheeler called for "discussions specific to Indigenous traditional intellectual history, or Indigenous historiography" that dealt with "how Indigenous peoples structure, organize, sift, retain and transmit knowledge of the past."[8] Oral history scholarship in the 1980s and 1990s had begun to take up these issues. Concerned with "writing down" Indigenous oral history, some emphasized the importance of oral history as a social process, especially as contextualized in relationships, places, and shifts in power, as problematized in statements of claim and reconstructions of the past, and as potentially subject to recolonization in pedagogical or museum content.[9] Consequently, they explored questions related to the performative qualities in the narrative art of oral history and their detachment from the dialogical process of the knowledge production in which meaning is made.[10]

Yet feminist and Indigenous scholars also asserted that oral history research, which inevitably involves decontextualized documentation, is also vital to advancing justice and sovereignty projects. For example, Julie Cruickshank maintained that "It may not be possible to produce seamless narratives about colonial encounters, but we *can* learn how the very act of constructing, remembering, and transmitting narratives continues to be a reassertion of autonomy."[11] Further to this, Linda Tuhiwai Smith wrote:

> Storytelling, oral histories, the perspectives of elders and of women have become an integral part of all indigenous research. Each individual story is powerful. But the point about the stories is not that they simply tell a story, or tell a story simply. These new stories contribute to a collective story in which every indigenous person has a place . . . The story and the story teller both serve to connect the past with the future, one generation to the other, the land with the people and the people with the story.[12]

Oral history research and its dissemination are woven into contemporary practice moving Indigenous sovereignty forward, in "storywork," as Joanne Archibald describes, through "the good power of interconnections within family, community, nation, culture, and land."[13] Women's oral history practice as cultural knowledge transmission is often centered within these interconnections, modeled powerfully in urban settings through direct and extended kin roles of grandmother, auntie, and sister.[14]

Other questions prompted by the 1998 panel and Wheeler's comments remain relevant: How might Indigenous oral history be translated or transformed by the collective and personal experiences of urbanization? How are urban Indigenous storytellers transmitting cultural knowledge in relation to life in the city? How are these processes politically charged and mediated in the production of research? Wheeler also noted that Indigenous peoples "can selectively adopt some of the colonizer's tools to enhance our ways of doing things," adding that "how we apply or use these tools will determine the degree to which we can continue to protect our respective cultural integrity."[15] For "First Story Toronto," digital technologies represent one of these tools, manifest in a mobile app created in 2012.[16]

The app utilizes an interactive map featuring historical points and current events, allowing users to access original stories, photographs, archival documents, and audio and video clips collected and housed in the "First Story" archive (see Figure 25.1). The digitization of oral history has been heralded for democratizing access, de-hierarchizing the power of gatekeepers and experts, and making them more accountable.[17] However, the process of generating content for the "First Story" app has also signaled the ways in which digitization may entail raising new gates and focusing energy on shifting the locale of authoritative knowledge in the processes of sharing. Diverse audiences accessing "First Story" content are not blank slates, and users may "fail to find a meaningful connection between their own ways of thinking and the stories they hear; their preconceptions may collide with the interviewee, history, or culture they hear," as Steve Cohen cautions.[18] This is an important consideration for "First Story," especially with regards to the inclusion of women's narratives, which as I describe below, relate multiple layers of interpretation

Figure 25.1 Screen shot of the "First Story Toronto" mobile phone app showing pins
marking historical and contemporary events

about the production of urban Indigenous community, and broader Indigenous
and non-Indigenous relations. This concern is further highlighted by the way
place may be overemphasized in decisions about where to "pin" oral history
narratives on urban interpretive map-based apps, as Mark Tebeau has noted in
his description of a similar app for Cleveland, Ohio.[19] Tebeau also considers
issues arising from a lack of resources and inequalities of access, and these too
resonate with "First Story" organizers, whose efforts to digitize and share
Indigenous oral history in the city often depend upon opportunistic and
unstable funding of special projects. As he concludes, "Ironically, digital
tools have presented us with new dilemmas precisely by presenting new
possibilities."[20]

Feminist discussions of digitization and the digital era more broadly have
tended to emphasize the potential to shift gendered power relations by creating
new possibilities for the construction of authoritative knowledge. This optimistic
premise was embodied in the cyberfeminism movement. However, in her
recent review of the apparent decline of cyberfeminism, Claire Evans writes

that: "[B]eing a woman online in 2014 comes with the same caveats and anxieties that have always accompanied being female in meatspace. Fears of being silenced, threatened, or bullied are as real in the digital realm as IRL."[21] With regard to smart phone apps, both feminist and Indigenist scholarship seems to focus on how women and Indigenous peoples use apps, not create them. Also, analyses of app use examine limited and expected domains: baby care, fitness, and finances for women, and how apps can get Indigenous peoples to comply with biomedical healthcare regimens.[22]

Moreover, in discussing ethical issues arising in the digital era, Mary Larson suggests that because social media has made younger generations more cavalier about privacy in general, some of the early worries of oral historians about putting everything online may be moot.[23] However, for Indigenous women, making their voices available online goes beyond shifting notions of privacy, and requires consideration of the range of their experiences as witnesses, orators, survivors, bearers of life broadly defined, and in colonial and decolonizing contexts. In what follows, I examine how "First Story Toronto's" production of women's and Indigenous people's knowledges accounts for these processes, extending earlier practices emergent in the transition of Indigenous orality in the urban context.[24]

"First Story Toronto": A personal-community relational research journey

Before pursuing scholarly research with Indigenous people in Toronto, I was co-founder with my late partner, Indigenous scholar, activist, historian, Rodney Bobiwash, of the Toronto Native Community History Project, now "First Story Toronto." A primary goal of this work was, and still is, to counter racism through the production of Indigenous research and representation. Between 1995 and 2003, I worked at the Native Canadian Centre of Toronto (NCCT) as a program director, where I edited the NCCT's publication, *The Native Canadian*, and coordinated "First Story". In addition, I volunteered in fundraising, membership, and on committees. In one way or another, all of this work revolved around community-based research. Eventually, this research provided data for *The Meeting Place: Aboriginal Life in Toronto*, a book I co-edited with a member of the NCCT board of directors and which privileges community members' research and writing. In this period, I also completed my PhD dissertation.[25] After Rodney Bobiwash's untimely death in 2002, I moved to Michigan but remain involved with "First Story," which continues due to the perseverance of community members, volunteers, scholars, and partnership projects.[26]

"First Story" research is directed by community-based researchers and within carefully conceived partnerships with academics, a dual strategy that has furthered its original vision and mandate "to speak our memory; to promote the history of Aboriginal people in the Toronto area from time immemorial to the present, and for the future; and to teach and share in the spirit of friendship, with the goal of eliminating racism and prejudice."[27] To carry out this mission, "First Story" projects prioritize research that provides capacity-building opportunities for Indigenous youth and for program development, and which promotes social action through positive relationships between Indigenous peoples and all of the communities in the Toronto area. The "First Story" collective includes community-based researchers and academic partners, both Indigenous and non-Indigenous, whose work together is grounded relationally, and guided by "responsibilities to each other within a context of sharing, respect, and care."[28] In stewarding the NCCT's now extensive collection of archival and other research materials, including oral histories, the main aim is to generate tools which disseminate representations of urban Indigenous people and transform relations by getting "people to govern their relationships with a different set of eyeballs," as Rodney Bobiwash once put it.[29]

Urban Indigenous women's orality, relationality, and refusal

Oral history projects have figured and continue to figure significantly in "First Story" activities as does women's leadership in community organizing. This is primarily because of the particular Indigenous research traditions already well established and utilized within the community for these same goals for at least half a century at the NCCT. Since the early days of Indigenous urban community building in Toronto, Indigenous people initiated or led numerous research projects to articulate social, economic, and cultural needs, and establish programs, but also to change broader representations of Indigenous peoples.[30] Oral history, as a methodology involving listening to people to learn about their experiences and understand Indigenous frameworks for wellbeing, has been and continues to be seen as the preeminent research tool. Examples include the "Indians in the City" project (1969–1971) carried out under the auspices of the Chiefs of Ontario, the "Native Canadian Oral History" project conducted as a collaboration between the NCCT and the Toronto Public Library (Spadina Branch) in 1982 and 1983, and a study of Elders' involvement in the NCCT in the 1980s.[31]

It is from the 1982–83 "Native Canadian Oral History" project that I take my title, "Shut the tape off and I'll tell you a story."[32] These are the words of Verna Johnston, one of the better known of the 28 Indigenous people interviewed for the project. Her life was the subject of the book *I Am Nokomis, Too*, published by anthropologist Rosamond Vanderburgh in 1977.[33] And, in 1972, Johnston herself published *Tales of Nokomis*, a collection of the stories told to her by her great-grandmother at the Chippewas of Nawash Unceded First Nation (Neyaashiinigmiing, formerly "Cape Croker").[34] From the 1940s until her death in 1996, Johnston lived primarily in Toronto, and was an important figure in Indigenous community building there. The work she did running a boarding home for Indigenous women coming to the city to pursue educational opportunities, and with Anduhyaun, the Indigenous women's shelter, was featured numerous times in the mainstream media.[35]

Despite her own extensive involvement in the process of recording and writing down Indigenous oral history, she was cautionary about how, why, and for whom this was done. In sharing her story for the 1982 "Oral History" project, Johnston chose to maintain the verbal integrity of her telling, and it matters that her young interviewer, Jocelyn Keeshig, was a Nawash relative. Her act expressed layers of significance and interconnections between personal narratives, oral histories, and collective identity for Indigenous people in the urban landscape. It embodied the duality of the Indigenous prerogative of refusal and the Anishinaabe imperative of sharing. And, it spoke to the power of story in the oratorical continuum, a term coined by Anishinaabekwe scholar Dawnis Kennedy, to describe how "women's experiences are storied together through the vitalizing power of Indigenous women's praxis."[36] In the oratorical continuum, Indigenous women's oral histories are "significant not only for historical value, but as living story which, conceptualized within an Indigenous traditional framework, engages intergenerationally to empower and inspire youth today and into the future."[37] Johnston's own engagement with oral history as an active process, in the parts of the interview reserved for those moments, and as gifts specifically for Jocelyn Keeshig, illustrates the dynamics

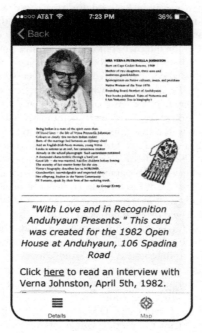

Figure 25.2 Screen shot of the "First Story Toronto" app page, featuring Verna Johnston

and vitality of oral history in the construction of Indigenous identity and community in the city.

How Indigenous oral history is defined is intimately tied to the concrete security of Indigenous peoples and their communities through its connection to Indigenous relationships with the land, other-than-human beings, and other human beings. As such, Johnston's words also reference the frictions of representational politics embedded in dispatching Indigenous voices to the front of efforts to transform the urban landscapes of erasure. In the 1980s, recording and sharing oral traditions met with criticism from within the community, but there were those, like Verna Johnston, who recognized the communicative value of transformations occurring in oral history processes through Indigenized publishing directed at members of the NCCT and which included a large non-Indigenous audience. The NCCT's *Beaver Tails* (1962–1968), *Toronto Native Times* (1968–1980), *Boozhoo Magazine* (1980–1984), and finally *The Native Canadian* (1985–present) established and continued a publishing tradition integral to the production of urban Indigenous community, and all reproduced oral history in the form of traditional stories, reminiscing, and biographical accounts. Also interviewed in the 1982 "Oral History" project, Elder Joe Sylvester related that while he was "getting so much flak" from community members who said he "should not write those sacred things in the paper," he persevered, feeling that "somehow we must pass these things on."[38]

Contestations continue to frame community-based efforts to share Indigenous knowledge for internal community-building purposes, and these are often entangled with social justice goals. Debates actively continue within the community about what constitutes Toronto's Indigenous history, by whom and with whom it may be shared, and why. However, content originating in Indigenous orality is generally seen as more accurate, and so the "First Story" app attempts to address these contestations by combining oral sources, including video and audio clips as well as transcript excerpts, with other forms of content.[39]

Regarding transcriptions, "First Story's" approach echoes the collective analysis generated in the 1990s by Toronto Indigenous women participants in a reading group. They read biographical works by and about Indigenous women, concluding that the transcript can convey the quality of being "like her lips to my ear" and result in transformative dynamics from the active ways in which the text is engaged by Indigenous and non-Indigenous readers.[40] The "First Story" app entry for Verna Johnston includes a transcript of an interview conducted with her in 1982 (see Figure 25.2). As the members of the reading group expressed, for Indigenous "First Story" users reading Johnston's transcript might be like listening "to my mother and her sisters talk like that, because on top of entertainment, it is history. It is a part of my history."[41] Because we can assume that non-Indigenous users may likely view content through the lens of stereotypes and tacit racism, in constructing women's content, "First Story" tries to re-orient their interpretations by presenting women's experiences, leadership, and power in unexpected places. By combining historical and current events, "First Story" app users are also invited to step beyond their remote engagement and attend, in person, Indigenous community-led events, with the hope of changing their relationships of co-existence in the city, and on Indigenous lands.

For example, another entry, which features Jeannette Corbiere-Lavell, is pinned on the "First Story" map to the location of the University Avenue courthouse where she first challenged sex discrimination in the Indian Act in 1971 (see Figure 25.3).[42] Corbiere-Lavell lived in Toronto in the 1960s and 1970s, worked at the NCCT, and was active in social movements. The entry includes text, photographs, links to a 1973 *Globe & Mail* article, and references to scholarly articles, including Cheryl Suzack's "Law Stories as Life Stories."[43] It also includes an 8-minute audio clip of Corbiere-Lavell recorded for a "First Story Toronto" project called "Indigenous Women, Memory and Power (IWMP)," the purpose of which was to gather and share the stories of Indigenous women in Toronto as leaders, activists, and community organizers. The IWMP project was initiated by Elder Pauline Shirt, along with Lee Maracle, Dawnis Kennedy, and Victoria Freeman in 2012, and received federal funding from Canadian Heritage in 2013–2014.

Maintaining the "oratorical continuum," as described earlier, structures the methodology of the IWMP project, in which young Indigenous women are mentored to facilitate a relational process of engagement between themselves and women with various experiences building Indigenous community in Toronto. Recording the women's oral histories is part of a multi-dimensional socio-cultural process, not its totality.[44] Although attention and resources supported training and equipment to ensure the quality of recording, the Corbiere-Lavell audio (and others) includes the din of rustling and commotion in the room, coughing, laughing, exclamations, and other emotive responses to the teller. These sounds highlight another kind of refusal with regards to the IWMP methodology and the value for posterity of this kind of oral history. It is the relational and intergenerational engagement within the oratorical process that is critical, displacing the primacy of recording quality.

In the Corbiere-Lavell audio selected for the "First Story" app, laughter erupts when Corbiere-Lavell says she cannot recall quite what happened to the 35-dollar cheque Indian Affairs sent her along with a notice ending her Indian status. The laughter, which is stimulated in part by Corbiere-Lavell's own tone, signals shared derision at the Canadian state for the paltry amount, and emphasizes the meaninglessness of the cheque. As Corbiere-Lavell continues, "That cheque apparently was all my rights, my band funds, membership, the allotment, and I just can't believe it." The cheque symbolized both everything that is important and everything that is wrong with the federal relationship in which one nation decides the "status" of the other, and which is embodied by Indigenous women. Corbiere-Lavell follows immediately with her description of her interaction with Judge B.W. Grossberg as he ruled against her:

> We went to County Court … this was right downtown Toronto on University. Judge Grossberg, he was just so arrogant, like we were wasting

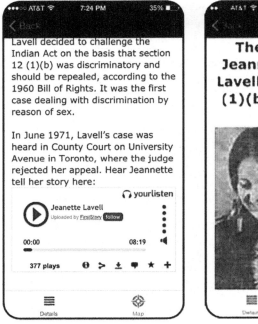
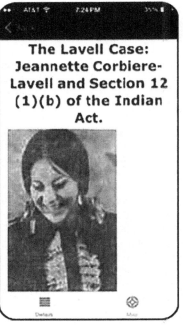

Figure 25.3 Two pages from the entry for Jeanette Corbiere-Lavell on the "First Story Toronto" app

his time. He was challenging me. He said: "Why are you challenging this? Everyone knows what reserves are . . . Why would you even consider this?" And I had to explain this—this is where I grew up, my family, all my relatives, this is who I am . . . The one question that I remember because it sort of hit me fairly hard. He said, "We all know what the Indian women are like, eh? There on the streets, like prostitutes." And then he said, "You should be glad a white man married you."

There is a burst of gasps in the room among the listeners and Corbiere-Lavell is briefly inaudible before stating: "I was devastated when he said that, you know."

By including this particular excerpt, "First Story Toronto" pays attention to how both Indigenous and non-Indigenous audiences may receive Corbiere-Lavell's oral history. It is framed within the "First Story" mission "to speak our memory," and to promote social action aimed at eliminating racism and prejudice. Focusing on Indigenous women's experiences and leadership make clearer how these aspects of the mission intersect with colonialism and misogynism. Judge Grossberg's words, spoken by Corbiere-Lavell, highlight the specific and continuing "caveats and anxieties" of being Indigenous and female in "meatspace."[45] The excerpt is historically contextualized with other sources, links, and images, but it is also linkable to ongoing current events in Toronto. These might include, for example, numerous sites pertaining to Indigenous Missing and Murdered Women such as protest-awareness actions, Facebook groups, and academic and public talks.

Conclusion

At the moment I am writing this, the Canadian government announced its intention to form an inquiry into Indigenous Missing and Murdered Women. Justice Minister Jody Wilson-Raybould emphasized that the extent of violence against Indigenous women and girls is not an Indigenous problem; "it's not simply a woman's issue" but "all Canadians are diminished by this national tragedy."[46] In sharing oral history on the "First Story" app, some of the reciprocal dimensions of Indigenous oral history may be lost. Storytellers and audiences do not share contexts, and some argue that the mere recollection of facts is no substitute for wisdom.[47] However, the Jeannette Corbiere-Lavell oral history illustrates the degree to which the recollection of personal facts provides wisdom for Indigenous women circulating within the ongoing structural and real violences of the contemporary Canadian settler state. Underlining how racism, colonialism, and misogynism intersect to produce such oppressive relations is crucial to changing these relations. Focusing on Indigenous people as active creators of digital oral histories underscores the significant role that Indigenous community-led research can play towards achieving this end. From this perspective, oral history produced and disseminated in digital forms may have more far-reaching implications than generally assumed for the urban Indigenous community and for non-Indigenous people living in the city on Indigenous lands.

The focus within the IWMP project on the process of oratorical continuum among Indigenous women highlights how oral history is transformed by the collective and personal experiences of urbanization, and the ways that urban Indigenous storytellers transmit cultural knowledge in relation to life in the city. As illustrated by Verna Johnston, refusal is as central a feature in oral history production sustaining Indigenous continuity as is recording. "Shutting the tape off" strengthens the power of memory shared among Indigenous women, and fortifies exponentially that which is shared more widely. Decolonizing oral history in this way is necessary to the production of social justice and co-existence to which we put oral history to work.

Notes

1 Sherna Berger Gluck and Daphne Patai, eds., *Women's Words: The Feminist Practice of Oral History* (New York: Routledge, 1991); Linda Tuhiwai Smith, *Decolonizing Methodologies: Research and Indigenous Peoples* (London: Zed Press, 1999), 144–145.

2 See Katherine Borland, "'That's Not What I Said': Interpretive Conflict in Oral Narrative Research," in *Women's Words*, 64; Marie-Francoise Chanfrault-Duchet, "Narrative Structures, Social Models, and Symbolic Representation in the Life Story," in *Women's Words*, 78.

3 See Rina Benmayor, "Testimony, Action Research, and Empowerment: Puerto Rican Women and Popular Education," in *Women's Words*, 164–165, 172–173; Claudia Salazar, "A Third World Woman's Text: Between the Politics of Criticism and Cultural Politics," in *Women's Words*, 103.

4 Heather A. Howard, "Dreamcatchers in the City: An Ethnohistory of Social Action, Gender, and Class in Native Community Production in Toronto" (PhD diss., University of Toronto, 2004), 8–9; 224–228; Heather Howard-Bobiwash, "'Like Her Lips to My Ear': Reading Anishnaabekweg Lives and Cultural Continuity in the City," in *Feminist Fields: Ethnographic Insights*, eds. Rae Bridgman, Sally Cole, and Heather Howard-Bobiwash (Peterborough: Broadview Press, 1999), 117–136; Diane Wolf, ed., *Feminist Dilemmas in Fieldwork* (Boulder: Westview Press, 1996); Susan Geiger, "What's So Feminist About Women's Oral History?" *Journal of Women's History* 2, no. 1 (Spring 1990): 169–182; Shulamit Reinharz, *Feminist Methods in Social Research* (New York: Oxford University Press, 1992); Joan Sangster, "Telling Our Stories: Feminist Debates and the Use of Oral History," *Women's History Review* 3, no. 1 (1994): 5–28; Bea Medicine, "American Indians and Anthropologists: Issues of History, Empowerment, and Application," *Human Organization* 57, no. 3 (Fall 1998): 253–257; Bea Medicine, *Learning to Be an Anthropologist and Remaining Native, Selected Writings* (Chicago: University of Illinois Press, 2001), 329–330.

5 Krystine Abel et al., "Indigenous Women, Memory, and Power: Igniting and Restoring an Oratorical Continuum Across Generations," in *Indigenous Women's Histories*, eds. Mary Jane McCallum and Susan Hill (Winnipeg: University of Manitoba Press, forthcoming); Heather Howard-Bobiwash, "Women's Class Strategies as Activism in Native Community Building in Toronto, 1950–1975," *American Indian Quarterly* 27, nos. 3/4 (Summer/Autumn 2003): 566–582; Howard-Bobiwash, "'Like Her Lips to My Ear.'" Also see Anderson et al., Chapter 12, Leddy, Chapter 7, as well as Couchie and Miguel, Chapter 16 in this volume.

6 See Kim Anderson, *A Recognition of Being: Reconstructing Native Womanhood* (Toronto: Sumach Press, 2000); Susan Lobo, *Urban Voices: The Bay Area American Indian Community* (Tucson: University of Arizona Press, 2002); Bonita Lawrence, *Real Indians and Others: Mixed-Blood Urban Native Peoples and Indigenous Nationhood* (Lincoln: University of Nebraska Press, 2004); Renya Ramirez, *Native Hubs: Culture, Community, and Belonging in Silicon Valley and Beyond* (Durham: Duke University Press, 2007). The "first wave" of studies dating to the 1960s and 1970s focused primarily on problem-centered issues, "(mal)adjustment" to city life, following major rural-urban population movements after World War II. For representations of this literature, see Arthur M. Harkins, *A Bibliography of Urban Indians in the United States* (Minneapolis: Center for Urban and Regional Affairs, University of Minnesota, 1971); Alan L. Sorkin, *The Urban American Indian* (Lexington: Lexington Books, 1978); Jack O. Waddell and Michael Watson, eds., *The American Indian in Urban Society* (Boston: Little, Brown, 1971).

7 The living history circle method followed Barbara Myerhoff's model of group interviewing with Jewish Holocaust survivors living in a seniors' residence in Venice, California, combined with the "sharing circle" form of group communication commonly used in the Toronto Indigenous community already for social, cultural, service, therapeutic, and other activities. See Myerhoff, *Number Our Days* (New York: E.P. Dutton, 1978); Heather A. Howard, "Canadian Residential Schools and Urban Indigenous Knowledge Production about Diabetes," *Medical Anthropology: Cross-Cultural Studies in Health and Illness* 33, no. 6 (2014): 529–545.

8 Winona Stevenson, "Indigenous Peoples' Oral Histories Raise Ethical Issues," *Oral History Association Newsletter* 33, no. 2 (June 1999): 7. Couchie and Miguel's chapter 16 in this volume provides a powerful example of a performative and dialogic approach rooted in Indigenous orality and epistemologies.

9 George J. Sefa Dei, "Rethinking the Role of Indigenous Knowledges in the Academy," *International Journal of Inclusive Education* 4, no. 2 (2000): 111–132; D. Cole, *Captured Heritage: The Scramble for Northwest Coast Artefacts* (Vancouver: Douglas & McIntyre, 1985); Julie Cruikshank, "Oral Tradition and Material Culture: Multiplying Meanings of 'Words' and 'Things,'" *Anthropology Today* 8 (June 1992): 5–9; Cruikshank, "Oral Tradition and Oral History: Reviewing Some Issues," *Canadian Historical Review* 75, no. 3 (September 1994): 403–418; Bruce Miller, *Oral History On Trial: Recognizing Aboriginal Narratives in the Courts* (Vancouver: University of British Columbia Press, 2011); Greg Sarris, *Keeping Slug Woman Alive: A Holistic Approach to American Indian Texts* (Berkeley: University of California Press, 1993).

10 Elizabeth Tonkin, *Narrating Our Past: The Social Construction of Oral History* (New York: Cambridge University Press, 1995).

11 Cruikshank, "Oral Tradition and Oral History," 418.

12 Smith, 144–145.

13 Joanne Archibald, *Indigenous Storywork* (Vancouver: University of British Columbia Press, 2008), ix.

14 Howard-Bobiwash, "'Like Her Lips to My Ear'"; Cara Krmpotich, Heather Howard, and Emma Knight, "From Collection to Community to Collections Again: Urban Indigenous Women, Material Culture and Belonging," *Journal of Material Culture* (18 October 2015 doi:10.1177/1359183515610362), accessed 14 November 2015; Rayna Green, "American Indian Women: Diverse Leadership for Social Change," in *Bridges of Power: Women's Multicultural Alliances*, eds. Lisa Albrecht and Rose M. Brewer (Philadelphia: New Society Publishers, 1990).

15 Stevenson, "Indigenous Peoples' Oral Histories Raise Ethical Issues," 7.

16 Native Canadian Centre of Toronto, "First Story Toronto App and Bus Tour," accessed 15 June 2015, http://ncct.on.ca/first-story-toronto-app-bus-tour/.

17 Mark Tebeau, "Listening to the City: Oral History and Place in the Digital Era," *Oral History Review* 40, no. 1 (Winter/Spring 2013): 25–35; Alistair Thomson, "Four Paradigm Transformations in Oral History," *The Oral History Review* 34, no. 1 (Winter/Spring 2007): 49–70; Mary Larson, "Steering Clear of the Rocks: A Look at the Current State of Oral History Ethics in the Digital Age," *Oral History Review* 40, no. 1 (Winter/Spring 2013): 36–49.

18 Steve Cohen, "Shifting Paradigms: New Questions for Oral History in a Digital Age," *Oral History Review* 40, no. 1 (Winter/Spring 2013): 161.

19 Tebeau, 30.

20 Tebeau, 33. See also, Lyndon Ormond-Parker and Robyn Sloggett, "Local Archives and Community Collecting in the Digital Age," *Archival Science* 12 (June 2012): 191–212. Mary Larson also makes this point in her chapter 22.

21 Claire L. Evans, "An Oral History of Cyberfeminism," *Motherboard*, last modified 11 December 2014, accessed 30 September 2015, http://motherboard.vice.com/read/an-oral-history-of-the-first-cyberfeminists-vns-matrix; Claire L. Evans, "'We Are the Future Cunt': Cyberfeminism in the 90s," *Motherboard*, last modified 20 November 2014, accessed 30 September 2015, http://motherboard.vice.com/read/we-are-the-future-cunt-cyberfeminism-in-the-90s.

22 This statement is based on Google Scholar searches in both domains and review of the abstracts produced on the first three pages of results. With regards to Indigenous peoples' smart phone use scholarship, one exception to the focus on healthcare compliance, was an article about an app that translated the Bible for Yoruba users.

23 Larson, 46.

24 I therefore situate First Story research methodologies in relation to other Indigenist approaches. See, for example, Shawn Wilson, *Research as Ceremony: Indigenous Research Methods* (Blackpoint: Fernwood, 2008); Margaret Kovach, *Indigenous Methodologies: Characteristics, Conversations, and Contexts* (Toronto: University of Toronto Press, 2010); Alexandra Kahsenniio Nahwegahbow, "Springtime in n'Daki Menan, the Homeland of the Teme-Augama Anishnabai: Babies, Cradleboards and Community Wrapping" (master's thesis, Carleton University, 2013); Heather Castleden, Vanessa S. Morgan, and Christopher Lamb, "'I Spent the First Year Drinking Tea': Exploring Canadian University Researchers' Perspectives on Community-based Participatory Research Involving Indigenous Peoples," *The Canadian Geographer/Le Géographe canadien* 56, no. 2 (Summer 2012): 160–179.

25 Howard, "Dreamcatchers"; Frances Sanderson and Heather Howard-Bobiwash, eds., *The Meeting Place: Aboriginal Life in Toronto* (Toronto: Native Canadian Centre of Toronto, 1997).

26 Krmpotich, Howard, and Knight, "From Collection to Community"; Lynne C. Howarth and Emma Knight, "To Every Artifact Its Voice: Creating Surrogates for Hand-Crafted Indigenous Objects," *Cataloging & Classification Quarterly* 53, no. 5–6 (2015): 580–595; Abel et al., "Indigenous Women, Memory, and Power"; Victoria Freeman, "'Toronto Has No History!' Indigeneity, Settler Colonialism, and Historical Memory in Canada's Largest City" (PhD diss., University of Toronto, 2010); Monica Bodirsky and Jon Johnson, "Decolonizing Diet: Healing by Reclaiming Traditional Indigenous Foodways," *Cuizine: The Journal of Canadian Food Cultures/Cuizine: revue des cultures culinaires au Canada* 1, no. 1 (2008), accessed 10 June 2010, www.erudit.org/revue/cuizine/2008/v1/n1/019373ar. html; Jon Johnson, "Pathways to the Eighth Fire: Indigenous Knowledge and Storytelling in Toronto" (PhD diss., York University, 2015); Jon Johnson, "The Great Indian Bus Tour: Mapping Toronto's Urban First Nations' Oral Tradition," in *The Nature of Empires and the Empires of Nature: Indigenous Peoples and the Great Lakes Environment*, ed. Karl Hele (Waterloo, ON: Wilfrid Laurier University Press, 2013), 302–320.

27 Stephanie M. Boissoneau and Heather Howard-Bobiwash, *Toronto Native Community History Project Policy and Procedures Manual* (Toronto: Native Canadian Centre of Toronto, 2000), 5.

28 Abel et al., "Indigenous Women, Memory, and Power"; Heather Howard, "Co-Producing Community and Knowledge: Indigenous Epistemologies of Engaged, Ethical Research in an Urban Context," *The Engaged Scholar Journal* 2, no. 1 (Spring 2016): 205–224; Leanne Betasamosake Simpson, "The Place Where We All Live and Work Together," in *Native Studies Keywords*, eds. Stephanie Nohalani Teeves, Andrea Smith, and Michelle H. Raheja (Tucson: University of Arizona Press, 2015), 18; Deborah McGregor and Sylvia Plain, "Anishinaabe Research Theory and Practice: Place-Based Research," in *Anishinaabewin NIIWIN Four Rising Winds*, eds. Alan Ojiig Corbiere et al. (M'Chigeeng: Ojibwe Cultural Foundation, 2013), 93–114.

29 TV Ontario, "Native Bus Tour," *Studio 2*, aired 25 March 2002.

30 Howard, "Co-Producing Community."

31 Howard, "Co-Producing Community"; Suzanne Stiegelbauer, "The Road Back to the Future: Tradition and the Involvement of Elders at the Native Canadian Centre of Toronto," (PhD diss., University of Texas Austin, 1990); "What Is an Elder? What Do Elders Do?: First Nation Elders as Teachers in Culture-based Urban Organizations," *Canadian Journal of Native Studies* 16, no. 1 (1996): 37–66.

32 "Native Canadian Oral History" project, Verna Johnston interviewed by Jocelyn Keeshig 1982, tape #OHT 82024, Spadina Road Library Branch of the Toronto Public Library, 3.

33 Rosamond M. Vanderburgh, *I Am Nokomis, Too: The Biography of Verna Patronella Johnson* (Don Mills, ON: General Publishing, 1977).
34 Verna P. Johnston, *Tales of Nokomis* (Don Mills, ON: Musson Book Co., 1975).
35 See M. Higgins, "Haven for Indian Girls," *Toronto Telegram*, 26 March 1968, and most recently, T. Alamenciak, "Remembering 'Grandma': Verna Johnston Smoothed the Transition to Toronto for Countless Native Kids," *Toronto Star*, 18 January 2015.
36 Abel et al., "Indigenous Women, Memory, and Power."
37 Abel et al., "Indigenous Women, Memory, and Power."
38 "Native Canadian Oral History" project, Joe Sylvester interviewed by Jocelyn Keeshig, 1982, tape #OHT 82023, Spadina Road Library Branch of the Toronto Public Library. Also note that Anishinaabe scholar John Borrows is Verna's great-great nephew and recognizes the value of keeping her stories alive in his book: *Canada's Indigenous Constitution* (Toronto: University of Toronto Press, 2010), 280.
39 These questions are elaborated and explored further in Heather Howard, Jon Johnston, and Victoria Freeman, "First Story: Indigenous Peoples' History as Smart Phone App," paper presented at the annual meeting of the American Anthropological Association, 21 November 2015.
40 Howard-Bobiwash, "'Like Her Lips to My Ear.'"
41 Howard-Bobiwash, "'Like Her Lips to My Ear,'" 132.
42 This is the 1876 federal Canadian law that governs the affairs of registered "Indians" and regulates "Indian" legal status. Until the 1980s, the Act enforced the extinguishment of a woman's Indian status if she married a man without Indian status, which meant loss of her rights under the Acts, including the right to live on her reserve.
43 Cheryl Suzack, "Law Stories as Life Stories: Jeannette Lavell, Yvonne Bedard, and Halfbreed," in *Tracing the Autobiographical*, eds., Linda Warley, Jeanne Perreault, and Susanna Egan (Waterloo, ON: Wilfrid Laurier University Press, 2005), 117–142.
44 Abel et al., "Indigenous Women, Memory, and Power."
45 Evans, "An Oral History of Cyberfeminism"; Evans, "'We Are the Future Cunt.'"
46 Canadian Press, "Ottawa to Consult Families on Inquiry into Missing, Murdered Indigenous Women," *The Star*, 8 December 2015, accessed 8 December 2015, www.thestar.com/news/canada/2015/12/08/ottawa-to-begin-consulting-families-on-inquiry-into-missing-murdered-indigenous-women.html.
47 Howard, Johnson, and Freeman, "First Story."

Index

Note: Text within figures is indicated by page citations in *italics*.

abolitionism 287
Aboriginal women 96: sterilization of
  107n10; *see also* Indigenous feminism,
  Anishinaabe and Anishinaabe
  womanhood
Aboriginal-English: 'Country' 181n10
abortion 85, 142, 315
Abrams, Lynn 3, 10, 12, 77, 100, 129,
  314
Abu-Lughod, Lila 137
Acholi tribal practices 201n18
activism 4: civil rights 109–10, 221;
  community 105; feminism in India
  109–22; feminist 212; human rights
  215n9; lesbians 131–2; ordinary
  people vs 131–2; political 68, 106,
  113, 219–21; racist 57–61
Addams, Jane 33
Adichie, Chimanada Ngozi 13
Adivasi women 116
adult literacy program: Spanish 28
affective engagement 239–40; *see also*
  social movements
affirmative action 54n11
African American civil rights 57
African Oral Narratives (AON) 312n18
Akello, Grace 5, 9, 153–4
Al-Ali, Nadje 5, 9, 79
Al-Anfal campaign (anti-Kurd) 140, 143
Albright, Madeleine. 143
alcoholism 43, 229, 294–5
Alexander, Marion 129
allanamientos (raids) 209
allohistory: definition 52
American Broadcasting Company 37n16

American imperialism 4; *see also*
  imperialism
American Pragmatism 33
ancient properties 175
ancient texts 112n26, 120
Anderson, Kathryn 10, 212–13, 299
Anderson, Kim 101
Anderson, Sue 4, 6, 151, 171, 179
andocentrism 288
Anglo-Indian community 38–46
Anglo-Indian schoolteachers 5, 29,
  38–46; *see also* positionality of narrators
  and interviewers
Anglophone dominance 4
Anishinaabe: ceremony 223, 225 233;
  creation stories, 226–7; Elders 13,
  95, 99–102, 104–6, 106n2, 230–2,
  328–9, 334n31; gender roles 101,
  104; teachings 102, 327; worldview
  104, 223, 225
Anishinaabe womanhood 6, 13, 95,
  101–4, 95–106, 107n16, 223, 225–6,
  235n7, 327: ceremony 223, 225;
  community strength and 17n22;
  Elders 13; grandfather teachings
  235n7; 'rascals' 235n7
anthropology 3, 49, 51, 63, 285: medical
  192, 198–9
anti-colonial women's oral history 16n16
"Anti-Eviction Mapping" project 238
Antikirinja women 171
anti-racist activism 256
Anzaldúa, Gloria 65, 69
apps: mobile phone 322–31
Arabic language 276n16

Arabization 79: policies 142–3
Arasu, Ponni 4, 79
Archibald, Joanne 323
archived oral histories 12, 313–18
"Archives of Lesbian Oral Testimony
    (ALOT)" project 281, 304, 306,
    308–9
archives 306: oral 205–7; terror 205–7
Argounova-Low, Tatiana 172
Aristide, Jean-Bertrand 186
Armenian: fountains 272; Genocide
    274, 275n7; language 275nn2, 9,
    276n15
Armitage, Susan 7, 289
Arshadi, Shahrzad 9, 219–20, 261
artistic installations 268
artwork 189fig, 191n16
ASCAP (American Society of Composers,
    Authors, and Publishers) 37n16
asylum rights 145
Attarian, Hourig 9, 219, 261
Audacity 304
audience 303n12
Australian Indigenous cultures; *see also*
    Indigenous feminism and Antikirinja
    women
authenticity 290–1
authoritarianism 145; *see also*
    dictatorship
authority 319n2
autobiographic ethnography 18n27,
    36n8, 63, 72n10, 192, 196, 237, 280,
    282n3
autonomy journeys 82
Aymara women 211

Ba'th regime 139, 141–2
Bachelet, Michelle 205
Baker, Khadija 9, 219, 261
Bakhtin, Mikhail 27, 33
Barker, Aunty June 171
Barker, Jimmie 175
Barker, Joanne 97
Barker, Lorina 4, 6, 151, 178–9
Barman, Jean 96
Barratt, Virginia 299
Becker, Carl 283, 291
Bedard, Yvonne 107n13
Behar, Ruth 49, 63, 200
Behrendt, Larissa 176
bell hooks 13, 176
Belliappa, Jyothsna Latha 5, 29
Benjamin, Jessica 33

Benmayor, Rina 2, 4, 27–8, 178, 204
Benson, Koni 177
Berkshire Conference of Women
    Historians 15n14
Bérubé, Alan 128
Bessarab, Dawn 174
Bhopal Group for Information and
    Action 246
Bhopal Movement Study Group (BMSG)
    245
Bi, Hamida 248
Bi, Hazra 247
Bi, Rabiya 248
Bi, Rashida 248–9
Bilici, Kumru 9, 219, 261
Black Lives Matter 253
Blasquez, Adélaïde 50
Blee, Kathleen 2, 29
blogs 309
Bobiwash, Rodney 325–6
"Bodies Across Borders: Oral and Visual
    Memory in Europe and Beyond
    (BABE)" project 20n36
bombing 275n1
borderlands consciousness: concept of
    69
Borges, Jorge Luis 53
Boris, Eileen 287
Borland, Katherine 2, 27–8, 50
Boulay, Nadine 306
Boyd, Nan Alamilla 128–9
Brah, Avtar 137
Brazil: oral history in 54n11; women
    17n24
breast cancer narratives 84, 92
Brewarrina Aboriginal Station 171
"Bringing Them Home Oral History"
    project 179
British Library 309
Brooklyn Historical Society (BHS)
    252–3, 256, 258n5
Bryman, Alan 197
Burgos, Elizabeth 51
Burkhas 248
Butalia, Urvashi 113

Cabrera-Murillo, Liliana 69
call backs 189
Cambodia 143, 190n2
"Cambodian Defenders" project (CDP)
    159, 167n1
Cambodian Women's Hearing (CWH)
    159–60

"Cambodian Women's Oral History" project (CWOHP) 5, 152, 155–67, 168n22, 205, 311n10
Campaign for Nuclear Disarmament (CND) 89–90
Canada: publishing tradition 328; *see also* "Montréal Life Stories" project
Carroll, Tamar 289
castes 110
Catholicism 42–3, 291–3
Ceili: definition 292
Center for Making and Saving History 240
Center for Story-Based Strategy 242n6
Central African Republic (CAR) 193
Centre for Indigenous Theatre (CIT) 233
Centre for Oral History and Digital Storytelling (COHDS) 190n2, 262, 270, 275n5
Cervantes, Herminia 67
Chakravarti, Uma 4, 79, 109–22, 124n25
Chandler, David 157
Chanfrault-Duchet, Marie-Françoise 34
Charlier, Ghislaine 187
Chenier, Elise 5, 134, 281, 314
childcare 139, 142, 144
childhood 194: concepts of 194; memory of 168n25, 263, 265
children: conceptualization as social actors 193–4; storytelling/yarning 173–4; wartime 143, 146n5, 192–200
Chile 5, 143, 152: archiving terror 205–7; female torture survivors 204–14; oral archive 205–7; oral history as a Gringa Chilena 210–12; survivors in Chile's different regions 207–10; Villa Grimaldi memory site 205–7; *Women's Words* and feminist oral history 212–14
Chippewas of Nawash Unceded First Nation 326–7
civil rights: activism 221, 309; India 110–21; organizations 114–15
Civil War (US) 52
cleansing rituals 201n18
clowning 234n3
CNI (National Information Agency, Chile) 205
Coast Salish territory 240
Coelho, Nelson 198
Cohen, Steve 323

coherence 37n15: system, definition 82
Cold War 104, 204
collaborative outcome 10
collective identity 242n12
collective storytelling 154
collective voice 302n2, 303n6
colonialism 8, 105, 286, 287, 330
Commanda, Orval 105
communism 50, 52
Communist Party (PC, Chile) 205, 215n8
communities 131, 184: community engagement 219–21; community memory: lesbians 126–34
composure 22n48
confessions 156–9; *see also* Khmer Rouge genocide
confidentiality 161, 215n14, 258n7
consent: concept of 117
Constitution of India 46n2
contentious performance 245, 249–50, 250n4; *see also* social movements
contraception 79, 90, 142
Contribute (plug-in) 310
Cooperative Commonwealth Federation (CCF) 127
Corbiere-Lavell, Jeanette 107n13, 329–31
Corless, Catherine 293
Correia, Caroline 283–4, 295
Couchie, Penny 6, 220–1
covert omission 299
creation stories 6, 224–6
Creative Commons license 308–9
critical consciousness 242n7
critiquing *testimonios* 66; *see also* emotion and pedagogy; *testimonios*
cross-cultural ethnographic studies 18n27
"Crossing Borders, Bridging Generations" (CBBG) project 252–8
crowd-sourcing 289
Cruikshank, Julie 172, 178, 322
Cuban rafter exodus 55n20
cultural heritage sites 275n8
cultural hybridity: concept of 252
cultural meaning 22n49
cultural myth 20n37
cultural theory 27
curating 285, 290, 306, 309
Cvetkovich, Ann 128
cyberactivism 302n6
cyberbullying 325

cyberfeminism 302, 324–5
cyborg feminism 279

D.B. 187
Da'wa party (Islamist Shi'i) 140–1
Dadirri (deep listening) 174–5, 178
Daesh (IS) 145
dancing 247
data protection 161
Dauphin, Monique 187
Davis, Madeleine 128
de Berg, Hazel 177
de Langis, Theresa 5, 9, 143, 151–2,
  205, 244, 309
death penalty 238
death squads 204
decentering and decolonizing:
  decolonization 7, 11, 14n4, 95,
  106n2, 180: decolonizing knowledge
  19n30; feminist oral history 151–4
Delhi University Discussion Society
  (DUDS!) 111
Delhi University Teachers Association
  112
D'Emilio, John 128
democracy 54n11
Democratic Republic of Congo (DRC)
  193
democratic rights movement 118
denuncia (denouncement) 204
deSouza, Sanchia 5, 29
developing world 311n5
Devil Baby Legends 36n8
Díaz, Junot 254
dictatorship 139, 143, 186, 209–10, 267
dictionaries 170, 314
difficult stories 22n47
Digital Humanities 282
digital revolution 284–5, 289
digital self-representation 5, 283–95
digital storytelling 27, 63–71, 241–2n6,
  279–82; *see also* emotion and pedagogy
digital technology 11–12, 300; 'afterlife'
  of oral histories 304–11
digitization: archival 319n7
DINA (National Intelligence Agency,
  Chile) 205
discomposure 37n15
displacement 190n4, 238, 275n13; *see
  also* refugees
distance: concept of 280
divorce 35; *see also* marriage
documentary film 121, 123n18, 309

"Documenting Ferguson" project 310
domestic violence 145, 238
domesticity *see* home in story
dreaming stories 172
Dunaway, David 300
Duvalier, Jean-Claude: dictatorship
  (1957–1986) 186

education 190n2
El Barrio Popular Education Program 63
elderly women 36n8
Elías-Morales, Ana 66–9
Ellingson, Laura 199
Ellis, Carolyn 199
Emergency period in India (1975–1977)
  112–16, 120
emotion 190n4, 209; centrality of 28;
  emotional experience 228–31;
  normative and 'outlaw' discourses of
  65
emotion and pedagogy 63–71, 190n4,
  209: context 71; critiquing
  testimonios 66; memory writes 66;
  pedagogies of emotion 65–7;
  performing story 67; presenting story
  70–1; producing story 67–9; story
  circles 66–7; texts of emotion 65;
  theorizing story 69–70; empathy 154:
  empathetic connection 61; empathetic
  enmeshment 192, 198
empowerment 28, 287
encounter killings 116–17
English language 160–1
enslavement 145
equal pay 90
equality and social justice 3–4, 7, 13
equality of opportunity 82
essentialism 3, 12
ethics 5, 12, 32: biomedical 216n25;
  ethical awareness 48–9; ethical conduct
  161
ethnicity: concept of 252, 254; ethnic
  discrimination 79
ethnography: auto- 196–200; feminist 8,
  213; social science methods 153; with
  wartime children 192–200
Etter-Lewis, Gwendolyn 176, 299
Evans, Claire 324–5
Everywoman clinics 83–4
eviction 238
Ewald, Holly 301
exclusivity 132–3
exile 204; *see also* refugees

Extraordinary Chambers in the Courts of Cambodia (ECCC) 158, 164, 166–7
Ezidi women 145

Facebook 11, 283, 289, 293, 304, 309
fact-finding 79–80, 124n25
family stories 269
Farsi language 275nn2, 9–10
Feisal II 141
female genital mutilation (FGM) 86, 145
feminine solidarity *see* women power and feminine solidarity
feminism: concept of 77, 82, 313–14; definition of 96; discussion 81–92
feminist critical ethnography 20n38
feminist oral history: past and present approaches 77–80
feminist standpoint theory 178
feminographies 84
festival culture 114, 123n18
festival poster *70*
fetishization of violence 158
fieldwork 219–21: field dilemmas 194–5; social movements 245
Fighting for my History: screen shots *68*
Figueiredo, Luis 198
Finch, Janet 41
"First Story Toronto" 7, 19n33, 281, 321–31, 330, 334n24; *see also* urban Indigenous community representations
first-wave feminism 314, 318
Flores, Catalina 208, 211–12
folklore 31–2
food 101–2, 275n12
forced disappearances 204, 205, 214n7
Forfreedom, Ann 313
Frank, Arthur W. 33
Fredericks, Bronwyn 176
Freeman, Victoria 329
Freire, Paolo 253
French, Marilyn 87
Freund, Alexander 71, 282n3, 300
Frisch, Michael 10, 177, 186, 190n2, 284, 286, 314
f-word 78, 86

Gabaccia, Donna 199
Gallardo, Jacquelyn 70–1
Gandhi, Indira 114, 124n28, 125n33
Garcia, Emmanuel 240
Garfield, Richard 146n5
Garner, Jeremy 290
Garza, José 71

gay women 126–34: finding 129–31; social historical approaches 135n7; *see also* lesbians
Geia, Lynore 173
gender: balance 134; equality 72n6; non-conformism 238; relations: Iraq 141–4; violence 208
gendered and racialized body 64
gendered state violence 143, 145
genocide: Khmer Rouge 155–67
ghost stories 294
Gifford, Brenda 176, 179
Gilligan, Carol 256
Gilmore, Glenda 287
Giorgi, Amadeo 200
Gluck, Sherna Berger 1–3, 11–12, 177, 200, 236, 256, 288–9, 310, 312n21, 313–14
Google Scholar 333n22
Grands récits: concept of 191n12
Great Depression 127
Great Lakes (Rwanda) 190n2
Green, Joyce 96
Greer, Germaine 87
Grele, Ronald 10
Gringa Chilena 9: definition 211–12; *see also* Chile
Groundswell: Oral History for Social Change network in Oregon 19n33, 239
group interviewing model 332n7
Guam 18n30
Guatemalan: Indigenous rights activism 18n27, 51
Gulf War (1991) 143
Gyavur mahallesi (neighborhood of the infidels) 275n8

Haiti 190n2: culture and history 186–7, 191n13; earthquake, impact of 190n5
Haksar, Nandita 113, 118
Hall-Carpenter Oral History Archive 78
Halloway, Immy 200
Hamilton, Jaimee 4, 6, 151, 178
Hamilton, Paula 178
hand-washing 274
Hanisch, Carol 302n1, 303n6
harrowing material 136nn19, 26
hate crime 55n17
Hatoum, Mona 268
Hawai'i 18n30
Hazel de Berg Award for Excellence in Oral History 177

heritage culture 5
hermeneutic approach 32–3
High, Steven 177, 284, 286
Hill, Susan 6, 11
Hindi language 112–13, 119, 123n13,
    124n32
Hiner, Hillary 5, 9, 143, 152–3, 155,
    244
historical content 240–1; *see also* social
    movements
historical research 19n30
History of Science 282
Hitler, Adolf 52
HIV/AIDs 72n6, 194, 198
Holocaust survivors 57, 332n7
Holy Bible 333n22
home and belonging: concept of
    276n16
home in story: kitchen table
    conversations 263–75; *see*king 261–75;
    washing/process-based performance
    261–3
homecoming 262: concept of 262;
    homeland lost 272
homeplaces *see* public homeplaces
homophobia 64, 258
honor killings 143, 145
housebound mothers 87
housework, politics of 288; *see also*
    laundry stories
Howard, Heather 6, 11, 280–1
human rights 72n6, 79, 168n23, 204:
    abuse of 143; activism 215n9
hunger strike 249, 287
Hussein, Saddam 137, 140, 142,
    143
Husserl, Edmund 197

Iacovetta, Franca 2, 199
identify as female 51
identity 33, 51, 53, 131: collective
    242n12; concepts of 252; ethnic
    and cultural 64; formation 27–8;
    home and 272; Indigenous 107n16;
    lesbian 126–34; multi-ethnic 254;
    multiracial 254; stories 254–8; *see also*
    public homeplaces
immigration 238
iMovie 304
imperialism 101, 145–6; *see also* American
    imperialism
inclusivity 132–3
independence: political 112

India: Anglo-Indian schoolteachers
    38–46; context 121–2; definition of
    feminism 79; education in 29;
    feminism and activism 109–22; civil
    rights 110–21; teachers' movement
    110–21; women's rights 110–21
Indian Act 97, 103–5, 107n12, 335n42
Indian heritage 97
Indian Homemakers' Club 95, 103
Indian subcontinent 16n16
Indigenous Elders xiv; 2; 6; 7; 171;
    174–175; 178–179; *see also*
    Anishinaabe
Indigenous: definitions 180n1
Indigenous feminism 3, 10, 77–8,
    170–80: context 179; definitions 13;
    Guatemala 18n27; life history model
    178–9; men's experiences 106n3;
    'new' field of study 176–8; oral
    traditions 172; oral history and 6–7,
    15n13, 95–106; orality in Indigenous
    and western social settings 172–6;
    recording data 175–6; western
    concepts 172–3; women's history
    19n30; yarning, importance of in
    contemporary contexts 173–5; *see also*
    urban Indigenous community
    representations
Indigenous knowledge 223–34
"Indigenous Women, Memory and
    Power" (IWMP) project 329, 331
industrial disaster 244–50; *see also* women
    power and feminine solidarity
"Inheriting Resistance" project 240
insider vs outsider status 48, 212, 214,
    245
InterClipper 22n57
intergenerational storytelling 224–6
internal stratification 134
International Federation for Research in
    Women's History 15n14
International Oral History Association
    (IOHA) 15n14, 17
Internet, the 11, 299, 310; *see also*
    cyberfeminism; digital technology;
    social media
internment 14n5
interpretive authority 27
intersectionality 40, 52, 288–9
intersubjectivity 10, 12, 33–4, 53, 153,
    195–6; intersubjective experiences *see*
    Uganda; intersubjective processes
    22n48

interview 33–4: as a conversational
  narrative 10; democratization of the
  10; process 10; *see also* positionality of
  narrators and interviewers
intimacy: concept of 280
Iran 79
Iraq 5, 79: changing women 141–4;
  gender relations 141–4; gender-based
  violence 144–6; memory, history, and
  contestations 137–46; Kawergosk
  Syrian refugee camp *268*
Iraqi communist party 141
Iraqi Kurdistan 264–5: Barika refugee
  camp *265*, *273*
Islamic Revolution in Iran (1979) 275n1
Islamic State/ISIS 264: sexual violence 5

Jack, Dana C. 10, 212–13, 299
Jamieson, Kathleen 99
Janke, Terri 172
Japanese Canadian women 14n5
Jennings, Rebecca 78
Johnston, Verna 326–8, 331
Jolly, Margaretta 256

Kali For Women 113
Kandiyoti, Deniz 137
Kartinyeri, Doreen 179
Kashmir 124n25
Keeshig, Jocelyn 327
Kennedy, Dawnis 327, 329
Khmer Rouge genocide 5, 8–9, 168n16,
  309: confessions 156–9; private
  memory 159–64; public power
  159–64; sexual and gender-based
  violence 155–67; women's voices
  164–7
kidnapping 145
kitchen table conversations 263–75;
  see also public homeplaces
Klapparoth, Daniele 180
Korinek, Valerie 3, 5, 78–9, 92
Kroløkke, Charlotte 287, 289
Ku Klux Klan 29, 56–61
Kumar, Krishna 45
Kuntsman, Adi 290
Kurdish: language 275n10; women 79,
  139

La Follette, Kristen 68
La Follette, Robert 68
labour and employment 104–5, 294; *see
  also* trade unionism

Langellier, Kristin 84
language 27, 48, 123n13, 124n32: of
  feminism 317–18; *see also* waves
  metaphor
Lapovsky Kennedy, Elizabeth 78, 128
Larochelle, A. 187
Larson, Mary A. 11–12, 279–81, 325
Latin American Recent History and
  Memory Studies 204
"Latin American Women's Oral History"
  project 308
Latina Life Stories 4, 27, 63–71, 72n4
Latina literature 63
Latino Studies 63
laundry stories 261–75
Lavalas movement 186, 191n13
Lawrence, Bonita 101
Lebanese Civil War (1975–1990) 263,
  275n1
Leddy, Lianne C. 6, 10, 77
legacy 231–2
Lehman, Greg 174
Lejeune, Philippe 50
lesbians 126–34: activism vs ordinary
  people 78, 131–2; context 133–4;
  inclusivity vs exclusivity 132–3;
  locating 129–31; setting the stage
  128–9
Letelier, Orlando 205, 215n9
letters 31–2, 36n1, 37nn19–20
Lewis, Frank 104–5
LGBTQ: communities 79; elders 240;
  histories 92; literature 15n13; voices 3
liberationist ideology 84
life history model 178–9; *see also*
  Indigenous feminism, Anishinaabe
  womanhood, *Material Witness*, and
  yarning
life-course format 93n5
Lindy, Jacob 198
listening skills 35–6
literacy rates 305
living history circle method 332n7
Llona, Miren 65
Loose, Sarah 4, 220–1
Lord's Resistance Army (LRA) 192–3,
  200n2
Lovelace, Sandra 107n13
Loving Day network 259n13
Luo 194

Māori 179
Maharawal, Manissa McCleave 255

Mahuika, Nepīa 180
majority world: definition 311n5
male scholarship citation 11
mamlakat (kingdom) 276n16
Manushi collective 113
Maoism 156
Mapuche 209, 211
Maracle, Lee 6, 329
margins: concept of 185
mark (sign, mark): definition 191n7
marriage 35, 42, 91, 248, 267: across
  caste 112; forced 79, 145, 158;
  marrying-out 97–9
Martelly, Stéphane 9, 151, 153
Marx, Karl 111
Marxist-Leninism 111, 123n9
"Mashapaug Pond" project 301
master status 57–8: concept of 29, 61; *see
  also* racist women
Material Witness: bundles 227–8; coming
  out 233–4; context 223; creation
  stories 224–6; emotional experience,
  continuously shifting 228–31; heaps
  227–8; intergenerational storytelling
  224–6; legacy 231–2; mounds 227–8;
  non-linear piles 227–8; time and space
  224–6; storyweaving, Indigenous
  knowledge, and process 221, 223–34
materialist approaches 137
maternity leave 90
MATRIX 310, 312n18
MAVIN Foundation 259n13
McCallum, Mary Jane 6
McIntosh, Peggy 254
Mead, George Herbert 27
meek dictator: concept of 45–6; *see also*
  positionality of narrators and
  interviewers
Meihy, José Carlos Sebe Bom 54n11
memory writes 66; *see also* emotion and
  pedagogy
memory: collective 138; cultural meaning
  and 22n49; emotion and 28; emphasis
  296n11; fact and 285; forgetting
  296n11; history and 138; individual
  and collective 53, 285; living 8;
  personal 36n8; projects 152–3; public
  269–70; selection 296n11;
  subconscious desire 154; subjective
  20n37; trauma and 8; truth and 152;
  violent manipulation of 159
Menchú 18n27
mental health 256

mentoring 19n30
Meriam 172
methodolatry 54n12
Mexican migrants 27
migration 64, 268
Miguel, Muriel 6, 220–1, 223, 234n2
Milroy, Gladys Idjirrimoonya 174
Milroy, Jill 174
mines 124n29
Minister, Kristina 78, 299
MIR (guevarist-inspired Revolutionary
  Left Movement) 205
misogynism 302n4, 331
Mitchell, Juliet 92
mixed heritage 254–5: concept of 254
mixed race 46–7n2: heritage 64
mobile phone apps 322–31
Moffitt, Ronni 205, 215n9
Mohanty, Chandra 139
Monarch Services 215n19
Montague-Chelmsford Reforms 39
"Montréal Life Stories" project 9, 19n33,
  153, 184–90, 259n20
Monture, Patricia 13
Moraga, Cherríe 65, 69
moral frameworks 259n21
Morales, Aurora Levins 65
Morales, Rosario 65
morality (*buenas costumbres*) 210, 256,
  267
Moreton-Robinson, Aileen 171, 173
"Mormon Women's" project 308
Morrison, Toni 176, 190n4
Moss, William 296n11
motherhood 42; *see also* abortion;
  contraception; single motherhood
moving beyond 1–11
moving forward 11–12
Mpyangu, Christine Mbabazi 201n18
Ms. Magazine 315
Mukherjee, Suroopa 5, 219
Multicultural History Society of Ontario
  (MHSO) 306
multi-ethnic organizations 259n13
multiraciality 255–6
murder 79, 176, 238, 310
music 68–9
Muslim women 247–8, 275n11: in post-
  9/11 America 55n20
Myerhoff, Barbara 332n7
mythical concepts 262, 272
myth-making *see* personal myth-making
myths: 21n46

Nadasen, Premilla 287
Nagar, Richa 177
narghile (water pipe) 270
narrative: ambiguity 238; form 237–9;
(mis)interpretation 31–6; term 52–3;
see also social movements
narrators *see* positionality of narrators and
interviewers
National Association for the
Advancement of Colored People
(NAACP) 51
National Childbirth Trust (NCT)
89–90
National Housewives' Register (NHR)
87, 89
National Library of Australia 177, 179
National Women's Register (NWR) 87,
89
Native American heritage 51
Native Canadian Centre of Toronto
(NCCT) 325–8
"Native Canadian Oral History" project
326–8
Naxalites 123n9
Nazism 60
neo-colonialism 145
neo-liberalism 145, 237
neo-Nazism 29
networked feminism 302n6
networks: social movements 242n17
neurobiology 53
New Democratic Party (NDP) 127
"New York City Trans Oral History"
project 18n26
New Zealand 18n30, 179–80
Ng'andu, Bridget 174
nihilism 9
"Nindibaajimomin" project 259n20
Nipissing First Nation 6
No One Is Illegal (anti-colonial migrant
justice group) 240
non-governmental organizations (NGOs)
193, 200n2, 212, 215n11
non-linear piles 227–8
non-linear time 6, 221
non-Western women 14n4, 30n8
Northern Ireland: Catholic women 5,
284; Northern Irish historiography of
'The Troubles' 291–5
nouveau solipsism 49, 53
NRIs (non-resident Indians) 111
nunca más (never again) discourse 153,
204, 207, 209

objective knowledge 15n11
objectivity 12, 221: feminist critiques of
20n39
Oinam Report 118
Okely, Judith 196
online feminist oral histories 11,
298–302
opacity of texts 191n6
Open Society Asia Justice Initiative
167n1
open source tools/software 22n57
Operation Blue Star 121, 124–5n33
Oral History Association 203n33
Oral History Australia 177
Oral History Metadata Synchronizer
(OHMS) 22n57
oral history: activism 27, 78–9, 120,
122n2, 221, 236; allure of 53–4;
analytical vs populist 20n36; archived
313–18; associations 17n19; digitizing
322–5; discipline of 50; emotional turn
64; essentialist definition 12; as an
exchange between individuals 239–40;
as generative process 237; history and
52; issues and essays 17n21; journals
17n19; as method for radical social
change 242n7; online 298–302; panels
14n8; performance and 21n45; as
private encounter 237; production of
specific knowledge 237; project design
252–8; social movements 236–41;
thematic issues 15n15; time as a
requirement for 236
oralista (oral history practitioner) 54n11
orality: Indigenous and western social
settings 172–6; *see also Material Witness*
and yarning
O'Reilly, Andrea 175
Organization of Family Members of
Disappeared Detained Persons 208–9
Otherness 156, 184, 194
Ottoman Turkish Empire 275n7
overt commission 299

Painter, Nell Irvin 50
Palestinian refugees 275n13
Pali 118
participant observation 250
Passerini, Luisa 1, 8, 20n37, 43, 65,
67–9, 154, 199–200, 210, 242n7, 317
Patai, Daphne 1–2, 7, 28, 177, 236
pathographies: definition 84
patriarchal culture 212

Patwardhan, Anand 115
pedagogy *see* emotion and pedagogy
Percy, Ruth 12, 280
performance 190n2, 219–21: oral history
  and 21n45; performing story 67; *see
  also* emotion and pedagogy
Perry, Adele 6
personal myth-making 43–5; positionality
  of narrators and interviewers
perspectival ambiguity 238–9
Peshmarga (Kurdish/Iranian freedom
  fighters) 264
Peterson, Eric 84
Philomena 294
philosophy 53
Pinochet, General 5, 9, 205, 207
Pitjantjatjara 180n4
PKK (Kurdistan Workers' Party) 275n8
playwriting 34, 37n16
Pol Pot regime 157
political activism 219–21
political constraints 249–50; *see also* social
  movements
political prisoners 143, 210
Polletta, Francesca 238–9, 242n10
Pollock, Della 270
polysemy 238–9
Popay, Jennie 197
popular education 28
Portelli, Alessandro 10, 177, 240, 285,
  296n11
Portland Immigrant Rights Coalition
  (PIRC) 239
positionality of narrators and interviewers
  9, 29, 38–46: evaluation 46; meek
  dictators 45–6; prefaces 41–3; private
  conversation 40–1; public performance
  40–1; personal myth making 43–5;
  self-disclosure 41–3
positivism 79
postcolonialism 122n5
posterity 134
post-modernism 3, 9, 15nn10–11,
  20n39, 54n13: post-modern
  ethnography 20n38
poststructuralist theory 15n11, 137
Potter, Claire Bond 288
poverty 153, 194, 294
PRAIS program (Chile) 207
prefaces 41–3; *see also* positionality of
  narrators and interviewers
presenting story 70–1; *see also* emotion
  and pedagogy

Prince, Ruth 194
prisoners: of conscience 123n18; self-
  incrimination 157
private conversation 40–1; *see also*
  positionality of narrators and
  interviewers
private memory 159–64; *see also* Khmer
  Rouge genocide
process-based performance 261–75
producing story 67–9; *see also* emotion
  and pedagogy
professional careers 85–6, 90–1
Progressive Era 33
proprietary tools/software 22n57
prostitution 330: forced 145
psychiatry 195
psychoanalysis 37n11
psychology 33, 53, 252, 256
psychosocial support 199
public homeplaces: collaboration and care
  in oral history project design 252–8;
  identity stories 254–8
public performance 40–1; *see also*
  positionality of narrators and
  interviewers
public power 159–64; *see also* Khmer
  Rouge genocide
PUCL (People's Union for Civil
  Liberties) 115
PUDR (Delhi-based People's Union for
  Democratic Rights) 115, 117, 119
Punjabi 124n32
purdah (women's seclusion) 110

Qassim, Abdelkarim 141
queer: terminology 129–30
queer historicism 5, 78, 126–34, 135n7;
  see also lesbians

race: concept of 252
racial extremism 29, 56–61
racism 64, 254–5, 258, 287, 330:
  organized 60; settler 96
racist women 238: context 60–1; feminist
  oral histories of 56–61; master status
  57–8; trauma 59–60
radical empathy: concept of 256
Ramirez, Horacio N. Roque 128–9
rape 55n17, 79, 115–18, 145, 158,
  164–7
Reagon, Bernice Johnson 257
rebellion 43–5
reciprocity 151, 170, 185

reconciliation 19n30
recording data: Indigenous settings
    175–6; recording techniques 34–5
recuperative work 20n35
reflexivity 3, 177
refugees 20n36, 190nn2, 5, 220: camps
    264–5, 268
reintegration 202n18
relational-cultural theory 256
relationality 6
remembrance 268
reparation 207, 211
Report of the National Inquiry into the
    Separation of Aboriginal and
    reproductivity 200
research in oral history 48–54: as
    objective, concept of 200; process
    196–9; researcher bias 55n20, 200;
    returning the research 28
respect 151, 170
restorative justice 17n23
Rettig Commission 207
rights: concept of 41
Rigney, Lester-Irabinna 176
Ritchie, Donald 177
Robb, Christina 252
Roe v. Wade Supreme Court case (1973)
    315
Romano, Renee 256
Roth, Benita 287
rupture: in feminist narratives 93n7
"Rural Organizing Voices Oral History"
    project 241

Said, Edward 268
sainthood 292
sameness: concept of 41–2
sanctions 79, 143–4, 146n5
Santhals 112
Saskatoon gay and lesbian activism
    126–34
Scandrett, Eurig 245
Schofield, Marella 97–103
Scott-Heron, Gil 271
search engines 258n7, 333n22
second wave feminism 10, 81, 280,
    287–9, 314, 318
secret/sacred knowledge 180n9
sectarianism 145
self-concept 34, 186
self-determination 92, 124n25
self-disclosure 41–3; *see also* positionality
    of narrators and interviewers

self-examination 37n15
self-reflexivity 48
self-representation 33, 46: concept of
    284; digital 283–95
semantic dissonance 238–9
sensitive oral history 303n16
"September 11, 2001 Oral History"
    project 19n33
Serpent River First Nation 6, 13
sexism 64, 89, 258
sexual abuse 60, 143
sexual harassment 145
sexual mutilation 158
sexual violence *see* violence
shared authority 177, 184, 186–7, 284:
    concept of 10, 153, 186, 190n2;
    'sharing authority' shared experiences
    196–9
Shea, Margo 5, 11, 280–1
Sheftel, Anna 283, 291
Shiosaki, Elfie 175, 179
Shirt, Pauline 329
'shoebox' problem: in relation to digital
    media 314
Shopes, Linda 49–50, 177–8, 284, 290,
    296n11
signs 33
Sikhs: killing of 119–21
silence 188: silent majority 134; silent
    pictures 37n16
Silman, Janet 97
Simcon, Dilip 111
single motherhood 292–3; *see also*
    motherhood
Sioux 6
sisterhood 117, 288: universal 123n20
"Sisterhood and After" project 93n3,
    309
Sitzia, Lorraine 177
Sivaraman, Mythily 111
slavery 158
Sliver, Marc 311n5
smart phone use 333n22; *see also* mobile
    phone apps 322–31
Smith, Linda Tuhiwai 175, 323
social actors: children as 193–4
Social Darwinism 173
social history: reconstruction of 36n8
social inclusion 54n11
social justice movements 68, 253–4, 310;
    see also social movements
social media 11, 239, 283–4, 289, 295,
    325: politicization of 302n6

social movements: affective engagement
239–40; context 241; historical
content 240–1; narrative form 237–9;
oral history for building 236–41; oral
history as a generative process 237;
oral history as a private encounter 237;
oral history produces specific
knowledge 237; oral history takes time
236
social psychology 285
social science methods 9–10, 34, 153
social stigmatization 129, 132
Socialist Party (PS, Chile) 205, 215n8
sociology 33, 57, 285
sodomy 210
solidarity, feminine *see* women power and
feminine solidarity
Sørensen, Anne Scott 287, 289
South African Sonke Gender Justice 72n6
South Asian literature 15n13, 16n16
Southern Exposure 221
"Southern Oral History" project 19n33
Southern Tenant Farmers Union 221
Spanish language 208, 210, 215n19
speech acts 34
Spiderwoman Theater 223, 234nn1, 4
Spivak, Gaytri 13n2
Srigley, Katrina 107n16
St. Denis, Verna 96
Stacey, Judith 8, 20n38, 20n39, 61, 156,
200, 212–13
Stanley, Liz 288
Starecheski, Amy 4, 220–1
state feminism 142
state impunity: concept of 79
state terrorism 207–9, 211
state-sponsored violence 191n13
Stein, Edith 197
stereotyping 250n3
Stewart-Harawira, Makere 101
Sto:lo 6
Stoll, David 51
Stories Matter 22n57, 311n9
story circles 66–7; *see also* emotion and
pedagogy
story-based model 242n6
StoryCorps app 289, 300
storytelling 237; *see also* yarning and
Material Witness
storyweaving 6, 223–34: definition
234n2; methodology of 220
Student Nonviolent Coordinating
Committee (SNCC) 257

subjective truths 33, 36n8
subjectivity 2, 10, 12, 33–4, 40, 65,
190n1, 317; *see also* intersubjectivity
subversion 49–50
Sudanese women 17n24
Sugiman, Pamela 2, 14n5
Sullivan, Sady 4, 220
Summerfield, Penny 7, 82, 315
superwomen 142
survivor testimony 55n18
Suzack, Cheryl 329
Swirl, Inc. 259n13
Sylvester, Joe 328
Syrian refugee camps *268*

Take-Back-the-Night marches 83
Tankink, Marian 194, 198
Tarkunde Commission 117
tas (bath bowl) 274–5, 276n15
tashts (traditional metal washtubs) 261–4,
274, 275n2
teachers' movement: India 110–21
teaching 19n30
Tebeau, Mark 324
terror: Chile 205–7
testimonios 4, 16n17, 17n20, 28, 51,
63–71, 73n19, 204–5, 215n17
"Texas After Violence" project 238
text messaging 289
"The Feminist History Research Project"
313–14
"The Nipissing Warriors" project 20n33
"The Voices of Feminism Oral History"
project 308
theorizing story 69–70; *see also* emotion
and pedagogy
Third Culture Kids 256
third wave feminism 289
third world 311n5
Third World feminism 14n4
Thompson, Paul 177
Thomson, Alistair 10–11, 177, 279, 284,
286
Thrasher, Sue 221
Thumin, Nancy 289
Thunderhawk, Madonna 6
time 122n5: concepts of 122n5, 178; and
space 48, 224–6
To You, With Love 32
Tobique First Nation 97
tola (a settlement) 112
Torres Strait Islander Children from their
Families 179

Torres Strait Islander People 173, 180, 181
torture 143, 145, 158, 293: female survivors in Chile 204–14
totalitarianism 191n13
toxic hotspots 244
trade unionism 313–17
trafficking 145
"Trans Oral History" project 18n26, 238
Trans Partner Oral History 18n26
transcreating 54n11
transcription methods 35
Transcultural Psychosocial Organization of Cambodia (TPO) 159–60
transference/counter-transference 195
transgender: bathroom wars 51; community 238; oral history 5
Transgender Law Center 242n6
"Transgender Oral History" project 129, 136n13
transition generation 82
translation theory 54n11, 163
transphobia 210, 258
trauma 109, 247: concept 29, 60; definition 29; identity and memory 188; racist women 59–60
trust 170: relationships of 220
truth 152, 154, 166–7, 283: concept of 174
Truth and Reconciliation Commission (Canada) 21n42, 234n5
TTC (Teacher Training Certificate in India) 45
Tuam Baby Home scandal 293–4
Tuck, Eve 7
Tuol Seng Genocide Museum 152, 156–7, 168n22, 205
Tur, Mona Ngitji Ngitji 171
Turkish language 275nn9–10, 276nn15–16
"Twentieth Century Trade Union Woman" project 313–14
Twitter 289, 295
Two-Axe Earley, Mary 107n13

Uganda, northern 5, 153: conceptualizing children as social actors 193–4; context 199–200; dilemmas in the field 194–5; ethnography with wartime children 192–200; intersubjectivity 195–6; research process 196–9; shared experiences 196–9

Uganda People's Defence Forces (UPDF) 192–3
Ukrainian communities of Sudbury, Canada 286–7
UNESCO's Memory of the World roster 157
UNICEF 200n2
Union Carbide Corporation (UCC) 244
Union Carbide India Limited (UCIL) 244
United Nations 79; *see also* UNESCO; UNICEF
United Nations High Commissioner for Refugees (UNHCR) 264–5
United Nations Security Council Cease Fire Resolution SCR 687 143
United Nations Special Committee (UNSCOM) 143
United Nations Statistics Division's report 305
United States Oral History Association 170
uranium industry 104, 106n4
urban Indigenous community representations 321–31: context 331; "First Story Toronto" 325–6, 330; urban Indigenous/digitizing oral history 322–5; urban Indigenous women's orality, relationality, and refusal 326–31

Vaid, Sudesh 117–18
Valech Commission 207
Valk, Anne 301
Vanderburgh, Rosamond 326
Velazquez, Elizabeth 257
Vickers, Emma 78
victimhood 159
video blogs 289
Villa Grimaldi memory site 205–7; *see also* Chile
Villa Grimaldi Oral History Archive (VGOA) 204, 206–13, 215nn11, 13–14, 216n25
Vimeo 309
violence: forms of 191n13; gender-based 144–6, 155–67; Iraq 144–6; Khmer Rouge 155–67; sexual 17n23, 21n43, 79, 151–2, 155–67, 207
Virtual Oral/Aural History Archive 312n21
VivesQ 240

voice 127–8, 189
Vysma, Marianne 194, 198

wartime children: ethnography with
    192–200
washing 261–75 *see also* home in story
waves metaphor 287; *see also* first wave
    feminism; second wave feminism; third
    wave feminism
weapons of mass destruction (WMDs)
    143
Weebly 309
western concepts 172–3, 194; *see also*
    Indigenous feminism and Anishinaabe
    womanhood
Western Desert culture 180n4
Western Kenya: Luo children 194
Wheeler, Winona 322–3
white supremacism 56–61, 254, 256
Whiteduck Liberty, Lorraine 13
whitestream feminism 10, 13
Wilson, John 198
Wise, Sue 288
Withers, Deborah 284, 290
Women in Resistance Movements 121
women power and feminine solidarity
    244–50: contentious performances
    249–50; doing fieldwork 245;
    feminism and feminine solidarity
    246–7; political constraints 249–50;
    see also Material Witness
women's narratives 247–9
"Women Who Rock" project 310

Women's Liberation Movement (1970s)
    77, 83, 89, 92, 309
women's narratives 247–9; *see also* social
    movements
women's rights: India 110–21
Women's Strike for Equality (1970) 315
Women's Studies 52
women's voices: Khmer Rouge 164–7
Women's Words: feminist oral history
    212–14; international reach 17–18n24;
    reflections on 27–30; reviews
    14–15n9; thematic issues 13n3, 14n7
Women's Trade Union League 315
WordPress 309
World Health Organization (WHO)
    168n20
World War II 52, 78, 128, 136n34, 267
Wuthathi 172

xenophobia 7

Yang, K. Wayne 7
Yankunytjatjara women 171, 180n4
yarning 4, 173–5: definition 170; telling
    yarns 180n4; *see also* Indigenous
    feminism and storyweaving
yearning 151
Yoruba 333n22
YouTube 304, 309

Zembrzycki, Stacey 2, 283–4, 286–7
ZOG (Zionist Occupation Government)
    56–7

Made in the USA
Las Vegas, NV
24 January 2023

66153780R00208